First World War
and Army of Occupation
War Diary
France, Belgium and Germany

9 DIVISION
South African Brigade
2 South African Infantry Regiment
1 January 1916 - 28 February 1918

WO95/1781

The Naval & Military Press Ltd
www.nmarchive.com
Published in association with The National Archives

Published by

The Naval & Military Press Ltd

Unit 10 Ridgewood Industrial Park,

Uckfield, East Sussex,

TN22 5QE England

Tel: +44 (0) 1825 749494

www.naval-military-press.com

www.nmarchive.com

This diary has been reprinted in facsimile from the original. Any imperfections are inevitably reproduced and the quality may fall short of modern type and cartographic standards.

Contents

Document type	Place/Title	Date From	Date To
Heading	From Egypt Delta & Western Form To 66 Div 1918 Sept		
Heading	2nd S. African Bn. Arrival Maroilles From Egypt 20.4.16. Diaries For April, May, & June 1916 Are Missing.		
Heading	War Diary Of 2nd Regiment, South African Infantry. From 1st. July. 1916 To 31st. July, 1916. Volume.		
War Diary	Grove Town	01/07/1916	01/07/1916
War Diary	Grovetown Valley Trigger Wood.	02/07/1916	04/07/1916
War Diary	Talus Boise.	05/07/1916	07/07/1916
War Diary	Talus Boise and Barnafay Wood	08/07/1916	08/07/1916
War Diary	Bernafay Wood	09/07/1916	10/07/1916
War Diary	Talus Boise	11/07/1916	14/07/1916
War Diary	Montabaun and Delville Wood	15/07/1916	15/07/1916
War Diary	Delville Wood	15/07/1916	19/07/1916
War Diary	Talus Boise	20/07/1916	20/07/1916
War Diary	Grovetown	21/07/1916	23/07/1916
War Diary	Long	24/07/1916	25/07/1916
War Diary	La Thieuloye	26/07/1916	27/07/1916
War Diary	Estree Cauchy	28/07/1916	31/07/1916
Heading	War Diary. of 2nd Regiment South African Infantry. From 1st August, 1916. to 31st August. 1916 Vol 5		
War Diary	Estree Cauchy.	01/08/1916	23/08/1916
War Diary	Camblain L'Abbe	24/08/1916	31/08/1916
War Diary	Trenches	31/08/1916	31/08/1916
Diagram etc	P.C.O.		
Diagram etc	XV Corps Communication. August 9th 1917		
Heading	15th Corps Attached to Signal.		
Map	Gauche Wood.		
Heading	War Diary for March To October 1916. 2nd Regt South African Infantry. Vol 7		
War Diary	Lignereuill	01/10/1916	04/10/1916
War Diary	Fortel	05/10/1916	06/10/1916
War Diary	Behencourt	07/10/1916	07/10/1916
War Diary	Mametz Wood	08/10/1916	08/10/1916
War Diary	Eaucourt L'Abbaye	09/10/1916	12/10/1916
War Diary	Bazentin & Grand	13/10/1916	18/10/1916
War Diary	Mametz Wood	19/10/1916	26/10/1916
War Diary	Millen Court	27/10/1916	27/10/1916
War Diary	Herissart	28/10/1916	29/10/1916
War Diary	Agnes Les Duisans	30/10/1916	31/10/1916
War Diary	Agnes Les Duisans and Lattre St. Quentin	01/11/1916	06/11/1916
War Diary	Agnes Les Duisans and Lattre St. Quentin	07/11/1916	09/11/1916
War Diary	Agnes Les Duisans and Lattre St. Quentin	10/11/1916	10/11/1916
War Diary	Agnes Les Duisans and Lattre St. Quentin	11/11/1916	19/11/1916
War Diary	Lattre St Quentin	20/11/1916	30/11/1916
Heading	To/ South African Brigade. Herewith War Diary for month of December, 1916. Lieut. colonel. Commanding 2nd Regiment S.A. Infantry. 1st January, 1917		
War Diary	Lattre St Quentin.	01/12/1916	02/12/1916

War Diary	Sub-Section J. II	03/12/1916	07/12/1916
War Diary	Reserve Billets.	08/12/1916	14/12/1916
War Diary	Sub-Section J. II	15/12/1916	31/12/1916
Operation(al) Order(s)	Operation Order No. 31. In The Field. 30th December, 1916	30/12/1916	30/12/1916
Operation(al) Order(s)	Operation Order No. 30. In The Field. 26th December. 1916	26/12/1916	26/12/1916
Operation(al) Order(s)	Operation Order No. 29. In The Field. 22nd December. 1916	22/12/1916	22/12/1916
Operation(al) Order(s)	2nd South African Infantry Order No. 27		
Miscellaneous	2nd Regiment South African Infantry Order No. 28	18/12/1916	18/12/1916
Operation(al) Order(s)	2nd South African Infantry Order No. 27	14/12/1916	14/12/1916
Operation(al) Order(s)	2nd Regiment South African Infantry. Operation Order No. 26	10/12/1916	10/12/1916
Operation(al) Order(s)	2nd Regiment South African Infantry. Operation Order No. 24		
War Diary		31/12/1916	31/12/1916
War Diary	Sub-Section J. II	01/01/1916	07/01/1916
War Diary	Arras, Forrester ND. St. Nicholas.	08/01/1917	11/01/1917
War Diary	Sub-Section J. II	12/01/1917	31/01/1917
Operation(al) Order(s)	Operation Order No. 32. In The Field, 3rd January. 1917	03/01/1917	03/01/1917
Operation(al) Order(s)	2nd South African Infantry Order No. 33	07/01/1917	07/01/1917
Operation(al) Order(s)	2nd South African Infantry Order No. 34		
Operation(al) Order(s)	Operation Order No. 36	19/01/1917	19/01/1917
Operation(al) Order(s)	Operation Order No. 35	17/01/1917	17/01/1917
Operation(al) Order(s)	Operation Order No. 37	21/01/1917	21/01/1917
Operation(al) Order(s)	Operation Order No. 38	23/01/1917	23/01/1917
Operation(al) Order(s)	Operation Order No. 39	25/01/1917	25/01/1917
Operation(al) Order(s)	Operation Order No. 40	28/01/1917	28/01/1917
Operation(al) Order(s)	Operation Order No. 41	29/01/1917	29/01/1917
Operation(al) Order(s)	Operation Order No. 42	31/01/1917	31/01/1917
War Diary	Sub Section J II	01/02/1917	09/02/1917
War Diary	Arras	14/02/1917	16/02/1917
War Diary	Sub Section Right Sector.	17/02/1917	17/02/1917
War Diary	Arras	10/02/1917	13/02/1917
War Diary	No 2 Section Right Sector	17/02/1917	25/02/1917
War Diary	Arras	26/02/1917	28/02/1917
Operation(al) Order(s)	Operation Order No. 43	02/02/1917	02/02/1917
Operation(al) Order(s)	Operation Order No. 44	04/02/1917	04/02/1917
Operation(al) Order(s)	Operation Order No. 45	06/02/1917	06/02/1917
Operation(al) Order(s)	2nd Regiment S.A. Infantry Order No. 47	10/02/1917	10/02/1917
Operation(al) Order(s)	2nd S.A. Infantry Order No. 48	16/02/1917	16/02/1917
Operation(al) Order(s)	192 Sector Order No. 49	18/02/1917	18/02/1917
Operation(al) Order(s)	Operation Order No. ?	12/02/1917	12/02/1917
Operation(al) Order(s)	Operation Order No. 61	22/02/1917	22/02/1917
Operation(al) Order(s)	Order No. 52	24/02/1917	24/02/1917
War Diary	Arras.	01/03/1917	03/03/1917
War Diary	Hermaville	04/03/1917	12/03/1917
War Diary	Monchy-Breton.	13/03/1917	14/03/1917
War Diary	Hermaville	08/03/1917	11/03/1917
War Diary	Monchy Breton	15/03/1917	22/03/1917
War Diary	No 2 Section Right. Sector	24/03/1917	25/03/1917
War Diary	Monchy Breton	23/03/1917	23/03/1917
War Diary	Y. Hutments	24/03/1917	24/03/1917
War Diary	No. 2. Section Right Sector	25/03/1917	31/03/1917

Operation(al) Order(s)	Order No. 53	02/03/1917	02/03/1917
Operation(al) Order(s)	Order No. 54		
Operation(al) Order(s)	Order No. 55	10/03/1917	10/03/1917
Operation(al) Order(s)	Order No. 56	20/03/1917	20/03/1917
Operation(al) Order(s)	Order No. 57	29/03/1917	29/03/1917
Operation(al) Order(s)	Order No. 58	24/03/1917	24/03/1917
Operation(al) Order(s)	Order No. 50	19/03/1917	19/03/1917
War Diary	Arras	01/04/1917	02/04/1917
War Diary	Y. Hutments	03/04/1917	07/04/1917
War Diary	Arras	08/04/1917	16/04/1917
War Diary	(ACQ) X. Huts	17/04/1917	21/04/1917
War Diary	Orlencourt	22/04/1917	27/04/1917
Miscellaneous	Index to Appendices.		
War Diary	Orlencourt	28/04/1917	30/04/1917
Operation(al) Order(s)	Operation Order No. 61. By Lieut. Col. W.E.G. Lanier. G.H.G. Commanding 3rd Regiment S.A. Infy. In The Field. 2nd April 1917	02/04/1917	02/04/1917
Operation(al) Order(s)	2nd Regiment South African Infantry. Order No. 62		
Operation(al) Order(s)	Order No. 63. In The Field. 6th. April 1917	06/04/1917	06/04/1917
Operation(al) Order(s)	2nd Regiment South African Infantry In The Field 7th April. 1917 Order No. 64	07/04/1917	07/04/1917
Operation(al) Order(s)	Order No. 65. In The Field 6th April, 1917	06/04/1917	06/04/1917
Operation(al) Order(s)	2nd South African Infantry Order No. 66. 20th April. 1917	20/04/1917	20/04/1917
Operation(al) Order(s)	Order No. 67 In The Field, 27th April 1917.	27/04/1917	27/04/1917
Operation(al) Order(s)	Order No. 65 A. In The Field 19-4-17	19/04/1917	19/04/1917
Miscellaneous	2nd Regiment South African Infantry. Report On Operations From 9th April, 1917 to 15th April, 1917. Appendix II.	09/04/1917	09/04/1917
Map	Sketch Map Operations At Fampoux April 12th 1917. Appendix IV		
War Diary	Monchy-Breton	01/05/1917	12/05/1917
War Diary	Orlencourt	13/05/1917	14/05/1917
War Diary	L'Abbaye De Neuville Farm	15/05/1917	21/05/1917
Operation(al) Order(s)	Order No. 70. In The Field. 12.5.17. App II A	12/05/1917	12/05/1917
War Diary	L'Abbaye De Neuville Farm	22/05/1917	31/05/1917
Operation(al) Order(s)	Order No. 68. In The Field 12.5.17	12/05/1917	12/05/1917
Operation(al) Order(s)	Order No. 69	12/05/1917	12/05/1917
War Diary	L'Abbaye De Neuville Farm	01/06/1917	01/06/1917
War Diary	Arras	02/06/1917	10/06/1917
War Diary	'Y' Huts	11/06/1917	14/06/1917
War Diary	Larasset	15/06/1917	30/06/1917
Miscellaneous			
Operation(al) Order(s)	Order No. 72	31/05/1917	31/05/1917
Operation(al) Order(s)	Order No. 75. App II	05/06/1917	05/06/1917
Operation(al) Order(s)	Order No. 75. App IV	10/06/1917	10/06/1917
Operation(al) Order(s)	Order No. 74. App III	10/06/1917	10/06/1917
Miscellaneous			
Miscellaneous	App V		
Miscellaneous	App VI		
Miscellaneous			
Operation(al) Order(s)	Order No. 76. App VII	14/06/1917	14/06/1917
Miscellaneous	App VIII		
Miscellaneous	App IX		
War Diary	Laresset	01/07/1917	06/07/1917
War Diary	Simencourt	07/07/1917	27/07/1917

War Diary	Neuville Bourjonval	28/07/1917	28/07/1917
War Diary	Trescault Trenches	29/07/1917	29/07/1917
War Diary	Trescault Section	30/07/1917	31/07/1917
Heading	2nd South African Infantry War Diary July 1917		
Operation(al) Order(s)	Order No. 77 Appendix 1	05/07/1917	05/07/1917
Operation(al) Order(s)	Order No 78	25/07/1917	25/07/1917
Operation(al) Order(s)	Order No. 79	28/07/1917	28/07/1917
Map	Appendix 2		
Miscellaneous	Entraining Table 28th July 1917	28/07/1917	28/07/1917
War Diary	Trescault Section	01/08/1917	03/08/1917
War Diary	Ytres Camp	04/08/1917	04/08/1917
War Diary	Ytres	05/08/1917	09/08/1917
War Diary	Trescault Section Left Sub Section	10/08/1917	12/08/1917
War Diary	Trescault Left Subsection	13/08/1917	14/08/1917
War Diary	Trescault Section Left Subsection	15/08/1917	17/08/1917
War Diary	Metz	18/08/1917	28/08/1917
War Diary	Achiet Le Petit	29/08/1917	31/08/1917
Heading	2nd Regiment South African Infantry. War Diary. August 1917		
Operation(al) Order(s)	Order No. 80. Appendix No 1	03/08/1917	03/08/1917
Operation(al) Order(s)	Order No. 1	09/08/1917	09/08/1917
Operation(al) Order(s)	Order No. 83.	16/08/1917	16/08/1917
Operation(al) Order(s)	Order No. 84	27/08/1917	27/08/1917
Operation(al) Order(s)	Correction To Order No. 82	15/08/1917	15/08/1917
Miscellaneous	Appendix No II Raid N.M. of 16/17 April. 1917		
Operation(al) Order(s)	Order No. 88	24/08/1917	24/08/1917
Operation(al) Order(s)	Instructions Issued in Connection With Order No. 83 of The 14/8/1917	14/08/1917	14/08/1917
Miscellaneous	C.Os Report South African Brigade.	06/08/1917	06/08/1917
Miscellaneous	2/lt Mills Report 17/8/1917. Report On Raid on Femy Scrub.	17/08/1917	17/08/1917
Miscellaneous			
Miscellaneous	There Were no Casualties		
Miscellaneous	1st South African Infantry Brigade. 9th Division.	06/08/1917	06/08/1917
Miscellaneous			
War Diary	Achiet Le Petit.	01/09/1917	12/09/1917
War Diary	Pear Tree Camp	13/09/1917	13/09/1917
War Diary	Erie Camp	14/09/1917	17/09/1917
War Diary	Ypres Area	17/09/1917	24/09/1917
War Diary	Winnezele	24/09/1917	26/09/1917
War Diary	Winnezeele to Arneke	27/09/1917	27/09/1917
War Diary	Arneke	28/09/1917	30/09/1917
Operation(al) Order(s)	Order No. 82	11/09/1917	11/09/1917
Operation(al) Order(s)	Instructions Issued in Connection With Order No. 85	11/09/1917	11/09/1917
Miscellaneous	March Table Issued In Connection With Order No. 86		
Operation(al) Order(s)	Order No. 86	13/09/1917	13/09/1917
Operation(al) Order(s)	Order No. 87	16/09/1917	16/09/1917
Miscellaneous	March Table Issued With Order No. 87	16/09/1917	16/09/1917
Operation(al) Order(s)	Order No. 88	14/09/1917	14/09/1917
Miscellaneous	Assembly		
Operation(al) Order(s)	Order No. 89		
Miscellaneous			
Miscellaneous	March Table Issued With Order No. 90		
Operation(al) Order(s)	Order No. 91	27/09/1917	27/09/1917
Operation(al) Order(s)	Order No. 90	24/09/1917	24/09/1917
Operation(al) Order(s)	Addendum To Order No. 91	27/09/1917	27/09/1917

Miscellaneous	2nd Regiment South African Infantry. Report On Operations East of Ypres Between The 19th and 22nd September, 1917,	09/09/1917	09/09/1917
Map	L. 3. Edition 1 Appendix II		
War Diary	Arneke	01/10/1917	04/10/1917
War Diary	Moulle	05/10/1917	10/10/1917
War Diary	Brake Camp.	10/10/1917	11/10/1917
War Diary	Reigersberg	11/10/1917	12/10/1917
War Diary	Ypres Canal Bank	13/10/1917	13/10/1917
War Diary	Ypres Front	14/10/1917	17/10/1917
War Diary	Irish Farm	18/10/1917	20/10/1917
War Diary	Reigersburg Camp	21/10/1917	23/10/1917
War Diary	Nouveau Monde To Worm Houdt	24/10/1917	25/10/1917
War Diary	Petit Synthe	26/10/1917	29/10/1917
War Diary	Coxyde Les Bains	29/10/1917	31/10/1917
Heading	2nd Regiment South African Infantry. War Diary. October, 1917		
Miscellaneous	March Table Issued Accordance With Order No. 92	04/10/1917	04/10/1917
Operation(al) Order(s)	Order No. 92	04/10/1917	04/10/1917
Operation(al) Order(s)	Order No. 93	09/10/1917	09/10/1917
Operation(al) Order(s)	Order No. 94	09/10/1917	09/10/1917
Miscellaneous	Entraining Table Issued in Connection with Order No. 94., 10.10.1917	10/10/1917	10/10/1917
Miscellaneous	Preliminary Instruction Issued In Connection With Move On 10/10/1917	10/10/1917	10/10/1917
Operation(al) Order(s)	Order No. 95	11/10/1917	11/10/1917
Miscellaneous	Preliminary Instructions In Connection With Move- 28.10.1917	28/10/1917	28/10/1917
Miscellaneous	Instruction In Reference To Move To-Morrow	28/10/1917	28/10/1917
Operation(al) Order(s)	Instruction Issued in Connection with Order No 96	11/10/1917	11/10/1917
Operation(al) Order(s)	Order No. 97	13/10/1917	13/10/1917
Operation(al) Order(s)	Order No. 99	17/10/1917	17/10/1917
Operation(al) Order(s)	Order No. 100	20/10/1917	20/10/1917
Miscellaneous	2nd S.A.I. Instruction Issued In Connection With Move 20-10-17	20/10/1917	20/10/1917
Miscellaneous		23/10/1917	23/10/1917
Operation(al) Order(s)	Order No. 103	24/10/1917	24/10/1917
Operation(al) Order(s)	Instructions Issued With Order 103	25/10/1917	25/10/1917
Operation(al) Order(s)	Order No. 104	29/10/1917	29/10/1917
Miscellaneous	March Table Issued With Order No. 104	29/10/1917	29/10/1917
Map	War Diary October 1917. Appendix II		
War Diary	Coxyde Les Bains	01/11/1917	10/11/1917
War Diary	Yorkshire Camp.	11/11/1917	16/11/1917
War Diary	Furnes Camp	17/11/1917	19/11/1917
War Diary	Ghyvelde	20/11/1917	20/11/1917
War Diary	Teteghem South and Goudekerque	21/11/1917	21/11/1917
War Diary	Wormhoudt	22/11/1917	22/11/1917
War Diary	Zermezeele	23/11/1917	23/11/1917
War Diary	Coubronne	24/11/1917	24/11/1917
War Diary	Avroult	26/11/1917	26/11/1917
War Diary	Bourthes	26/11/1917	30/11/1917
Operation(al) Order(s)	Order No. 105	09/11/1917	09/11/1917
Operation(al) Order(s)	C.Os Report. South African Brigade.	15/11/1917	15/11/1917
Operation(al) Order(s)	Order No. 107	18/11/1917	18/11/1917
Operation(al) Order(s)	Order No. 108	19/11/1917	19/11/1917
Miscellaneous	March Table "A" Issued In Connection With Order 108	20/11/1917	20/11/1917

Miscellaneous	March Table "B" Order 108	20/11/1917	20/11/1917
Miscellaneous	March Table "C" Order 108	21/11/1917	21/11/1917
Miscellaneous	March Table "D" Order 108	22/11/1917	22/11/1917
Miscellaneous	March Table "E" Order 108	24/11/1917	24/11/1917
Miscellaneous	March Table "F" Order 108	25/11/1917	25/11/1917
War Diary	Bourthes	01/12/1917	01/12/1917
War Diary	Verchin	02/12/1917	03/12/1917
War Diary	Moislains	03/12/1917	04/12/1917
War Diary	Couzeaucourt	05/12/1917	05/12/1917
War Diary	Couzeaucourt Trenches	06/12/1917	10/12/1917
War Diary	Couzeaucourt	10/12/1917	15/12/1917
War Diary	Reserve Camp WC 3	16/12/1917	19/12/1917
War Diary	Gouzeaucourt	20/12/1917	20/12/1917
War Diary	Gouzeaucourt Trenches	21/12/1917	31/12/1917
Heading	2nd Regiment South African Infantry War Diary & Appendices For December, 1917		
Miscellaneous	Movement Table Issued In Connection With Order 109		
Operation(al) Order(s)	Order No. 109	01/12/1917	01/12/1917
Operation(al) Order(s)	Order No. 111	04/12/1917	04/12/1917
Operation(al) Order(s)	2nd S.A.I. Order No. 110	02/12/1917	02/12/1917
Operation(al) Order(s)	Order No. 110 A	02/12/1917	02/12/1917
Miscellaneous	Administration Instructions Issued With Order 111	04/12/1917	04/12/1917
Operation(al) Order(s)	Order No. 112	08/12/1917	08/12/1917
Operation(al) Order(s)	Order No. 113	10/12/1917	10/12/1917
Operation(al) Order(s)	Order No. 115	15/12/1917	15/12/1917
Operation(al) Order(s)	Order No. 116	19/12/1917	19/12/1917
Operation(al) Order(s)	Operation Order No. 117	22/12/1917	22/12/1917
Operation(al) Order(s)	Operation Order No. 118	24/12/1917	24/12/1917
Operation(al) Order(s)	Operation Order No. 119	26/12/1917	26/12/1917
Operation(al) Order(s)	Operation Order No. 120	30/12/1917	30/12/1917
Heading	The 1st 2nd & 4th South African Infantry Battalions Were Formed Into South African Composite Battalion On 24th April 1918		
War Diary	Gouzeaucourt Trenches	01/01/1918	08/01/1918
War Diary	Gouzeaucourt Support Trenches.	09/01/1918	12/01/1918
War Diary	Gouzeaucourt Support	12/01/1918	14/01/1918
War Diary	Heudicourt	14/01/1918	17/01/1918
War Diary	Sorrel Le Grand	18/01/1918	20/01/1918
War Diary	Sorrel	20/01/1918	23/01/1918
War Diary	Gouzeaucourt Trenches.	24/01/1918	27/01/1918
War Diary	Hutments W.2.C. Ne Fins.	28/01/1918	31/01/1918
Operation(al) Order(s)	Order No. 121	03/01/1918	03/01/1918
Miscellaneous	Instructions Issued With Order No. 121	03/01/1917	03/01/1917
Operation(al) Order(s)	Order No. 122	07/01/1918	07/01/1918
Operation(al) Order(s)	Operation Order No 123		
Operation(al) Order(s)	Operation Order No. 123B.	18/01/1918	18/01/1918
Operation(al) Order(s)	Order No. 124	22/01/1918	22/01/1918
Operation(al) Order(s)	Order No. 125	26/01/1918	26/01/1918
Operation(al) Order(s)	Order No. 126	30/01/1918	30/01/1918
Miscellaneous	Administrative Instruction No. 1 Issued With Order No. 126	31/01/1918	31/01/1918
Operation(al) Order(s)	Instructions Issued With Order No. 124	22/01/1918	22/01/1918
Map	Gouzeaucourt.		
Miscellaneous			
War Diary	Suzanne	07/02/1918	28/02/1918
Miscellaneous	Order. Reference Sheet 62c. N W. 1/20000		

Heading	Appendix Vol III Diary Of Composite Company 5th To 14th May By Capt. E.C. Bryant Of Commdg Composite Company 2. S.A.I.
Map	Edition 4 A., Appendix III.
Map	On no account to fall in hands of enemy.
Map	Gouzeaucourt.
Map	
Map	51b N.W.3 (Edition 4 A) C. 2
Map	On no account to fall in hands of enemy.
Map	
Miscellaneous	9
Map	St Idesbald Sector

FROM EGYPT

DELTA WESTERN FORCE

TO 66 DIV

1918 SEPT

2nd S African Bn.

Arrived Marseilles from Egypt 20.4.16.

Diaries for April, May, & June 1916 are missing

2nd S A Bn July
Vol 4

9

CONFIDENTAL.

War Diary.

of.

2nd Regiment. South African Infantry.

FROM 1st. July, 1916 TO. 31st. July, 1916.

(VOLUME. 4).

Instructions regarding War Diaries and Intelligence Summaries are contained in F.S. Regs. Part II and the Staff Manual respectively. Title pages will be prepared in manuscript.

War Diary

or

~~Intelligence Summary~~

Army Form C 2118.

Place	Date	Hour	Summary of Events and Information	Remarks and Reference to Appendices
Grovetown	1. 7. '16	—		
Grovetown	2. 7. '16	5.0 P.M.	Regiment marched from Grovetown to Trigger Wood Valley, "X" route.	
Trigger Wood Valley	3. 7. '16	4.30 A.M.	Regiment in reserve - sustained one casualty.	
D°	4. 7. '16	4.30 P.M.	Regiment marched from Trigger Wood Valley to vicinity of Talus Boise and Cambridge Copse (trench area). Regiment acting in Divisional Reserve, relieving the 21st Brigade.	
Talus Boise	5. 7. '16			
Talus Boise	6. 7. '16			
Talus Boise	7. 7. '16			
Talus Boise and Bernafay Wood	8. 7. '16	5.30 P.M.	Headquarters, "A" and "C" Companies proceeded to Bernafay Wood, taking over the front line from portions of 16th Royal Scots and 6th K.O.S.B. Approximately 37 casualties. "B" and "D" companies remained at Talus Boise.	
Bernafay Wood	9. 7. '16	9.0 P.M.	Consolidating Position. "D" Coy arrived from Talus Boise, taking over part of line. Approximate Casualties:- 138. Capt. H.E. Clifford. wounded (died of wounds, 12.7.16) Lieut. B.N. Macfarlane, wounded. Lieut C.L.H. Mulcahy. wounded (died of wounds, 12.7.16)	
Bernafay Wood	10. 7. '16		Regiment relieved by 4th S.A. Infantry, returning to old camp at Talus Boise. Approximate casualties:- 12.	
Talus Boise	11. 7. '16		Detachment of one reserve Officer, two N.C.O's and ten men left Talus Boise to represent regiment at French National Review in Paris. Six casualties, caused indirectly by enemy searching for our batteries.	
Talus Boise	12. 7. '16		} Regiment lying in reserve. Three casualties.	
Talus Boise	13. 7. '16			
Talus Boise	14. 7. '16	4.0 P.M.	Regiment moved up to vicinity of Montabaun, sleeping the night in old German trenches immediately in rear of Montabaun. Considerable discomfiture caused by enemy tear shells, but only one casualty.	
Montabaun and Delville Wood	15. 7. '16	3.0 A.M.	Regiment marched, through Montabaun, to Longueval and Delville Wood to force enemy out of portions of the wood he still held. Capt. Adjutant H.M. Bamford, wounded,	

Instructions regarding War Diaries and Intelligence Summaries are contained in F.S. Regs. Part II. and the Staff Manual respectively. Title pages will be prepared in manuscript.

War Diary

or

Intelligence Summary

Army Form C 2118

Place	Date	Hour	Summary of Events and Information	Remarks and References to Appendices
Delville Wood	15.7.16		Capt C. R. Heenan, wounded; Capt E. Barlow, wounded; Capt. H. E. F. Creed, killed; Capt W. Gray, killed; 2nd Lieut. J. W. Bro de Wold, killed; 2nd Lieut R. G. Miller, killed. 2nd Lieut. E. V. Tatham, acting adjutant. Approximate casualties – 64.	
Delville Wood	16.7.16		Holding and consolidating ground won previous day. Fairly numerous casualties caused by enemy snipers who remained concealed in wood in rear of our positions, also making it awkward for regimental ration and ammunition carriers. Great difficulty in passing orders along the line owing to large gaps caused by casualties, and position being exposed to enemy. Approximate Casualties:– 48.	
Delville Wood	17.7.16.		Entrenching and making good positions. Lieut. W. J. Hill, killed; 2nd Lieut. A. T. Wales, wounded and died of wounds, Lieut Col W. E. C. Tanner, C.M.G. wounded; Capt Heptroff, W.J, temporarily in command. Approximate Casualties:– 84.	
		Noon	Major H. H. A. Gee assumed command of regiment.	
Delville Wood	18.7.16	do.	Strong German counter-attack, after heavy bombardment by guns of all calibre, compels regiment to evacuate positions on edge of wood, falling back on Battalion Headquarters and trench on outer edge of village of Longueval. Capt W. J. Hoptroff, killed; Lieut C. J. K. Letchford, killed; 2nd Lieut. R. V. Tatham, killed; 2nd Lieut. W Hammer, killed; Capt. L. Greene, wounded; Lieut W. J. Perkins, wounded; Lieut. R. Beverley, wounded; Lieut. R. Knibbs, wounded; 2nd Lieut and actg. Adjutant E. V. Tatham, wounded (since reported missing); 2nd Lieut. B. N. Fenix, wounded	
		Late afternoon	Being relieved by fresh troops, the majority of the regiment retired on Brigade dump, and were mustered by 2nd Lieut. King, under orders from Brigade Headquarters. Approximate casualties: – 221.	
Delville Wood	19.7.16		Details of Regiment still in wood, under command of Major H. H. A. Gee and O.C., 3rd S.A. Infantry. Major H. H. A. Gee, wounded ~~and died~~ of wounds; Lieut J. Connock (Trench Mortar Battery) killed; 2nd Lieut. G. G. Green, wounded, slight, to duty in	

Instructions regarding War Diaries and Intelligence Summaries are contained in F.S. Regs. Part II and the Staff Manual respectively. Title pages will be prepared in manuscript.

War Diary
or
Intelligence Summary

Army Form C 2118

Place	Date	Hour	Summary of Events and Information	Remarks and References to Appendices
Delville Wood	19.7.16		charge ~~[illegible]~~ of details of Regiment. Approximate Casualties:- 24. Majority of Regiment returned to Talus Boise, where Major F. H. Heal, (1st S.A. Infantry) assumed command.	
Talus Boise	20.7.16		Regiment marched to Grovetown. Detachment of 1 officer, and 12 other ranks, who attended French National Review, rejoined Regiment.	
Grovetown	21.7.16		Various details, thought missing, reported back to camp from Delville Wood, under command of 2nd Lieut. G. G. Green.	
Grovetown	23.7.16	8.0 a.m.	Regiment marched to Mericourt where it entrained. Detrained at Longpré; and marched to Long.	
Long.	24.7.16		Regiment at Long.	
Long.	25.7.16		Regiment marched to Longpré, where it entrained.	
La Thieuloye	26.7.16		Regiment marched to La Thieuloye, after detraining at Brias.	
La Thieuloye	27.7.16		Regiment marched from La Thieuloye to Estree Cauchy.	
Estree Cauchy ~~La Thieuloye~~	28th 7.16		Regiment re-organizing at Estree Cauchy.	
Estree Cauchy ~~La Thieuloye~~	29th 7.16		Regiment re-organizing at Estree Cauchy.	
Estree Cauchy ~~La Thieuloye~~	30.7.16		Regiment re-organizing at Estree Cauchy.	
Estree Cauchy.	31.7.16		Regiment re-organizing at Estree Cauchy.	

CONFIDENTIAL

WAR DIARY

of

2ND REGIMENT SOUTH AFRICAN INFANTRY.

FROM 1st. August, 1916. to 31st August, 1916.

Vol 5

Instructions regarding War Diaries and Intelligence Summaries are contained in F. S. Regs. Part II and the Staff Manual respectively. Title pages will be prepared in manuscript.

War Diary

or

Intelligence Summary.

Army Form C.2118.

Place	Date	Hour	Summary of events and Information	Remarks and reference to appendices
Eshee Cauchy	1st August 1916	-	Regiment re-organizing and training. Routine.- 6.45 am to 7.15 am. Physical Training. 9.30 am. to 11.30 am. Bombing, Bayonet fighting, Trench Warfare, etc. 2 pm. to 4 pm. Route March.	
Eshee Cauchy	2nd Aug. 1916		Draft arrived from Base. 18. O.R.	
Eshee Cauchy	3rd Aug. 1916	-		
Eshee Cauchy	4th Aug 1916	3.0. am.	Regiment inspected at Frevillers by 4th Corps Commander.	
Eshee Cauchy	5th Aug 1916		Draft arrived from Base 1 officer (Capt. A. A. Sullivan) and 16 O.R. Routine training.	
Eshee Cauchy	6th Aug 1916	8.45 am	Church Parade. Capt. A. A. Sullivan takes over temporary command of the Regiment from date, Major F. H. Heal returning to the 1st Regiment South African Infantry.	
Eshee Cauchy	7th Aug 1916	6.15 to 6.45 AM	Physical training	Specialists training:-
Eshee Cauchy	8th Aug 1916	8.30 to 11.30 AM	Bombing and Bayonet fighting, Trench	8.30 am to 11.30 am. Detached with R. E. Tunnelling Coy. 55. O.R.
Eshee Cauchy	9th Aug 1916		Warfare, Gas precautions, Wiring etc.	Lewis Gunners, Signallers.
Eshee Cauchy	10th Aug 1916	2 pm. to 4 pm	Route march	Stretcher Bearers, Snipers
Eshee Cauchy	11th Aug 1916			and Observers.
Eshee Cauchy	12th Aug 1916			
Eshee Cauchy	13th Aug 1916	8.45. A.M	Church Parade.	
Eshee Cauchy	14th Aug 1916		Routine training and Specialists training as above.	
Eshee Cauchy	15th Aug 1916		Routine training. Draft of two officers from Base. (Major Symmes and 2nd Lieut J. E. B. D. Cochrane) Major Symmes takes over temporary command of the Regiment. 194 O.R. arrived from Base	
Eshee Cauchy	16th Aug 1916		Routine training and Specialists training. Following officers arrived from Base:- Lieut Col. E. Christian, Capt B. Burne, Capt F. E. Cochran, Lieut T. H. Symons, Lieut. R. C. Knight. Lieut. Colonel E. Christian assumes command of Regiment from date. Major H. C. Symmes appointed second in command.	
Eshee Cauchy	17th Aug 1916		Routine and Specialists training as above. Carrying party of 3 officers and 300 O.R. furnished for work in MAESTRE LINE.	
Eshee Cauchy	18th Aug 1916		Ditto. Ditto. Working party of 2 officers and 100 O.R. supplied for work on Signal communications. MAESTRE LINE.	
Eshee Cauchy	19th Aug 1916		Routine and Specialists training as above.	

Place	Date	Hour	Summary of Events and Information	Remarks and References to Appendices
Estree Cauchy.	20th August '16	8.45 A.M.	Church Parade. Bathing. Further working party of 1 officer and 120 O.R. supplied for work under Royal Engineers, MAESTRE LINE.	
Estree Cauchy.	21st August '16		Routine and Specialists training. Working party of 1 officer and 100 O.R. returned to camp from MAESTRE LINE.	
Estree Cauchy.	22nd Aug. '16		Routine and Specialists training.	
Estree Cauchy. Camblain L'Abbe	23rd Aug. '16	8.30 to 11.30.	Routine training. Regiment marched from Estree Cauchy to reserve billets at CAMBLAIN L'ABBE. Working party of 3 officers and 300 O.R., and Working party of 1 officer and 100 O.R. returned to camp from MAESTRE LINE.	
Camblain L'Abbe ~~Estree Cauchy~~	24th Aug. '16		Training 6.15–6.45 am Physical Drill, 8.30 to 11.30 am Company Drill. 1 O.R. (Miner) KILLED.	
Camblain L'Abbe ~~Estree Cauchy~~	25th Aug. 1916		Bayonet fighting and extended order drill. 2 pm to 4 pm Route march.	
Camblain L'Abbe	26th Aug. 1916		Specialists training. Lewis Gunners, Signallers, Snipers, etc. 6 pm. Working party of 4 officers and 150 O.R. supplied for work in MAESTRE LINE.	
Camblain L'Abbe	27th Aug 1916	8.45 am	Church Parade. Working party of 4 officers and 152 O.R. supplied MAESTRE LINE.	
Camblain L'Abbe	28th Aug. 1916		Routine training and Specialists training. 3 O.R. Casualties in Working party.	
Camblain L'Abbe	29th Aug. 1916		Ditto Ditto.	
Camblain L'Abbe	30th Aug. 1916		Ditto Ditto.	
Camblain L'Abbe Trenches.	31st Aug. 1916	6 am - 7 am	Regiment marched up to trenches and relieved 4th Regiment, South African Infantry, in front line. BERTHONVAL I. Situation on relief - que[illegible] 1 O.R. casualty on patrol duty.	

[illegible]

Lieut. Colonel, Commanding.
2nd Regiment South African Infantry.

31st August 1916.

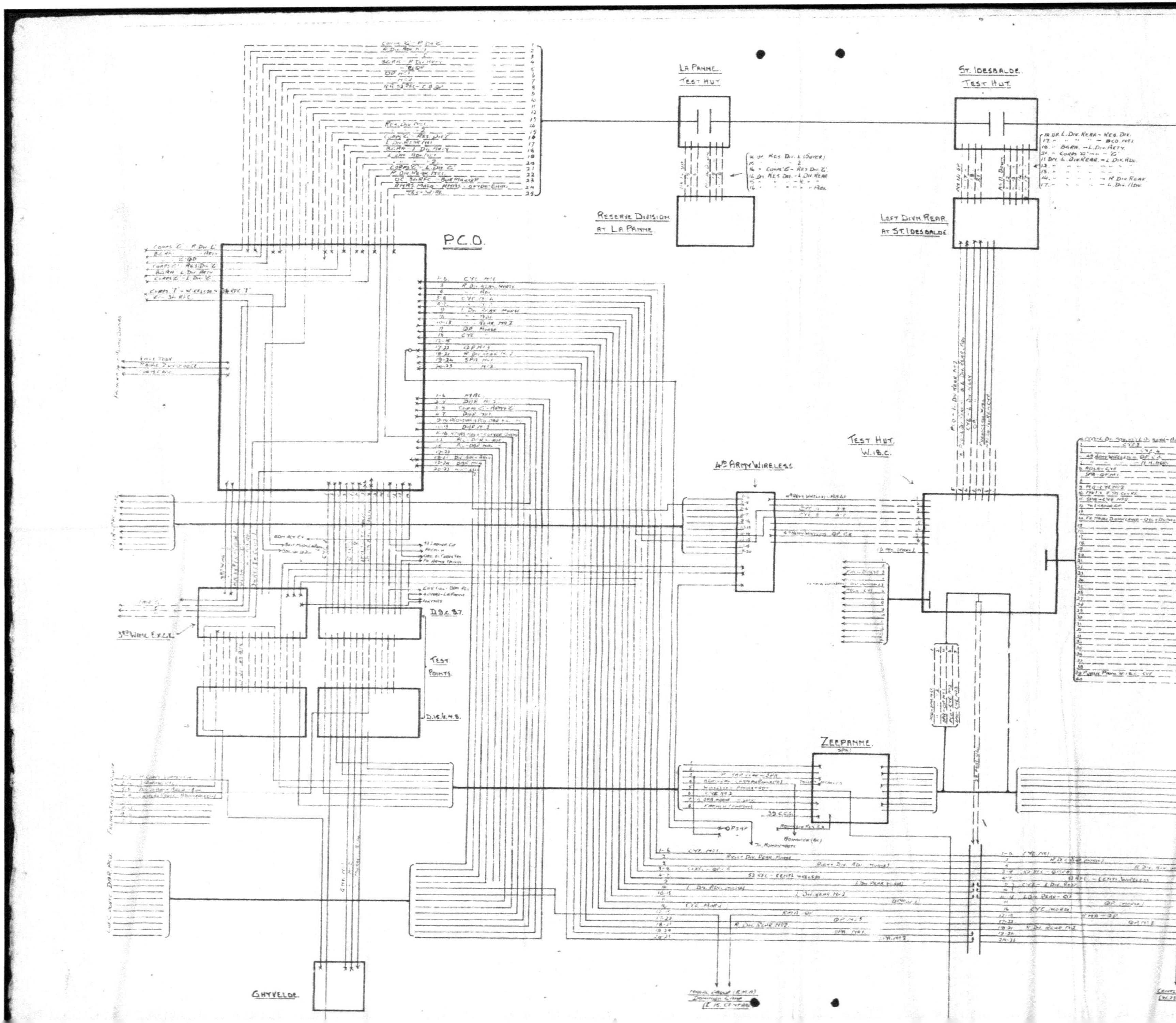

La Panne Test Hut
St. Idesbalde Test Hut
Reserve Division at La Panne
Left Divn. Rear at St. Idesbalde
P.C.O.
Test Hut. W.I.B.C.
4th Army Wireless
3rd Wing Exce.
D.9 & B.7.
Test Points.
D.16 & 48.
Zeepanne
Ghyvelde

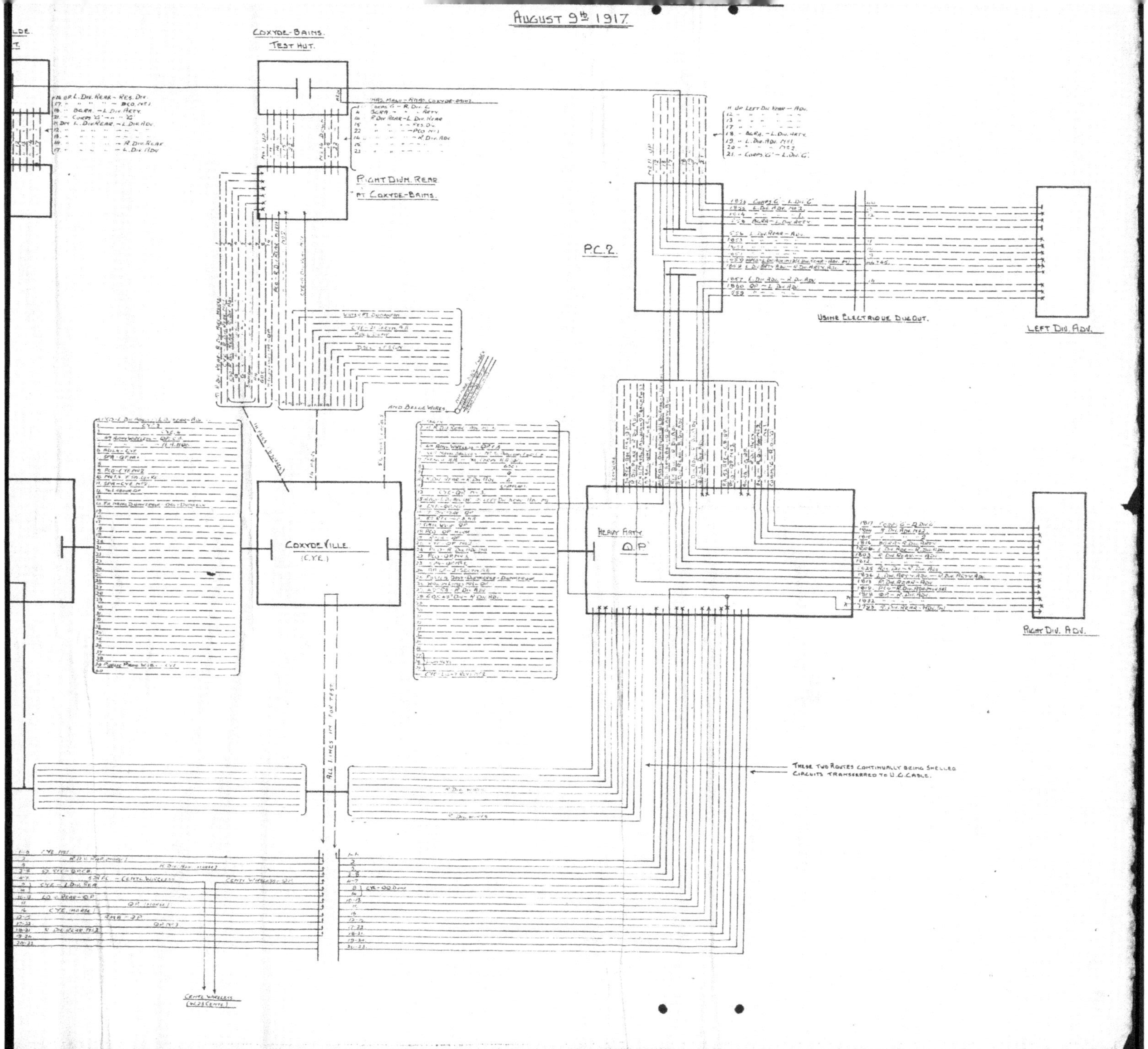
AUGUST 9th 1917.
COXYDE-BAINS.
TEST HUT.
RIGHT DIVN. REAR
AT COXYDE-BAINS.
P.C.2.
USING ELECTRIQUE DIV. OUT.
LEFT DIV. ADV.
COXYDE VILLE
(C.Y.E.)
HEAVY ARTY
O.P.
RIGHT DIV. ADV.
AND BELGE WIRES
ALL LINES IN FOR TEST
THESE TWO ROUTES CONTINUALLY BEING SHELLED
CIRCUITS TRANSFERRED TO U.G. CABLE.
CENTL WIRELESS
(W.23 CENTL)

15 Corps
attach to Signals

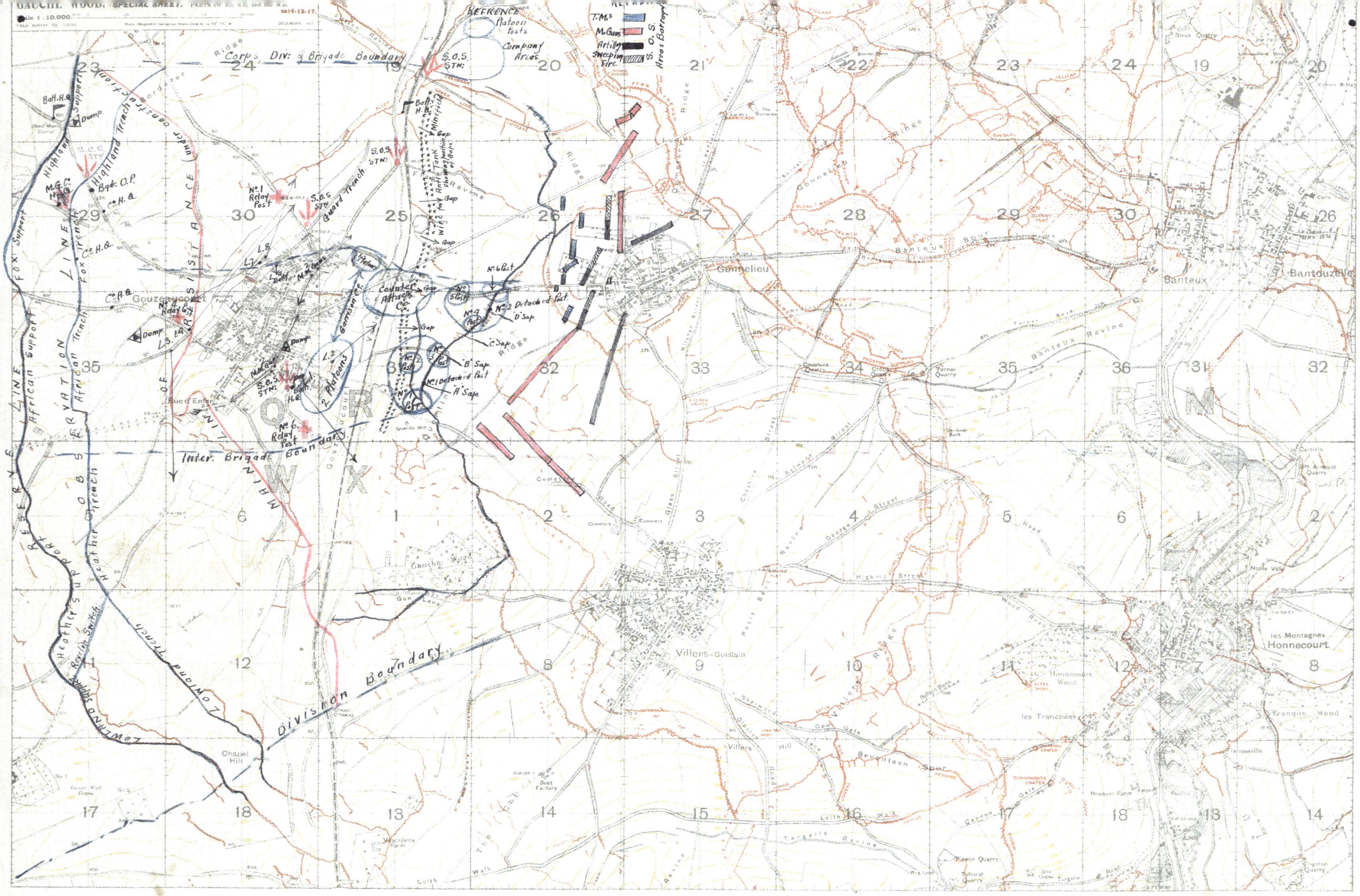
GAUCHE WOOD. SPECIAL SHEET.
Scale 1 : 10,000.
1919-12-17.
REFERENCE
Platoon Posts
Company Areas
T.M.s
M.Guns
Artillery
Sweeping Fire
S.O.S. Areas Barrage
Corps, Div: & Brigade Boundary
S.O.S. STN:
Inter. Brigade Boundary
Division Boundary
RESERVE LINE
OBSERVATION LINE
MAIN LINE
RESISTANCE (under construction)
Fox Support
African Support
African Trench
Fox Trench
Highland Support
Highland Trench
Heather Support
Heather Trench
Lowland Support
Lowland Trench
Revelon Switch
Guard Trench
Garrison Co.
Counter Attack Co.
2 Platoons
Bgde. O.P.
Batt. H.Q.
Co. H.Q.
M.G.Co. H.Q.
Dump
No. 1 Relay Post
No. 6 Relay Post
No. 2 Detached Post
No. 1 Detached Post
No. 6 Post
No. 5 Post
No. 4 Post
No. 3 Post
No. 2 Post
Anti Tank Minefield
Wire showing position of Gaps
Gap
'A' Sap
'B' Sap
'C' Sap
'D' Sap
Gouzeaucourt
Gonnelieu
Villers-Guislain
Banteux
Bantouzelle
Honnecourt
les Montagnes
Gauche Wood
Chapel Hill
Banteux Spur
Banteux Ravine
Seventeen Spur
Targelle Ravine
Leith Walk
Quentin Ridge
Gun Lane
Highland Ridge
Villers Ridge
Honnecourt Wood
les Tranchées
Francqueville
Bosquet Farm
Pigeon Quarry
Turner Quarry
Cheshire Quarry
Beet Factory
Vaucellette Farm
Gauche Wood
Cemetery
Q R W X M

War Diary

for Month of

October 1916.

2nd Regt South African Infantry.

Place	Date	Hour	Summary of Events & Information	Remarks & references to Appendices
LIGNEREUIL	October 1st		The Regiment in billets. All attended Church Parade.	
	2nd		The Regiment proceeded by companies to GRAND RULLECOURT for baths. All Coys training, Specialists on special training. All Officers on tactical scheme with the O.C. from 2pm to 4 30pm.	
	3rd		Raining, Coys attended lectures. Iron Rations & Gas Helmets inspected.	
	4th		Owing to rain, route march cancelled, all men on lectures.	
FORTEL	5th		Regiment transferred to IV ARMY, XV CORPS. Battalion marched out 46 Officers & 731 OR strong at 8am. Route via FREVENT & BONNIERES to FORTEL, distant about 14 miles, arrived at FORTEL late in afternoon & went into billets.	Bde Op Ord 61.
	6th		Transport left for BEHENCOURT in advance, Regiment resting	Bde Op Ord 62.
BEHENCOURT	7th		Regiment left by busses for BEHENCOURT arriving there at dusk. Route via AMIENS	Bde Op Ord 63.
MAMETZ WOOD	8th		Regiment marched out at 10am en route for railway station at MEAULTE. Entrained about 4pm for MAMETZ WOOD arriving there after dark. 35 men were left at BEHENCOURT. Regiment took over trenches & dugouts for the night.	Bde Op Ord 64.
EAUCOURT L'ABBAYE	9th		Regiment marched out 20 Officers & 578 OR, halted at HIGH WOOD & went on at dusk to the trenches at EAUCOURT L'ABBAYE held by 21st & 22nd London Regiment. Relief effected. Certain specialists, second in command of Regiment & Coys, with other Officers were left behind at the 1st Line Transport. During the night front line trenches were dug & repaired.	Bde Op Ord 65.
	10th		Regiment in the line. Patrols out during the previous evening reconnoitring & collecting information. Throughout the day the enemy steadily shelled us on front line, supports & in vicinity of Battalion HeadQuarters. Our Artillery very active throughout the day. 35 men of new draft reported at 1st Line Transport & were immediately placed on duty at the Brigade Dump. Casualties 1 OR killed, 11 OR wounded, 1 OR slightly wounded & returned to duty.	

II.

War Diary

2nd South African Infantry

Place	Date	Hour	Summary of Events and Information	Remarks and references to Appendices
EAUCOURT L'ABBAYE	Oct 11th		Enemy artillery fairly active on front line, supports & vicinity of Battn. H.Q. Our artillery replied with usual activity, also putting up intense bombardment from 3.15 pm to 3.35 pm., enemy retaliation slight. Many wounded men of the London Regt were brought in by us, casualties 1 Offr wounded 4 O.R. killed 3 O.R. missing, 24 O.R. wounded 2 O.R. slightly wounded & returned to duty.	
	12th		The usual active bombardment by our guns, with slight retaliation from enemy. The Regiment attacked at 2.5 pm with 4th S.A.I. in support. The Regiment was on left of division – with 26th Bgde on right & 44th Bgde on left. Boundary between 26th Bgde & S.A.I. Bgde was a line running between M23 A68 & M17 B37. There were two objectives, First objective the enemy trench in M17C; second objective enemy trench from M17 B37 to the LE SARS-BAPAUME ROAD including the BUTTE de WARLENCOURT. The first objective was not attained, the advance being brought to a standstill by heavy machine gun fire from left front. Lieut Pearce & 75 men dug themselves in some 150 yds from enemy trench. During the night all available men assisted in bringing in the wounded. The Regiment with the exception of Lieut Pearce's party was relieved by the 3rd S.A.I. Known casualties 1 Offr killed 4 Offrs wounded 150 O.R. wounded	Ref. Op. Ord. 66. Map 57C, SW, ED 3A
BAZENTIN le GRAND	13th		All men with the exception of Lieut Pearce's party proceeded to BAZENTIN le GRAND. Marching out strength was 5 Offrs & 126 O.R. excluding Lieut Pearce's party. During the night 13th–14th Lieut Pearce & party of 75 men were relieved & returned to camp. Total estimated casualties 2 Captns, 13 Lieuts, & 316 O.R.	
	14th		Parties were sent out to assist to bring in the wounded & to fetch great coats left in line before proceeding to attack. Casualties NIL. Alteration to previous lists 1 Offr reported believed killed now reported killed, 1 Offr reported missing now reported killed, 3 Offrs reported missing, now reported wounded & missing, 1 Offr reported wounded, now reported Died of wounds, 1 Offr reported wounded now reported killed.	
	15th		Arms, Gas helmet inspection. New kit issued & great coats distributed. Stretcher parties provided, also party of men for work on dug outs with R.Es. Casualties NIL. Correction to previous list. 1 Offr reported wounded & missing now reported wounded, 1 Offr reported missing now reported killed.	

War Diary

2nd Regt South African Infantry

Place	Date	Hour	Summary of Events & Information	Remarks & references to Appendices
	Oct			
BAZENTIN LE GRAND	17th		Stretcher parties & carrying fatigues provided, Casualties 1 OR wounded. ~~Draft of~~	
	18th		177 O.R. arrived at 1st Line Transport. (New Draft). Stretcher parties & carrying parties provided, Casualties 3 OR missing, 1 OR died of wounds, 1 OR wounded	
MAMETZ WOOD	19th		Regiment moved out at 11AM for MAMETZ WOOD where they took over tents & dugouts from the 11th ROYAL SCOTS. All in new lines by 4 pm, Casualties NIL.	Bde Op Ord 69
	20th		177 OR of New Draft reported for duty. Stretcher party of 50 men to "Millers Post", this party to be relieved daily. 100 men supplied for road work under REs Casualties 1 OR wounded 1 OR died of wounds.	
	21st		Stretcher party of 50 OR to MILLERS POST	
	22nd		50 OR to MILLERS POST. 1 Off & 30 men to BAZENTIN CIRCUS for work under REs 2 Offs & 133 OR to S8 A&S. as working party under REs (Canada), Inspection of Gas Helmets. Casualties NIL	Map 57C SW & 3 & 4
	23rd		50 OR to MILLERS POST, 2 Offs & 108 OR to 1st 90th Field Coy REs at RE Dump S3 D47, remainder fatigues in camp.	do.
	24th		2 Offs & 100 OR to REs for road work (Reserve recalled). Stretcher, Dump & Burial Parties recalled. Battn moved to lines of 5th YORKSHIRE REGT. Move completed by 3.30 pm	Bde Op Ord 71
	25th		Working party of 4 Offs & 190 OR left at 9.30 am to report to REs at BOTTOM WOOD CORNER RE Dump.	
	26th		Working parties of 3 Offs & 300 OR on road work under REs.	
MILLENCOURT	27th		The Regiment marched out at 7.45 am for MILLENCOURT via CONTALMAISON & ALBERT arriving at 1 pm. Marching out strength 31 Offs 528 OR	Bde Op Ord 72
HERISSART	28th		The Regiment left MILLENCOURT at 9 am & arrived at HERISSART 1.30 pm	Bde Op Ord 73
	29th		The Regiment marched out at 7 am & proceeded 1 mile NW of HERISSART. The Regt embussed at 9 am & arrived at AGNES LES DUISANS at 7 pm. Marching in state 28 Offs 479 OR. Transport & Lewis Gun Carts left HERISSART at 6 am arriving at DOULLENS at 12 noon, strength 3 Offs 79 OR.	Bde Op Ord 74
AGNES LES DUISANS	30th		Regiment in billets. AB & C Coys bathed. Foot Inspection by M.O. General parades for inspection of equipment, clothing & arms. Transport & Lewis Gun Carts arrived at 4 pm, marching in state 3 Offs 79 O.R.	

IV

War Diary

Army Form C. 2118.

2nd Regt. South African Infantry.

Place	Date	Hour	Summary of Events & Information	Remarks & References to Appendices
AGNES LES DUISANS	Oct. 31st		Regiment in billets. 40 men fatigue on roads. Specialists training. Casualties (Correct) during the Regiments tour in the trenches at FAUCOURT L'ABBAYE; 5 Offs killed, 3 Offs died of wounds, 2 Offs missing, 6 Offs wounded, 57 O.R. killed, 225 O.R. wounded, 55 O.R. missing, 12 O.R. wounded & missing, 20 O.R. died of wounds. Total – Casualties – 16 Offs, 369 O.R.	

Edwdd Christian

Lieut.-Colonel,
Commanding 2nd Regt. S.A. Infantry

Army Form C. 2118.

WAR DIARY
or
INTELLIGENCE SUMMARY.
(Erase heading not required.)

Instructions regarding War Diaries and Intelligence Summaries are contained in F. S. Regs., Part II. and the Staff Manual respectively. Title pages will be prepared in manuscript.

2nd S. A. I. Vol 8

Place	Date	Hour	Summary of Events and Information	Remarks and references to Appendices
[illegible]	1.7.16 [illegible]		Regt. in billets. Strength 34 officers 607 O.R. Hd Qrs and [illegible] bathing. 50 O.R. fatigues. Specialists training. Remainder under Company arrangements.	
	2.		40 O.R. fatigues. Remainder as yesterday	
	3.		40 O.R. fatigues. Specialists training, C and D Coys. bathing and afterwards a route march. Remainder Coy. arrangements.	
	4.		50 O.R. on fatigue. Specialists training. Remainder Coy. arrangements.	
	5.		10. O.R. on fatigue. Court martial of PTE WAGNER. Church parades for C. of E. and R. Cs.	
	6.		50 ORs fatigues. Draft of 40 men arrived. Specialists Training. Remainder Coy Arrangements.	
and	7.		50 O.Rs. fatigues, Specialists training. Remainder Coy. arrangements.	Regtl Op. Order No 22
LATTRE ST QUENTIN	8.		At 9 A.M. 8 Officers 162 O.R. left for LATTRE ST. QUENTIN (A and C. Coys less sick and specialists who remained behind.	
	9.		41 O.Rs. fatigues AGNES. All available men on fatigue at LATTRE. Specialists Training. Remainder Coy. Arrangements.	

T2134. Wt. W708—776. 500000. 4/15. Sir J. C. & S.

Instructions regarding War Diaries and Intelligence Summaries are contained in F. S. Regs., Part II. and the Staff Manual respectively. Title pages will be prepared in manuscript.

WAR DIARY
or
INTELLIGENCE SUMMARY. 2nd S.A. INFANTRY.
(Erase heading not required.)

Army Form C. 2118.

Place	Date	Hour	Summary of Events and Information	Remarks and references to Appendices
AGNES-LES-DUISANS and	10/11/16		48 O.R. on fatigue at AGNES. All available men on fatigue at LATTRE. Specialists training. Remainder Coy arrangements. Men belonging to A and C Coys at AGNES together with details from B and D bathing.	
LATTRE-ST. QUENTIN.	11		63. ORs. fatigues at AGNES. Specialists training. Remainder Coy arrangements. All available men on fatigue at LATTRE.	
	12		57. O.R. fatigues AGNES. Remainder Church Parade. At LATTRE Church Parade	
	13		34 O.Rs. fatigues AGNES. Remainder Coy arrangements. Specialists training. All available men at LATTRE on fatigue.	
	14.		25 ORs. fatigues Agnes. All available men at LATTRE on fatigue. Coy arrangements remainder. B. Coy less specialists and sick, moved out to LATTRE. Strength 3 Officers and 68 ORs. Capt Heenan left on Coy. Cmdrs. Course ~~[illegible]~~, 2nd Lt THORBURN took over A. Coy.	
	15.		23 O.R fatigues AGNES, Specialists training, Remainder Coy arrangements. 40 ORs on fatigue at LATTRE	

T2134. Wt. W708-776. 500000. 4/15. Sir J. C. & S.

Instructions regarding War Diaries and Intelligence Summaries are contained in F. S. Regs., Part II. and the Staff Manual respectively. Title pages will be prepared in manuscript.

WAR DIARY
or
INTELLIGENCE SUMMARY.
(*Erase heading not required.*)

2ND S.A.I

Army Form C. 2118.

Place	Date	Hour	Summary of Events and Information	Remarks and references to Appendices
AGNES LES DUISANS	16/11/16		31 O.Rs. fatigues at AGNES. Specialists Training. 19 O.R. to base as unfit. 40 O.Rs. fatigue at LATTRE. Remainder Coy arrangements.	
and	17.		18 O.Rs. fatigues at AGNES. Specialists Training. 25 O.Rs. fatigue at LATTRE. Remainder company arrangements.	
LATTRE ST QUENTIN	18.		13. O.R. fatigues at AGNES. Specialists training. 25 O.R. Fatigues at LATTRE Remainder Coy arrangements. LORD MILNER visited Bde. H.Qrs and met officers of the Regt. Lt Col TANNER C.M.G and Capt BAMFORD arrived from England.	
	19.		11 O.R. fatigues AGNES. Specialists Training. O.Rs fatigues LATTRE. Remainder Coy arrangements. Lt Col CHRISTIAN relinquished Command of the Regt. Capt Cochran Actg Adjt posted to B Coy as OC. Lt Col TANNER C.M.G. resumed command. Capt BAMFORD took over his duties as ADJUTANT again.	
LATTRE ST QUENTIN.	20		Remainder of Regt. proceeded to LATTRE. 25 O.Rs. on fatigues. Draft of 35 men arrived from base.	REGTL. O. ORDER NO 23.

T2134. Wt. W708—776. 500000. 4/15. Sir J. C. & S.

Instructions regarding War Diaries and Intelligence Summaries are contained in F. S. Regs., Part II. and the Staff Manual respectively. Title pages will be prepared in manuscript.

IV

WAR DIARY
or
INTELLIGENCE SUMMARY. 2ND S. A. I

(Erase heading not required.)

Army Form C. 2118.

Place	Date	Hour	Summary of Events and Information	Remarks and references to Appendices
LATTRE ST QUENTIN	22/11/16		34 O.R fatigues. General Training. Gens. Haldane and Furse inspected the work. Games in the afternoon. Specialists under own instructors.	
	23/11/16		43 O.R fatigues. Box respirators tested and fitted. Training as per programme. Specialists under own instructors. Draft of 2 men reported	
	24/11/16		21 O.R. fatigues. Training as per programme. Specialists as yesterday. Night operations for Coys. Football in the afternoon. 2ND LT BROOK returned off a course (general training)	
	25/11/16		41 O.R. fatigues. Training as per programme. Specialists under own Instructors. Football in the afternoon.	
	26/11/16		21 O.R. fatigues. Church parade. 2nd Lt GREEN went to DIV SCHOOL as INSTRUCTOR. Football in the afternoon. Lt Col TANNER left to attend a Conference of Comdg Officers at 3rd ARMY School at AUXI LE CHATEAU. Maj Symmes temporarily Comdg Regt. 2nd Lt McLean left for a sniping Course.	

T2134. Wt. W708–776. 500000. 4/15. Sir J. C. & S.

Instructions regarding War Diaries and Intelligence Summaries are contained in F. S. Regs., Part II. and the Staff Manual respectively. Title pages will be prepared in manuscript.

WAR DIARY or INTELLIGENCE SUMMARY.

(Erase heading not required.)

2ND S.A.I.

Army Form C. 2118.

Place	Date	Hour	Summary of Events and Information	Remarks and references to Appendices
LATTRE ST QUENTIN	27/11/16		Training as per programme. Specialist Training. 20 O.R. on fatigues R.F.C.	
	28/11/16		40 O.R. fatigue on Bayonet Assault Course and 20 O.R. to R.F.C for fatigue duty. Remainder training as laid down. Remainder of men having box respirators tested. 2nd Lt. Walsh left for Divisional Hd Qrs to act as Temp. Aide de Camp to Gen FURSE.	
	29/11/16		20 O.R. Fatigues. Specialists training under own Instructors. Remainder as laid down in Programme. Lt Pearse and 2nd Lt. Adendorff on a Coy Cmdrs Course. 2nd Lt. Ross on a bayonet fighting course. Capt Bamford proceeded to Hd Qrs of 27th Inf Bde for Staff duty. During his absence Capt Cochrane is appointed acting Adjutant. 2nd Lt Dowling O.C. B Coy during the absence of Capt Cochrane. 2nd Lt James O.C. D Coy during the absence of Lt Pearse.	

T2134. Wt. W708—776. 500000. 4/15. Sir J. C. & S.

VI

Instructions regarding War Diaries and Intelligence Summaries are contained in F. S. Regs., Part II. and the Staff Manual respectively. Title pages will be prepared in manuscript.

WAR DIARY
or
INTELLIGENCE SUMMARY.
(Erase heading not required.)

2nd S. A. I

Army Form C. 2118.

Place	Date	Hour	Summary of Events and Information	Remarks and references to Appendices
LATTRE ST QUENTIN	30/11/16		20 O.R. fatigue R.F.C. Training as per programme. Regiment marched to Wanquetin by Coys. and practised firing from the hip, 10 rounds per man. Strength 24 Officers 585 men.	

H. P. Symmes Major
Commanding 2nd Regt. S.A. Infantry

To/

South African Brigade.

Herewith WAR DIARY for month of DECEMBER, 1916.

for F. E. Cochran Capt & adj.
Lieut. Colonel,
Commanding 2nd Regiment S. A. Infantry.
Temp absent

1st January, 1917.

2nd Regiment South African Infantry.

Instructions regarding War Diaries and Intelligence Summaries are contained in F. S. Regs., Part II. and the Staff Manual respectively. Title pages will be prepared in manuscript.

WAR DIARY
or
INTELLIGENCE SUMMARY.
(Erase heading not required.)

Army Form C. 2118.

Place	Date	Hour	Summary of Events and Information	Remarks and references to Appendices
	Decr.			
LATTRE ST QUENTIN.	1st.		Forty other ranks on fatique. All specialists training under own Instructors. Remainder training in accordance with programme laid down. During the afternoon competitions were held, including guard mounting, best turned out man in full marching order, and a long distance race.	
	2nd.		Bathing carried on and in the intervals training as laid down. O.C. and Company Commanders went to the line to look over Sector to be taken over.	
SUB-SECTION I. II	3rd		Advance party of four Company officers, Signalling officer, R.S.M. all Company Sergeant Majors and 16 other ranks left at 8. am. to proceed to Sub Section I.II.- At 3.30 pm the Regiment embussed, arriving in the line after dusk. The Battalion relieved the 14th GLOUCESTERS.- and took over Sub Section I.II. Limits of front held by Battalion were Trench 95 CLARENCE CRATER exclusive to Trench 89 inclusive. "B" Coy occupied 89-92 inclusive in front line and "C" Company 93-95 CLARENCE CRATER exclusive.- "A" Company 89-"B" Works inclusive in support, and "D" Company in BRITTANIA WORKS and vicinity. Headquarters at G.17.a.1.7. Detachment at Candle Factory. Relief was	O.O. No 214.- (attached) Map. Ref ARRAS 51B NW 3 1/10,000

T2134. Wt. W708-776. 500000. 4/15. Sir J. C. & S.

Instructions regarding War Diaries and Intelligence Summaries are contained in F. S. Regs., Part II. and the Staff Manual respectively. Title pages will be prepared in manuscript.

WAR DIARY
or
INTELLIGENCE SUMMARY.
(Erase heading not required.)

Army Form C. 2118.

Place	Date	Hour	Summary of Events and Information	Remarks and references to Appendices
SUBSECTION J. II	3rd (Cont)		complete at 9.25 p.m. The 1st S.A. Infy are on the right, 3rd on the left, and 4th in ARRAS in Reserve. 106 O.R. employed wiring, repairs to trenches etc. 108 other ranks on carrying work.-	
	4th		Two patrols out during the night inspecting the wire. Two parties engaged wiring. Others general work and carrying parties. Enemy quiet.	
	5th		Communication Trenches being repaired and revetted, also repair work being carried out on saps, and Dug-out of Headquarters, Right Company. Enemy was slightly active on right using Trench Mortars without doing any material damage. Also fired on our patrols about 3 or 4 am but without ~~effect~~ harm. Our machine guns active. Our artillery - fairly active at intervals.- Our Trench Mortars ranging.-	
	6th		All available men employed on general repairs and constructional work, wiring and carrying parties.- Posts for snipers and observers under construction. Two officer's patrols were out inspecting our wire.- Casualties - one other rank wounded.- Enemy attitude quiet.-	

Instructions regarding War Diaries and Intelligence Summaries are contained in F. S. Regs., Part II. and the Staff Manual respectively. Title pages will be prepared in manuscript.

WAR DIARY
or
INTELLIGENCE SUMMARY.
(Erase heading not required.)

Army Form C. 2118.

Place	Date	Hour	Summary of Events and Information	Remarks and references to Appendices
SUB.SECTION J.II	7th		The Regiment was relieved by the 4th. S.A. Infantry and went into reserve. Battalion Headquarters, HOTEL UNIVERSE, ARRAS; "B" and "C" Coys billeted at Convent; "A" Coy, less one platoon at St. NICHOLAS, one platoon, "A" Coy" at BOSKY REDOUBT. "D" Company, less two platoons, at NICHOLLS REDOUBT, & two platoons of "D" Coy at FORRESTIER REDOUBT. During the relief the enemy put over a number of Trench mortars, rifle grenades and a few minenwerfer, without, however, causing any casualties.- Usual work was carried out during the day prior to relief commencing.- Relief commenced 4.30 pm and finished 6.30 p.m.	Regtl. O.O. No. 25. (attached)
RESERVE BILLETS.	8th		Two officers and 100 men working under the R.E's on general work in the line.- Remainder of men at the REDOUBTS repairing, revetting, etc.- in the vicinity of their posts.- Lewis Gunners and signallers were working under their own instructors, and were stationed at Battalion Headquarters.-	

Instructions regarding War Diaries and Intelligence Summaries are contained in F. S. Regs., Part II. and the Staff Manual respectively. Title pages will be prepared in manuscript.

WAR DIARY
or
INTELLIGENCE SUMMARY.
(Erase heading not required.)

Army Form C. 2118.

Place	Date	Hour	Summary of Events and Information	Remarks and references to Appendices
RESERVE BILLETS	9th		Two officers and 100 men on fatigue with R.E's. Same work as yesterday.- "B", "C" and Headquarters bathed at S.A.M.C. baths in ARRAS. All available men in Redoubts - general work at their posts.- Signallers and Lewis Gunners - training.	
	10th		Two officers and 100 men employed as yesterday.- Headquarter Detachment, "B" and "C" Companies at the convent on Church Parade	
	11th		Two officers and 104 men employed as yesterday with R.E's.- "B" Company relieved "D" Company at FORRESTIER and NICHOLL REDOUBTS.- "D" Company came into the Convent. Casualties - one other rank, slight, shrapnel.- Signallers and Lewis Gunners training.-	Regtl O.O. No. 26 (attached)
	12th		Three officers and 156 other ranks on working and carrying parties under R.E's.- "D" Coy bathing. Remainder of men available at Redoubts on work in the vicinity of their posts.- All available men at Battalion Headquarters included in above fatigue.-	
	13th		Three officers and 147 other ranks to R.E's for working and.	

Instructions regarding War Diaries and Intelligence Summaries are contained in F. S. Regs., Part II. and the Staff Manual respectively. Title pages will be prepared in manuscript.

WAR DIARY
or
INTELLIGENCE SUMMARY.
(Erase heading not required.)

Page 5

Army Form C. 2118.

Place	Date	Hour	Summary of Events and Information	Remarks and references to Appendices
RESERVE BILLETS (Cont)	13th		carrying parties, this includes all available men from Headquarters. Available men at Redoubts working in the vicinity of their posts.	-
	14th		Three officers and 150 men to R.E.'s as yesterday.- Headquarter men included: Remainder of available men at Redoubts - General repairs in vicinity of their posts.-	
SUB-SECTION J.II.	15th		The Regiment relieved the 4th S.A. Infantry in Sub Section J. II, relief commenced 2. pm and completed 4.45 p.m. Disposition of Companies on relief - Left company in front line "A" Company.- "D" Company right company in front line.- "C" Coy in Support. "B" Company in BRITTANIA WORKS and vicinity.- The band and other details attached to Headquarters were stationed at Candle Factory. Battalion Headquarters at G.17.a.1.7.-	Regtl. O.O. No. 27. (attached)
	16th		Enemy quiet generally with exception of a few minenwerfers which fell in vicinity of JULY and Support trench. Our Artillery active from 2.30 to 3.30 p.m. Our Trench Mortars active between 2.45 pm and 3.30 p.m. One patrol out at night. "A" and "D" Companies	

T2134. Wt. W708-776. 500000. 4/15. Sir J. C. & S.

WAR DIARY
or
INTELLIGENCE SUMMARY.
(Erase heading not required.)

Place	Date	Hour	Summary of Events and Information	Remarks and references to Appendices
SUB-SECTION J II	16th (cont.)		to Candle Works for Bathing. 135 other ranks on repair, construction and carrying work. - Casualty. One other rank wounded. -	
	17th		Enemy Trench Mortars slight activity, also six minenwerfers fell in our lines. Enemy were generally more active than on previous days. Some aerial torpedoes came over between front line and support - no damage. - Our artillery fairly active in the afternoon. Also Trench Mortars, which latter shelled the enemy front line. - An officers patrol was out during the night, patrolling front. 169 other ranks employed general work, Repairs, revetting construction and carrying. - 1 Off. (2nd Lieut. James) - wounded and Two other ranks wounded. -	
	18th		Quiet generally. - 160 other ranks employed clearing, cleaning, revetting, and repairing trenches, wiring and carrying parties. -	
	19th		Enemy 18 pounders did a little damage in AUGUST AVENUE; a few shells fell in support line, but no damage. Enemy machine guns fairly active from 9.30 am. to 11.30 am. About 15 minenwerfers and	

Instructions regarding War Diaries and Intelligence Summaries are contained in F. S. Regs., Part II. and the Staff Manual respectively. Title pages will be prepared in manuscript.

WAR DIARY
or
INTELLIGENCE SUMMARY.
(Erase heading not required.)

Army Form C. 2118.

Page 7

Place	Date	Hour	Summary of Events and Information	Remarks and references to Appendices
SUB-SECTION S.II	19th cont		and 40 aerial torpedoes fell in our lines during the day.- Our artillery active from 10.30 am. to 11. a.m. shelling the enemy front line, apparently with good effect. 18 pounders and 60 pounders were used. Our Stokes Trench Mortars also bombarded from 10.30 a.m. to 11. a.m. An officers patrol was out during the night inspecting our wire. 170 other ranks on duty cleaning, revetting and repairing trenches,- and communication trenches; also construction of saps and wiring. At 11.30 p.m. a German working party was observed and dispersed by our Lewis Gun fire.- Inter Company relief carried out. "C" relieved "A" Company in the Front Line. "A" Company going into Support. "B" relieved "D" Company in Front Line, "D" Company going into reserve.- Relief completed by 2. p.m.	Regtl. O.O. No. 28 (attached.)
	20th		Enemy attitude agressive - Enemy shelled AUGUST AVENUE and Support Line with light shells.- Trench Mortars and their aerial Torpedoes also active. Several heavy minenwerfers	

Instructions regarding War Diaries and Intelligence Summaries are contained in F. S. Regs., Part II. and the Staff Manual respectively. Title pages will be prepared in manuscript.

WAR DIARY
or
INTELLIGENCE SUMMARY.
(Erase heading not required.)

Army Form C. 2118.

Page 8

Place	Date	Hour	Summary of Events and Information	Remarks and references to Appendices
SUB-SECTION S.II.-	20th (cont)		fell in the rear of CUTBERT CRATER, slightly damaging trench. Enemy aircraft active from 9.30 am to 10.30 a.m. Our aircraft engaged that of the enemy, which eventually returned to its own lines, followed by the fire of our anti-aircraft guns.- Our artillery active, also Trench Mortars, who fired on enemy front opposite our right. Machine guns active with indirect fire during the night. Wiring parties out during the night also an Officers patrol.- 184 other ranks engaged clearing, revetting, construction and wiring.-	
	21st		Enemy's artillery - slight activity, shelling the support line with light shells - damage slight.- His machine guns slightly active during the night.- Our artillery active throughout the day, shells seem to burst along the enemy parapet with good effect. Trench Mortars also very active, apparently with good results.- 108 other ranks on general work as yesterday.-	

WAR DIARY
or
INTELLIGENCE SUMMARY.
(Erase heading not required.)

Page 10

Instructions regarding War Diaries and Intelligence Summaries are contained in F. S. Regs., Part II. and the Staff Manual respectively. Title pages will be prepared in manuscript.

Place	Date	Hour	Summary of Events and Information	Remarks and references to Appendices
SUB-SECTION J.II.	23rd (Cont.)		in Front line, D Company relieved "B" Company in Front line. "C" Company relieved "A" Coy in Support Line, "B" Company relieved "D" Company in BRITTANIA WORKS and vicinity.	
	24th		Enemy attitude quiet. About 2. p.m. 6 minenwerfer shells came over - no damage. An enemy plane approached our line but was driven off by our planes and returned to its own lines. Our artillery fairly active about 10. a.m. Our Trench Mortars active on enemy front line between 1.30 and 2.30 p.m. Twenty rounds were fired from our 2" Trench Mortars and appeared mostly to fall beyond enemy front line. During the morning our aircraft was active. At night an officers patrol was out inspecting enemy wire. 115 other ranks clearing, cleaning, revetting, carrying, wiring etc.-	
	25th		During the night enemy used more Very Lights than usual and it was noticed they had a longer range and appeared brighter. Enemy artillery active during the afternoon. Our support line was damaged in two places. he ceased artillery fire at 3.30 p.m. It appeared to be retaliation for our shoot. Enemy Trench Mortars fired on our support line in the afternoon, also a few minenwerfers. Our artillery very active during afternoon. Our 2 inch and Stokes Trench Mortars bombarded enemy front line at 2.15 p.m. Our Machine Guns	

A5834 Wt. W4973/M687 750,000 8/16 D. D. & L. Ltd. Forms/C.2118/13.

2nd Regiment South African Infy.

Instructions regarding War Diaries and Intelligence Summaries are contained in F. S. Regs., Part II. and the Staff Manual respectively. Title pages will be prepared in manuscript.

WAR DIARY
or
INTELLIGENCE SUMMARY.
(Erase heading not required.)

Army Form C. 2118.

Place	Date	Hour	Summary of Events and Information	Remarks and references to Appendices
SUB-SECTION I. II	22nd		Enemy activity slight in afternoon. Shelled our Communication Trenches with light shells, also put over a few minenwerfer without effect. At night whilst our wiring parties were out, enemy machine guns were active.- Our artillery fairly active during afternoon shelling enemy front line and also some distance behind it.- Our Trench Mortars fairly active at intervals. Machine guns firing during the night. indirect fire.- Casualties 1 other rank wounded. 161 other ranks on general work, extending Saps, clearing, revetting etc and also wiring and carrying.-	
	23rd		Enemy shelling our support lines with light shells about 11. a.m. Enemy Trench Mortars active about noon, slightly damaging one place in Support Line. During afternoon about 40 - 18-pounder shells fell around AUGUST and NOVEMBER, of which a good percentage were blind. In the afternoon 9 minenwerfers fell in near of CUTBERT CRATER between Support and Front line.- Our artillery active during morning and afternoon. Trench Mortars very active with apparent good results on enemy front line. about 300 rounds expended. Machine Guns active throughout night with overhead fire. Two officer patrols out during night to examine enemy wire, and to see what damage had been done by our Trench Mortar fire. 164 other ranks carrying, general construction work, wiring etc. "A" Company relieved "C" Coy	Regt. operation order No. 29 (attached)

A5834 Wt. W4973/M687 750,000 8/16 D. D. & L. Ltd. Forms/C.2118/13.

Instructions regarding War Diaries and Intelligence Summaries are contained in F. S. Regs., Part II. and the Staff Manual respectively. Title pages will be prepared in manuscript.

WAR DIARY
or
INTELLIGENCE SUMMARY.
(Erase heading not required.)

Army Form C. 2118.

Place	Date	Hour	Summary of Events and Information	Remarks and references to Appendices
SUB-SECTION 1.II.	25th (Cont)		guns also assisted. Our aircraft were active. An enemy plane was observed flying low over CLARENCE CRATER. — Machine guns and anti-aircraft guns were used and they all returned to their own lines. - 111 other ranks general work, carrying, construction, repairing, etc. 15 other ranks wiring. Casualties 1 officer (2ND LIEUT. - BURLEY) killed, and Two other ranks killed. -	
	26th.		Enemy artillery quiet. Enemy put 6 minenwerfer shells between Support and Front Line. Enemy aircraft were up about 11.30 am., but were driven off by our machine and anti-aircraft guns. - During the night more activity was shewn by the enemy in use of rifles and very lights. Enemy machine guns rather more active, and aerial Torpedoes sent over at intervals. Our artillery more active from 2. pm to 2.30 pm. and again during the night, shelling enemy lines in rear at intervals. Our aircraft engaged enemy planes about 11.30 am. and drove them back to their own lines. - At intervals during the day we put over a number of rifle grenades. - 198 other ranks were on general work connected with Sap and Trench Construction, repairs and carrying parties. - 1 officer and 16 other ranks were wiring. -	
	27th		Company reliefs were carried out during the day. "C" relieved "A" Company in front line and "B" relieved "D" Company in the front line.	Regtl. O.O. No. 30 (attached)

A5834 Wt. W4973/M687 750,000 8/16 D. D. & L. Ltd. Forms/C.2118/13.

Instructions regarding War Diaries and Intelligence Summaries are contained in F. S. Regs., Part II. and the Staff Manual respectively. Title pages will be prepared in manuscript.

WAR DIARY
or
INTELLIGENCE SUMMARY.
(Erase heading not required.)

Page 12.

Army Form C. 2118.

Place	Date	Hour	Summary of Events and Information	Remarks and references to Appendices
SUB-SECTION I. II.	27th. (cont.)		"D" Company relieved "A" Coy in Support line and "A" relieved "B" Company in BRITTANIA WORKS. Enemy artillery put 10 long range shells in the vicinity of NICHOLLS REDOUBT. About 9.30 am several enemy Heavy Trench Mortar shells came over, no damage. Enemy artillery very active at 11 p.m. and finishing at 3.30 am (28/12/16) putting gas shells continuously into ARRAS. Enemy Trench Mortars slight activity, - 2.30 pm. to 4.30 pm. Our artillery active, - Our Trench Mortars also active. A fair number of rifle grenades were put over by us. 137 other ranks on working and carrying parties. 1 off and 11 other ranks wiring. -	
	28th.		Enemy artillery active with gas shells from 11 pm (27/12/16) to 3.30 am. shelling ARRAS. Enemy's trench mortars fairly quiet. During the day enemy artillery inactive. Between 3 pm and 4 pm 11 minenwerfer shells fell on right and left of JULY AVENUE, damage done to JULY in one place. Our artillery active firing on enemy front and support lines. - Our trench mortars active especially the Stokes between 3 pm. and 4.15 pm. A fair number of rifle grenades were put over by us during the day. 102 other ranks on working and carrying parties. 1 off. 12 other ranks wiring. Our machine guns overhead fire during night. -	
	29th.		Enemy artillery quiet except for a few long range shells. His trench Mortars and Minenwerfer also quiet. - Our artillery very active for a short time during afternoon and after that, bursts of gunfire at irregular intervals during the early part of the night.	

Instructions regarding War Diaries and Intelligence Summaries are contained in F. S. Regs., Part II. and the Staff Manual respectively. Title pages will be prepared in manuscript.

WAR DIARY
or
INTELLIGENCE SUMMARY.
(Erase heading not required.)

Page 13.

Army Form C. 2118.

Place	Date	Hour	Summary of Events and Information	Remarks and references to Appendices
SUB-SECTION J. II	29th (Contd.)		Our Trench Mortars active on enemy front and support lines. - 215 men Working and Carrying parties. 1 officer and 9 other ranks wiring. During the day Rifle Grenades were fired by us at intervals. -	
	30th		Enemy artillery quiet, except for a few long range shells dropped in rear of our support line. - No damage done. - Enemy Trench Mortars and machine guns quiet. Our artillery and Trench Mortars fairly active - Our machine guns were active. - An officer and two men patrolled "NO MANS LAND", but did not meet or hear any of the enemy. - Twenty six rifle grenades were expended on enemy front line. - 170 other ranks on clearing, revetting and Repairing Front line and Support Trenches. 1 off. 9 other ranks wiring our front line. -	
	31st		Inter Company reliefs. - "A" relieving "C" Company in Front Line. "D" relieving "B" Company in front line. - "B" relieved "D" Company in Support Line, and "C" relieved "A" Company in BRITTANIA WORKS and vicinity. - Relief completed by 2.15 p.m. Enemy artillery and Trench Mortars were active immediately after relief was effected without causing any casualties. -	Regtl. Operation Order No. 31 (attached)

A5834 Wt. W4973/M687 750,000 8/16 D. D. & L. Ltd. Forms/C.2118/13

SECRET. Copy No. 8.

OPERATION ORDER NO: 31.

IN THE FIELD,
30th December, 1916.

Ex. I.
Map Reference
Trench Map
1/10,000.

No. 1. RELIEF. The following reliefs will take place to-morrow, the 31st instant. -
"A" Coy. will relieve "C" Coy. in FRONT LINE.
"D" Coy. will relieve "B" Coy. in FRONT LINE.
"B" Company on relief will occupy the SUPPORT LINE.
"C" Company on relief will occupy BRITTANIA WORKS and vicinity.

Company Commanders will arrange with the Company Commanders they relieve the method of relief and submit proposals for approval to the Commanding Officer.

No. 2. INFORMATION. Our Artillery and Trench Mortar Batteries will not, as far as is known, operate.

No. 3. LEWIS GUNS "A" and "D" Companies will each be augmented by two extra Lewis Guns for the period which these Companies are in the Front Line. Detachments for these guns will report to O.C. "A" and "D" Companies at 9.30 a.m. on the 31st instant.

No. 4. TRENCH STORES. These will be taken over and receipts obtained.

No. 5. LOG BOOKS. Log Books completed will be taken over.

No. 6. COMPLETION OF RELIEF.
Relief to be completed by 2.15. p.m.
Completion of relief will be reported in writing to Orderly Room.

No. 7. ACTION IN CASE OF ATTACK.
O.C.'s "B" and "C" Companies will remain in command of their respective fronts until completion of the relief.

McLean

Captain & A/Adjutant,
2nd Regiment S. A. Infantry.

Copy No. 1.	File.
Copy No. 2.	"A" Coy.
Copy No. 3.	"B" Coy.
Copy No. 4.	"C" Coy.
Copy No. 5.	"D" Coy.
Copy No. 6.	Commanding Officer.
Copy No. 7.	2nd in Command.
Copy No. 8.	War Diary.

SECRET.

Copy No. 8.

OPERATION ORDER No: 30.

IN THE FIELD,
26th December, 1916.

Map Reference
Trench Map
1/10,000.

No. 1. RELIEF. The following reliefs will take place to-morrow the 27th instant.-
"C" Company will relieve "A" Company in FRONT LINE.
"B" Company will relieve "D" Company in FRONT LINE.
"D" Company on relief will occupy the SUPPORT LINE.
"A" Company on relief will occupy BRITTANIA WORKS and vicinity.

Company Commanders of "C" and "B" Companies will arrange with the Company Commander they relieve the method of relief and submit proposals for approval to the Commanding Officer.

No. 2. INFORMATION. Our Artillery and Trench Mortar Batteries will not operate ~~unless otherwise advised~~ as far as is known.

No. 3. LEWIS GUNS. "B" and "C" Companies will each be augmented by two extra Lewis Guns for the period which these Companies are in the Front Line. Detachments for these guns will report to O.C. "B" and "C" Companies at 9.30. a.m. on the 27th instant.

No. 4. TRENCH STORES. These will be taken over and receipts obtained.

No. 5. LOG BOOKS. Log Books completed will be taken over.

No. 6. COMPLETION OF RELIEF.
Completion of relief will be reported in writing to Orderly Room.

No. 7. ACTION IN CASE OF ATTACK. O.C's. "A" and "D" Companies will remain in command of their respective fronts until completion of the relief.

E Cochran
Captain & A/Adjutant,
2nd Regiment S. A. Infantry.

Copy	No. 1.	File.
	No. 2.	"A" Coy.
	No. 3.	"B" Coy.
	No. 4.	"C" Coy.
	No. 5.	"D" Coy.
	No. 6.	Commanding Officer.
	No. 7.	Second in Command.
	No. 8.	War Diary.

Copy No. 8.

OPERATION ORDER NO: 89.

[illegible] IN THE FIELD,
22nd December, 1916.

Map Reference
Trench Map
1/10,000.

No. 1. RELIEF. The following reliefs willx take place to-morrow, the 23rd instant:-
"A" Company will relieve "C" Company in FRONT LINE.
"D" Company will relieve "B" Company in FRONT LINE.
"C" Company on relief will occupy the SUPPORT LINE.
"B" Coy. on relief will occupy BRITTANIA WORKS and vicinity.

Company Commanders of "A" and "D" Companies will arrange with the Company Commander they relieve the method of relief and submit proposals for approval to the Commanding Officer.

No. 2. [illegible]. Our Artillery and Trench Mortar Battery will operate on enemy lines at 2.45 p.m. on the 23rd inst.

No. 3. LEWIS GUNS. "A" and "D" Companies will each be augmented by two extra Lewis Guns for the period which these Companies are in the front line. Detachments for these guns will report to O.C. "A" and "D" Coys. at 9.30 a.m. on 23.12.1916.

No. 4. TRENCH STORES. These will be taken over and receipts obtained.

No. 5. LOG BOOKS. Logx books completed will be taken over.

No. 6. COMPLETION OF RELIEF. Completion of relief will be reported in writing to Orderly Room.

No. 7. [illegible] ATTACK. O.C.'s "B" and "C" Companies will remain in command of their respective fronts until completion of the relief.

Captain & A/Adjutant,
2nd Regt. S. A. Infantry.

Copy No. 1 - File.
Copy No. 2. "A" Coy.
Copy No. 3. "B" Coy.
Copy No. 4. "C" Coy.
Copy No. 5. "D" Coy.
Copy No. 6. Commanding Officer.
Copy No. 7. 2nd in Command.
Copy No. 8. War Diary.

2nd SOUTH AFRICAN INFANTRY ORDER No 27. Page 2.

Vacated/

7 WORKING PARTIES.	Work will be carried out in accordance with special order issued.
8 TRENCH STORES.	Trench Stores will be taken over and receipts in duplicate,obtained.One card will be sent in to Battalion H.Q. by 9.0.p.m. 15th inst.
9. TELEPHONES.	In accordance with orders in force regarding the use of telephones,no message whatever wik will be sent over the line regarding the xxix relief excepting the code word reporting relief complete.
10. COMPLETION OF RELIEF.	Completion of relief will be reported by telephone to Battalion H.Q. by code word "BILLY".
11 MOVEMENT IN ARRAS.	Orders regarding movement in ARRAS must be strictly adhered to.

F.E. Ochrun

Captain.&A/Adjutant.
2nd Regiment.S.A.I.

No 1 Copy to "A" Coy by Orderly.
2 Copy to "B" Coy by Orderly.
3 Copy to "C" Coy by Orderly
4 Copy to "D" Coy by Orderly.
5 Copy to Commanding Officer.
6 Copy to 2nd in Command.
7 Copy Office File.
8 Copy to S.A.Brigade.
9 Copy to 4th S.A.Infty.
10. Copy for War Diary.

2nd REGIMENT SOUTH AFRICAN INFANTRY ORDER No 28.

Map referance
Trench Map
1/10.000.

18-12-16.

Copy...6 8.......

No 1
RELIEF

"C" Company will relieve "A" Coy in FRONT LINE.

"B" Company will releive "D" Coy in FRONT LINE on the 19-12-16.
"A" Coy on relief will ocupy the SUPPORT LINE.
"D" Coy on relief will ocupy BRITTANIA WORKS and vicinity.

Company Commanders of "B" and "C" Coy's will ~~xxxx~~ arrange with the Company Commander they relieve the method of relief and submit proposals for approval to the Commanding Officer.

No2
INFORMATION.

OUR ARTILLERY and T.M.B. will operate on ENEMY LINES at 10.30.a.m. to 11.0.a.m. on the 19-~~xxx~~6.

No 3
LEWIS GUNS.

"B" and "C" Cy's will each be augmented by two extra LEWIS GUNS for the period which these Coy's are in the fron t line.Detachments forthese guns will report to O.C. "B" and "C" coy's at 9.30. a.m. on 19-12-16.

No 4.
TRENCH STORES.

These will be taken over and receipts obtained.

No 5
LOG BOOKS%

Log Books completed will be taken over.

No 6
COMPLETION OF RELIEF.

Completion of relief will be reported in writing to Orderly Room.

No 7
ACTION IN CASE OF ATTACK.

O.C's "A" and "D" Coy's will remain in command of their respective fronts until completion of ~~xx~~ relief.

Lt. for Captain & A/Adjutant.
2nd Regiment South African Infantry.

Copy No 1 to "A" Coy.
Copy No 2 to "B" Coy
Copy No 3 to "C" Coy.
Copy No 4 to "D" Coy.
Copy No 5 to Commanding Officer.
Copy No 6 to 2nd in Command.
Copy No 7 to Office File.
Copy No. 8. War Diary.

2nd SOUTH AFRICAN INFANTRY ORDER No 27. Copy..10....

Map reference.
Trench Map. ARRAS.
1/10,000.

14-12-16.

1
RELIEF. The Battalion will relieve the 4th S.A.Infantry on the 15th in Sub - Section.J.2

2
DISTRIBUTION. "A" Coy will relieve the LEFT Coy in the front line
"D" Coy will relieve the RIGHT Coy in the front line.
"C" Coy will relieve the SUPPORT Coy in the Support line.
"B" Coy will relieve the RESERVE Coy in BRITANNIA WORKS and vicinity.

3
LEWIS GUNS. Lewis G uns of "A" "D" and "C" Companies will relieve Lewis Guns of 4th S.A.Infantry in front and support lines at 12.0.noon.
"A" and "D" Companies will each be augmented bytwo extra Lewis Guns for the period which these Coy's are in the front line.These detachments will report to the Company Commanders at 9.30.a.m. tomorrow.
The relief of the remainder of the Battalion will commence at 1.0.p.m. in the following order:-
1 Platoon and 1 Lewis Gun of "B" Coy from FORRESTIER REDOUBT will relieveReserve Company,4th S.A.I. in BRITTANIA WORKS at 1.0.p.m.
"C" Coy will relieveSupport Coy,4th S.A.I. at 1.40. p.m.
"A" Coy,less one platoon,will relieve Left Coy 4th S.A.I. at 2.10.p.m.

"D" Coy will relieve Right Coy,4th S.A.I. at 2.50. p.m.
"B" Coy,less 1 platoon,will move to BRITTANIA WORKS and vicinity on relief in FORRESTIER REDOUBT and NICHOLL'S REDOUBT by 3rd S.A.I. at 3.30.p.m.

1 platoon of "A" Company at DUSKY REDOUBT will be relieved by 1 platoon of 3rd S.A.I. at 2.0.p.m. and will move forward via AUGUST AVENUE,to Front Line to its position as alloted by O.C."A" Coy.

4
ROUTES. The relief will be carried out in succession of platoons at intervals of 10 minutes.
Lewis Gunners will move in via JULY AVENUE.
"C" Coy will move in via JULY AVENUE.
"A" Coy " " " " " "
"D" Coy will move in via MAY AVENUE.

5
GUIDES. No guides will be supplied.

6
LOG-BOOKS,etc. Companies will take over,Log-books,Maps,etc,and hand over these for position being vacated.

7

2nd S.A. INFANTRY ORDER No 25. COPY No 8. War Diary.
--- 6-12-16.

Map reference.
Sketch plan of trenches.

1 RELIEF. The Battalion will be relieved by the 4th S.A. Infantry on the 7th inst in Sub-Section J.2. The Battalion will take up duties of Reserve Battalion.

2 The Lewis Guns of "B" and "C" Companies will be relieved at 1.p.m. and will withdraw via July Avenue to Candle Factory where a guide will meet the detachments and conduct them to the Convent, ARRAS.
"A" Company will be relieved at 1.p.m. and the Company (less two platoons) will move to NICHOLS REDOUBT. The remaining two platoons to FORESTIER REDOUBT.
The relief of the remainder of the Battalion will commence at 4.30.p.m. in the following order.
"Headquarters Detachment"
"C" Company.
"B" Company.
"A" Company.

3 The relief will be carried out in succession of platoons at an interval of 5 minutes.

4 ROUTES. (a) The relieving unit will move up via JULY AVENUE
(b) "C" Company will withdraw via AUGUST AVENUE.
(c) "B" Company " " " MAY "
(d) "A" Company (less two platoons) will withdraw via AUGUST AVENUE.
(e) Two platoons of "A" Company will withdraw via MAY Ave.
(f) One Platoon of "A" Company and Lewis Guns to BOSKY REDOUBT.

5 GUIDES. One guide from each platoon of "A", "B" and "C" Companies will report to Battalion Headquarters at 2.p.m. and will be prepared to guide the relieving platoons to their several positions.
Guides for "B" and "C" Companies will meet the platoons of these Companies and end of MAY and AUGUST AVENUES, and guide them to the Convent at ARRAS, where they will be billetted.

6 Log Books completed will be handed over to relieving Companies.

7 Trench Stores will be handed over, Trench Store cards will be made out in triplicate and handed in to Regimental Orderly Room by 9.0.a.m the 8th inst.

8 Company Commanders are reminded that until relief is complete they are responsible for the relief of their lines and will act in such capacity during the relief.

9 Completion of relief will be reported by the code word "SAXON" on the telephone.

F. E. Cochran (?)
Captain & A/Adjutant.
2nd Regiment S.A. Infantry.

Copy No 1 "A" Coy.
" No 2 "B" Coy.
" No 3 "C" Coy.
" No 4 "D" Coy.
" No 5 Commanding Officer.
" No 6 Second-in-Command.
" No 7 File.
" No. 8. War Diary. -

2nd REGIMENT SOUTH AFRICAN INFANTRY. Copy No.6.
War Diary.

Map reference.
Trench map,
ARRAS 1/10000.

Operation Order No. 26.

10. 12. 16.

No. 1. RELIEF. "D" Coy. less two platoons will be relieved in NICHOLL'S REDOUBT by "B" Coy less two platoon on 11th inst, and two platoons of "D" Coy. will be relieved by two platoons of "B" Coy. in FORRESTIER REDOUBT on the 11th inst.

No. 2. The Lewis guns of "D" Coy will be relieved by the Lewis guns of "B" Coy at 11.0.am. and will withdraw via JULY AVENUE to CANDLE FACTORY where a guide will meet them and conduct them to the CONVENT ARRAS. The relief of the remainder of "D" Company will commence at 3.0.pm. in the following order.-

"D" Coy. less two platoons.

Two platoons of "D" Company.

The relief will be carried out in succession of platoons at intervals of 10minutes.

No. 3. ROUTES. "B" Coy less two platoons will move in via SEPTEMBER.

Two platoons of "B" Coy will move in via MAY.

"D" Coy less two platoons will withdraw via NOVEMBER.

Two platoons of "D" Coy will withdraw via APRIL.

No. 4. GUIDES. One guide from each platoon of "D" Coy will meet relieving platoons at map reference G.16.d.4½.10. and will be prepared to guide relieving platoons to their respective positions.

Guides for each platoon of "D" Coy. will meet platoons at end of APRIL and NOVEMBER near CANDLE FACTORY and guide them to the CONVENT ARRAS where they will be billeted.

No. 5. LOG BOOKS completed will be handed over to relieving Company.

No. 6. TRENCH STORES. Trench stores will be handed over. Trench cards will be made out in duplicate.

No. 7. DUTIES. Trench wardens and other duties. These duties at present found by "D" Coy. will be taken over by "B" Coy.

No. 8. COMPLETION OF RELIEF. Completion of relief will be reported by wire to the Battalion Headquarters by the code word "JONES".

sgd. F.E.Cochran.

Captain & A/Adjutant.

2nd S.A. Infantry.

Copy No. 1. File.
Copy No. 2. "B" Coy.
Copy No. 3. "D" Coy.
Copy No. 4. C.O.
Copy No. 5. 2nd in Command.
Copy No. 6. War Diary.

" A "

2nd REGIMENT SOUTH AFRICAN INFANTRY.

Operation Order No. 24.

"C" Company.	Will relieve "Y" Company in front line on left. On relief will occupy from CUTBERT'S CRATER inclusive to 93 inclusive.
"B" Company.	Will relieve "X" Company in front line on right. On relief will occupy 89 inclusive to 92 inclusive.
"A" Company.	Will relieve "W" Company in support line and on relief will occupy from Point "G.11.D.6.2. inclusive to "B" WORK inclusive.
"D" Company.	Will relieve "Z" Company in reserve line at BRITANNIA WORKS.
"Headquarters"	Will be situated at G. 17.a.1. 7.

All movement during occupation will be along "JULY" AVENUE.
"MAY" and "AUGUST" avenues will be used only for evacuation.

GUIDES.- Guides will meet Unit at Entrance to ARRAS at G. 27.A.2.9½.

Copy No. 8., War Diary.

OPERATION ORDER NO. 24.

By

Major H. C. Symmes, Commanding 2nd Regiment South African Infantry.
In the Field, Saturday, 2nd December, 1916.

Map Reference,
Sheet 51c. N.E.
" 51b N.W.

No. 1. MOVE. The Regiment, less advanced parties, will move to ARRAS to-morrow to relieve the 14th Battalion GLOUCESTERS, according to attached Schedule marked "A".

No. 2. BUSSING. The Regiment will enbus at road junction J.23.B. 1.4. at 3.0. p.m. The Regiment will march to this point at 2.30. p.m.
Order of march:-
"C" Company.
"B" Company.
"A" Company.
"D" Company.
Headquarters.
Starting point - cross roads at J. 23.D.6.8. Head of Regiment will pass starting point at 2.30. p.m.

No. 3. OFFICERS. Officers will enbus with their respective Companies.

No. 4. BLANKETS. Further orders will be issued regarding blankets.

No. 5. BILLETS. All companies will be clear of billets by 2.p.m. and a written report will be handed to Adjutant that they are in a clean and sanitary condition.

No. 6. DRESS. Full marching order - greatcoats will be worn.

No. 7. TRANSPORT. No regimental transport will pass east of L.3.C. or of WAIRUS before 4.15. p.m. Transport will remain in lines at present occupied until further orders.

No. 8. TRENCH STORES. Trench Store cards will be made out in ~~duplicate~~ triplicate, and duplicate copies forwarded to Battalion Orderly Room after taking over.

No. 9. COMPLETION OF RELIEF. Companies will report when relief is completed by code word "JAMES".

No. 10. COOKING UTENSILS. All boilers, roasters, and camp kettles will be carried under Company arrangements.

No. 11. LEWIS GUN AMMUNITION. Lewis guns and magazines will be carried into line by Companies. Lewis Gun Carts will be parked at transport lines by 10.a.m.

No. 12. BATTALION HEADQUARTERS. Battalion Headquarters in line will be situated at G.17. A.1.7.

J. E. Cochran

Captain & A/Adjutant,
2nd Regiment S. A. Infantry.

Instructions regarding War Diaries and Intelligence Summaries are contained in F. S. Regs., Part II. and the Staff Manual respectively. Title pages will be prepared in manuscript.

WAR DIARY
or
INTELLIGENCE SUMMARY.
(Erase heading not required.)

Army Form C. 2118.

Place	Date	Hour	Summary of Events and Information	Remarks and references to Appendices
	31st. (Cont.)		Our artillery fairly active. Trench Mortars fairly active especially Stokes Guns.- 1 N.C.O. and 2 men patrolled "NO MAN'S LAND" from 11 pm to 12.25 am;- reporting everything quiet.- 136 other Ranks engaged on repairing, revetting and clearing Trenches.- Carrying Party of 1 off. and 30 other ranks supplied to Trench Mortar Battery.-	

W. Tanner Lieut. Colonel.
Commanding 2nd Regt. S.A. Infantry

A5834 Wt. W4973/M687 750,000 8/16 D. D. & L. Ltd. Forms/C.2118/13.

No 1

2nd SOUTH AFRICAN INFANTRY

WAR DIARY
or
INTELLIGENCE SUMMARY.
(Erase heading not required.)

Army Form C. 2118.

Instructions regarding War Diaries and Intelligence Summaries are contained in F. S. Regs., Part II. and the Staff Manual respectively. Title pages will be prepared in manuscript.

Vol 10

Place	Date	Hour	Summary of Events and Information	Remarks and references to Appendices
SUB-SECTION J II	JANUARY 1st		Regiment in the line. Disposition shown in War Diary for December. A Company and D Company in front line. B Company in support line. C Company in Brittania Works in Reserve. Band, pioneers, police and others attached to HEAD QUARTERS all at or in vicinity of CANDLE FACTORY. Enemy showed slight activity using H.E and Shrapnel but with no effect. They also sent over a few T.Ms. Enemy Machine Guns fairly active between 3 p.m. and 4.30 p.m. Our Artillery fairly active also heavy T.Ms and Stokes. Machine Guns usual activity. One patrol N.C.O and 2 men left sap at 95 trench at 2 A.M. and patrolled No. MANS LAND. Nothing observed, but movement was difficult owing to bursts of Enemy Machine Gun fire and the mud. One officer and 165 men engaged on general Trench repairs etc and carrying parties. 14 Rifle Grenades were fired by us. Strength of Regiment in trenches Officers 15. Other ranks 446. Casualties Nil. 2/Lieut Manlleur returned off leave. 3 other ranks have proceeded on leave to England. 2nd Lieutenant E. J. Brooks returned off leave. also 1 other rank. 2/Lieut Begley E.R. and 2/Lieut Forth W. proceeded on a Course of General Trench Warfare from 1st JANUARY 1917 to 7th January 1917 at 9th Divisional School. 2/Lieut Britton Course Bayonet Fighting at 9th Divisional School from 1st January to 11th January 1917. Lieut Knight R.C. Course of Signalling.	
	2nd		Enemy attitude quiet generally but active between 4.45 A.M. and 5.30 A.M. Artillery slightly active between 4.45 A.M. and 5.30 A.M., no damage done. Our artillery fairly active, also Heavy Trench Mortars and Stokes. Our Machine Guns firing as usual. An Artillery test was carried out at 10.32 p.m. Trench 95 time 40 seconds. Our Stokes Mortars particularly active on enemy front line between 3.15 p.M. and 5.15 p.M. An N.C.O.s patrol left Sap 92 at 10.55 p.M. and patrolled No mans land returning at 12.35 A.M. via Sap 95. Reported all quiet and enemys wire ~~are~~ in very good order. Another patrol left SAP 90 at 11.15 P.M. remaining out for an hour. Nothing observed and all quiet. 22 Rifle Grenades were fired at enemy front line by us. 156 Other ranks on General Trench repairs and revetting work. 17 Other Ranks employed wiring in Front Line. Strength of Regiment in trenches Officers 16. Other ranks 444. Casualties other ranks 3. 1 killed and 2 wounded. ~~2 Other ranks have proceeded on leave to England.~~	
	3rd		Enemy attitude quiet. Enemy Artillery quiet except at 9.45 p.M when he fired 12 long range shells between Jelly and August Avenues, 8 of these were blind and no damage was done. Our Artillery active, between 5 p.M and 5.50 p.M particularly so. Our Heavy Trench Mortars and Stokes Guns active at intervals throughout the day on enemy front and support lines. Our Machine Guns usual activity. A Raid on Enemy lines at Map Ref G.6. C.5.0. ~~[illegible]~~ (ARRAS. 51 B.N.W.3) Edition 4A) was carried out by 3rd S.A.I. ZERO being at 5 P.M. Our Lewis Guns co-operated by firing on enemy front line on flank of section raided. 38 Rifle Grenades were fired by us. 179 Other Ranks General work in trenches, Carrying parties, Cleaning bombs, Clearing and revetting etc. 1 Officer and 15 other ranks employed wiring in front of front line. Casualty One man died of wounds ~~[illegible]~~ and 2 wounded other ranks. 2/Lieut Whelan proceeded on leave. 2/Lieut M.S. Whelan proceeded on leave to England, also 2 other ranks. 4 other ranks returned off leave.	

2nd SOUTH. AFRICAN. INFANTRY

WAR DIARY
or
INTELLIGENCE SUMMARY.
(Erase heading not required.)

Army Form C. 2118.

Instructions regarding War Diaries and Intelligence Summaries are contained in F. S. Regs., Part II. and the Staff Manual respectively. Title pages will be prepared in manuscript.

Place	Date	Hour	Summary of Events and Information	Remarks and references to Appendices
SUB-ECTION J II	JANUARY 4th		Enemy attitude quiet. Enemy artillery fairly quiet. Our Artillery was active between 5 P.M. and 5.30 P.M. and TRENCH MORTARS did some good work on enemy front and support line. 190 other ranks General work in trenches, repairs, revetting etc including carrying parties. 1 officer 13 other ranks wiring at front line. The intercompany relief was carried out in accordance with operation order 32 attached. Strength of Regiment in trenches officers 15 other ranks 447. Casualties NIL.	
	5th		Enemy attitude quiet. Enemy artillery quiet generally till 10.15 pm when he shelled ARRAS with gas shells from 10.30 to 11.30 No gas shells fell in Sub-Section. Enemy Trench mortars inactive except at 2.50 P.M when they put 3 light Trench mortar shells into our support line right of July Avenue. One enemy plane observed. at 7 P.M about a dozen bright lights were sent up by the enemy, each light exploded into 5 white lights, ~~nothing~~ no action followed. Our Artillery active from 10.15 P.M on Enemy Gas Shell Batteries which were soon silenced. our bombardment was kept up intermittently till 12.30 A.M (5 and 6th). Otherwise our artillery was fairly active, also Trench Mortars and Stokes Guns. Our Machine Guns usual activity. Several of our aircraft were over enemy lines between 10 A.M. and 11.30 AM, they were fired on by the enemy without success. 115 other ranks working parties on General repairs to trenches, and carrying parties. 11 other ranks wiring. Strength of Regiment in trenches. Officers 15 other ranks 447. Casualties NIL. 2nd Lt N. Beddy returned off leave also 2 other ranks. 1/Lieut Harvey J.N. Course of Musketry at VI Corps Camiers.	
	6th		Enemy attitude fairly active. Enemy artillery fired gas shells into ARRAS from 10.30 P.M. to 11.30 P.M. No gas shells fell in sub-section. Enemy fired several Heavy Trench mortars at intervals during the afternoon on our front and support line. The right coy front line was damaged considerably. Green lights were sent up by enemy at about 4.45 P.M. No action followed. Our artillery fairly active generally, but during enemy's gas shelling it became very active. Our Trench Mortars slightly active. Our Machine Guns as usual. We put over 26 Rifle Grenades. An N.C.O patrol left Sap 90 at 11 P.M and formed a listening post west out in No man's land returning at 12.20 AM, nothing observed. A similar Post lay out to right of Cuthbert Crater [illegible] usual observed. 130 other ranks General work on trenches. Cleaning [illegible] carrying parties. 16 other ranks wiring parties in front of front line. [illegible] other ranks 441. Casualties Nil.	

A5834 Wt. W4973/M687 750,000 8/16 D. D. & L. Ltd. Forms/C.2118/13.

2nd SOUTH AFRICAN INFANTRY

Instructions regarding War Diaries and Intelligence Summaries are contained in F. S. Regs., Part II. and the Staff Manual respectively. Title pages will be prepared in manuscript.

WAR DIARY
or
INTELLIGENCE SUMMARY.
(*Erase heading not required.*)

Army Form C. 2118.

Place	Date	Hour	Summary of Events and Information	Remarks and references to Appendices
Sub-SECTION. J II	JANUARY 7th		Enemy attitude fairly active. Enemy shelled July and August Avenues between 10.45 p.m and 11.15 p.m. and continued at intervals throughout the day. Between 9 a.m and 12 noon light Trench Mortar shells and Rifle Grenades fell in vicinity of Cuthbert. At 4 pm enemy put 7 Heavy Trench Mortar shells over at minute intervals. Enemy machine Gun slightly active between 7.30 p.m and 7.45 p.m on left of Cuthbert. Our artillery active generally, especially from 3 pm to 4.30 pm. Our Trench mortars fairly active at intervals. Machine Guns as usual but with increased activity from 6.15 pm to 9.30 pm. We put over 10 Rifle Granades. Our Aircraft active throughout the day. 121 other ranks General work on Trenches, Cleaning, Bombs and Carrying parties. 14 other ranks wiring outside front line. Strength of Regiment in trenches. officers 16. other ranks 441. Casualties Nil. Captain T.H. Symons proceeded on leave to England, also 2 other ranks. 2/Lieut Middleton H.G.N. returned off leave, also 2 other ranks.	
ARRAS, FORRESTIER and ST. NICHOLAS.	8th		Battalion relieved by the 4th South African Infantry and on completion of relief took up the duties of Reserve Battalion. Operation Order 33 attached. Relief Complete at 12-30 p.m. Strength of Regiment. Officers 17 other ranks 440. Casualties Nil.	O. O. No 33 attached
	9th		234 men supplied for working parties in the line. One other rank killed accidently. available men training and bathing. Strength of Regiment Officers 17. other ranks 433. Casualties one other ranks accidently killed. Lieut R.C. Knight proceeded on leave to England, also 3 other ranks. 2/Lieut G.G. McLean returned off leave, also 3 other ranks.	
	10th		234 men supplied for working parties in the line. Guards and duties found in ARRAS. Strength of Regiment. Officers 19 other ranks 431. Casualties nil.	
	11th		234 men supplied for working parties in the line. Guard and duties found in ARRAS. Strength of Regiment. Officers 19. other ranks 424 - Casualties One other ranks wounded. 2/Lieut H. W. S Terry proceeded on leave to England. 3 other ranks returned off leave. 2/Lieut Bowling B. 2/Lieut Burley M.F. 2/Lieut Harvey J.N. course of Gas at 9th Divisional School.	

A5834 Wt. W4973/M687 750,000 8/16 D. D. & L. Ltd. Forms/C.2118/13.

Instructions regarding War Diaries and Intelligence Summaries are contained in F. S. Regs., Part II. and the Staff Manual respectively. Title pages will be prepared in manuscript.

Army Form C. 2118.

2nd South African Infantry ~~WAR DIARY~~
or
INTELLIGENCE SUMMARY.
(Erase heading not required.)

Place	Date	Hour	Summary of Events and Information	Remarks and references to Appendices
Sub-Section J II	January 12th		234 Men supplied for working parties in the line. Guards and duties found in ARRAS. Strength of Regiment. Officers 19. other ranks 421. Casualties Nil. 2/Lieut Brooks. J. and 4th Kirsten E.J. proceeded on a Course of General Trench Warfare at 9th Divisional School from 12th January 1917 to 23rd January 1917. Broddy N. Course Bayonet Fighting at 9th Divisional School from 12th January to 22nd January 1917.	
	13th		234 Men supplied for working parties in the line. Guards and duties found in ARRAS. Strength of Regiment. Officers 19 other ranks 429 Casualties Nil. 2/Lieut E R Bigby proceeded on leave to England, also 1 other ranks. 3 other ranks returned off leave.	
	14th		234 Men supplied for working parties in the line. Guards and duties found in ARRAS. Strength of Regiment. Officers 17 other ranks 425 Casualties Nil.	
	15th		234 Men supplied for working parties in the line. Guards and duties found in ARRAS. Strength of Regiment. Officers 18 other ranks 426 Casualties Nil. 3 other ranks proceeded on leave to England. 3 other ranks returned off leave.	
	16th		The Battalion relieved the 4th South African Infantry in J II Sub Section in accordance with operation order 34 attached. Relief completed at 12·30 am. Officer patrol left Sap 89 to inspect enemy wire in front, whilst at German wire a party of Germans were observed wiring about 50 yards to the left front. A great number of very lights were put up by enemy. Enemy artillery and Trench Mortars fairly active. Our artillery and Trench Mortars fairly active. Strength of Regiment. 36 officers 695 other ranks. In trenches 19 officers and 441 other ranks. 56 other ranks General trench work. 25 other ranks wiring outside front line. Strength of Regiment. Officers 18. other ranks 416. Casualties Nil.	

Instructions regarding War Diaries and Intelligence Summaries are contained in F. S. Regs., Part II. and the Staff Manual respectively. Title pages will be prepared in manuscript.

Army Form C. 2118.

2nd SOUTH AFRICAN INFANTRY ~~WAR DIARY~~ or INTELLIGENCE SUMMARY.

(Erase heading not required.)

Place	Date	Hour	Summary of Events and Information	Remarks and references to Appendices
SUB-SECTION. J II	JANUARY 17th		Enemy operations fairly quiet. Enemy artillery slight activity. About mid-day all light shells falling in supports. Enemy Trench Mortars fairly active shelling April. Also slight activity with minenwerfer. Our artillery and Trench Mortars fairly active. Our Stokes were firing at intervals on Enemy front line. 24 Rifle Grenades sent over by us. 150 other ranks employed general work in the trenches. 4 other ranks wiring outside front line. Snowing. Strength of Regiment in trenches Officers 18 Other ranks 435. Casualties Nil. 2/Lieut V. Beeton proceeded on leave to England, also 2 other ranks. 2/Lieut M. S. Whelan returned off leave, also 2 other ranks.	
	18th		Enemy operations attitude active. Enemy Artillery more active than usual during the last 3 days. At 10.30 AM. The Newtut was shelled with Shrapnel in several places but with no effect, a few shells were also fired at BOSKY REDOUBT. At 2 PM the Right Battalion was rather heavily shelled with 4.2 and 5.9 shells. Enemy active with minenwerfers on head of August Avenue between 10 A.M. and 11.30 AM., also sent over a few fish tail bombs between supports and front line right of July. Slight Enemy Machine Gun activity at 5.30 AM opposite 93. Our artillery active from 10 AM to 12 noon shelling support lines, again in the afternoon at intervals with light shells, mostly. At 10 AM and again in afternoon our Trench Mortars and Stokes fired on enemy front line opposite 94, about 100 shells in all were fired. One of our aeroplanes flew low over Enemy lines at 5 pm. Weather, slight snow and rain. 146 other ranks General work in Trenches. 10 other ranks wiring in vicinity of Trench 91. Company reliefs were carried out in accordance with operation order 35. Strength of Regiment in trenches officers 19 other ranks 440. Casualties Nil.	
	19th		Enemy operations. attitude aggressive. BASKY REDOUBT and BRITTANIA WORKS were shelled with light shells about 2 p.m. Enemy Trench Mortars ~~were~~ more active, about 50 Minenwerfers fell north of August Ave in left Bn Sub Section between 10 AM and 12 Noon. 5 enemy Heavy Trench Mortar shells fell in vicinity T90 and T91 and one near support line damaging July. Several Fish tail bombs were also sent over. An enemy plane came along our front line at a very low altitude, our Lewis Guns opened on it as soon as it came within range, and it at once retired to its own line. Enemy active with rifle fire at night. Our artillery actively shelled enemy front and support lines with light shells during morning and afternoon. From 7.30 PM to 9 PM our long range guns and howitzers fired on points in rear of enemy lines. 25 Grenades were put over by us. 129 other ranks General work in Trench. 13 other ranks wiring outside front line. Strength of Regiment in trenches officers 19 other ranks 441. Casualties Nil. 3 other ranks proceeded on leave to England.	

A5834 Wt. W4973/M687 750,000 8/16 D. D. & L. Ltd. Forms/C.2118/13.

Instructions regarding War Diaries and Intelligence Summaries are contained in F. S. Regs., Part II. and the Staff Manual respectively. Title pages will be prepared in manuscript.

2nd South African Infantry ~~WAR DIARY~~ or INTELLIGENCE SUMMARY.

(Erase heading not required.)

Army Form C. 2118.

Place	Date	Hour	Summary of Events and Information	Remarks and references to Appendices
Sub Section J II	1917 January 20th		Enemy alert and aggressive. Very little artillery activity. 2 heavy shells and several light ones fell in vicinity of CUTHBERT WORKS. Enemy Trench Mortars very active from 9 AM to 10.30 AM bombarding our support line. T92.93.94 were blown up and considerable damage done to that part of the line. July and August were also damaged in vicinity of Supports. 3 enemy planes observed but were driven off by Lewis Guns and rifle fire, though no damage was caused. A few bursts of enemy Machine Gun fire came from opposite T90. Enemy snipers becoming rather active, but we were unable to locate their positions. Our artillery intermittently shelled enemy front line and supports up till 12 midnight. At night we shelled points in rear of the enemy's lines with long range shells. Our Trench Mortars and Stokes were active during the morning, and again in the evening. Machine Guns fired on enemy planes, and later carried out indirect fire during the night. We sent over 30 Rifle Grenades during the period. 136 other ranks general work on trenches and carrying parties. 6 other ranks wiring left of Sap 93. Strength of Regiment in trenches. Officers 19. other ranks 435. casualties Nil.	
	21st		Enemy attitude fairly quiet. Enemy artillery. Slight activity between 9 AM and 11 AM. A few shells were put in the vicinity of BOSKY REDOUBT. Enemy Trench Mortars and Minenwerfer shells were sent over at intervals between 9 AM and 12.20 PM. A few bursts of machine gun fire was directed at our lines from enemy parapet. One enemy plane was observed from our lines but soon disappeared. Our operations. Our artillery shelled enemy front line and supports at frequent intervals with High Explosive and Shrapnel. Our Hows fired intermittently searching for enemy Heavy Trench Mortar emplacements. Our Stokes Mortars fired on enemy front line opposite the Right and Left Sector. 2 of our planes patrolled our lines from 10.30 AM to 12 Noon and again in the afternoon. We sent over 31 rifle-grenades. 142 other ranks general work in the trenches. 2 Officers 15 men in front trenches 89 & 93. Strength of Regiment in trenches. Officers 18 other ranks 434. Casualties Nil. 3 other ranks proceeded on leave to England. Captain J. H. Symons returned off leave, also 2 other ranks.	
	22nd		Enemy attitude fairly quiet. A few light shells were fired in vicinity of BOSKY REDOUBT. 2 or 3 long distance shells came over at 10 AM. Enemy Trench Mortars active in the morning blowing in our front line in 3 places along T90 and 91. One enemy plane passed along front but was driven off by Lewis Gun fire. A snipers plate has been erected at A12 C59 and a few shots have been fired. Enemy fired several bursts of fire from apparently mobile machine Guns during the night. Our operations. During the afternoon our 18 pounders and heavy guns fired on enemy front and support line. Our Stokes fired on the enemy in the afternoon and evening at intervals. Machine Guns fired indirect fire as usual. Several of our planes patrolled our line during the day. We sent over 43 Rifle grenades. 122 other ranks General work on trenches. 14 other ranks wiring in front trench 89. Inter-Company Reliefs were carried out during the day. Operation order 37 attached. Strength of Regiment Officers 19 other ranks 429. Casualties Nil.	

A5834 Wt. W4973/M687 750,000 8/16 D. D. & L. Ltd. Forms/C.2118/13.

2nd SOUTH. AFRICAN INFANTRY. ~~WAR DIARY~~

or

INTELLIGENCE SUMMARY.

(Erase heading not required.)

Army Form C. 2118.

Instructions regarding War Diaries and Intelligence Summaries are contained in F. S. Regs., Part II. and the Staff Manual respectively. Title pages will be prepared in manuscript.

Place	Date	Hour	Summary of Events and Information	Remarks and references to Appendices
1917 Sub. [illegible]CTION [illegible]II	JANUARY 23rd		Enemy exceptionally quiet. A few light shells were fired at BOSKY REDOUBT. and November Avenue at about 10 p.m. At 11 AM. enemy sent about 20 Trench mortars into supports and July. Enemy aircraft flying high were engaged by our planes and Anti Aircraft Guns. Enemy Machine Guns were used against our planes with no effect. Our operations, our heavies shelled enemy Trench mortar positions at intervals during the day especially in afternoon, a few light shells were fired on enemy front line. In afternoon and morning our Anti Aircraft Guns were in action against enemy planes. Our Stokes Guns were active shelling several points along enemy front line. Throughout the day our air-craft were active and several times engaged enemy planes. We sent over 60 Rifle Grenades. 147 other ranks general work in trenches, 17 other ranks wiring front of Cuthbert Sap 90, and T89. Strength of Regiment in trenches. Officers 16 other ranks 426 Casualties Nil. 3 other ranks proceeded on leave to England. Lieut R. C. Knight returned off leave, also 3 other ranks. 2/Lieut Humphrey J. T. and 2/Lieut Ross J.M. proceeded on a course of General Trench Warfare from 23rd January 1917 to — at 9th Divisional School. 2/Lieut Middleton H.G.H. Course Bayonet Fighting at 9th Divisional School.	
	24th		Enemy attitude quiet. Enemy artillery slightly active from 9AM to 11·45 AM with light shells on BOSKY. REDOUBT. A few gas shells and Inflammatory shells also a few 77MM. were sent over by the enemy's from 12 Noon to 1·30 PM, some fell short of our wire, others went clean over us doing no damage. Enemy planes were observed flying at great height. Our light guns several times shelled the enemy lines our heavies searched for position of enemy Trench mortars. Stokes mortars active at all hours. Aircraft active in all directions throughout the day. Enemy threw several bombs into his own wire. We sent over 30 rifle grenades. Company reliefs were carried out during the day. Operation Order 38. 190 other ranks general trench work – carrying etc. 16 other ranks wiring in front of 91 and 94. Strength of Regiment Officers 19 other ranks 436. Casualties Nil.	
	25th		Enemy artillery quiet exception of Anti Aircraft Guns and a few light shells which fell into November. About 20 Heavy Trench Mortars fell into the vicinity of the Right Company's lines and in support line left of July Avenue. Our wire was slightly damaged by some which fell short, and our front line was blown in once in the morning, and once in the afternoon. Several enemy planes came over our lines during the morning but were forced to return by the bombardment of our Anti-Aircraft guns. Enemy working parties were heard during the night and were fired on by the Stokes Mortars. Our Artillery carried out intermittent shelling of enemy front line and supports. Anti-Aircraft guns very active. Our Trench mortars and Stokes Mortars active. Our aircraft very active and were fired on by the enemy whenever within range. 12 Rifle Grenades sent over. 191 other ranks general work in trenches and carrying. 17 other ranks wiring. Strength of Regiment in trenches Officers 20 other ranks 433. Casualties One other ranks accidently wounded. One other ranks shell shock. Lieut W. Thorburn proceeded on leave to England, also 2 other ranks. 3 other ranks returned off leave.	

A5834 Wt. W4973/M687 750,000 8/16 D. D. & L. Ltd. Forms/C.2118/13.

2nd SOUTH. AFRICAN. INFANTRY
~~WAR DIARY~~
or
INTELLIGENCE SUMMARY.
(Erase heading not required.)

Army Form C. 2118.

Instructions regarding War Diaries and Intelligence Summaries are contained in F. S. Regs., Part II. and the Staff Manual respectively. Title pages will be prepared in manuscript.

Place	Date	Hour	Summary of Events and Information	Remarks and references to Appendices
Sub-SECTION J II	1917 JANUARY 26th		Enemy attitude aggressive. Shelled July avenue and BOSKY. REDOUBT with 77MM shells. Enemy Heavy Trench Mortars bombarded support, August and July Avenues damaged, the latter being blown in twice. Fish-tail bombs and shrapnel were also sent over by the enemy: about 80 Heavy Trench mortar shells were fired in all. One enemy plane was driven back by our guns. Our artillery actively shelled enemy lines throughout the day and part of the night. Our Stokes Mortars also active. Our Aeroplanes patrolled our front as usual and were shelled frequently. 26 Rifle Grenades were used by us. 188 other ranks General Trench work, carrying etc. 18 other ranks wiring front of 90, 93, 94 and CUTHBERT. Strength of Regiment in Trenches Officers 19 Other ranks 426 Casualties other ranks 1 killed and 3 wounded.	
	27th		Enemy attitude fairly quiet. Artillery inactive except in reply to our organised shoot from 1PM. A few enemy Heavy Trench Mortars fell around support line between 1 PM and 3 PM, slightly damaging support line in one place. Occasional bursts from enemy machine guns. One enemy plane driven down behind his own line at 11 AM. Our operations. Artillery put up an organised shoot from 1 PM to 3 PM intermittent shelling was carried out. Trench Mortars slightly active during morning and again from 1 PM to 8 PM shelling enemy front line. Our machine guns carried out an unusual amount of indirect fire. Our planes very active. 165 other ranks general Trench work, carrying parties etc. 18 other ranks wiring in front of trench 90 and CUTHBERT. Strength of Regiment in trenches officers 19 other ranks 425 Casualties Nil. 2/Lieut. L. W. S. Terry. 2/Lieut. E. R. Begley returned off leave, also 1 other rank.	
	28th		Company inter-relief in accordance with attached ~~[illegible]~~ operation order 40. Enemy artillery occasionally shelled BOSKY REDOUBT and communication trenches during the morning. About 25 Trench Mortars fell in our support lines damaging it slightly. Many fish tail bombs came over, most often falling near August Avenue. Flash lights were observed in enemys lines about 6.30 P.M. apparently a signal of some kind. Our artillery intermittently shelled enemy positions during the 24 hours. Our Stokes Mortars fired many shells into enemy front. Our planes actively patrolling. Our Machine Guns usual activity. An officer Patrol out examining enemy wire and searching for enemy sentry posts. 37 Rifle grenades used. 196 other ranks on General trench repairs, carrying parties etc. 22 other ranks wiring in front of trenches 91 and 92 and also on left of sap 93. Strength of Regiment in trenches Officers 20 other ranks 426 Casualties Nil.	

A5834 Wt. W4973/M687 750,000 8/16 D. D. & L. Ltd. Forms/C.2118/13.

Army Form C. 2118.

Instructions regarding War Diaries and Intelligence Summaries are contained in F. S. Regs., Part II. and the Staff Manual respectively. Title pages will be prepared in manuscript.

WAR DIARY
or
INTELLIGENCE SUMMARY.

(Erase heading not required.)

Place	Date	Hour	Summary of Events and Information	Remarks and references to Appendices
Sub Section J II	1917 January 29th		Enemy operations. Occasional shelling of BOSKY REDOUBT. and communication trenches during the morning. 25 Trench mortars were sent over, most of them falling near support lines damaging it slightly in one place. There was a fair amount of activity with fish tail bombs up to 11.30 pm. most of these falling near August Avenue. Our operations. Intermittent shelling of enemy positions was carried out for the last 24 hours. Trench mortar stokes guns fired a considerable of shells into enemy front. Air Craft. Our planes actively patrolled enemy lines and were heavily fired on by Anti-Air-Craft guns and by machine guns whenever within range, no damage was done. Usual amount of indirect fire by machine guns. Strength of Regiment in trenches officers 20 other ranks 434 Casualties. 2 other ranks wounded. 3 other ranks returned off leave. 156 other ranks General trench work, carrying Etc.	
	30th		Enemy operations. Attitude aggressive. Very little artillery activity for the last 24 hours. Minenwerfers active from 11 AM to 4 PM slight damage was done to front line and support line Considerable amount of fish-tail bombs were sent over. An occasional ~~[illegible]~~ burst was fired from enemy emplacements during the night. Our operations. 18 pounders and 4.5 howitzers fired a fair amount of shells on enemy front line, and places in rear of line. Trench Mortar Stokes actively shelled enemy front line at intervals during the day. Usual indirect firing by our Machine Guns. Strength of Regiment in trenches Officers 22 other ranks 434. Casualties. 3 other ranks wounded. 104 other ranks general trench work carrying etc. 18 other ranks wiring in front of 90, 91, & 93.	
	31st		Enemy operations. Artillery slightly active. Trench Mortars showed activity at midnight Shelling front line and support, and doing some damage to the head of August Avenue. Aircraft. An enemy Aeroplane flew very low over our front and support lines at 2.30 pm Machine and Lewis Guns opened fire, the plane returning to its lines over SUBSECTION J I General attitude Very quiet. Our operations. Artillery active. Machine Guns, Stokes, were active Rifle Grenades being particularly so. An officer patrol left Trench 92 and patrolled to the German wire – nothing occurred. The German wire is fairly thick especially at the head of Saps. Strength of Regiment in Trenches Officers 22 other ranks 445. Casualties Nil. 126 other ranks general trench work carrying etc. 10 other ranks wiring in front of 93 & 94.	

W R Heenan Major
Temp Cmdg 2 S A I

A5834 Wt. W4973/M687 750,000 8/16 D. D. & L. Ltd. Forms/C.2118/13.

SECRET. Copy No.....1.... W.D.

OPERATION ORDER NO: 32.

IN THE FIELD,
3rd January, 1917.

Map Reference,
Trench Map.
1/10,000.

No. 1. RELIEF. The following reliefs will take place to-morrow, the 4th instant:-
"C" Company will relieve "A" Company in Front Line.
"B" Company will relieve "D" Company in front line.
"A" Company will relieve "B" Company in Support Line.
"D" Company will relieve "C" Company in BRITTANIA WORKS and vicinity.

Company Commanders will arrange with Company Commanders they relieve the method of relief and submit proposals for approval to the Commanding Officer.

No. 2. INFORMATION. Our Artillery and Trench Mortar Batteries will not, as far as is known, operate.

No. 3. LEWIS GUNS. "C" and "B" Companies will each be augmented by two extra Lewis Guns for the period which these Companies are in the Front Line. Detachments for these guns will report to O.C. "B" and "C" Companies at 9.30 a.m. on the 4th instant.

No. 4. TRENCH STORES. These will be taken over and receipts obtained.

No. 5. LOG BOOKS. Log Books completed will be taken over.

No. 6. COMPLETION OF RELIEF. Relief to be completed by 2.15. p.m. Completion of relief to be reported in writing to Orderly Room.

No. 7. ACTION IN CASE OF ATTACK.
O.C's. "A" and "D" Companies will remain in command of their respective fronts until completion of the relief.

Captain & A/Adjutant,
2nd Regiment South African Infantry.

Copy No. 1. File.
Copy No. 2. "A" Coy.
No. 3. "B" Coy.
No. 4. "C" Coy.
No. 5. "D" Coy.
No. 6. Commanding Officer.
No. 7. War Diary.

Ptle

2nd SOUTH AFRICAN INFANTRY ORDER NO: 33.

Copy No.....

7. 1. 1917.

Map Reference
Trench Map ARRAS
1/10,000.

No1. RELIEF.

The Battalion will be relieved by the 4th South African Infantry on the 8h. in Sub-Section J. 2. The Battalion on relief will take up duties of Reserve Battalion.

"C" Company, less two platoons, will relieve "C" Company, less two platoons, 4th S. A. Infantry, in St. NICHOLAS.

2 platoons of "C" Company will relieve two platoons of "C" Company, 4th S.A.I. in FORRESTIER REDOUBT.

"D" Company, less 1 platoon, will move to Billets in BARBED WIRE SQUARE, ARRAS.

1 Platoon of "D" Company will relieve 1 platoon of "D" Company, 4th S.A.Infantry, in ST. NICHOLAS.

"B" and "A" Companies will move to billets in CONVENT, ARRAS.

Headquarters will move to HOTEL UNIVERSE, ARRAS.

No. 2. ORDER OF RELIEF.

Lewis Guns will be relieved by Lewis Guns of the 4th S.A.Infantry at 9.A.M.

The Relief of the remainder of Regiment will commence at 9.30.A.M. in the following order:-

Headquarters Detachment.
"B" Company.
"C" Company.
"A" Company.
"D" Company.

No. 3. LEWIS GUNS.

Two Platoons of "C" Company will be augmented by one Lewis Gun and detachment.

No. 4. ROUTES.

The relieving Unit will move up JULY AVENUE.

"B" Company will withdraw via MAY AVENUE.

"C" Company will withdraw via JULY, SUPPORT LINE and AUGUST.

"A" Company less two platoons, will withdraw via AUGUST.

Two Platoons of "A" Company will withdraw via MAY AVENUE.

"D" Company will withdraw via AUGUST AVENUE.

No. 5. MOVEMENT.

The Relief will be carried out in succession of platoons at intervals of 5 minutes.

From the CANDLE FACTORY into ARRAS the movement will be in parties of EIGHT at a minutes interval.

No. 6. LOG BOOKS, etc.

Log Books completed, Company and Battalion Defence Schemes, Maps, etc. will be handed over to Relieving Battalion.

No. 7. TRENCH STORES.

Trench Stores will be taken over and trench cards handed into Regimental Orderly Room by 6 p.m. on the 8th instant.

P.T.O.

Page 2. Operation Order No. 33.

In accordance with orders in force regarding the use of the telephone, etc. no message whatever will be sent over the lines regarding this relief, excepting the codeword reporting relief complete.

Completion of relief will be reported to Battn.
F Headquarters by the codeword ~~XXXXX~~ "JACK" on the telephone.

Company Commanders are reminded that until relief is complete they are responsible for the ~~safety~~ defence of their lines and will act in such capacity during the relief.

Orders regarding movement in ARRAS must be strictly adhered to.

F.E. Cochran

Captain & A/Adjutant,
2nd Regiment S. A. Infantry.

Copy No. 1.	File.
Copy No. 2.	O.C. "A" Coy.
Copy No. 3.	O.C. "B" Coy.
Copy No. 4.	O.C. "C" Coy.
Copy No. 5.	O.C. "D" Coy.
Copy No. 6.	Commanding Officer.
Copy No. 7	War Diary.
Copy No. 8.	Lieut. Knight.
Copy No. 9.	Quartermaster & Transport Officer.

By Orderly ......p.m. 7.1.17.

War Diary

2nd SOUTH AFRICAN INFANTRY ORDER No. 34. Copy No. 8

Map Reference
ARRAS
1/10000.

No. 1.
RELIEF.

The Battalion will relieve the 4th S. A. Infantry on the 16th instant in Sub-section J. 2.

"D" Coy. will relieve Right Coy. ("B" Coy. 4th S.A.I.) in the Front Line at 10.30. a.m.
"A" Coy. will relieve Left Coy. ("C" Coy. 4th S.A.I.) in the front line at 11.a.m.
"C" Coy. will relieve "D" Coy. 4th S.A.I. in the Support Line at 9.30 a.m.
"B" Coy. will relieve "A" Coy. 4th S.A.I. in BRITTANIA WORKS and vicinity at 9.45 a.m.
Headquarter Detachment at 9.30 a.m.

No. 2.
LEWIS GUNS.

Lewis Guns will relieve Lewis Guns of 4th S. A. Infantry at 9.a.m. "A" and "D" Companies will each be augmented by 2 extra lewis guns for the period these companies are in the front line.
These detachments will report to the Company Commanders at 8.a.m. tomorrow.

No. 3.
MOVEMENT.

From ARRAS to CANDLE FACTORY the movement will be in parties not larger than eight (8) at minute intervals. From the CANDLE FACTORY to positions in LINE, the parties will be not larger than platoons at five (5) minutes interval.

No. 4.
ROUTES.

"D" Company will move in via JULY and NEW CUT.
"A" Company will move in via JULY.
"C" Company less one platoon will move in via JULY.
One platoon of "C" Company will move in via JULY and NEW CUT.
"B" Company will move in via JULY.

No. 5.
LOG BOOKS, etc.

Companies will take over Log Books, Defence Schemes, Maps, etc. and will hand these over for positions being vacated.

No. 6.
TRENCH STORES.

Trench Stores will be taken over and receipts in TRIPLICATE made out. Duplicate receipts will be handed in to Battalion Headquarters by 6.p.m. on the 16th.

No. 7.
TELEPHONES.

In accordance with orders in force regarding the use of the telephone, etc. no message whatever will be sent over the lines regarding this relief, excepting the code word reporting relief complete.

No. 8.
COMPLETION OF RELIEF.

Completion of relief will be reported to Battalion Headquarters over the telephone by the code word "BLACK".

[illegible] Cochrane,
Captain & A/Adjutant,
2nd Regiment S.A.Infantry.

Copy No. 1. File.
Copies No. 2-5 O.C. Companies.
Copy No. 6. C.O.
Copy No. 7. Transport Officer - [illegible].
Copy No. 8. War Diary.✓
Copy No. 9. Second in Command.

Issued by orderly at 11 a.m. on the 15th Jan. 19[illegible].

OPERATION ORDER No 36.

Map Reference. Trench Map. 1/10000.

Copy No. 8 War Diary

No 1 RELIEFS.

The following reliefs will take place tomorrow the 20th inst..
"A" Coy will relieve "C" Company in Front Line.
"D" Coy will relieve "B" Company in Front Line.
"B" Coy will relieve "D" Company in Support Line.
"C" Coy will relieve "A" Company in Brittania Works and vicinity..
Reliefs will commence at 1.p.m. and will be completed by 2.p.m. Company Commanders will arrange with the Company Commanders they relieve the method of relief and submit proposals for approval to the Commanding Officer..

No 2. INFORMATION.

Our Artillery and Trench Mortars will operate as under.
10.a.m. 6" Howitzers only.
2.30.p.m. 18 pdrs and T.M's the H.T.M. will operate on CT. G. 18.C.3½.9½. at 2.30.p.m.

No 3. LEWIS GUNS.

"A" and "D" Companies will each be augmented by two extra Lewis Guns for the period which these companies are in the front line. Detachments for these guns will report to O.C. "A" and "D" Companies at 12.30. p.m. on 20th inst..

No 4 TRENCH STORES.

These will be taken over and receipts obtained.

No 5. LOG BOOKS.

Log Books completed will be taken over.

No 6 COMPLETION of RELIEF.

Completion of relief will be reported by the code word "FRED" over telephone to Battalion H.Q.

No. 7. ACTION IN CASE OF ATTACK.

O.C's "B" and "C" Companies will remain in command of their respective fronts until completion of relief.

[signature]
Captain & A/Adjutant,
2nd Regiment S. A. Infantry.

Copy No. 1. File.
Copy No. 2. "A" Coy.
Copy No. 3. "B" Coy.
Copy No. 4. "C" Coy.
Copy No. 5. "D" Coy.
Copy No. 6. Commanding Officer.
Copy No. 7. Second in Command.
Copy No. 8. War Diary. ✓
Copy No. 9. Corps Intelligence Officer.

Issued by Orderly at..1.0.p.m. on 19.1.17.1917.

OPERATION ORDER NO: 35. Copy No. 8

War Diary

Map Reference,
Trench Map,
1/10000.

No. 1.
RELIEF.

The following reliefs will take place to-morrow the 18th instant.-

"B" Company will relieve "D" Company in Front Line.
"C" Company will relieve "A" Company in Front Line.
"D" Company will relieve "C" Company in Support Line.
"A" Company will relieve "B" Company in BRITTANIA WORKS and vicinity.

Company Commanders will arrange with Company Commanders they relieve the method of relief and submit proposals for approval to the Commanding Officer.

No. 2.
INFORMATION.

Our Artillery and Trench Mortars will operate on enemy C. T. G.13.C.4½, 9½. between 11.a.m. and 4. p.m.

No. 3.
LEWIS GUNS.

"B" and "C" Companies will each be augmented by Two extra Lewis Guns for the period which these Companies are in the Front Line. Detachments for these guns will report to O.C. "B" and "C" Companies at 9.a.m. on the 18th instant.

No. 4.
TRENCH STORES.

These will be taken over and receipts obtained.

No. 5.
LOG BOOKS.

Log Books completed will be taken over.

No. 6.
COMPLETION OF RELIEF.

Completion of relief to be reported by Code Word "HENRY" over telephone to Battalion Headquarters.

Relief to be completed by 9.a.m.

No. 7.
ACTION in CASE OF ATTACK.

O.C.'s. "A" and "D" Companies will remain in command of their respective fronts until completion of the relief.

G. Cochran.
Captain & A/Adjutant.
2nd Regiment South African Infantry.

Copy No. 1. File.
Copy No. 2. "A" Coy.
Copy No. 3. "B" Coy.
Copy No. 4. "C" Coy.
Copy No. 5. "D" Coy.
Copy No. 6. Commanding Officer.
Copy No. 7. Second in Command.
Copy No. 8. War Diary.-

✓ 17.1.17.

OPERATION ORDER NO. 37. Copy No. ...3... War Diary

21/1/1917.

Map Reference
Trench Map
1/10,000.

No. 1.
RELIEFS.

The following reliefs will take place to-morrow, the 22nd instant.
"C" Company will relieve "A" Coy. in front line.
"B" Company will relieve "D" Coy. in front line.
"A" Company will relieve "B" Coy. in Support Line.
"D" Company will relieve "C" Company in BRITTANIA WORKS and vicinity.

Reliefs will commence at 1.p.m. and will be completed by 2.p.m.
Company Commanders will arrange with the Company Commanders they relieve the method of relief and submit proposals for approval of the Commanding Officer.

No. 2.
INFORMATION.

Our artillery and trench mortars will operate as under:-

2.p.m. to	18 prs.	Cover Trench Mortars.
3.30 p.m.	9.45 T.M.	Selected Target.
	2" T.Ms.	Trenches G.12a.6.4. to G. 12.a.6.8.
	3" Stokes.	DITTO.
During evening.	3" Stokes.	DITTO. To catch any enemy repairing parties.

No. 3.
LEWIS GUNS.

"B" and "C" Companies will each be augmented by two extra Lewis Guns for the period which these companies are in the front line. Detachments for these guns will report to O.C. "B" and "C" Companies at 12.30 p.m. on the 22nd inst.-

No. 4.
TRENCH STORES.

These will be taken over and receipts obtained.

No. 5.
LOG BOOKS.

Log Books completed will be taken over.

No. 6.
COMPLETION OF RELIEF.

Completion of relief will be reported by the code word "FRANK" over telephone to Battalion Headquarters.

No. 7.
ACTION IN CASE OF ATTACK.

O.C's. "A" and "D" Companies will remain in command of their respective fronts until completion of relief.-

F.E. Cochran
Captain & A/Adjutant,
2nd Regiment S.A.Infantry.

Copy No. 1 to No. 4. Retained.
Copy No. 5. O.C. "A" Coy.
Copy No. 6. O.C. "C" Coy.
Copy No. 7. O.C. "D" Coy.
Copy No. 8. O.C. "B" Coy.

Issued by Orderly at........p.m. 21/1/1917.

OPERATION ORDER NO: 36. Copy No.....1.....

23/1/1917.

War Diary

Map Reference
Trench Map.
1/10,000.

No. 1.
RELIEFS.

The following reliefs will take place to-morrow the 24th instant.-

"A" Company will relieve "C" Company in Front Line.
"D" Company will relieve "B" Company in Front Line.
"C" Company will relieve "A" Company in SUPPORT LINE.
"B" Company will relieve "D" Company in BRITTANIA WORKS and vicinity.

Reliefs will commence at 1.p.m. and will be completed by 3.p.m.

Company Commanders will arrange with the Company Commanders they relieve the method of relief and submit proposals for approval of the Commanding Officer.-

No. 2.
INFORMATION.

Our artillery and trench mortars will not operate, as far as it is known, unless otherwise advised.

The 4th S.A.I. will relieve the 1st S.A.I. in "XXXXXXXX J.1. sub-section at an hour to be notified later.

XXXXX
XXXXXXXXXX

Two companies 4th S.A.I. will pass along the Support Line.

No. 3.
LEWIS GUNS.

"A" and "D" Companies will each be augmented by two extra Lewis Guns for the period which these Companies are in the front line. Detachments for these guns will report to O.C. "A" and "D" Companies at 12.30 p.m. on the 24th instant.

No. 4.
TRENCH STORES.

These will be taken over and receipts obtained.

No. 5.
LOG BOOKS.

Log Books completed will be taken over.

No. 6.
COMPLETION OF RELIEF.

Completion of relief will be reported by the Code Word "RICHARD" over telephone to Battalion Headquarters.

No. 7.
ACTION IN CASE OF ATTACK.

O.C's. "B" and "C" Companies will remain in command of their respective fronts until completion of relief.

F.E. Cochrane
Captain & A/Adjutant,
2nd Regiment S.A.Infantry.

Copy Nos. 1 to 4.	Retained.
Copy No. 5.	O.C. "A" Coy.
Copy No. 6.	O.C. "B" Coy.
Copy No. 7.	O.C. "C" Coy.
Copy No. 8.	O.C. "D" Coy.

Issued at ....p.m. 23/1/17 by Orderly.

OPERATION ORDER NO: 39.

Copy No ......3...... War Diary

25/1/1917.

Map Reference,
Trench Map
1/1[illegible],000.

No. 1.
RELIEFS.
The following reliefs will take place tomorrow, the 26th instant.
"C" Company will relieve "A" Company in Front Line.
"B" Company will relieve "D" Company in Front Line.
"D" Company will relieve "C" Company in Support Line.
"A" Company will relieve "B" Company in BRITTANIA WORKS and vicinity.

Reliefs will commence at 1. p.m. and will be completed by 2. p.m.
Company Commanders will arrange with the Company Commanders they relieve the method of relief and submit proposals for approval of the Commanding Officer.-

No. 2.
INFORMATION.
Our artillery and trench mortars, as far as it is at present known, will not operate tomorrow.

No. 3.
LEWIS GUNS.
"B" and "C" Companies will each be augmented by two extra Lewis Guns for the period which these Companies are in the front line. Detachments for these guns will report to O.C. "A" and "D" Companies at 12.30 p.m. on the 26th inst.

No. 4.
TRENCH STORES.
These will be taken over and receipts obtained.

No. 5.
LOG BOOKS.
Log Books completed will be taken over.

No. 6.
COMPLETION OF RELIEF.
Completion of relief will be reported by the Com Pers "ALLEN" over telephone to Battalion Headquarters.

No. 7.
ACTION IN CASE OF ATTACK.
O.C's. "A" and "D" Companies will remain in command of their respective fronts until completion of relief.

Marlean
Captain & Adjutant,
2ndRegiment S. A. Infantry.

Copy Nos. 1 to 3.	Retained.
Copy No. 4.	O.C. "A" Coy.
Copy No. 5.	O.C. "B" Coy.
Copy No. 6.	O.C. "C" Coy.
Copy No. 7.	O.C. "D" Coy.

Issued by Orderly at ......p.m. 25/1/1917.

OPERATION ORDER NO: 40.

Copy No...2....War Diary.

26/1/1917.

Map Reference
Trench Map
1/10000.

No. 1.
RELIEFS.

The following reliefs will take place to-morrow, the 28th instant:-
A Company will relieve "C" Company in Front Line.
"D" Company will relieve "B" Company in Front Line.
"B" Company will relieve "D" Company in Support Line.
"C" Company will relieve "A" Company in BRITTANIA WORKS and vicinity.-

Reliefs will commence at 1. p.m. and will be completed by 2. p.m.
Company Commanders will arrange with the Company Commanders they relieve the method of relief and submit proposals for approval of the Commanding Officer.

No. 2.
INFORMATION.

Our artillery and trench mortars, as far as it is present known, will not operate to-morrow.

No. 3.
LEWIS GUNS.

"A" and "D" Companies will each be augmented by two extra Lewis Guns for the period which these Companies are in the front line. Detachments for these guns will report to O.C. "A" and "D" Companies at 12.30 p.m. on the 28th instant.

No. 4.
TRENCH STORES.

These will be taken over and receipts obtained.

No. 5.
LOG BOOKS.

Log Books completed will be taken over.

No. 6.
COMPLETION OF RELIEF.

Completion of relief will be reported by the Code Word "JIMMIE" over telephone to Battalion Headquarters.

No. 7.
ACTION IN CASE OF ATTACK.

O.C's. "B" and "C" Companies will remain in command of their respective fronts until completion of relief.

F. E. Cochran
Captain & Adjutant,
2nd Regiment S. A. Infantry.

Copy Nos 1 to 3.	Retained.
Copy No. 4.	O.C. "A" Coy.
Copy No. 5.	O.C. "B" Coy.
Copy No. 6.	O.C. "C" Coy.
Copy No. 7.	O.C. "D" Coy.

Issued by Orderly at ....p.m. 27/1/17.

OPERATION ORDER NO: 41.

Copy No. ..3.. War Diary.

29th January, 1917.

Map Reference,
Trench Map
1/10,000.

No. 1.
RELIEFS.

The following reliefs will take place to-morrow, the 30th instant.
"C" Company will relieve "A" Company in Front Line.
"B" Company will relieve "D" Company in Front Line.
"A" Company will relieve "B" Company in Support Line.
"D" Company will relieve "C" Company in BRITTANIA WORKS and vicinity.

Reliefs will commence at 1.p.m. and will be completed by 2. p. m.
Company Commanders will arrange with the Company Commanders they relieve the method of relief, and submit proposals for approval of the Commanding Officer.

No. 2.
INFORMATION. Our Artillery and Trench Mortars, as far as it is at present known will not operate tomorrow.

No 3.
LEWIS GUNS. "B" and "C Companies will each be augmented by two extra Lewis Guns for the period when these Companies are in the front line, Detachments for these guns will report to O.C. "B" and "C" Companies at 12.30.p.m. on 30th inst.

No 4.
TRENCH STORES. These will be taken over and receipts obtained.

No 5
LOG BOOKS. Log Books completed will be taken over.

No 6.
COMPLETION OF RELIEF. Completion of Relief will be reported by the code word "TOM" over telephone to Battalion Headquarters.

No 7.
ACTION IN CASE OF ATTACK. O.C's "A" and "D" Companies will remain in command of their respective fronts until completion of relief.

[signature]
Lt. for Captain & A/Adjutant.
2nd Regiment. S.A. Infantry.

Copy Nos 1 to 3.	Retained. ✓
Copy No 4.	O.C. "A" Coy.
Copy No 5.	O.C. "B" Coy
Copy No 6.	O.C. "C" Coy.
Copy No 7	O.C. "D" Coy.

Issued by Orderly at..8:10....p.m. 29.1.17.

OPERATION ORDER NO: 42.

Copy No...2.... War Diary

31st January, 1917.

Map Reference,
Trench Map
1/10,000.

No. 1. **Reliefs.** The following reliefs will take place to-morrow, the 1st February, 1917.
"A" Company will relieve "C" Company in Front Line.
"D" Company will relieve "B" Company in Front Line.
"C" Company will relieve "A" Company in Support Line.
"B" Company will relieve "D" Company in BRITTANIA WORKS and vicinity.

Reliefs will commence at 1.p.m. and will be completed by 2.p.m.
Company Commanders will arrange with the Company Commanders they relieve the method of relief, and submit proposals for approval of the Commanding Officer.-

No. 2. **INFORMATION.** Our Artillery and Trench Mortars, as far as it is at present known, will not operate to-morrow.
The 1st Regiment will relieve the 4th Regiment S.A.I. in Sub-Section J.1. to-morrow.

No. 3. **LEWIS GUNS.** "A" and "D" Companies will each be augmnted by two extra Lewis Guns for the period which these Companies are in the front line. Detachments for these guns will report to O.C. "A" and "D" Companies at 12.30 p.m. on the 1st February.

No. 4. **TRENCH STORES.** These will be taken over and receipts obtained.

No. 5. **LOG BOOKS.** Log Books completed will be taken over.

No. 6. **COMPLETION OF RELIEF.** Completion of Relief will be reported by thecode word "MACK" over telephone to Battalion Headquarters.

No. 7. **ACTION IN CASE OF ATTACK.** O.C's. "B" and "C" Companies will remain in command of their respective fronts until completion of relief.

F. E. Cochran

Captain & A/Adjutant,
2nd Regiment S. A. Infantry.

Copies Nos. 1 to 3.	Retained.
Copy No. 4.	O.C. "A" Coy.
Copy No. 5.	O.C. "B" Coy.
Copy No. 6.	O.C. "C" "
Copy No. 7.	O.C. "D" ".

Issued by Orderly at........p.m. 31.1.17.

2nd SOUTH AFRICAN INFANTRY

WAR DIARY
or
INTELLIGENCE SUMMARY.
(Erase heading not required.)

Army Form C. 2118.

Instructions regarding War Diaries and Intelligence Summaries are contained in F. S. Regs., Part II. and the Staff Manual respectively. Title pages will be prepared in manuscript.

Vol XI

Place	Date	Hour	Summary of Events and Information	Remarks and references to Appendices
Sub SECTION J II	1917 FEBRUARY 1st		Enemy Operations. Artillery quiet. a few 77 MM shells were sent over but no damage was done. Trench Mortars. particularly active at 6pm and 10 pm. and again active at 7.30 AM. a little damage near the top of July AVENUE. Our Operations. Artillery active and apparently effective in retaliation on Trench Mortars. Stokes and Rifle Grenades active during the day. 50 Rifle Grenades fired. Wiring in front of trench 90. Aircraft particularly active. Patrol. an officer patrol between 2AM and 4AM along practically the whole of J II SECTOR encountered no opposition. The German wire is in fairly good condition. Strength of Regiment in trenches Officers 21 other ranks 444 Casualties Nil. 2 officers 138 other ranks engaged on general trench repairs etc.	
	2nd		Enemy Operations. Artillery shelled towards BOSKY REDOUBT also front line. Trench Mortars. Rather more active than usual, doing considerable damage to the front line. Aircraft active. (Company relief as per attached order) Our Operations. Artillery active in retaliation enemy trench mortars. Trench Mortars and Stokes were active. Stokes doing good work particularly in front of trench 89. 25 Rifle Grenades fired. Wiring in front of trench 90.	O.O. attached No. 43

2nd REGIMENT SOUTH AFRICAN INFANTRY.

WAR DIARY
or
INTELLIGENCE SUMMARY.
(*Erase heading not required.*)

Army Form C. 2118.

Instructions regarding War Diaries and Intelligence Summaries are contained in F. S. Regs., Part II. and the Staff Manual respectively. Title pages will be prepared in manuscript.

Place	Date	Hour	Summary of Events and Information	Remarks and references to Appendices
19	1917			
SUB SECTION J II	Feby 2nd		Aircraft very active. Strength of Regiment in trenches Officers 19 other ranks 443. Casualties 3 other ranks killed & wounded. 3 returned off leave. Captain & Adj J.E. COCHRAN. LIEUT. V.E. ADENDORFF proceeded on leave to ENGLAND. LIEUT. COLONEL W.E.C. TANNER. C.M.G. assumed command of the Regiment. MAJOR C.R. HEENAN relinquished command of the Regiment. 1 officer 189 other ranks engaged on general trench repairs and carrying etc.	
	3rd		Enemy Operations. Artillery 4 MM shells fell in JULLY AVENUE at SUPPORT LINE. Trench Mortars. 25 L.T.M.s and 10 H.T.M.s were fired into AUGUST AVENUE between 9 & 10 pm. General Attitude very quiet. Aircraft slightly active. Our Operations. Our artillery active. Trench mortars and Stokes active with good effect on German front line and supports. Rifle Grenades 50 were fired. Wiring carried out as usual. Aircraft very active. Strength of Regiment in trenches Officers 17 other ranks 435. Casualties Nil. LIEUT & QMR. W.PYMM. 2/LIEUT RICHES and 1 other rank proceeded on leave to ENGLAND. LIEUT. KING & 2/LIEUT COOPER proceeded on a course of General trench warfare at 9th Div School. 4 other ranks proceeded on a	

A5834 Wt. W4973/M687 750,000 8/16 D. D. & L. Ltd. Forms/C.2118/13.

2nd REGIMENT. SOUTH AFRICAN INFANTRY.

WAR DIARY
or
INTELLIGENCE SUMMARY.
(*Erase heading not required.*)

Army Form C. 2118.

Instructions regarding War Diaries and Intelligence Summaries are contained in F. S. Regs., Part II. and the Staff Manual respectively. Title pages will be prepared in manuscript.

Place	Date 1917	Hour	Summary of Events and Information	Remarks and references to Appendices
SUB SECTION J II	Feby 3rd		course of General Trench warfare at 9th Divisional School. 171 other ranks engaged on general trench repairs & etc.	
	4th		Enemy Operations. Artillery quiet. Trench Mortars 11 & 3 ins into supports vicinity of AUGUST AVENUE and front line. Rifle Grenades about 40 were fired along our line during the day. Attitude exceptionally quiet. (Company reliefs as per attached order.) Our Operations Artillery active. Trench Mortars active especially on enemy front wire. Rifle Grenades 55 fired. Aircraft active. Patrol an officer patrol along the whole of J II front, had nothing to report. Strength of Regiment in trenches Officers 22 Other ranks 442 Casualties Nil. 30 other ranks returned off leave. 140 other ranks engaged on General trench repairs, carrying & etc.	O.O. attached No. 44
	5th		Enemy Operations Artillery quiet. Trench Mortars. 16 & 6. T Ms fell in vicinity of top of JULY, AUGUST, and SUPPORTS between 12 noon	

(Contd)

A5834 Wt. W4973/M687 750,000 8/16 D. D. & L. Ltd. Forms/C.2118/13.

Instructions regarding War Diaries and Intelligence Summaries are contained in F. S. Regs., Part II. and the Staff Manual respectively. Title pages will be prepared in manuscript.

2nd REGIMENT SOUTH AFRICAN INFANTRY
WAR DIARY or INTELLIGENCE SUMMARY.

(Erase heading not required.)

Army Form C. 2118.

Place	Date 1917	Hour	Summary of Events and Information	Remarks and references to Appendices
SUB SECTION J II	Feby 5th		and 4 pm. 20 L T Ms fell near front line. Aircraft a German Aeroplane was observed very high up between 4 pm and 5 pm. driven off by shell fire. Our Operations Artillery action. Trench Mortars active. Wire. 2 parties were out examining our own wire. Patrol 1 officer and 2 OR patrolled NO MANS LAND. they were fired on with no effect. Strength of Regiment in trenches officers 22 other ranks 444 Casualties Nil. MAJOR C.R. HEENAN and 2 other ranks on leave to ENGLAND. 146 other ranks engaged on general trench repairs etc.	
	6th		Enemy Operations Artillery about 11.45 AM 7 MM shells fell in vicinity of trench 89. At 10.20 AM 20 shells towards BOSKY REDOUBT and 1.35 PM 8 shells towards BOSKY REDOUBT. Trench Mortars 6 H.T.M. shells fell near front line and top of AUGUST AVENUE. Aircraft slightly active. Our Operations. Artillery action. Trench mortars active. Rifle Grenades 20 fired. Aircraft very active. General. 2 enemy working parties were dispersed by rifle and Lewis Gun fire.	O.O. attached

A5834 Wt. W4973/M687 750,000 8/16 D. D. & L. Ltd. Forms/C.2118/13.

2nd REGIMENT, SOUTH AFRICAN INFANTRY

Instructions regarding War Diaries and Intelligence Summaries are contained in F. S. Regs., Part II. and the Staff Manual respectively. Title pages will be prepared in manuscript.

WAR DIARY
or
INTELLIGENCE SUMMARY.
(Erase heading not required.)

Army Form C. 2118.

Place	Date 1917	Hour	Summary of Events and Information	Remarks and references to Appendices
Sub SECTION J II	July 6		Strength of Regiment in trenches Officers 22. Other ranks 441. Casualties NIL. 3 other ranks returned off leave. 3 other ranks on leave to ENGLAND 171 other ranks on general trench repairs. Company reliefs as per attached order	O.O. No 45
	7th		Enemy Operations. Artillery At 12pm. 3. 77 MM shells fell near top end of AUGUST. AVENUE. Trench Mortars 7 H.T.M.s fell in Support line near AUGUST AVENUE and near CUTHBERT CRATER. Aircraft slightly active. Our Operations. Artillery active. Trench Mortars active with good effect on enemy front line and wire. Aircraft very active. General enemy working party was dispersed by Lewis Gun fire opposite trench 93 at 8 pm. Strength of Regiment in trenches Officers 21 other ranks 434 Casualties NIL. LIEUT. T.F. PEARSE proceeded on a course of General Trench Warfare at 3rd ARMY SCHOOL. 1 officer & 181 other ranks on general trench repairs.	
	8th		Enemy Operations. Artillery slightly more active. between 11 AM and 1 pm. about 30 light shells were fired into area between	

Instructions regarding War Diaries and Intelligence Summaries are contained in F. S. Regs., Part II. and the Staff Manual respectively. Title pages will be prepared in manuscript.

2nd REGIMENT SOUTH AFRICAN INFANTRY

WAR DIARY
or
INTELLIGENCE SUMMARY.
(*Erase heading not required.*)

Army Form C. 2118.

Place	Date 1917	Hour	Summary of Events and Information	Remarks and references to Appendices
Sub SECTION J II	FEBY 8		between front line and SUPPORTS, and a few towards C. WORKS. Trench Mortars & 76 T.Ms were fired into vicinity of SUPPORTS, end of JULY. AVENUE. Rifle Grenades. About 30 fell along our front line during the day. Aircraft slightly active. Our Operations. Artillery active throughout the day. Trench Mortars active as usual with good effect especially on area facing CUTHBERT CRATER. Aircraft active. Wiring as usual. Strength of Regiment in trenches officers 21 O.R. 438. Casualties OR 1 killed and 4 wounded. LIEUT. W. THORBURN and 2 OR returned off leave. 3 OR proceeded on leave to ENGLAND. LIEUT. WALSH 2/LT WHELAN 2/LT. FORTH on one days Gas Lecture at NOYELLE VION. 149 O.R. on general trench repairs and Carrying. Company relief as per attached order.	O.O. No. 45
	9th		Battalion relieved by the 4th SOUTH AFRICAN INFANTRY and on completion of relief took up duties of RESERVE BATTALION in Arras. Relief complete at 12.30 p.m. Disposition of BATTALION in accordance with O.O. No. 45 attached. Strength of Regiment in trenches Officers 21 O.R. 430 Casualties Nil. 175 OR on general trench repairs.	

A5834 Wt. W4973/M687 750,000 8/16 D. D. & L. Ltd. Forms/C.2118/13.

2nd REGIMENT SOUTH AFRICAN INFANTRY

WAR DIARY
or
INTELLIGENCE SUMMARY.
(Erase heading not required.)

Instructions regarding War Diaries and Intelligence Summaries are contained in F. S. Regs., Part II. and the Staff Manual respectively. Title pages will be prepared in manuscript.

Army Form C. 2118.

Place	Date	Hour	Summary of Events and Information	Remarks and references to Appendices
ARRAS	Feby 14th		150 men supplied for working parties in the line. Guards and duties found in ARRAS. Strength of Regiment Officers 19. Other ranks 506. Casualties Nil. LIEUT. ADENDORFF returned off leave.	
	15th		150 men supplied for working parties in the line. Guards and duties found in ARRAS. Strength of Regiment Officers 23 other ranks 513. Casualties Nil. LIEUT & QMR. W. PYMM. 2/LT. RICHES and one other rank returned off leave.	
	16th		150 men supplied for working parties in the line. Guards and duties found in ARRAS. Strength of Regiment officers 24 other ranks 511. Casualties Nil. CAPT & ADJ. F.E. COCHRAN returned off leave. Regimental relief as per attached order.	O.O. attached No 48
No 2 SECTION RIGHT SECTOR.	17th		The Regiment relieved the 4th SOUTH AFRICAN INFANTRY in No 2 section Right SECTOR. Relief commenced 9.30 AM and completed 12 NOON. The name of sector has now been changed to Right Sector, and Battalion front slightly altered Right Coy ~~[illegible]~~ from 90 to 93. Left Coy ~~[illegible]~~	map attached

A5834 Wt. W4073/M687 750,000 8/16 D. D. & L. Ltd. Forms/C.2118/13.

2nd REGIMENT SOUTH AFRICAN INFANTRY.

Instructions regarding War Diaries and Intelligence Summaries are contained in F. S. Regs., Part II. and the Staff Manual respectively. Title pages will be prepared in manuscript.

WAR DIARY
or
INTELLIGENCE SUMMARY.
(*Erase heading not required.*)

Army Form C. 2118.

Place	Date	Hour	Summary of Events and Information	Remarks and references to Appendices
ARRAS	FEBY 10th		150 men supplied for working parties in the line. Guards and duties found in ARRAS men bathing. Strength of Regiment Officers 20 other ranks 427 Casualties Nil. 2/LT. KIRK and 20 other ranks proceed on leave to ENGLAND.	O.O. attached
	11th		150 men supplied for working parties in the line. Guards and duties found in ARRAS. men bathing. Strength of Regiment Officers 18 other ranks 424 Casualties Nil.	
	12th		150 men supplied for working parties in the line. Guards and duties found in ARRAS. Strength of Regiment Officers 18 other ranks 430 Casualties Nil. Draft from Base taken on Strength of Regiment 1 Officer 75 O. Ranks.	
	13th		150 men supplied for working parties in the line. Guards and duties found in ARRAS. Strength of Regiment Officers 19 other ranks 509. Casualties Nil.	

Instructions regarding War Diaries and Intelligence Summaries are contained in F. S. Regs., Part II. and the Staff Manual respectively. Title pages will be prepared in manuscript.

2nd REGIMENT. SOUTH AFRICAN INFANTRY

WAR DIARY
or
INTELLIGENCE SUMMARY.
(Erase heading not required.)

Army Form C. 2118.

Place	Date	Hour	Summary of Events and Information	Remarks and references to Appendices
No 2 SECTION RIGHT SECTOR	FEBY 17th		front 94 to 97. Support in B. C. & D. WORKS and home St PANCRUS. exclusive to S90	
			General Attitude. Quiet.	
			Enemy Operations. Between 10.10 and 10.45 A.M. about 20 77MM shells fell about supports and near NEW CUT. Trench Mortars 30 ~~Enemy~~ Heavy Trench mortar shells into Cannon St and Front Line between 2.50 and 3.45 p.m. 10 Heavy Trench Mortar shells into same vicinity between 6 pm and 7 pm. Fishtails. A considerable number of fishtail bombs were dropped along our front line between 3 & 5 pm and 8 and 9 pm.	
			Our Operations. Artillery action. Trench Mortars very active on enemy front line opposite trench 90 and 91. Machine Guns Active Aircraft Quiet. Patrols 1 Battalion patrol of 1 officer and 20 other ranks patrolled NO MANS LAND nothing to report. 1 officer and 1 OR on wire patrol. Strength of Regiment in trenches officers 27 OR 520. Casualties 2 other ranks wounded (Gas)	
			Major C. R. HEENAN and 2 other ranks returned off leave.	
			254 other ranks on General trench repairs and carrying.	

2nd REGIMENT. SOUTH AFRICAN INFANTRY

Army Form C. 2118.

WAR DIARY
or
INTELLIGENCE SUMMARY.
(Erase heading not required.)

Instructions regarding War Diaries and Intelligence Summaries are contained in F. S. Regs., Part II. and the Staff Manual respectively. Title pages will be prepared in manuscript.

Place	Date 1917	Hour	Summary of Events and Information	Remarks and references to Appendices
No 2 SECTION RIGHT SECTOR	FEBY 18th		Enemy Operations. Between 2.45 and 4.30 pm. 12. 77 MM shells fell on JULY AVENUE and AUGUST near supports. Trench motors 20 light Trench Mortar shells fell into support lines near CANNON ST between 11.45 and 12.30 pm. 12 Heavy Trench Mortars near the Front line in the vicinity of CLAUDE CRATER between 3 and 3.30 pm. 12 heavy trench mortars fell near CANNON ST between 5 pm and 5.30 pm. no damage done. Machine Guns active at times. Signal. At 5.55 pm a red light was used in German sector opposite CLAUDE CRATER - No action followed. Fishtail bombs were fired along our front doing no damage. Our Operations. Artillery active. Trench Mortars showed considerable activity and appeared to be doing some damage. Machine Guns showed the usual activity. Rifle Grenades 15 fired. General. At 9.30 as the mist lifted an enemy working party was observed. They were dispersed by Lewis Gun fire. an enemy search light observed in the direction of BLANGY Strength of Regiment Officers 28 O.R. 516. Casualties Nil. 411 OR on General Trench repair and Carrying etc. Company reliefs as per attached order.)	O.O attached No.49

A5834 Wt. W4973/M687 750,000 8/16 D. D. & L. Ltd. Forms/C.2118/13

2nd REGIMENT SOUTH AFRICAN INFANTRY

WAR DIARY
or
INTELLIGENCE SUMMARY.
(Erase heading not required.)

Army Form C. 2118.

Instructions regarding War Diaries and Intelligence Summaries are contained in F. S. Regs., Part II. and the Staff Manual respectively. Title pages will be prepared in manuscript.

Place	Date 1917	Hour	Summary of Events and Information	Remarks and references to Appendices
No 2 SECTION RIGHT SECTOR	FEBY 19th		Enemy Operations shells fell at the back of trenches 90-93 and 96 during the day. Trench Mortars a little damage was done to Coy H.Qrs by Heavy Trench mortars. Between 2pm and 4pm our artillery retaliated. Fishtail bombs about 40 were fired along our line no damage.	
			Our Operations. Artillery active. Trench and Stokes Mortars - active with good effect. Rifle Grenades 50 were fired. General usual patrols in NO MANS LAND nothing to report. Strength of Regiment in trenches Officers 27 O.R. 518. Casualties 2 O.R. wounded. 325 OR on general trench repairs.	
	20th		Enemy Operations. Attitude more active than usual. Artillery — between 9AM and 12 NOON about 40-77MM shells fell in front line and Support line. Trench Mortars. 11 Heavy trench mortars fell near Support Trench 98 between 9 and 10AM no damage. 20 Heavy trench mortars and light trench mortars fell near front line rear of CLAUDE CRATER no damage. Fishtail bombs active as usual along the SECTOR.	

Contd

Instructions regarding War Diaries and Intelligence Summaries are contained in F. S. Regs., Part II. and the Staff Manual respectively. Title pages will be prepared in manuscript.

2nd REGIMENT SOUTH AFRICAN INFANTRY.

WAR DIARY
or
INTELLIGENCE SUMMARY.
(Erase heading not required.)

Army Form C. 2118.

Place	Date 1917	Hour	Summary of Events and Information	Remarks and references to Appendices
No 2 SECTION RIGHT SECTOR.	FEBY 20th		Our Operations. Artillery very active retaliated with effect on enemy Heavy Trench mortars. Stokes Mortars fired on enemy front line and wire. Rifle Grenades 30 fired. General. An Officer and 2OR patrolled NO MANS LAND between CLAUDE and CUTHBERT-CRATER. nothing was encountered. Strength of Regiment in trenches Officers 30 OR. 513. Casualties 1OR died of wounds. 406 O.R. on general trench repairs carrying etc. 3 OR returned off leave. (~~Trench Mortars~~) Draft from Base taken on strength of Regiment 1 Officer 10. O Ranks.	
	21st		Enemy Operations. Attitude fairly quiet. Trench Mortars about 30-77MM shells fell in our line during the day. Our Operations. actively shelled enemy front line and supports Trench Mortars. a number of heavies were fired into enemy wire opposite Sap. 90. Stokes Mortars. also very active on enemy wire, front line and supports. Rifle Grenades 80 were fired. General. An enemy working party in supports between CLARENCE and CUTHBERT were dispersed by Lewis gun & Rifle fire. Strength of Regiment in trenches Officers 31. O.R 520. Casualties Nil. 246 OR on general trench repairs. Company relief as per attached order.	OO attached No. 50.

A5834 Wt. W4973/M687 750,000 8/16 D. D. & L. Ltd. Forms/C.2118/13.

2nd REGIMENT SOUTH AFRICAN INFANTRY

WAR DIARY
or
INTELLIGENCE SUMMARY.
(Erase heading not required.)

Army Form C. 2118.

Instructions regarding War Diaries and Intelligence Summaries are contained in F. S. Regs., Part II. and the Staff Manual respectively. Title pages will be prepared in manuscript.

Place	Date	Hour	Summary of Events and Information	Remarks and references to Appendices
	1917			
No 2 SECTION RIGHT SECTOR	FEBY 22nd		Enemy Operations. Artillery quiet. Trench Mortars 10 Heavy trench mortars fell near Cannon St and AUGUST and 4 Heavy Trench mortars near CLAUDE – CRATER. The enemy was active with fishtail bombs but no damage was done. Our Operations. Artillery quiet. Trench Mortars active. General The rising of the mist at 10AM disclosed 2 working parties. One in supports and the other in the wire, both these parties were dispersed by Lewis Gun and Rifle fire. Sniping Two Germans were seen walking along ridge opposite SAP.91. They were fired on and one appeared to be hit. Strength of Regiment in Trenches Officers 32 OR 531. Casualties 1 OR killed. 324 OR on general Trench repairs. 2/LIEUT KIRK and 2 OR returned of leave.	
	23rd		Enemy Operations. Artillery quiet. Trench Mortars 6 Heavy trench mortars fell between supports and front line slight damage to top of AUGUST AVENUE between 2.30 and 3.30 pm. 15 light Trench mortars fell near front line no damage was done. Rifle Grenades 50 were fired along our front line without effect. Our Operations. Artillery active. Trench Mortars active on wire and (Contd)	O.O attached

A5834 Wt. W4973/M687 750,000 8/16 D. D. & L. Ltd. Forms/C.2118/13.

2nd REGIMENT. SOUTH AFRICAN INFANTRY.

WAR DIARY
or
INTELLIGENCE SUMMARY.
(*Erase heading not required.*)

Army Form C. 2118.

Instructions regarding War Diaries and Intelligence Summaries are contained in F. S. Regs., Part II. and the Staff Manual respectively. Title pages will be prepared in manuscript.

Place	Date 1917	Hour	Summary of Events and Information	Remarks and references to Appendices
No 2 SECTION RIGHT SECTOR	FEBY 23rd		and front line. Rifle Grenades 41 were fired. Machine Guns active. Strength of Regiment in trenches Officers 32 OR 527 Casualties Nil. 262 OR on general trench repairs. Company relief as per attached order.	O.O. No. 51
	24th		Enemy Operations. About 50. 77 MM. shells fell in and near our lines little damage. Trench Mortars. At 4 pm. 4 Heavy trench mortars fell near JULY AVENUE and supports. Rifle Grenades 30 fell along our front line. Sniping active opposite the CRATERS. Our Operations. Artillery active. Trench Mortars Stokes medium and heavy were active with good effect. General. 3 working parties were seen and fired on by our Lewis guns and rifles at the following hours 6.45 AM. 7 AM. and 7.15 AM opposite CLARENCE CRATERS. Patrols. 1 Officer and 2 OR patrolled the entire Battalion frontage along the enemy wire. There were ample signs of the enemy being still in occupation of the entire front line opposite this Battalion. The enemy wire was found to be practically intact. Strength of Regiment in trenches Officers 32 OR. 523. Casualties 1 OR killed. 256 OR on general trench repairs. Battalion Relief as per attached order.	O.O. attached No 52

2nd REGIMENT. SOUTH AFRICAN INFANTRY

Instructions regarding War Diaries and Intelligence Summaries are contained in F. S. Regs., Part II. and the Staff Manual respectively. Title pages will be prepared in manuscript.

WAR DIARY
or
INTELLIGENCE SUMMARY.
(Erase heading not required.)

Army Form C. 2118.

Place	Date 1917	Hour	Summary of Events and Information	Remarks and references to Appendices
No 2 SECTION RIGHT SECTOR	FEBY 25th		Battalion relieved by the 4th SOUTH AFRICAN INFANTRY, and on completion of relief took up the duties of RESERVE BATTALION in ARRAS. all coys at the CONVENT. Head Quarters at hotel Univers. Relief complete at 12 pm. Strength of Regiment officers 32 OR 529. 60 men supplied for working parties in the line. 2 O.R proceeded on snipers Course. Draft from Base taken on strength of Regiment 4. O. Ranks.	
ARRAS	26th		260 supplied for working parties in the line. Guards and duties found in ARRAS. Strength of Regiment officers 33 OR 531. Casualties Nil.	
	27th		230 men supplied for working parties in the line. Guards and duties found in ARRAS. Strength of Regiment officers 33 OR 520 Casualties Nil. 10 OR ~~[illegible]~~ on pigeon course. Draft from Base taken on strength of Regiment 2 Officers 18 O. Ranks.	
	28th		230 men supplied for working parties in the line. Guards and duties found in ARRAS. Strength of Regiment officers 35 OR 541 Casualties Nil	

CR Heenan Major

A5834 Wt. W4973/M687 750,000 8/16 D. D. & L. Ltd. Forms/C.2118/13.

OPERATION ORDER NO: 43.

Copy No. ...3... War Diary

2nd February, 1917.

Map Reference,
Trench Map.
1/10,000.

No. 1.
RELIEFS.

The following reliefs will take place to-morrow, the 3rd February, 1917.

"C" Company will relieve "A" Company in Front Line.
"B" Company will relieve "D" Company in Front Line.
"D" Company will relieve "C" Company in Support Line
"A" Company will relieve "B" Company in BRITTANIA WORKS and vicinity.-

Reliefs will commence at 1.p.m. and will be completed by 2.p.m.
Company Commanders will arrange with the Company Commanders they relieve the method of relief, and submit proposals for approval of the Commanding Officer

No. 2.
INFORMATION.

Our artillery and trench mortars will operate as follows to-morrow, between 9 a.m. and 10.a.m.

18 prs. Cover fire of T.M.S.
4.5" Hows. Haystack at H.14.A.10.82. Destroy work.
2" T.M. G.6.C.90.05.
3" Stokes. Trenches.G.12.7.7. G.12.A.73.20 and support trenches in rear,

No. 3.
LEWIS GUNS.

"B" and "C" Companies will each be augmented by two extra Lewis Guns for the period which these Companies are in the front. Detachments for these guns will report to the O.C. "C" and "B" at 12-30 pm. on the 3rd February.

No. 4.
TRENCH STORES.

These will be taken over and receipts obtained.

No. 5.
LOG BOOKS.

Log Books completed will be taken over.

No. 6
COMPLETION OF RELIEF.

Completion of Relief will be reported by the code word JOHN "[redacted]" over telephone to Battalion Headquarters.

No. 7.
ACTION IN CASE OF ATTACK.

O.C.'s, "A" and "D" Companies will remain in command of their respective fronts until completion of relief.

Lieut. Actg. Adjutant.
2nd Regiment, S.A.Infantry.

Copies Nos. 1 to 3 Retained.
Copy No. 4 to 7 O.C. "A" Coy.- "D" Coy.

B. War Diary

OPERATION ORDER No. 44.

Copy No.....

4th February, [illegible]

Map Reference
Trench Map.
1/[illegible]

No. 1
RELIEFS.

The following reliefs will take place to-morrow, the 5th February 1917.

"A" Company will relieve "B" Company in Front Line.
"D" Company will relieve "B" Company in Front Line.
"B" Company will relieve "D" Company in Support Line.
"C" Company will relieve "A" Company in [illegible] WOOD and vicinity.

Reliefs will commence at 1 p.m. and will be completed by 5 p.m.
Company Commanders will arrange with the Company Commanders they relieve the method of relief, and submit proposals for approval of the Commanding Officer.

No. 2
[illegible].

Our Artillery and Trench Mortars will operate as follows to-morrow, between 3.30 p.m. and 4.30 p.m.

18 prs.	Cover T.M.s.
9.45" T.M.s	Front Line [illegible] to [illegible]
2" T.M.s	Wire at [illegible]
3" Stokes	From [illegible] to [illegible]
	From [illegible] to [illegible]

No. 3.
LEWIS GUNS.

"A" and "D" Companies will each be supported by two extra Lewis Guns for the period which those Companies are in the front. Detachments for these guns will report to the O.C. "A" and "D" at 12.30. p.m. on the 5th February.

No. 4.
TRENCH STORES.

These will be taken over and receipts obtained.

No. 5.
LOG BOOKS.

Log Books completed will be taken over.

No. 6
COMPLETION OF RELIEF.

Completion of Relief will be reported by the code word "[illegible]" over telephone to Battalion Headquarters.

No. 7.
ACTION IN CASE OF ATTACK.

O.C.s "B" and "C" Companies will remain in command of their respective fronts until completion of relief

[signature]
Lieut. & A/g. Adjutant.
2nd Regiment, S.A. Infantry.

Copies Nos 1 to 3	Retained.
Copy No. 4	O.C. "A" Coy.
Copy No. 5	O.C. "B" Coy.
Copy No. 6	O.C. "C" Coy.
Copy No. 7	O.C. "D" Coy.

OPERATION ORDER No. 45.

Copy...3...War Diary

6th February 1917.

Map Reference
Trench Map
1/10,000

No. 1.
RELIEFS.

The following reliefs will take place to-morrow, the 7th February 1917.

"C" Company will relieve "[illegible]" Company in Front Line
"B" Company will relieve "[illegible]" Company in Front Line
"A" Company will relieve "[illegible]" Company in Support Line
"D" Company will relieve "C" Company in [illegible] WORKS and vicinity.

Reliefs will commence at 1 p.m. and will be completed by 2 p.m.
Company Commanders will arrange with the Company Commanders they relieve the method of relief, and submit proposals for approval of the Commanding Officer.

No. 2.
[illegible].

Our artillery and Trench Mortars will operate as follows to-morrow, between 10 and 11 a.m.

18 prs.	Cover T.M.s
9.45" T.M.B.	Trench G.10.A.2.5. to G.10.C.5.7.
2" T.M.B.	Wire and Sap. G.1[illegible] 4.5.
3" Stokes	Support trench G.1[illegible].9. to G.12. A.[illegible].35.

No. 3
LEWIS GUNS.

"B" and "C" Companies will each be augmented by two extra Lewis Guns for the period which these Companies are in the front line. Detachments for these guns will report to the O.C. "B" and "C" at 12.30 p.m. on the 7th February.

No. 4
TRENCH STORES. These will be taken over and receipts obtained.

No. 5
[illegible]. Log Books completed will be takenover.

No. 6
COMPLETION OF RELIEF

Completion of Relief will be reported by the code word "PERCY" over telephone to Battalion Headquarters.

No. 7
Action in case of Attack

O.Cs "A" and "D" Companies will remain in command of their respective fronts until completion of relief.

Lieut & Act. Adjutant.
2nd Regiment S.A.Inf.

Copies 1 to 3	retained.
Copy No. 4	O.C. "A" Coy.
Copy No. 5.	O.C. "B" Coy
Copy No. 6	O.C. "C" Coy
Copy No. 7	O.C. "D" Coy.

Copy No.

2nd REGIMENT S. A. INFANTRY ORDER NO: 47.

10. 2. 1917.

No. 1.
RELIEF.

"B" Company, less two platoons, in St. NICHOLAS will be relieved by two Platoons of the 3rd Regiment S. A. Infantry to-morrow, the 11th inst. Two Platoons of "B" Company in FORRESTIER REDOUBT will be relieved by two platoons of the 3rd S. A. I.
One Platoon of "A" Company in St. NICHOLAS will be relieved by 1 platoon of the 3rd S. A. I.

The relieving platoons of the 3rd Regiment S. A.I. will move into Forrestier and St. Nicholas at 10. a.m.
As practically all men will be on fatigues, O.C. "B" Coy. will arrange for all kit etc. to be stacked outside the billets in one place, and a guard of light duty men put over this kit. On completion of ~~relief~~ fatigues, "B" Company and the one platoon of "A" Company will move into ARRAS and take over billets assigned to them at the CONVENT. The guards will not be dismounted until ~~xxxxxxxxxxxx~~ relieved by guards of the 3rd S.A.I.
"A" Company, less one platoon, at Barbed Wire Square will move and take over billets in CONVENT, ARRAS. O.C. "A" Coy. will arrange to have all kit stacked outside, and left under a guard before proceeding on fatigue in the morning. On return of the fatigue parties, the movement into new billets will be completed.

No. 2.
TRENCH WARDENS.

O. C. "B" Coy. will be responsible for withdrawing all trench wardens after they have been relieved by the 3rd Regiment wardens. List of their various posts attached herewith. On completion of relief, trench wardens will rejoin their respective companies.

No. 3.
MOVEMENT.

Movement will be by the usual small parties, care being taken that control is kept by the N.C.O's.

No. 4.
TRENCH STORES, etc.

Trench stores, etc. will be handed over and receipts obtained. A certificate ~~xx~~ will also be obtained, stating that the billets were handed over in a clean and sanitary condition.

No. 5.
COOKING ARRANGEMENTS.

Company Commanders will be responsible for cooking arrangements.
All light duty men should be used to carry kits, cooking utensils, etc. to the new company billets.

No. 6.
COMPLETION OF RELIEF.

O.C's. "A" and "B" Companies will report in writing to Orderly Room when finally settled in new billets at the CONVENT.

[signature]
Lieut. & Act. Adjutant,
2nd Regt. S.A.I.

By orderly, ...a.m. 11.2.1917.

2nd S.A. Infantry Order No. 48.

Copy No. 2.......

16/2/1917.

Map Reference
French Map ARRAS
1/10,000.

No. 1.
RELIEF.

The Battalion will relieve the 4th S.A. Infantry on the 17th instant in No. 2 Section, Right Sector.

"A" Company will relieve Left Company ("C" Coy. 4th S.A.I.) in front line at 9.30 a.m.
"B" Company will relieve Right Company ("B" Coy. 4th S.A.I.) in front line at 10 a.m.
"C" Company will relieve Support Company ("D" Coy. 4th S.A.I.) in Support Line at 10.30 a.m.
"D" Company will relieve Reserve Company ("A" Coy. 4th S.A.I.) in Brittania Works and vicinity.

No. 2.
DISPOSITION ON RELIEF.

On relief "A" Company will occupy Trench 94 inclusive to Trench 97 inclusive.
"B" Company will occupy Trench 90 inclusive to Trench 93 inclusive.
"C" Company will occupy "B" WORK and ST. PANCRAS inclusive to ~~Ex~~ S. Trench 90 inclusive.
"D" Company will occupy BRITTANIA WORKS and vicinity.

No. 3.
LEWIS GUNS.

Lewis Guns and teams will relieve Lewis Guns of the 4th South African Infantry at 9 a.m.
"A" and "B" Companies will each be augmented by 2 extra Lewis Guns for the period these companies are in the front line.
These detachments will report to Company Commanders at 8 a.m. to-morrow.

No. 4.
ADVANCE PARTIES.

Company Commanders will arrange for one officer and 2 N.C.O's. to proceed half-an-hour in advance of their Companies to take over stores. Company Gas N.C.O's. will accompany these parties.

No. 5.
ROUTES.

Two platoons of "A" Company will move up AUGUST to Front Line.
"A" Company less two platoons will move up AUGUST SUPPORT LINE and [illegible] STREET.
"B" Company less two platoons will move up JULY AVENUE.
Two platoons of "B" Company will move up JULY and [illegible] CUT.
"C" Company less one platoon will move up AUGUST.
One Platoon of "C" Company will move up JULY.
"D" Company will move up [illegible] AVENUE.

No. 6.
MOVEMENT.

The movement will be carried out in parties of 6 at intervals of one minute, as far as CANDLE FACTORY.
From CANDLE FACTORY the movement will be by platoons at intervals of 5 minutes.

No. 7.
LOG BOOKS,
MAPS, etc.

Log Books, Maps, etc. will be taken over.

No. 8.
TRENCH
STORES.

Trench stores will be taken over and duplicate receipts forwarded to Battalion Headquarters by 2 p.m.

No. 9.
COMPLETION OF RELIEF.

Completion of Relief will be reported to Battalion Headquarters by the code word "JACK" over the phone.

Captain & Adjutant,
2nd Regiment South African Infy.

Copies Nos. 1 - 4.	Retained.
Copy No. 5.	"A" Coy.
Copy No. 6.	"B" Coy.
Copy No. 7.	"C" Coy.
Copy No. 8.	"D" Coy.

Issued by Orderly at ......p.m. 16.2.17.

OPERATION ORDER No. 49.

Copy No. 2 War Diary

18th Feby. 1917.

Map Reference
Trench Map.
1/10,000

No. 1.
RELIEFS.

The following reliefs will take place to-morrow, the 19th February 1917.
"C" Company will relieve "A" Company in Front Line
"B" Company will relieve "D" Company in Front Line.
"D" Company will relieve "B" Company in Support Line.
"A" Company will relieve "C" Company in Brittania Works and vicinity.

Reliefs will commence at 1 p.m. and will be completed by 3 p.m.
Company Commanders will arrange with the Company Commanders they relieve the method of relief, and submit proposals for approval of the Commanding Officer.

No. 2.
INTIMATION.

As far as it is at present known there will be no Artillery or Trench Mortar shoot to-morrow.

No. 3
LEWIS GUNS

"C" and "B" Companies will each be augmented by two extra Lewis Guns for the period which these Companies are in the front line. Detachments for these guns will report to the O.C. "B" and "C" Coys. at 12.30 p.m on the 19th February 1917.

No. 4
TRENCH STORES. These will be taken over and receipts obtained.

No. 5
LOG BOOKS. Log Books completed will be taken over.

No. 6
COMPLETION OF RELIEF.

Completion of Relief will be reported by the code word "[illegible]" over telephone to Battalion Headquarters.

No. 7
ACTION IN CASE OF ATTACK.

O.C.s "A" and "D" Companies will remain in command of their respective fronts until completion of relief.

R. C. Knight
Lt. for Captain & Adjutant
2nd R egt. S.A.Inf.

Copies Nos. 1-4	retained
Copy No. 5	O.C. "A" Coy.
Copy No. 6	O.C. "B" Coy.
Copy No. 7	O.C. "C" Coy
Copy No. 8	O.C. "D" Coy.

OPERATION ORDER No. [illegible]

Copy No. 3

Map Reference.
Trench Map.
1/10,000.

20th February 1917.

No. 1.
RELIEFS.

The following reliefs will take place to-morrow, the 21st February 1917.
"A" Company will relieve "C" in the front line.
"D" Company will relieve "B" in the front line.
"C" Company will relieve "D" Coy. in Support line.
"B" Company will relieve "A" Coy. in Britannia Works and vicinity.

Reliefs will commence at 1 p.m. and will be completed by 3 p.m.
Company Commanders will arrange with the Company Commanders they relieve the method of relief, and submit proposals for approval of the Commanding Officer.

No. 2.
INFORMATION.

As far as it is at present known there will be no Artillery or Trench Mortar shoot to-morrow.

No. 3.
LEWIS GUNS.

"A" and "D" Companies will be each augmented by two extra Lewis Guns for the period which these Companies are in the front line. Detachments for these guns will report to the O.C. "A" and "D" Coys. at 12 noon on the 21st February 1917.

No. 4.
TRENCH STORES.

These will be taken over and receipts obtained.

No. 5
LOG BOOKS.

Log Books completed will be handed over.

No. 6.
COMPLETION OF RELIEF.

Completion of Relief will be reported by the code word "[illegible]" over telephone to Battalion Headquarters.

No. 7.
ACTION IN CASE OF ATTACK.

O.C.s "B" and "C" Companies will remain in command of their respective fronts until completion of relief.

Captain & Adjutant.
2nd Regiment, S.A. Inf.

Copies 1- 3	Retained.
Copy No. 4	O.C. "A" Coy.
Copy No. 5	O.C. "B" Coy
Copy No. 6	O.C. "C" Coy
Copy No. 7	O.C. "D" Coy.
Copy No. 8.	O.C. [illegible].

OPERATION ORDER No. 61.

Wardiary

Copy No. ....

Map Reference
French Map.
1/10,000.

22nd February 1917.

No. 1
RELIEFS.

The following reliefs will take place to-morrow, the 23rd February 1917.
"[illegible]" Company will relieve "A" Company in Front Line.
"[illegible]" Company will relieve "[illegible]" Company in Front Line.
"A" Company will relieve "[illegible]" Company in Support Line.
"[illegible]" Company will relieve "[illegible]" Company in Britannia Works and vicinity.

Reliefs will commence at 1 p.m. and will be completed by [illegible] p.m.
Company Commanders will arrange with Company Commanders they relieve the method of relief, and submit proposals for approval of the Commanding Officer.

No. 2
INFORMATION.

As far as it is at present known there will be no Artillery or Trench Mortar Shoot to-morrow.

No. 3
LEWIS GUNS.

"[illegible]" and "[illegible]" Companies will be each augmented by two extra Lewis Guns for the period which these Companies are in the Front Line. Detachments for these guns will report to the O.C. "[illegible]" and "[illegible]" Companies at 10 noon on the 23rd February 1917.

No. 4
TRENCH STORES.

These will be taken over and receipts obtained.

No. 5.
LOG BOOKS.

Log Books completed will be handed over.

No. 6.
COMPLETION OF RELIEF.

Completion of Relief will be reported by the code word "[illegible]" over telephone to Battalion Headquarters.

No. 7.
ACTION IN CASE OF ATTACK.

O.C. "A" and "[illegible]" Companies will remain in command of their respective fronts until completion of relief.

[illegible signature]
Lt for Captain & Adjutant.
2nd Regiment, S.A. Inf.

Copies Nos. 1-3 Retained.
Copy No. 4 O.C. "A" Coy.
Copy No. 5 O.C. "[illegible]" Coy
Copy No. 6 O.C. "[illegible]" Coy
Copy No. 7 O.C. "[illegible]" Coy
Copy No. 8 O.C. "[illegible]"

ORDER NO: 52.

Copy No....[illegible]....
War Diary.

24/3/1917.

Map Reference
Trench Map ARRAS,
1/10000.

No. 1.
RELIEF.

The Battalion will be relieved in the line by the 4th S.A. Infantry on the 25th instant.
Lewis Guns, Signallers and Snipers will be relieved at 9.a.m.
"A" Coy. 4th S.A.I. will relieve "C" Company at 9.15. a.m.
"C" Coy. 4th S.A.I. will relieve "B" Company at 10. a.m.
"B" Coy. 4th S.A.I. will relieve "A" Company at 10.45. a.m.
"D" Coy. 4th S.A.I. will relieve "D" Company at 11.30 a.m.
Headquarters will be relieved at 12. a.m.
On relief the Battalion will take up the positions and duties of Reserve Battalion.
Companies on relief will be situated ~~at xxxxx~~ in billets at Convent, ARRAS.
Headquarters on relief will be situated at HOTEL UNIVERS.

No. 2.
ROUTES.

"C" Company less two platoons will withdraw via CANNON STREET and AUGUST AVENUE.
Two Platoons of "C" Company will withdraw via AUGUST AVENUE.
"B" Company less two platoons will withdraw via JULY AVENUE.
Two platoons of "B" Company will withdraw via NEW CUT and JULY.
"A" Company, less three platoons, will withdraw via JULY AVENUE.
Three platoons of "A" Company will withdraw via AUGUST AVENUE.
"D" Company will withdraw via AUGUST AVENUE.

No. 3.
MOVEMENT.

The movement as far as the CANDLE FACTORY will in platoons at five minutes interval.
From the Candle Factory to the billets in ARRAS in parties of EIGHT, at one minutes interval.
Orders as regards movement in ARRAS must be strictly adhered to.
2nd Lieut. HARVEY will control the movement from the Candle Factory.

No. 4.
TRENCH STORES.

Trench Stores will be handed over and duplicate receipts obtained and forwarded to Battalion Headquarters by 3.p.m.

No. 5.
LOG BOOKS, etc.

Log Books, Maps, etc. will be handed over complete.

No. 6.
COMPLETION OF RELIEF.

Completion of Relief will be reported to Battalion Headquarters by the code word "[illegible]", over the phone.

[signature] for Captain & Adjutant,
2nd Regiment S.A. Infantry.

Copies 1-4 Retained. 5 - 8 O.C. Companies.

Instructions regarding War Diaries and Intelligence Summaries are contained in F. S. Regs., Part II. and the Staff Manual respectively. Title pages will be prepared in manuscript.

Army Form C. 2118.

2nd REGIMENT SOUTH AFRICAN INFANTRY WAR DIARY

or

~~INTELLIGENCE SUMMARY.~~

(Erase heading not required.)

Vol 12

Place	Date	Hour	Summary of Events and Information	Remarks, and references to Appendices
ARRAS.	1st MARCH		230 men supplied for working parties in the line. Guards and duties found in ARRAS. Strength of Regiment Officers 34 OR 533. Casualties Nil.	
	2nd		240 men supplied for working parties in the line. Guards and duties found in ARRAS. Strength of Regiment Officers 33 OR. 535. Casualties Nil. 3 OR. proceeded on Lewis Gun Course at Etaples.	Operation Orders No 53 attached
	3rd		The Battalion moved out of ARRAS 9 AM and arrived at Y. Hutments at 12 noon where they remained for the night. Strength of Regiment Officers 33 OR 533. Captain R. Beverley proceeded on Lewis Gun Course at G.H.Q. Etaples.	
HERMAVILLE	4th		The Regiment moved from Y. Hutments at 9·30 AM. arrived at HERMAVILLE at 11·30 AM. 3 Companies A. B and D billeted in HERMAVILLE and C Company at TILLOY-LES-HERMAVILLE. 4 Officers 200 OR on working parties. Strength of Regiment Officers 42 OR. 724.	Operation Order No 54 attached

Instructions regarding War Diaries and Intelligence Summaries are contained in F. S. Regs., Part II. and the Staff Manual respectively. Title pages will be prepared in manuscript.

2nd Regiment South African Infantry.

WAR DIARY

or

~~INTELLIGENCE SUMMARY.~~

(Erase heading not required.)

Army Form C. 2118.

Place	Date	Hour	Summary of Events and Information	Remarks and references to Appendices
	1917			
HERMAVILLE	5th MARCH		4 Officers 166 O.R. supplied for working parties. Guards found in HERMAVILLE. men bathing. Strength of Regiment officers 42 O.R. 724. LIEUT COL TANNER C.M.G. returned off leave and assumed Command of the Reg. MAJOR C. R. HEENAN relinquished command of the Regiment.	
	6th		5 Officers 300 O.R. supplied for working parties. Guards and duties found in HERMAVILLE. men bathing. Strength of Regiment Officers 42 O.R. 724.	
	7th		4 Officers 263 O.R. supplied for working parties. Guards and duties found in HERMAVILLE. A football match took place at HERMAVILLE between the R.A.M.C. and 2nd REGIMENT South AFRICAN INFANTRY which resulted in a win in favour of the SOUTH AFRICANS 3 Nil. Each member of the winning team received a medal. This was the final match played for the cup presented by Major General Furse to the 9th Division. The cup was handed to the winning team by MAJOR GENERAL LUKIN. D.S.O. C.M.G. Strength of Regiment Officers 42 O.R. 717.	

Instructions regarding War Diaries and Intelligence Summaries are contained in F. S. Regs., Part II. and the Staff Manual respectively. Title pages will be prepared in manuscript.

2nd REGIMENT SOUTH AFRICAN INFANTRY
WAR DIARY
or
~~INTELLIGENCE SUMMARY.~~
(Erase heading not required.)

Army Form C. 2118.

Place	Date	Hour	Summary of Events and Information	Remarks and references to Appendices
HERMAVILLE	12 3/7		2 officers 100 OR supplied for working parties. The Regiment moved out of HERMAVILLE at 9-30 AM. ROUTE) from HERMAVILLE in a N.W direction to junction of main ARRAS-ST-POL road south of SAVY STA thence to VILLERS-BRULIN then through GUESTREVILLE, thence in a NW direction HERLIN-LE-VERT: arriving at MONCHY BRETON at 2 pm. Strength of Regiment officers 42 OR 715. Captain F.E. COCHRAN from 2nd Reg S.A INF to be STAFF CAPTAIN. S.A. BRIGADE.	
MONCHY-BRETON.	13 3/7		Regiment in Billets at MONCHY. BRETON. ROUTINE) Rouse 6-30 AM Roll Call 7 AM from 10 AM to 11 AM Close order drill. 11 to 12 AM Rifle Grenade practice 12 to 12-30 pm Bayonet fighting and practice firing from hip. 1-30 to 2-30 pm platoon attack practice. 2-30 to 4 pm Bombing. Specialists under their own Instructors. Strength of Regiment officers 42 OR 715.	
	14 3/7		Regiment in Billets. Routine) 10 to 11 AM close order drill 11 AM to 12-30 pm Bayonet fighting 1-30 to 2-30 pm company attack practice. 2-30 to 4 pm physical exercises specialists under their own instructors. Strength of Regiment officers 41 OR 711.	

Instructions regarding War Diaries and Intelligence Summaries are contained in F. S. Regs., Part II. and the Staff Manual respectively. Title pages will be prepared in manuscript.

Army Form C. 2118.

2nd REGIMENT SOUTH AFRICAN INFANTRY.
WAR DIARY
or
~~INTELLIGENCE SUMMARY.~~
(Erase heading not required.)

Place	Date	Hour	Summary of Events and Information	Remarks and references to Appendices
HERMAVILLE	8th MARCH		4 Officers 222 O.R. supplied for working parties. Guards and duties found in HERMAVILLE men bathing. 1 O.R. proceeded on Lewis Gun Course at XVII Corps. Strength of Regiment Officers 42 O.R. 718.	
	9th		4 Officers 269 O.R. supplied for working parties. Guards and duties found. Strength of Regiment Officers 42 O.R. 718.	
	10th		4 Officers 300 O.R. supplied for working parties. Guards found in HERMAVILLE men bathing. 2 O.R. returned from Auxi-le-Chateaux off Snipers Course. Strength of Regiment Officers 42 O.R. 715.	Operation Order No 55 attached
	11th		4 Officers and 200 O.R. supplied for working parties. Guards found in HERMAVILLE Captain R. BEVERLEY [M.C.] returned off Lewis Gun Course. Strength of Regiment Officers 42 O.R. 715.	

Instructions regarding War Diaries and Intelligence Summaries are contained in F. S. Regs., Part II. and the Staff Manual respectively. Title pages will be prepared in manuscript.

Army Form C. 2118.

2nd Regiment South African Infantry.
WAR DIARY
or
~~INTELLIGENCE SUMMARY.~~
(Erase heading not required.)

Place	Date	Hour	Summary of Events and Information	Remarks and references to Appendices
MONCHY BRETON	15 7/17		Routine.) Rouse 6·30 AM Roll Call 7AM. 10 to 11 close order drill 11 to 12·30 PM Bayonet fighting 1·30 to 2·30 PM Company attack practice. 2·30 to 4 PM Physical exercises. Specialists under their own instructors. Strength of Regiment Officers 41 OR. 711.	
	16 7/17		Routine 10 to 11 AM close order drill. 11 AM to 12·30 PM company attack practice 1·30 to 2·30 pm Bayonet fighting. 2·30 to 4 pm Physical exercises. Throughout the day Lewis Gun training, Rifle Grenade practice. Stokes gun Instruction. Signalling, Shutters and Lamps under their own instructors. Strength of Regiment Officers 41 OR 711.	
	17 7/17		Training as yesterday. Strength of Regiment Officers 42 OR 710.	
	18 7/17		Routine Rouse 6·30 Roll Call 7AM Church parade 8AM. Strength of Regiment Officers 42 OR 707.	

Instructions regarding War Diaries and Intelligence Summaries are contained in F. S. Regs., Part II. and the Staff Manual respectively. Title pages will be prepared in manuscript.

Army Form C. 2118.

2nd Regiment South African Infantry
WAR DIARY
or
~~INTELLIGENCE SUMMARY.~~

(Erase heading not required.)

Place	Date	Hour	Summary of Events and Information	Remarks and references to Appendices
MONCHY BRETON	19 3/17		Routine. Rouse 6-30 AM Roll Call 7 AM. 2 to 3 pm bombing. 3 to 3-30 Bayonet fighting 3-30 to 4-30 Company attack practice. Strength of Regiment officers 42 O.R. 707.	
	20 3/17		Brigade day. 2nd Lieut E J RICHES and 5 O.R. proceeded on Lewis Gun Course at XVII Corps. Strength of Regiment officers 42 O.R. 693.	operation Order No 56 attached Q
	21 3/17		The Regiment moved out of MONCHY-BRETON ~~... S.E.~~ at 9-30 AM. from MONCHY BRETON in a S.E direction to CHELERS thence South to TINCQUES, thence East along the main ARRAS-ST. POL road as far as the A in SAVY STA, from SAVY south east to HERMAVILLE. arriving 2 p.m. Strength of Regiment officers 41 O.R. 692.	
	22 3/17		Parades. Companies at the disposal of Company Commanders. Guards and duties found in HERMAVILLE. men bathing. Strength of Regiment officers 41 OR 692.	

Instructions regarding War Diaries and Intelligence Summaries are contained in F. S. Regs., Part II. and the Staff Manual respectively. Title pages will be prepared in manuscript.

WAR DIARY
or
~~INTELLIGENCE SUMMARY~~.
(Erase heading not required.)

Army Form C. 2118.

Place	Date	Hour	Summary of Events and Information	Remarks and references to Appendices
No 2 SECTION RIGHT SECTOR	24 7/17		enemy wire - returning to our trenches via SAP 89. the wire appeared to be in good condition. 1 officer and 2 OR patrolled our wire and NO MANS LAND from trench 89 to 92 - a dead German was found but no identification was obtainable. CAPTAIN R. C. KNIGHT. and 5 OR. proceeded on an Aeroplane Signalling Course at SAVY. 2 OR on Gas Course at HERMAVILLE. Strength of Regiment in trenches Officers 33 OR 534.	
	25 7/17		<u>Enemy Operations</u> Artillery Between 12 NOON and 2 PM 48 77 MM Shells fell in vicinity of front line trench 89. Between midnight and 4 AM 90-77 MM and 36-10·5 SM Shells fell in vicinity of front line and supports of trenches 87 and 89. Between 7 AM and 12 NOON 20-77 MM and 9-10·5 SM Shells fell in vicinity of trench 89. Machine Guns active between 9 and 11 pm. Trench Mortars Quiet Aircraft Active. <u>Our Operations</u>. Artillery very active. Trench mortars active Aircraft active. Patrols 2 patrols 1 officer and 3 OR and 1 Senior ~~of~~ N.C.O and 2 OR left SAP 87 and proceeded along enemy wire	

T2134. Wt. W708—776. 500000. 4/15. Sir J. C. & S.

Instructions regarding War Diaries and Intelligence Summaries are contained in F. S. Regs., Part II. and the Staff Manual respectively. Title pages will be prepared in manuscript.

WAR DIARY

Army Form C. 2118.

2ND REGIMENT. SOUTH AFRICAN INFANTRY ~~INTELLIGENCE SUMMARY.~~

(Erase heading not required.)

Place	Date	Hour	Summary of Events and Information	Remarks and references to Appendices
MONCHY BRETON	23 3/17		The Battalion moved out of HERMAVILLE 10AM and arrived at Y. HUTMENTS at 12.30 PM. Strength of Regiment Officers 41 OR 692.	Operation Orders No 57 attached
Y. HUTMENTS	24 3/17		The Battalion moved from Y. HUTMENTS at 4 pm arrived in trenches 7 PM. The Battalion relieved the 27th Brigade in No 2 SECTION RIGHT SECTOR. Relief commenced at 7 pm and completed 9 pm Companies in SECTION from 89 to 91.	Operation Orders No 58 attached
			<u>Enemy Operations</u> Artillery 8 to 9 pm 18 77 MM shells fell between front line and supports 8 to 8.30 AM 5 77 MM shells fell near front line, and again at 10 AM 3 77 MM shells fell in the same vicinity. Trench Mortars Quiet. Machine Guns Quiet. Aircraft at 8.25 3 – machines above our lines – one dropped a red light, but nothing occurred.	
			<u>Our Operations</u> Artillery very active mostly on enemy wire. Trench Mortars active on enemy wire. Aircraft active. Patrols 1 Officer and 3 OR left SAP 87 and crossed to the	

(Contd)

Instructions regarding War Diaries and Intelligence Summaries are contained in F. S. Regs., Part II. and the Staff Manual respectively. Title pages will be prepared in manuscript.

WAR DIARY
or
~~INTELLIGENCE SUMMARY~~.
(Erase heading not required.)

Army Form C. 2118.

Place	Date	Hour	Summary of Events and Information	Remarks and references to Appendices
No. 2 SECTION RIGHT SECTOR	25 3/7		returning to our line at SAP 89. They reported that wire was still in very good state - and no gaps were seen. No enemy patrols were encountered. 2 OR on LEWIS GUN COURSE at 3rd ARMY SCHOOL. 5 Officers 350 OR engaged on general trench repairs Carrying etc. Strength of Regiment in trenches 31 Officers 523 OR. Casualties Nil.	
	26 3/7		Enemy Operations. Artillery Between 1 pm and 4 pm 10·77 MM shells fell near JULY AVENUE. Between 5·30 and 6·30 19·77 MM shells fell near Supports in rear of trenches 90 and 91. at 9·15 AM 8·10·5 CM Shells fell between front line and Support trenches 90 and 91. Between 1 pm and 4 pM. 15·77 MM shells and 24 10·5 CM Shells fell between front line and supports vicinity of trenches 88 and 89. Trench Mortars Quiet. Machine Guns Nil. Our Operations Artillery active Trench Mortars active. Patrols 2 officers and 2 Senior N.C.O. patrols visited the German wire during the night and report the wire still thick - although that portion facing our trench 90 and part 91 could be cleared by intense wire (Contd)	

WAR DIARY
or
~~INTELLIGENCE SUMMARY~~.
(Erase heading not required.)

Army Form C. 2118.

Place	Date	Hour	Summary of Events and Information	Remarks and references to Appendices
H02 SECTION RIGHT SECTOR	26 7/7		cutting of a few hours. 357 OR engaged on general trench repairs carrying etc. Strength of Regiment in trenches officers 31 OR 496. Casualties Nil. 2/Lieut ARNOLD and ~~2~~ 73 OR, draft from Base taken on Strength of Regiment.	
	27 7/7		*Enemy Operations* Artillery Between 3pm and 5pm 25.77 MM shells fell between front line and Support line of trenches 90 and 91. Between 12 Midnight and 1AM 20. 10.5 CM shells fell in vicinity of NICHOLAS REDOUBT and CHALK FARM. Between 11 AM and 12 Midday 15 10.5 CM Shells fell between front line and ~~Supports~~ trenches 89 and 90. Trench Mortars 7 light Trench Mortars fell near our Support line but did no damage. Machine Guns Quiet. Aircraft active.	
			Our Operations Artillery very active Trench Mortars active. Patrols 2 Officers and 2 N.C.O. patrols visited NO MANS LAND and enemy wire during the night and report several gaps between SAP 89 and 91. The enemy wire has been badly battered - but in parts it is still very thick. One of our patrol parties was fired on. An enemy party was heard working in trench just south of SAP VII.	
			(Contd)	

Instructions regarding War Diaries and Intelligence Summaries are contained in F. S. Regs., Part II. and the Staff Manual respectively. Title pages will be prepared in manuscript.

WAR DIARY
or
~~INTELLIGENCE SUMMARY.~~
(Erase heading not required.)

Army Form C. 2118.

Place	Date	Hour	Summary of Events and Information	Remarks and references to Appendices
No2 SECTION RIGHT SECTOR	27 3/7		5 Officers and 355 OR engaged on general trench repairs Carrying etc. Casualties 1 OR slightly wounded and returned to duty. Strength of Regiment in trenches officers 32 OR 561.	
	28 3/7		Enemy Operations Artillery fairly quiet during the day but very active during the night with heavy and light shells. From 2 AM to 5 AM enemy shelled the front line with light shells blowing it in in several places. Between 12 noon and 7 pm. enemy shelled front line and supports with 77 MM and 10.5 shells. Trench mortars Quiet Machine Guns Quiet. Aircraft active hours of 11 AM to 5 PM and slightly active from 5 pm to sundown Our Operations. Our artillery active throughout the day shelling enemy front line and wire with good effect. Trench Mortars active from 11 AM to 5 pm firing on enemy wire. Machine Guns slightly active. Aircraft active through the day. Patrols 1 officer and 2 OR left head of JULY AVENUE at 1·30 AM moving East until they came in	

2353 Wt. W2544/1454 700,000 5/15 D. D. & L. A.D.S.S./Forms/C. 2118.

Instructions regarding War Diaries and Intelligence Summaries are contained in F. S. Regs., Part II. and the Staff Manual respectively. Title pages will be prepared in manuscript.

WAR DIARY
or
~~INTELLIGENCE SUMMARY~~.
(Erase heading not required.)

Army Form C. 2118.

Place	Date	Hour	Summary of Events and Information	Remarks and references to Appendices
No 2 SECTION RIGHT SECTOR	28 3/17		in contact with enemy wire opposite SAP 91. wire very thin with quite a number of gaps between the thick balls of wire. entanglements which have not yet been touched ~~by~~ by our fire. South between SAP 91 and 90 there is a very large gap and also in the vicinity there are a number of large shell craters about 70 yards from enemy line. Head Quarters of the 2nd Reg S.A.I. took over Head Quarters of the 26th Brigade near CANDLE FACTORY. 5 Officers and 353 O.R engaged on general trench repairs carrying etc. Casualties 1 OR wounded. Strength of Regiment in trenches Officers 33 OR 573	
	29 3/17		Enemy Operations Artillery 120 77 MM shells fell in vicinity of front line and supports during the afternoon and morning. Between 1 and 2 pm 15 CM shells fell near T.M. emplacement behind trench 90. Between 8 AM and 10 AM 10 15 CM shells fell top end of NEW CUT damaging trench slightly. Between 8 AM and 12 Noon 40 · 10.5 cm and 15 cm	

(Contd)

2353 Wt. W2544/1454 700,000 5/15 D. D. & L. A.D.S.S./Forms/C. 2118.

Instructions regarding War Diaries and Intelligence Summaries are contained in F. S. Regs., Part II. and the Staff Manual respectively. Title pages will be prepared in manuscript.

WAR DIARY
or
~~INTELLIGENCE SUMMARY.~~
(Erase heading not required.)

Army Form C. 2118.

Place	Date	Hour	Summary of Events and Information	Remarks and references to Appendices
No 2. SECTION RIGHT SECTOR	29/7/17		shells fell in vicinity of CHALK FARM and NICHOLAS REDOUBT. Between 10 and 11-30 AM 20 · 15 CM Shells fell in vicinity of CANDLE FACTORY. Between 10 and 10 30 AM 20 · 15 CM Shells on BRITTANIA WORKS. Rifle Grenades a few fell along our front line. Aircraft very active 7 flew very low along front line between 10 AM and 12 NOON. Our Operation Artillery very active. Trench Mortars active with very good results on enemy wire - where several gaps are now noticeable. Machine Guns Usual indirect fire - action against enemy aircraft. Patrols Four patrols were out during the night - and report that the enemy wire has been badly shattered and several gaps are noticeable. The enemy threw bombs and also fired at one officer patrol between 10 and 11 pm. 4 Officers 345 OR engaged on general trench repairs. Casualties 1 O.R. killed. Strength of Regiment in Trenches Officers 33 OR 571.	

2353 Wt. W2544/1454 700,000 5/15 D. D. & L. A.D.S.S./Forms/C. 2118.

Instructions regarding War Diaries and Intelligence Summaries are contained in F. S. Regs., Part II. and the Staff Manual respectively. Title pages will be prepared in manuscript.

WAR DIARY

or

~~INTELLIGENCE SUMMARY.~~

(*Erase heading not required.*)

Army Form C. 2118.

Place	Date	Hour	Summary of Events and Information	Remarks and references to Appendices
No 2 SECTION RIGHT. SECTOR	30 7/17		Enemy Operations. Artillery 58-77MM shells fell in vicinity of front line and Supports during the afternoon. Between 4 and 6 p.m. 10 cm shells fell in vicinity of CANDLE FACTORY. Trench Mortars Quiet. Our Operations Artillery very active. Trench Mortars active on enemy wire. Machine Guns Quiet. Battalion relieved by 3rd SOUTH AFRICAN INFANTRY. and on completion of relief took over duties of RESERVE BATTALION. Relief commenced 7.15 pm and complete 10 p.M. Desposition of BATTALION in accordance with operation Order attached. 1 OR proceeded on a COURSE of Cookery at 3rd ARMY SCHOOL. 4 officers and 300 OR engaged on general trench repairs. Strength of Regiment in trenches Officers 33 OR. 564.	operation Order No 60 attached
	31 7/17		4 officers 170 men supplied for working parties in the line. Guards found in ARRAS. Strength of Regiment in Bn Reserve Officers 33 OR. 561. Casualties. Nil.	

W. Dawson[?]

Lieut Colonel

Commanding 2nd Reg. S. A. Inf.

ORDER NO. 53.

Copy No......War Diary

Map Reference,
LENS II
Scale 1/100,000.

2nd March, 1917.

No. 1. RELIEF.

The Battalion will be relieved by the 8th Black Watch on the 3rd instant.

No. 2. MOVEMENT.

The Battalion will move to new area by March route.

The movement from ARRAS to "Y" Hutments will be by platoons at intervals of 400 yards.

Movement through ARRAS will be in single file.

No. 3. ORDER OF MARCH.

Headquarters.
"A" Company. Starting at about 9.30
"B" Company.
"C" Company.
"D" Company.

No. 4. STARTING POINT.

CONVENT GATE for Companies.

"A" Company will move off on arrival of 1st platoon of 8th BLACK WATCH, and the movement will be continued at the interval named above.

No. 5. GUIDES.

Each Company will detail 4 guides to meet incoming Regiment. These guides will report to 2nd Lieutenant RICHES at Battalion Headquarters at 8.45 a.m. on 3rd.

2nd Lieutenant RICHES will report to the Adjutant for instructions at 8 p.m. to-night.

No. 6 BILLETS

Reports to be sent by Runner to Battalion Headquarters as soon as Companies are clear of Billets. A separate report must be sent stating that Billets vacated are left in clean condition.

The Battalion will be billeted in "Y" HUTMENTS on night of 3rd.

No. 7 LEWIS GUNS.

Lewis Guns will be carried out by Companies. 20 magazines per gun will be carried. The balance of Lewis gun magazines and boxes will be stacked near Gate of Convent and will be loaded on to transport on evening of 3rd. Each Company will detail 3 men to load and accompany this gear.

No. 8 BATTALION HEADQUARTERS.

Battalion Headquarters will remain at Hotel De L'UNIVERS until "D" Company reports clear. Headquarters will then move to "Y" HUTMENTS.

No. 9 FURTHER MOVE.

The Battalion will move by March Route to HERMAVILLE on the 4th instant under further orders to be issued later.

[signature]

Captain & Adjutant,
2nd Regiment South African Infantry.

Copy No. 1-4 Retained.
Copy No. 5. O.C."A"Coy.
Copy No. 6. "B" Coy.
Copy No. 7. "C" Coy.
Copy No. 8. "D" Coy.

ORDER NO: 34.

Map Reference
LENS. 11.
Scale 1/100,000.

Copy No....3... War Diary

No. 1. MOVE. The Battalion, less Working Parties, will march to HERMAVILLE and TILLOY Les HERMAVILLE on the 4th instant.

No. 2. ORDER OF MARCH.
"A" Company.
"C" Company.
Headquarters.
"B" Company.
"D" Company.

No. 3. STARTING POINT. X Roads 400 yards west of "Z" in ETRUN.

No. 4. ROUTE. X Roads - west along south edge of BOIS d'HABARCQ to HERMAVILLE and TILLOY Les HERMAVILLE.

No. 5. TIME. "A" Company will pass starting point at 9.30 a.m. on the 4th instant.

No. 6. MOVEMENT. The movement will be by Companies, at intervals of 400 yards.

No. 7. BILLETS. All Hutments must be left clean. Certificates to this effect will be rendered direct to Adjutant.

No. "A" and "C" Companies will march to and be billeted at TILLOY les HERMAVILLE.
Headquarters, "B" and "D" Companies will be billetted at HERMAVILLE.

No. 8. COMMAND. Captain SYMONS will be in command of detachment at TILLOY les HERMAVILLE.

No. 9. REPORTS. All states and reports will be rendered as soon as Companies arrive at billets.

No. 10. WORKING PARTIES. Working Parties will report as per special orders issued.

No. 11. KITS & BLANKETS. Further orders will be issued.

No. 12. LEWIS GUNS. Further orders will be issued.

No. 13. FURTHER ORDERS. Company Commanders, Transport Officer and Quartermaster will report to the Adjutant at "Y" Hutments at 4.p.m. on the 3rd instant for further instructions.

Captain & Adjutant,
2nd S.A.I.

Copy Nos. 1 - 4. Retained.
Copy No. 5. "A" Coy.
Copy No. 6. "B" Coy.
Copy No. 7. "C" Coy.
Copy No. 8. "D" Coy.

ORDER NO: 55.

Copy No...3.. War Diary

10/3/1917.

Map Reference,
LENS II.
1/100000.

No. 1. INTENTION. The O.C. intends to march to MONCHY BRETON to-morrow.

No. 2. DISTRIBUTION. The Companies (less working parties) will march in the following order with a distance of 400 yards between each (approximately 5 minutes).

Headquarters, Band, and "A" Company will pass the starting point at	9.15.a.m.
"B" Company. at	9.20 a.m.
"D" Company at	9.25 a.m.

"C" Company will join the column in rear of "D" Company at X roads ¼ mile N.E. of TILLOY les HERMAVILLE at 9.45 a.m.

No. 3. STARTING POINT. Sentry Box, Depot Battalion Guard, West of HERMAVILLE.

No. 4. ROUTE. From HERMAVILLE in a N.W. direction to junction of main ARRAS - ST.POL road at a point south of the "A" in SAVY STA. thence along main road for 400 yards thenc e in a N.W. direction to VILLERS BRULIN, thence to GUESTREVILLE, thence in a N.W. direction to HERLIN LE VERT, thence in a westerly direction to Cross roads 600 yards S.E. of the H in MONCHY BRETON, thence south to first cross road, then North-west to MONCHY BRETON.

No. 5. BILLETS. Everyone will be clear of billets by 9.a.m. Usual certificates will be rendered to Adjutant at 9.a.m. Second in Command and Medical Officer will inspect billets, commencing at 9.a.m.

No. 6. STATES. Marching in states will be rendered to Adjutant immediately on arrival, stating number of men who fell out on line of march.

No. 7. REPORTS. Reports to the head of the Battalion.

[signature]
Captain & Adjutant,
2nd Regiment S. A. Infantry.

Copies Nos. 1 - 5.	Retained.
Copy No. 6.	"A" Coy.
Copy No. 7.	"B" Coy.
Copy No. 8.	"C" Coy.
Copy No. 9.	"D" Coy.

ORDER NO: 56.

Copy No....1

Map Reference
LENS II.
1/100000.

20. 3. 17.

No. 1.
INTENTION.

The O.C. intends to march to HERMAVILLE to-morrow.

No. 2.
DISTRIBUTION.

The Companies (less fatigues parties and sick) will march in the following order, with a distance of 400 yards (approximately 5 minutes) between each company:-

"Headquarters, Band and "A" Company will pass the starting point at 9.30 a.m.
"B" Company. at 9.35 a.m.
"D" Company. at 9.40 a.m.
"C" Company. at 9.45. a.m.

No. 3.
STARTING POINT.

Church in MOCHY BRETON.

No. 4.
ROUTE.

From MONCHY BRETON in a S.E. direction to CHELERS from CHELERS south to TINCQUES, thence EAST along the main ARRAS-ST.POL road as far as the "A" in SAVY STA.; from Savy south-east to HERMAVILLE.

No. 5.
BILLETS.

Everyone will be clear of Billets by 9.a.m. Usual certificate will be rendered to Adjutant by 9.[illegible]. a.m.
Second in Command and Medical Officer will inspect billets commencing at 9.15. a.m.

No. 6.
HALTS.

No halts other than the authorized halt every hour is to be made along the main ARRAS-ST.POL road.

No. 7.
REPORTS.

Reports to the head of the column.

No. 8.
MARCHING IN STATES.

Marching in states to be handed to the Adjutant immediately on arrival at HERMAVILLE, stating the number of men who fell out on the line of march.

R Beasley

Captain & A/Adjutant,
2nd Regiment S.A.Infantry.

Copies Nos. 1 - 4. Retained.
5. "A" Coy.
6. "B" Coy.
7. "C" Coy.
8. "D" Coy

Issued by orderly at.....12-30 AM. 21-3-17

ORDER NO. 57.

Copy No...7.. *War Diary*

Map Reference,
LENS II.
1/100000.
------

22. 3. 17.

No. 1.
~~XXXXXXXX~~
INTENTION.

The O.C. intends to march to "Y" HUTS to-morrow.

No. 2.
DISTRIBUTION.

Companies will march in the following order, with a distance of 200 yards (approximately five minutes) between each company.

Band, Headquarters and "A" Company will pass the starting point at		9.30 a.m.
"C" Company	at	9.35 a.m.
"B" Company	at	9.40 a.m.
"D" Company	at	9.45 a.m.

No. 3.
STARTING POINT.

Cross road by St. GEORGE Farm.

No.4.
ROUTE.

From Hermaville due EAST to the main ARRAS-ST.POL road, thence direct to "Y" HUTS.

No. 6.
BILLETS.

All men will be clear of billets by 9.a.m. Second in Command and Medical Officer will inspect Billets at that hour.

Usual certificate will be sent in by Company Commanders by 9.a.m.

No. 7.
REPORTS.

Reports to the head of the column.

No. 8.
MARCHING IN STATES.

Marching in states to be handed to Adjutant immediately on arrival at "Y" Huts, shewing the number of men who fell out on the line of march.

R.P. Beverley

Captain & A/Adjutant.
2nd South African Infantry. ....

Copyes Nos. 1-4 retained.
Copy No. 5. "A"
6. "B"
7. "C" ✓
8. "D"

Issued by orderly at ...... on the ...March, 191

......

ORDER NO: 10.

Copy No..2.. War Diary

Map Reference
51c 1/40,000.
and
51B N.W. 3.
1/10,000.

No. 1.
[illegible]. The Battalion will relieve two companies of the 8th ~~xxxx~~ Black Watch and two companies of the 9th Scottish Rifles ~~xxxxxxxxxxxxxxxxxxxxxxxx~~ in trenches 87-91 inclusive in Brittannia Works, and in the Candle Factory.

"D" Company will relieve one company of the 8th Black Watch in the front line.

"A" Company will relieve one company of the 9th Scottish Rifles in the front line.

"C" Company will relieve one company of the 9th Scottish Rifles in BRITTANNIA WORKS.

"B" Company will relieve one company of the 5th Cameron Highlanders in the Candle Factory.

Headquarters detachment will take over the left Battalion headquarters, "J" Sector.

The reliefs will commence at 6.30 p.m. to-day.

No. 2.
[illegible]. From "Y" Huts to the [illegible], ARRAS, the movement will take place in platoons at 400 yards interval. Intervals must be strictly adhered to.

Companies will move in the following order, commencing at 4.15. p.m.

"A" Company.
"D" Company.
"C" Company.
"Headquarters.
"B" Company.

The first platoon of "A" Company will move off at 4.15. p.m. sharp, followed by the remaining platoons ~~xx~~ in order of Companies as named, at 5 minutes interval.

No. 3.
[illegible]. From "Y" Huts to [illegible] - thence to [illegible], from [illegible] to St. [illegible] BRIDGE ST. [illegible], and from there to the [illegible].

GUIDES At the [illegible] guides will meet all companies commencing at 6.30 p.m.

No. 4.
LEWIS GUNS. Lewis Guns and magazines will be carried into the line ~~xxxxxxxxxxxxxxxxxxxxxxxx~~, by companies.

No. 5.
COMPLETION OF RELIEF. Completion of relief will be reported to Battalion Headquarters by the code word "[illegible]" over the telephone.

R.B[illegible]

Captain & A/Adjutant,
2nd Bat.

Copies Nos.	1 - 3.	Retained.
Copy No.	4.	"A"
Copy No.	5.	"B"
	6.	"C"
	7.	"D"

Issued by orderly at ...p.m. on the 24.3.17.

ORDER NO. 60.

Copy No..4...

Map Reference
Trench Map ARRAS
1/10000.

30/3/1917.

No. 1.
RELIEF.

The Battalion will be relieved in the line by the 3rd S.A.Infantry to-night, the 30th inst.
"D" Coy. 3rd S.A.I. will relieve "D" Company in the Candle Factory by platoons at 5 minutes interval, commencing at 7.15 p.m.
"A" Coy. 3rd SAI. will relieve "A" Company in BRITTANNIA WORKS by platoons at 5 minute s interval commencing at 7.35 p.m.
"C" Company 3rd SAI will relieve "C" Company in Front Line commencing at ~~XXXX~~ 7.55 p.m. by platoons at 5 mins intervals
"B" Company 3rd SAI. will relieve "B" Company in Front Line commencing at 8.15 p.m. by platoons at 5 mins intervals
Headquarters - 7.15 p.m.
Signallers on all stations will be relieved at 7.15 p.m.
Lewis Gunners will be relieve d with their Companies.
Companies on relief will be in billets at ARRAS.
On relief Battalion will be in Brigade Reserve.

No. 2.
ROUTES.

"A" Company will withdraw from BRITTANNIA WORKS down AUGUST AVENUE.
"C" Company. - platoon in Support will withdraw along SUPPORT LINE and down JULY AVENUE. Front Line platoons will withdraw dow n JULY. The whole will enter AUGUST AVENUE by Trench leading past th e Regimental Aid post, an d continue withdrawal along AUGUST AVENUE.
"B" Company will withdraw via NEW CUT, JULY and AUGUST AVENUE passing the Regimental Aid post en route.

Company Commanders must pay special attention to the movement of platoons to avoid congestion.
JULY AVENUE and NEW CUT are to be as near as possible left clear fo r the passage of the 3rd S.A.I.

No. 3.
MOVEMENT.

The movement as far as the CANDLE FACTORY will be in platoons at five minutes interval.
From the Candle Factory to the billets in ARRAS in parties of EIGHT, at one minutes interval.
Orders as regards movement in ARRAS must be strictly adhered to.
Lieut. KING will control movement from the Candle Factory.

No. 4.
TRENCH STORES.

Trench Stores will be h anded over and duplicate receipts obtained and fo rwarded to Battalion Headquarters by 9.a.m. to-morrow.

No. 5.
LOG BOOKS.

Log Books, Maps. etc. will be handed over complete.

No. 6.
COMPLETION OF RELIEF.

Completion of relief will be reported to Battalion Headquarters in ARRAS by memo.

R.Beverley

Captain & A/Adjutant.
3rd S.A.I.

Copies 1 - 4 - Retained.
Copies 5 - 8 - "A" - "D" Companies.

Issued by orderly at.... a.m. 30/3/17.

Army Form C. 2118.

WAR DIARY

2nd REGT. SOUTH AFRICAN INFANTRY ~~or INTELLIGENCE SUMMARY.~~

(Erase heading not required.)

Instructions regarding War Diaries and Intelligence Summaries are contained in F. S. Regs., Part II. and the Staff Manual respectively. Title pages will be prepared in manuscript.

Place	Date 1917	Hour	Summary of Events and Information	Remarks and references to Appendices
ARRAS	1/4/17		3 Officers and 230 OR supplied for working parties in the line. Guards and duties found in ARRAS. Weather cloudy light showers in early morning. Strengths of Regiment Officers 33 OR 559. Casualties nil.	~~Orders~~ ORDER FILE APPENDIX I
	2/4/17		4 Officers and 250 OR supplied for working parties in the line. Guards and duties found in ARRAS. Weather cloudy heavy showers during the afternoon. The Battalion moved out of ARRAS 7-30 pm arriving at Y. HUTMENTS at 11 pm. Strengths of Regiment Officers 33 OR 561. Casualties 1 OR wounded.	O.O. No 6 I attached
Y. HUTMENTS	3/4/17		Regiment Billeted in Y. HUTMENTS. Guards found. Church parade at 11 AM. Captain F.M. DAVIS and 8 OR. draft from Base taken on strength of Regiment. Strengths of Regiment officers 42 OR 750.	Y Huts at Sheet 51 C 1/40000 L 2 C central.
	4/4/17		Regiment at Y. HUTMENTS. Weather overcast. Guards found. MAJOR SYMMES & batman returned from ENGLAND. Strengths of Regiment Officers 43 OR 759.	

2353 Wt. W2544/1454 700,000 5/15 D. D. & L. A.D.S.S./Forms/C. 2118.

Instructions regarding War Diaries and Intelligence Summaries are contained in F. S. Regs., Part II. and the Staff Manual respectively. Title pages will be prepared in manuscript.

Army Form C. 2118.

WAR DIARY
or
~~INTELLIGENCE SUMMARY.~~
(Erase heading not required.)

Place	Date	Hour	Summary of Events and Information	Remarks and references to Appendices
Y. HUTMENTS	5 4/17		Regiment in Y. HUTMENTS. Guards found. Church parade. Strengths of Regiment Officers 43 OR 759.	
	6 4/17		The Battalion was inspected by GENERAL SMUTS together with 3rd and 4th S.A.I. at Y. HUTMENTS. Strength of Regiment Officers 42 OR 760. Order No 62	Order No 62 attached
	7 4/17		The Regiment marched out Officers 20 OR 519 from Y. HUTMENTS. at 10.30 pm en route for ARRAS arriving about 12.30. Details remaining at first line Transport ETRUN 10 Officers 128 OR under the command of Major HEENAN.	B.O No 65 attached
ARRAS	8 4/17		During the whole day the Regiment lay in Billets in ARRAS. Various war material was drawn from dumps and distributed amongst companies. Orders for assembly in the trenches were issued in the afternoon order No 64. The assembly commenced at 10.30 pm and was carried out by platoons at two minutes interval. The weather during the day was warm & clear. The enemy artillery was fairly active and a few heavy shells fell in ARRAS.	Order No 64 attached

Army Form C. 2118.

Instructions regarding War Diaries and Intelligence Summaries are contained in F. S. Regs., Part II. and the Staff Manual respectively. Title pages will be prepared in manuscript.

WAR DIARY
~~or~~
~~INTELLIGENCE SUMMARY.~~
(Erase heading not required.)

Place	Date	Hour	Summary of Events and Information	Remarks and references to Appendices
	9/4/17		By 1 AM the whole Battalion was assembled in the allotted positions in the trenches in the sector J II of the ARRAS line. Three casualties occurred during the night in A Coy in the assembly trenches. At Zero the artillery creeping barrage burst forth and the two leading Coys of the Battalion viz D & A followed the 4th S.A.I. to the attack. The attack was eminently successful and was carried out according to operation order No 63 issued on April 6th.	Order 63 attached.
			Vide Report of Commanding officer dated 20-21-17. The troops opposed to us during the day were principally BAVARIANS 8th BAV Infantry Reg. and 125 Reserve Infantry Reg. Not a large number enemy dead were found in the positions taken, but the surrenders were numerous. Several dug-outs were blown in and it is presumed that numbers of the enemy perished in this manner. The greater number of casualties apparently ~~had~~ been caused by artillery fire. Our casualties during the day were MAJOR SYMMES killed LIEUT THORBURN 2/LIEUT WHEDAN, COOPER, MIDDLETON wounded and 82 OR killed wounded and missing. 2/LIEUT HARDWICK who had been attached to Brigade for special duty was severely wounded and succumbed shortly (contd)	

Instructions regarding War Diaries and Intelligence Summaries are contained in F. S. Regs., Part II. and the Staff Manual respectively. Title pages will be prepared in manuscript.

WAR DIARY

or

~~INTELLIGENCE SUMMARY.~~

(Erase heading not required.)

Army Form C. 2118.

Place	Date	Hour	Summary of Events and Information	Remarks and references to Appendices
	9/4/17		shortly afterwards. The Battalion was relieved at the appointed time by the troops of the 4th Division. During the attack the 26th Brigade and 27th Brigade were on our right and left respectively. On relief the C O received orders to occupy a position in the BLACK LINE. The night was therefore spent in that position. MAP reference 51B NW3 Ed YA 1/20000.	COs report Appendix II MAP 1/5000 51B NW3} 51A NW3} Appendix III
	10/4/17		The Battalion remained in position in this line during the whole day. The day was spent in cleaning rifles and equipment and replenishing ammunition. All rifles and equipment in the rear of our position were collected and salvage dumps were established. The weather was cold and a strong wind was blowing from the N.W. The night was spent in this position. The following officer reinforcements joined during the day. 2/LIEUT CRAGG. ROSS. TOOKE. McLEAN. HENNESSY. LIEUT. SINCLAIR.	
	11/4/17		At 4 AM orders were received from Brigade to proceed to a position in the BROWN LINE. This order was duly executed and the Battalion was in position by 6-45 AM. At 8 AM information was received that the 4th Division were to carry out an attack	

Instructions regarding War Diaries and Intelligence Summaries are contained in F. S. Regs., Part II. and the Staff Manual respectively. Title pages will be prepared in manuscript.

WAR DIARY
or
~~INTELLIGENCE SUMMARY~~.
(Erase heading not required.)

Army Form C. 2118.

Place	Date	Hour	Summary of Events and Information	Remarks and references to Appendices
	11/4/17		attack at 12 NOON. In consequence of further orders received we moved up to a forward position under cover of a ridge some 500 yards behind the green line. In this position we remained in immediate support to the GREEN LINE. After dark in consequence of orders received the Battalion occupied EFFIE TRENCH. The 4th S.A.I. were on our left and the 1st S.A.I. on our right. Vide report of C.O. dated 20th April. The night was cold and snow fell fairly heavily. The troops slept in the open as there was no dug-out accomodation. Five casualties occurred from shell fire.	Reference. 51B N.W. EFFIE TRENCH APPENDIX III
	12/4/17		At 10.15 AM the C.O. was summoned to a meeting of C.Os at Brigade Head Quarters. Orders were received that we were to carry out an attack on the enemy line EAST of FAMPOUX at 5 PM. At 3 pm the Battalion moved its position in EFFIE TRENCH and followed the 4th S.A.I. to the position of assembly in FAMPAUX. This movement could not fail to be observed by the enemy and we were subjected to a bombardment of heavy shells while assembling in FAMPAUX, which caused a large number of casualties	

(Contd)

Instructions regarding War Diaries and Intelligence Summaries are contained in F. S. Regs., Part II. and the Staff Manual respectively. Title pages will be prepared in manuscript.

WAR DIARY

or

~~INTELLIGENCE SUMMARY.~~

(Erase heading not required.)

Army Form C. 2118.

Place	Date	Hour	Summary of Events and Information	Remarks and references to Appendices
	12 4/17		The leading Companies when moving from the assembly positions in the village were also subjected to a heavy Machine Gun and Rifle fire. The attack commenced at 5 pm and resulted in a few survivors reaching points varying from 150 - 200 yds east of the line held by the 4th Division. Of a total of 20 Officers and 400 OR who took part in this engagement 16 Officers and 280 OR became casualties. Battalion Head Quarters was established in a house in FAMPAUX. The 4th S.A.I. supported the 1st and 2nd S.A.I. in this attack. The 3rd SAI was held in reserve and rendered aid in the collection of the wounded during the night of 12th and 13th April 1917.	Map shewing Operations at FAMPOUX Appendix IV
	13 4/17		The Battalion was withdrawn to the GREEN LINE PHYSIC TRENCH at 4 AM and remained there in support of the FAMPAUX LINE. During the day several men who had been isolated during the attack returned from the line. Overcoats were collected and the trench deepened and shelters were built during the day. The line was shelled intermittently during the day with 10 CM and 15 CM shells no casualties occurred. The weather was cold and there was a slight rain during the ~~day~~ evening. The 3rd S.A.I. were in front, the 4th S.A.I. on our right. (Contd)	FAMPOUX Map Appendix IV

Instructions regarding War Diaries and Intelligence Summaries are contained in F. S. Regs., Part II. and the Staff Manual respectively. Title pages will be prepared in manuscript.

WAR DIARY

or

~~INTELLIGENCE SUMMARY.~~

(Erase heading not required.)

Army Form C. 2118.

Place	Date	Hour	Summary of Events and Information	Remarks and references to Appendices
	13 4/17		right in the same trench and the 1st S.A.I. some 200 yards to our rear. CAPT DAVIS LIEUT PEARSE 2/LIEUT MERRIMAN arrived as reinforcements 5 pm.	
	14 4/17		The Regiment remained in position in PHYSIC TRENCH. Rations were abundant and rum was issued. The field kitchen arrived enabling the men to obtain a hot meal. Trenches were improved. MAJOR GENERAL LUKIN. C.B. CMG DSO. visited the troops. At about 10-11 pm the enemy bombarded ATHIES some 500 yards in rear of our line with gas shells. The gas was perceptible in our lines. The usual precautions were taken and no casualties occurred.	
	15 4/17		Still in the same possession in PHYSIC TRENCH. We were shelled intermittently with heavy shells during the day, no casualties occurred. At 8-30 pm in consequence of orders previously received the Regiment was relieved by the 5th GORDONS of the 51st Division. We then marched to billets in ARRAS via ATHIES and the Canal. We arrived in ARRAS at 12 midnight. ORDER 65 A	Order 65 A Appendix I

Instructions regarding War Diaries and Intelligence Summaries are contained in F. S. Regs., Part II. and the Staff Manual respectively. Title pages will be prepared in manuscript.

Army Form C. 2118.

WAR DIARY

or

~~INTELLIGENCE SUMMARY.~~

(Erase heading not required.)

Place	Date	Hour	Summary of Events and Information	Remarks and references to Appendices
	16/7/17		The Battalion marched out of ARRAS billets at 12 NOON en route for ACQ. ~~Len~~ (MAP.REF) LENS 11 Edition 2. 1/100000. The route taken was through St CATHERINE and along the North bank of the River SCARPE to ACQ. where we arrived at 3·30 p.m. Here the Regiment was joined by the details who remained at first line Transport and the Transport. Strength of Regiment from trenches Officers 7, OR 126. Strength of details including Transport Officers 6 OR 144.	O.O No 65 B attached. Appendix I
(ACQ) X. HUTS	17/7/17		Regiment resting in Billets X Huts near ACQ. Strength of Regiment Officers 13 OR 275.	
	18/7/17		Regiment billeted in X HUTS. Weather overcast. 2/LIEUT TERRY formerly Transport officer now appointed acting officer commanding D Coy. Strength of Regiment Officers 13 OR 282.	
	19/7/17		Regiment in billets X HUTS. Raining. 2/LIEUT EGAN rejoined unit from Trench Mortar Course 3rd ARMY SCHOOL. 2/LIEUT ARNOLD is appointed Regimental Transport officer. Strength of Regiment officers 13 OR 312.	

Army Form C. 2118.

Instructions regarding War Diaries and Intelligence Summaries are contained in F. S. Regs., Part II. and the Staff Manual respectively. Title pages will be prepared in manuscript.

WAR DIARY
or
~~INTELLIGENCE SUMMARY.~~
(Erase heading not required.)

Place	Date	Hour	Summary of Events and Information	Remarks and references to Appendices
(A C Q) X HUTS.	20/7		Regiment in billets X HUTS. 2/LIEUT CRAGG left for Trench Mortar Course 3rd ARMY School. Strength of Regiment Officers 14 OR 312.	~~O.O. No 66~~ ~~attached~~ ~~Appendix~~ I
	21/7		Regiment marched from X HUTS as per attached ~~[illegible]~~ Order No 66. No men fell out en Route. Distance march 12 miles. South African Brigade also billeted at ORLENCOURT. (MAP REF) LENS.11. Edition 2 1/100,000. Strength of Regiment officers 19 OR 394.	Order No 66 Appendix I.
ORLENCOURT	22/7		Regiment in billets at ORLENCOURT. Church parade 10.45 AM. Present with Regiment Officers 13 OR 318. Detached Officers 1 OR 48 not with unit officers 5 OR 28. Strength of Regiment Officers 19 OR 394.	
	23/7		Regiment at training in ORLENCOURT. Battalion parade from 9.30 AM to 12.30 PM. All specialists parading with their respective companies. Strength of Regiment Off 19 OR. 383.	

Army Form C. 2118.

WAR DIARY
~~or~~
~~INTELLIGENCE SUMMARY.~~
(Erase heading not required.)

Instructions regarding War Diaries and Intelligence Summaries are contained in F. S. Regs., Part II. and the Staff Manual respectively. Title pages will be prepared in manuscript.

Place	Date	Hour	Summary of Events and Information	Remarks and references to Appendices
ORLENCOURT	24/4/17		Battalion Parade from 9.30 AM on MONCHY BRETON training ground, all specialists parading with their respective companies. Strength of Regiment Off 19 OR 378.	
	25 4/17		Battalion training as yesterday. A full marching order competition was held between the companies of this Regiment - and prizes given - B Company won this competition. Draft from Base 6.O.R. ~~the~~ taken on strength of Unit. Strength of Regiment Off 19 OR 376.	
	26 4/17		Regiment at training under company arrangements. Bathing at ROCOURT. Strength of Regiment Off 19 OR 386.	
	27 4/17		Regiment at training - Rifle practice rapid firing on range MONCHY BRETON. Bathing at ROCOURT. Strength of Regiment Off 19 OR 383.	~~[illegible]~~ ~~[illegible]~~ Appendix I

INDEX to APPENDICES.

APPENDIX I Copies of Orders. 61 - 67 (incl)

" II Report on Operations from April 8th - April 16th 1917. (incl)

" III Map referring to Operations from April 9th - April 11th 1917 (incl).

IV Map referring to Operations in front of FAMPOUX April 12th 1917, showing also trench occupied by 2nd S.A. Inf. after action at FAMPOUX.

Instructions regarding War Diaries and Intelligence Summaries are contained in F. S. Regs., Part II. and the Staff Manual respectively. Title pages will be prepared in manuscript.

Army Form C. 2118.

WAR DIARY
~~or~~
~~INTELLIGENCE SUMMARY.~~
(Erase heading not required.)

Place	Date	Hour	Summary of Events and Information	Remarks and references to Appendices
ORLENCOURT	28 4/7		The Regiment moved from ORLENCOURT to MONCHY BRETON. Thirty one signallers on course of signalling at Brigade Head Quarters under Brigade Instructor. Ten O.R. left for HERMAVILLE as prisoner of war guard. Strength of Regiment off 19 OR. 383. 2 OR. returned off course 3rd ARMY. SCHOOL.	Order No 67 Appendix I
	29 4/7		Church parade at 10 AM. Strength of Regiment off. 19 OR. 383. 2nd Lieut CRAGG returned off course 3rd ARMY. SCHOOL. Bathing at ROCOURT.	
	30 4/7		Regiment at training. Bathing. Strength of Regiment with unit off 13 OR. 289. not with unit Off. 6. OR. 43. detached OR. 51.	

C R Heenan Major
~~Lieut Colonel~~
Temp Commanding 2nd Regt. S. A. Infantry.

2353 Wt. W2544/1454 700,000 5/15 D. D. & L. A.D.S.S./Forms/C. 2118.

61 APPENDIX I

OPERATION ORDER NO. [illegible]

BY

Lieut. Col. W.E.C. Tanner, C.M.G. Commanding 2nd Regiment S.A. Infy.

Map Reference
Trench Map
51C N.W. 1/20,000.
& N.W. 3.
1/10,000.

IN THE FIELD, 2nd APRIL, 1917.

Copy No. 1...

No. 1. RELIEF. The Regiment will be relieved by the 11th Royal Scots at 7.30 p.m. to-day and on relief will march to "Y" HUTS.

No. 2. DISTRIBUTION. Companies on relief by the corresponding Company of the 11th Royal Scots will march out of billets by platoons at 6 minutes interval. The order of marching out will be dependent on the order of the relieving unit.

Lieut. ARENDORFF will direct the movement of Companies at the starting point.

No. 3. STARTING POINT. Convent, ARRAS.

No. 4. ROUTE. From the Convent to the Main Gate of ARRAS thence along the ARRAS - ST.POL Road to "Y" HUTS.

No. 5. BILLETS. All troops will be clear of Billets by 6.45 p.m. The Medical Officer will inspect the billets at that hour. Usual certificate to be handed to Battalion Orderly Room at 7 p.m.

No. 6. REPORTS. Reports to the head of the column.

No. 7. MARCHING IN STATES. Marching in States to be handed to the Battalion Orderly Officer immediately on arrival at "Y" HUTS shewing the number of men who fell out on route.

R. Beverley

Captain & A/Adjutant.
2nd Regiment S. A. Infantry.

Copy No. 1.- 4 Retained.
5 "A" Coy.
6 "B" Coy.
7 "C" Coy.
8. "D" Coy.

3

Issued by orderly at [illegible] p.m. on the 2/4/17.

2nd Regiment South African Infantry.

Order NO . 62

(I) The Ist South African Brigade, less Ist Regiment, will be inspected to-day by Lieut.General the Hon.J.Smuts, K.C.at II.45 a.m.

(2) The Battalion will parade ready to march off at I/.45 a.m. in close column of companies, on the ground North of the Camp.

Companies will be sized and equalized on parade .

Every available man to parade .

(3)Markers Battalion markers will report to the R.S.M.on par parade ground at II a.m.

Brigade markers will report at the Orderly Room at II.a.m.for instructions..

(4)Dress Fighting order. Officers ordinary uniform and fighting equipment as laid down for all ranks.

Dismounted officers will wear boots and putties.

Steel helmet, and P.H.Gas Helmet onlywill be worn.

(5)Parade States .Parade states to be at Orderly Room by I0.30.a.m.

R Brunsby

Captain & A/Adjutant
2nd Regiment South African Infantry.

63

Retained

ORDER NO. [illegible]

Copy No......1..
IN THE FIELD.
8th April, 1917.

Reference
Marked Sheet
51b N.W.3. Edition 7a.
1/20000.

No. 1.(a) INFORMATION. The 1st S.A.Brigade will be the centre brigade in an attack by the 9th Division between the river SCARPE and ... and will have the 26th Infantry Brigade on its right and the 27th Infantry Brigade on its left.

(b) The boundaries of the S.A.Brigade are those marked in green on the Reference.

(c) The three objectives, viz: the BLACK, BLUE and BROWN LINES will be attacked in three distinct bounds.

(d) The S.A.Brigade will attack on a two battalion front. The two leading battalions attacking the BLACK and BLUE LINES, supported by the remaining two battalions, thereafter the two supporting battalions will pass through the leading battalions and attack the BROWN LINE.
The division of the Brigade frontage allotted to each battalion is that shown in yellow on the reference.

(e) The 3rd S.A.I. on the right and the 4th S.A.I. on the left will attack the BLACK and BLUE LINES.

(f) The 1st S.A.I. will follow the 3rd S.A.I. and the 2nd S.A.I. the 4th S.A.I. to the attack of the BROWN LINE.

(g) The attack will be preceeded by an artillery bombardment for five days.

No. 2. INTENTION. The C.C. intends to support the left leading battalion, viz: the 4th S.A.I. with two companies as far as the BLACK LINE, and with the whole Battalion as far as the BLUE LINE, thereafter the battalion will carry out the attack on the S.A.Brigade left sub-section of the BROWN LINE.

No. 3. (a) DISTRIBUTION. The battalion will assemble in the normal formation in Support Trenches 89, 90 and 91, and ARTILLERY TRENCH and BRITTANNIA WORKS in the following order:-
"D" Company from 89 to 90.3 inclusive.
"A" Company from 90.4 to 91 inclusive.
"C" Company in Artillery trench between Mill Cut and SUPPORT LINE (less one platoon).
"B" Company (less one platoon) in BRITTANNIA WORKS.

No. 3. DISTRIBUTION (Continued).

(b) One platoon from each of "B" and "C" Companies will be temporarily detached for MOPPING-UP duties under the instructions of the 4th S.A.Infantry. These platoons will be employed on the trenches BRESLAUER and PETER GRABEN, and will rejoin their respective Companies upon the arrival of these Companies at these trenches.

No. 4. ZERO.

Zero will be at

and all units will be assembled at minus 15 minutes.

No. 5. ATTACK. FIRST OBJECTIVE. BLACK LINE.

(a) The 2nd Battalion will move to the BLUE LINE in normal artillery formation, unless required to assist the leading battalion in the taking of this line or the BLACK LINE.

(b) At ZERO the 3rd and 4th S.A.Infantry will advance as close as possible to our artillery barrage, which will open 50 yards in front of the German front line, and lift on to their front line at plus 2 minutes, and remain on the front line until plus 4 minutes.

(c) At plus 4 minutes the barrage will move forward until it reaches a line 300 yards beyond the BLACK LINE and will be closely followed by the attacking infantry.

(d) The first two waves of the 3rd and 4th S.A.Infantry will go to the BLACK LINE and consolidate, and the remaining two waves of these battalions, unless required to reinforce, will occupy the SUNKEN ROAD immediately xxxx WEST of the BLACK LINE.

(e) "D" and "A" Companies of the 2nd S.A.Infantry will move at ZERO from the support trench in normal artillery formation, "D" Company on the right, "A" Company on the left, and follow the 4th S.A.I. as far as PETER GRABEN and BRESLAUER GRABEN, where, unless required for the Support of the 4th S.A.Infantry, they will remain and consolidate these trenches until the attack on the BLUE LINE is launched.

No. 6. ATTACK : SECOND OBJECTIVE. BLUE LINE.

(a) At ZERO plus 1 hour and 45 minutes the two rear waves of the 3rd and 4th S.A.Infantry will advance from the SUNKEN ROAD and deploy in front of the BLACK LINE, and at ZERO plus 2 hours will advance under a creeping barrage and supported by the remaining two waves of these battalions to attack the BLUE LINE.

(b) At Zero plus 1 hour 30 minutes, "B" and "C" Companies, 2nd S.A.I. (less one platoon each) will assemble in the Support Line, "C" Company via ARTILLERY TRENCH

No. 6. (b) Continued.

"B" Company via JULY AVENUE and NEW CUT, and occupy Support trench as detailed for "D" and "A" Companies in para. 3. sub-section (a). "B" Company on the RIGHT, "C" Company on the LEFT.

(c) At ZERO plus 2 hours "D" and "A" Companies 2nd S.A.I. will advance in normal artillery formation to the BLACK LINE, and "B" and "C" Companies (less one platoon each) will advance from our Support line to the SUNKEN ROAD immediately WEST of the BLACK LINE. "B" and "C" Companies will be rejoined en route by the platoons detached as MOPPERS-UP.

(d) The artillery will then carry out a concentrated bombardment on the BROWN LINE.

No. 7. (a) ATTACK, THIRD OBJECTIVE, BROWN LINE.

At ZERO plus 6 hours 15 minutes the 2nd Battalion will advance from the BLACK LINE in normal artillery formation, with "D" Company on the right, supported by "B" Company, "A" Company on the left supported by "C" Company, to the valley immediately WEST of the BLUE LINE.

(b) The Battalion will halt in this valley until ZERO plus 7 hours, when the Battalion will move forward to a ~~xx~~ position in which the FIRST WAVE will have passed through the BLUE LINE and the remaining waves in rear of this line, with their correct distances. The first wave will be correctly aligned on the third objective, BROWN LINE, viz: with its right immediately EAST of the railway embankment and the left approximately 100 yards in advance of this embankment.

(c) The barrage will move forward from a line 300 yards in front of the BLUE LINE at ZERO plus 6 hours 46 minutes and continue to a line 300 yards behind the BROWN LINE.

(d) At ZERO plus 6 hours ~~36~~ 46 minutes the barrage will lengthen a 100 yards every 2 minutes until it reaches the line H.8.b.5.9½. H.8.d.0.4., H.8.c.7.0., H.14.a.9.1.

(e) At ZERO plus 7 hours 11 minutes a proportion of smoke shells will be fired, and this will be the signal to the Battalion that the barrage is going to move forward in 4 minutes time, viz: 7 hours 15 minutes from the co-ordinates given in the foregoing sub-paragraph.

(f) At ZERO plus 7 hours 15 minutes ~~xxxx~~ the Battalion will move forward to the attack of the BROWN LINE from the position described in para. 7.(b).

(g) During the attack on the BROWN LINE a smoke barrage will be placed on the ridge H.10.c. H.16.B. H.16.d.

(h) On reaching the BROWN LINE the first waves of "D" and "A" Companies will proceed to LAUREL TRENCH, and their second waves to the road immediately WEST of that trench. The first waves of "B" and "C" Companies will proceed to LADLE TRENCH, and their second waves to KICK and KEEN TRENCHES.

Para 7. (b) Continued.

This distribution will be naturally dependant on the opposition met with, and Company Commanders will deal with the situation as they find most suitable, to secure and hold the whole objective.

No. 8. CONSOLIDATION.

(a) Selected localities in the captured line to be immediately consolidated and put into a state of defence, and every preparation made to withstand a possible immediate counter-attack which the enemy may launch.

(b) A section of the 34th Field Coy. R.E. will assist in the consolidation of ~~xx~~ the BROWN LINE in the most westerly line of the German third system. viz KEEN TRENCH.

No. 9. COMMUNICATION TRENCH.

A communication trench will be constructed by the Pioneers from a Sap south of Sap 91 to the German front line at V.10. and joined up with MANGFALL TRENCH and MINDEL TRENCH. This will form a Brigade communication trench.

No. 10. MACHINE GUNS.

Upon the capture of the BLUE LINE half a section of the 28th Machine Gun Company will take up a position in the BLACK LINE, and upon the capture of the BROWN LINE half a section of these guns will go forward to the POINT DU JOUR, or to H.8.c.5.7.

No. 11. SIGNAL COMMUNICATIONS.

(a) Two main visual receiving stations will be established at -
    (1) G.22.c.9.8.
    (2) G.10.c.9.4.

(b) Daylight lamps will be used throughout.

(c) The B.A.B. Trench code will be used.

(d) Runners will be employed.

(e) Contact aeroplane. In addition to the foregoing means of communication, Contact aeroplanes will be employed to receive signals from Brigade and Battalion headquarters by means of:-
    (1) Ground signal panels.
    (2) Lamps.
    (3) Flares. (from attacking infantry)

No. 12. PRISONERS OF WAR.

Prisoners captured by the fighting troops will be sent under as small a guard as possible to ST. NICHOLAS, where they will be taken over by the A.P.M.

Walking wounded should be utilized for escorts as far as possible.

No. 13. MEDICAL ARRANGEMENTS.

(a) AID POSTS. G.11.d.8.7. - JULY AVENUE.
(b) COLLECTING POSTS. G.17.c.4.9. MARCH AVENUE. also G.11.d.2.5. AUGUST AVENUE.
(c) ADVANCED DRESSING STATION. G.16.c.4.9. ST. NICHOLAS.

No. 14. **DUMPS.**
(a) R.E. Divisional Dump - G.16.d.3.7.
(b) Brigade Dump. Head of GUNNER TRAMWAY.
(c) Battalion Dump. Dugout 28 near Trench 89.
To move with Battalion headquarters to BLUE LINE.

No. 15. **RESERVE DIVISION.**
(a) The 4th Division will be held in reserve.

(b) From the BLUE LINE the attacking brigades of the 4th Division will follow up the 9th Division, so as to reach the German third system of trenches at ZERO plus 6 hours 40 minutes.

(c) They will pass through the 9th Division on the BROWN LINE at ZERO plus 9 hours 40 minutes and proceed to the attack of the German fourth system.

(d) The consolidation of the BROWN LINE by the troops of the 9th Division will be continued until they are relieved by the troops of the 4th Division other than those who pass through them to the attack of the GREEN LINE.

(e) Units of the 1st South African Infantry Brigade will not leave the BROWN LINE until properly relieved by troops of the 4th Division.

No. 16. **STOKES GUN.**
One Stokes gun will be attached to the Battalion to assist in the capture of the BROWN LINE, and will follow in rear of the centre of the Battalion during the attack, and on reaching the BROWN LINE the officer in charge will select a position in the objective to assist in holding it.

No. 17. **REPORTS.**
Reports to Battalion headquarters as follows:-
(a) From ZERO to plus 2 hours - No. 28 Dug-out.
(b) From plus 2 hours to plus 7 hours - No. 28 Dug-out (Front Line in 89 Trench).
(c) From plus 7 hours - a selected position in the BLUE LINE.
(d) From plus 8 hours 20 minutes - HIGH TRENCH.

Issued at 9 pm on 6th April 1917.

R Bursby

Captain & A/Adjutant,
2nd Regiment South African Infy.

Copies Nos. 1 - 2 Retained.
Copy No. 3 "A" Company. handed to Lt THORBURN
No. 4 "B" Company. " " Capt TURNER
No. 5 "C" Company. " " Capt SYMONS
No. 6 "D" Company. " " Lt WALSH.
No 7 Adjutant
No 8 Handed to Major SYMMES
~~Issued by orderly at......... on the...............~~
No 9 Handed to Major HEENAN
No 10 Handed to Brigade Major by Adjutant.

Reference
TRENCH MAP.
Sheet 51b N.W.
Edition 6A.
1/20000.

2nd REGIMENT SOUTH AFRICAN INFANTRY

In THE FIELD
7th APRIL.1917

ORDER NO.64

NO.1 INFORMATION. The Brigade with one section 90th Field Company. R.E. and half a company. Seaforth Pioneers, will assemble in the trenches on Y/Z night (8/9th inst.)

NO.2. INTENTION It is the intention of the O.C. to move into the trenches to the assembly positions at 10.30 p.m. on Y/Z night (8/9th inst.)

NO.3. DISTRIBUTION. The Battalion willmove out of billets in ARRAS by plato platoons at 2 minutes interval in the following order
"A" Company at 10.30 p.m.
"B" Company at 10.40 p.m.
"C" Company (lessatone platoon) at 1.30 a m.
"B" Company (less one platoon) at 1.40 a.m.
THE Companies will assemble in normal formation in support trenches 89.4. 91. ARTILLERY TRENCH. and BRITT BRITTANIA WORKS as followers:-
"A" Company from 90.4. 91 inclusive.
"D" Company from 89 - 90.3 inclusive.
"C" Company (less one platoon) in ARTILLERY TRENCH between NEW CUT and SUPPORT LINE.
"B" Company (less one platoon) in BRITTANNIA WORKS.

Battalion Headquarters will move at 1.45 a.m. and occupy dug-out35 J II SECTOR.

NO.4. COMPLETION OF MOVE. Completion of move will be reported to Battalion Headquarters in dug-out 35 by the word MEGANTIC in writing by a runner.

NO. 5 COMMUNICATION TRENCHES. If communication trenches are blocked, platoons will reach their assembly positions over the open.

NO.6 REPORTS. Reports to Battalion Headquarters at NO.35 Dug-out J II SECTOR.

Issued at 6p.m. onthe 8th April,1917

R.Bruby.
Captain A/Adjutant
2nd S.A.Inf.

ORDER NO. 65.

Copy NO.I.

Reference
Sheet 51B N.W.
Sheet 51C N.W.
1/20000.

In THE FIELD,
6th April, 1917

NO.I.
INTENTION

The O.C. intends to march to ARRAS at 8.15.p.m. to-morrow night.

NO.2.
DISTRIBUTION

The Regiment will pass the starting point at an interval of three minutesbetween companies in the following order.

Headquarters	8.15. p.m.
"D" Company	8.18. p.m.
"A" Company.	8.21. p.m.
"B" Company.	8.24. p.m.
"C" Company.	8.27. p.m.
M.O. and party.	8.27. p.m.
Transport.	(as detailed)

NO.3.
Starting Point

The starting point will be the CROSS ROADS south eat of"Y" HUTS on the main ARRAS-ST-POL road.

NO.4.
ROUTE.

BY the route along the SOUTH BANK of the river SCARPE as reconnoitted by officers.

NO.5.
BILLETING PARTIES.

Billeting parties as detailed will pmoceed in advane of the Regiment.

NO.6.
TRANSPORT.

The following vehicles will accompany the Regiment
Lewis gun carts.
Cookers.
Water Carts.
Mess Carts.
Medical Carts.
On arrival in ARRAS all vehicles,except Lewis Gun carts ,and all animals will return to the Transport lines.

NO.7.
COMPLETION OF MOVE.

Completion of move will be reported by an officer of each company to Battalion Headquarters.

NO.8.
DRESS.

Fighting order. Overcoats and one blanket will be carried.

NO.9.
REPORTS.

Reports to head of column.

R Bramley

Captain & A/Adjutant
2nd Regiment S.A.Infantry.

Copy Nos I-4. REtained.
Copy No.5. "A" Coy.
Copy No.6. "B".Coy
Copy No.7. "C".Coy.
Copy No.8. "D".COy.

Issued by orderly at II-30.p.m. on April 6th 1917.

Copy No...1.

2nd SOUTH AFRICAN INFANTRY ORDER NO: 66.

20th April, 1917.

Map Reference
LENS 11
1/100000.

No. 1. INTENTION. It is the intention of the C.O. to march to ORLANCOURT to-morrow at 10.15. a.m.

No. 2. DISTRIBUTION. Companies will pass the starting point in the following order, commencing at 10.15. a.m.

Band,Headquarters, and "B" Coy.	10.15.a.m.
"C" Company.	10.19. a.m.
"D" Company.	10.23 a.m.
"A" Company.	10.27 a.m.

Transport will follow immediately in rear of "A" Company.
Intervals of 400 yards, i.e. about 4 minutes, will be maintained during the march.

No. 3. STARTING POINT. The starting point will be the Bridge over the RIVER SCARPE immediately SOUTH of ACQ.

No. 4. ROUTE. Through ACQ thence WEST by route reconnoitred by officers.

No. 5. DRESS. Full marching order for all ranks except mounted officers.

No. 6. BILLETS. All men will be clear of Billets by 9.30 a.m. Usual certificates of cleanliness to be handed to the Adjutant by 9.30 a.m.
The Second in Command and the Medical Officer will inspect billets at 9.30 a.m.

No. 7. STATES. Marching out states will be handed to the Adjutant by 9.30 a.m.
Marching in states immediately on arrival in Billets at ORLANCOURT. This state should show the number of men who fell out on the line of march.

No. 8. REPORTS. Reports to the head of the column.

Issued at Orderly Room at 6.30 p.m. April 20th, 1917.

Captain & A/Adjutant,
2nd S.A.I.

Copy No. 1.	Retained.
Copy No. 2.	Retained.
Copy No. 3.	"A" Coy.
Copy No. 4.	"B" Coy.
Copy No. 5.	"C" Coy.
Copy No. 6.	"D" Coy.
Copy No. 7.	R.S.M.
Copy No. 8.	Transport Officer.
Copy No. 9.	C.O.

File

ORDER No. 67. Copy. No....1.....

IN THE FIELD, 27th April 1917.

Map Reference
LENS 11, Ed. 2.
1/100,000.

No. 1. INTENTION. It is the intention of the O.C. to march to MONCHY BRETON to-morrow.

No. 2. DISTRIBUTION. The Regiment will parade in the following order of Companies:- Drums, Headquarters, "A" Coy. "B" Coy. "C" Coy. "D" Coy., Transport., in front of the Head-quarter Mess. The head of the column will pass the starting point at 10 a.m.

No. 3. STARTING POINT. Starting point will be the gate at the Headquarter Mess.

No. 4. ROUTE. Along the main road to MONCHY BRETON.

No. 5. BILLETS. All men will be clear of billets by 9.15 a.m. Usual certificates to be handed to the Adjutant by 9.30. a.m. Second in Command and Medical Officer will inspect billets at 9.15 a.m.

No. 6 STATES. Marching out states to be handed in by 9.30. a.m. Marching in states to be rendered immediately on arrival in Billets at MONCHY BRETON.

No. 7. BAGGAGE. Blankets, Lewis Guns and Company Stores to be piled outside Company Quarters by 8.45 a.m. ready for loading on Transport.

No. 8. MEN UNABLE TO MARCH. Men unable to march will parade at 9.15 a.m. at the Orderly Room.

No. 9. REPORTS. Reports to the head of the column.

Issued at Orderly Room at 10.30. p.m. 27.4.1917.

R Beverley

Captain & A/Adjutant.
2nd Regt. S.A.Infantry.

Copy No. 1	Retained.
Copy. No. 2	O.C."A" Coy.
Copy. No. 3	O.C."B" Coy.
Copy. No. 4	O.C."C" Coy.
Copy. No. 5	O.C."D" Coy.
Copy No. 6	Major Heenan.
Copy. No. 7	Transport Officer.

Order 65 A. War Diary

In the Field

15 - 4 - 17

(1) Intention It is the intention of the O.C. to march to ARRAS tonight

(2) Distribution On relief the Battalion will march out in the following order of Companies Head quarters A, B, C, D,

(3) Route FAMPOUX - ATHIES Road to road junction at ATHIES, thence SOUTH to the River SCARPE tow-path to ARRAS.

(4) Billets On arrival at ARRAS. they will be billeted at 15 RUE GAMBETTA, other parts of the HOSPICE DES VEILLARDS.

Guides for billets will meet the regiment at the SCARPE BRIDGE near ST NICHOLAS on the old TRENCH ROUTE

(5) Marching in states Marching in states will be handed to the Adjutant on arrival at ARRAS Billets

(6) Reports. Reports to the head of the Column.

Issued at 6.30 pm 15.4.17

R Bunting Capt & Adj

2nd S.R.

Copy No 1 retained
2 Capt Dam
3 Capt Humphreys
4 retained

Order No 65 B

In the Field

16 - 4 - 1917

(1) Intention It is the intention of the O.C to march to the Camp at Acq.

(2) Distribution) The Battalion will leave the starting point as follows
Head Quarters. A. B. C & D Companies.

(3) Starting Point The HOSPICE-des-VEILLARDS.

(4) Route. From ARRAS through St. CATHERINE to the main ARRAS - St POL road thence along the main road as far as HAUTE AVESNES from there north to Acq.

(5) Billets Billets will be left in a clean and sanitary condition and a certificate of cleanliness handed to the Adjutant by 11-45

(6) Marching in States. Marching in states will be handed to the Adjutant on arrival in Billets in Acq.

Issued at 11 AM 16-11-1917

R Bunting Capt & Adj 2nd S.R.

APPENDIX II.

2nd REGIMENT SOUTH AFRICAN INFANTRY. COPY.

REPORT ON OPERATIONS FROM 9th APRIL, 1917 to 15th APRIL, 1917.

1. THE In accordance with the plan the battalion marched from "Y" Huts on the night of the 7th April and billeted in ARRAS during that night and the following day.

2. On the night of the 8th April, and early hours of the 9th the battalion assembled in our trenches as follows.-
"D" and "A" Companies in 89,90 and 91 Support Trenches.
"C" Company in Artillery trench WEST of NEW CUT, and
"B" Company in BRITTANNIA WORKS.
Battalion Headquarters at J.II Battalion Headquarters.

3. All ranks were assembled in the line by 1a.m. on Z day the 9th instant.

4. At ZERO, viz 5.30 a.m. our artillery barrage burst forth like a thunder clap on the enemy front line followed by various coloured light signals from the distressed Bavarians who, it had been reported, had come many long miles to hurl back our impending attack.

5. "D" and "A" Companies followed on the heels of the 4th S.A.I. and occupied the trenches immediately in rear of the German front line trench, which they at once proceeded to consolidate as a supporting point to the attack on the BLACK LINE.

6. Just prior to the attack on the BLUE LINE at ZERO plus 1 hour 45 minutes the remaining two companies, "B" and "C" assembled in the Support Line and Headquarters moved to 89 Trench. At the hour for the attack on the BLUE LINE, viz. ZERO plus 2 hours, these Companies moved to the SUNKEN ROAD preceeded by the two leading companies from the German front line to the BLACK LINE.

7. The consolidation of the BLACK LINE was at once proceeded with to provide a supporting point to the attack on the BLUE LINE.

8. When my leading companies arrived at the BLACK LINE they were fired on by several of the enemy who had concealed themselves there; however this little burst of Bavarian energy was quickly and effectively suppressed. Major SYMMES who was leading one of these Companies was fired on by two of these scoundrels but managed by careful manouvring to despatch them both with his revolver.

9. Our artillery bombardment had completely destroyed the enemy front line system of trenches and very

little trace of his wire was to be found here.

10. A few minutes after ZERO in response to the various light signals the enemy put up an artillery barrage down on our front line and on "NO MANS LAND", it was feeble and wild; however, a number of casualties were caused by it in my two leading companies as they issued from our sup-port line, and crossed "NO MANS LAND".

11. The capture of the BLUE LINE was carried out by the leading Battalions in splendid style.

12. The wire on the slope WEST of the BLUE LINE was still a difficult obstacle, and had there been any servious opposition on this line it would have been the cause of much loss as it was only negotiable via a small number of enemy prepared paths.

13. Half an hour before the attack on the BROWN LINE I moved the battalion up through the BLUE LINE and formed up for the attack and as the barrage moved forward the line advanced close up to it until we arrived at the enemy wire i n the valley immediately in front of the BROWN LINE.

14. This wire was very strong indeed and quite impassable except at two points, viz: via a communication trench and an enemy prepared passage.

15. Fortunately there was no opposition met with here otherwise this wire would have seriously held up the attack.

16. The BROWN LINE trenches were found in good condition having suffered very little from our bombardment.

17. FromThe BROWN LINE the enemy could be seen in the vicinity of the GREEN LINE passing along the sky line in a southerly direction towards FAMPOUX.

18. At the appointed time the troops of the 4th Division passed through the BROWN LI NE and advanced to the attack on the GREEN LINE. Shortly afterwards my battalion was relieved by a Battalion of the 4th Division and my Companies moved back en route to St. NICHOLAS. However ~~in the BLACK LINE~~ we received orders whilst en route to occupy a position in the BLACK LINE, and we moved there that evening, the 9th April, and remained in this position until the morning of the 11th April.

19. On the morning of the 11th April I received orders to proceed to a position in the BROWN LINE, - this was carried out andthe battalion in position at 6.45 a.m.

20. At 8 a.m. I received information from you that the 4th Division were to carry out an attack at 12 noon

and at 9.45 a.m. a further message to the effect that if there were any signs of the enemy retiring I was to press on immediately and keep touch with the troops in front on me.

21. I, at once sent up an officer to the GREEN LINE to ascertain what the situation was there but nothing definite could be obtained as to the situation, and at 12 noon, as our guns were particularly active, it appeared to me the Battalion was too far back to be of immediate assistance so I moved it up under cover of the ridge within some 500 yards of the GREEN LINE.

22. I went up to the GREEN LINE to find out if it we were wanted further on, but discovered we were not required further forward, so arranged the Battalion along a parallel line in rear of the GREEN LINE partly in EFFIE TRENCH and partly in shell holes. In this position we remained as an immediate support to the GREEN LINE until after dark when I was ordered to withdraww my left from the shell holes, and occupy EFFIE TRENCH back to its junction with the BROWN LINE.

23. Up to and including this night of the 11th April the weather had been very severe indeed and the men, who had been exposed to this extreme cold and wet for three days and four nights were suffering from exhaustion, and want of hot food.

24. At 10.15 a.m. on the 12th April I was summoned to attend a C.O.'s meeting at Brigade Headquarters at 10.15.a.m

25. At this meeting we were given details of an attack we were called upon to carry out EAST of FAMPOUX at 5 p.m. that afternoon.

26. At 3 p.m. my Battalion moved from its position in EFFIE TRENCH and followed by the 1st S. A. Infantry to the position of assembly in FAMPOUX.

27. As this movement could not fail to be observed by the enemy we were received in FAMPOUX by a bombardment of heavy shells which caused a number of casualties and the moment the leading companies showed their noses outside the eastern edge of the village they were met by heavy machine gun fire.

28. Up to this time 4.30 p.m. when the deployment began our artillery had not opened, and the numerous enemy machine guns and his artillery were particularly active on our deploying line.

29. The position as discovered upon reaching the ground was that the line held by the 4th Division through which the attach was to pass, some 250 yards EAST of FAMPOUX, could only be approached by passing over the whole of this distance in full view of the enemy and under the full blast of his artillery and numerous machine guns.

30. Our artillery barrage which opened at ZERO - 5 p.m.- did so some 500 yards EAST of the line held by the 4th Division, beyond the first enemy line of defence.

31. From this it will be seen that our men were required to cross some 750 yards of open ground under a destructive fire before they could even come up with the barrage.

32. The attack began at 5 p.m. and resulted in a few survivors reaching points varying from 150 yards to 200 yards east of the line held by the 4th Division troops.

33. Owing to the difficulty in obtaining any definite information regarding progress of the attack I despatched the battalion Intelligence Officer, Lieut. G.G.GREEN, M.C. at 6.30 p.m. to gain touch with one or other of the officers, and obtain some definite information.

34. This officer, finding no unwounded officers, proceeded to reconnoitre the position and returned at 8.30. p.m. with the definite information regarding our points reached carefully marked on his map, and upon this I was in a position to report to you the exact position.

35. As an example of the dash and splendid soldierly bearing of all ranks in their efforts to carry out this task I wish to draw your attention to the fact that before the attack was brought to a stand still 16 officers and 290 N.C.O. and men had become casualties and this from a total of 400 of all ranks employed in this attack.

36. The Battalion was withdrawn to the GREEN LINE on the morning of the 13th April and remained there in support of the FAMPOUX FRONT until the evening of the 15th April when we were withdrawn to ARRAS.

37. I should like to record our appreciation of the great services rendered my Battalion by the 3rd S.A.Infantry in recovering and removing our wounded comrades from the batt lefield in the face of an active enemy, during the night of 12th April.

38. I regret that owing to the very large number of casualties I am unable at the present moment to submit a full list of my recommendations for awards, and shall be glad if provision can be made for these to be rendered at a later date.

39. For the present I submit the names of three officers one N.C.O. and 1 man, particulars of which I am in possession of.

40. I cannot speak too highly of the magnificient spirit and gallantry displayed by all ranks throughout these very trying operations.

(sgd). W.Tanner.
Lieut. Colonel.
Commanding, 2nd Regiment, S.A.Infantry.

20.4.1917.

True copy

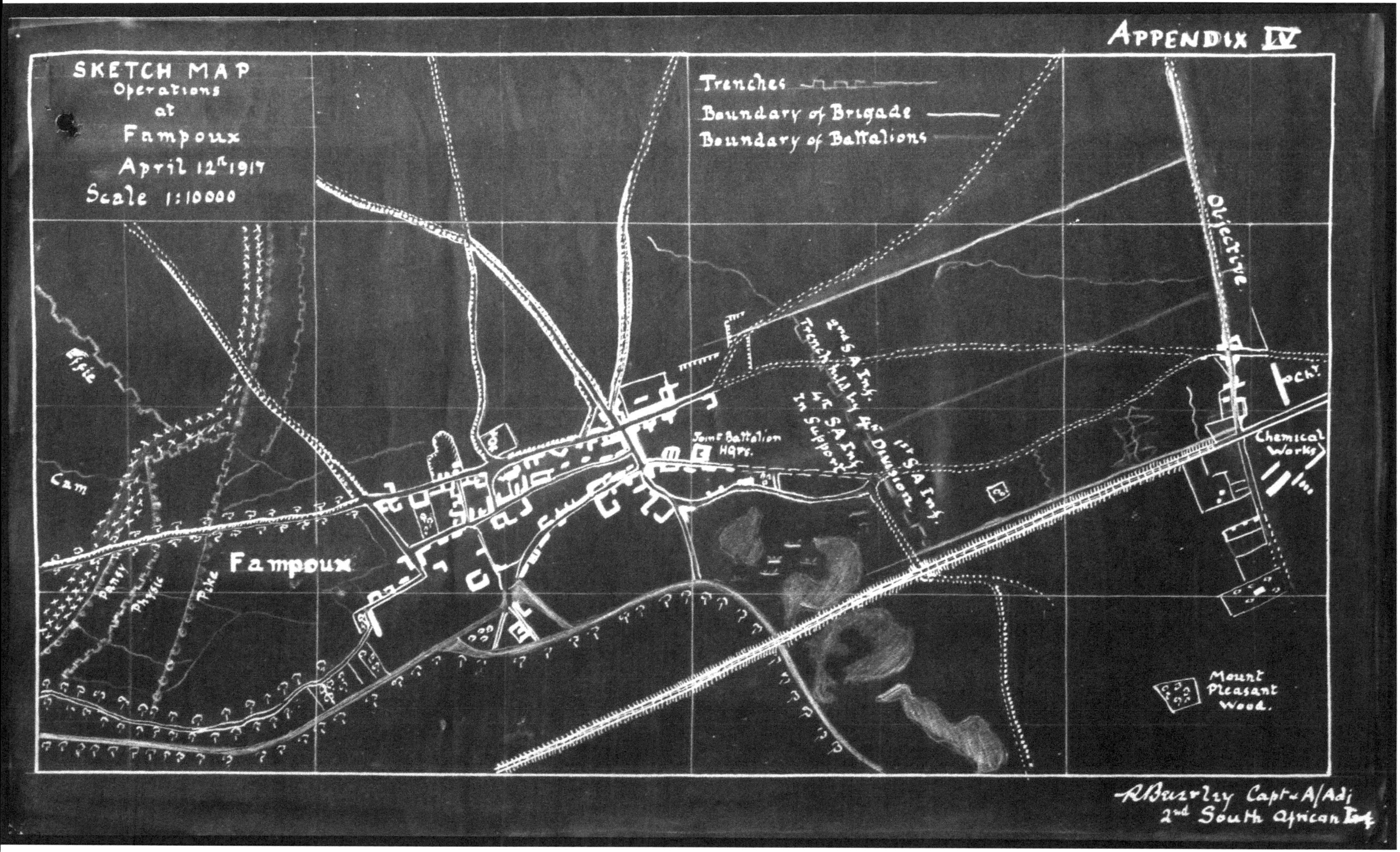

APPENDIX IV
SKETCH MAP
Operations
at
Fampoux
April 12th 1917
Scale 1:10000
Trenches
Boundary of Brigade
Boundary of Battalions
Objective
2nd S A Inf.
1st S A Inf.
Trench held by 4th Division
4th S A Inf
In Support
Joint Battalion HQrs.
Chemical Works
Mount Pleasant Wood.
Fampoux
Effie
Cam
Pansy
Physic
Pike
2nd South African Inf

Summaries are contained in F. S. Regs., Part II. and the Staff Manual respectively. Title pages will be prepared in manuscript.

INTELLIGENCE SUMMARY.

(Erase heading not required.)

Place	Date	Hour	Summary of Events and Information	Remarks and references to Appendices
MONCHY-BRETON.	1.5.17		Regiment at training on MONCHY-BRETON training ground. Lt E.C. BRYANT and 20. O.R. formed firing party at funeral of Lt R.B. DAVIES. of the 4th NORTHUMBERLAND FUSILIERS, attached R.F.C. in MONCHY-BRETON churchyard. The REV. H. HARRIS. officiated. Strength of regiment:- With Unit. Not with Unit. Detached. TOTAL Officers. 13 5 1 19 Other Ranks 287 44 52 383 Weather - fine, warm.	
	2.5.17		Regiment at training. Weather fine and warm. Strength Officers 19. OR 384	
	3.5.17		Regiment training on MONCHY-BRETON training ground. All ranks fired GROUPING practice on range. Strength - Officers 19. OR 384.	
	4.5.17		Regiment at training under company arrangement. Bathing at ROCOURT. Composite company formed consisting of 4 Officers and 116 O.R.. O.C. Lt E.C. BRYANT. with 2nd Lts C.V. MERRIMAN, E.J. BROOK, H.H.S. TERRY.. 3 men detailed for duty at 9th DIVISION BATHS, ROCOURT. Strength Officers 19. O.R. 381	

Instructions regarding War Diaries and Intelligence Summaries are contained in F. S. Regs., Part II. and the Staff Manual respectively. Title pages will be prepared in manuscript.

WAR DIARY

2nd REGT. SOUTH AFRICAN INFANTRY.

~~INTELLIGENCE SUMMARY~~.

(Erase heading not required.)

Army F

Place	Date	Hour	Summary of Events and Information
MONCHY-BRETON	5.5.17		Inspection of composite company. 330 PM composite company paraded under MAJOR WEBBER, 3rd SAI, officer commanding composite battalion of S.A.I. BRIGADE; this composite company embussed 445 PM at crossroads MONCHY-BRETON for ARRAS via TINCQUES. Two signallers detailed to report to A.P.M. ARRAS for duty. Strength Officers 19. O.R 381. Weather fine and dry.
	6.5.17		Usual church services. 6 men, runners and signallers, detailed for duty with composite company. Strength Officers 19. O.R 381. Weather very fine.
	7.5.17		Training at MONCHY-BRETON training ground. One man detailed for duty at Prisoner of War cage ARRAS. One limber and driver detailed for duty with composite company. DRAFT consisting of 62 O.R. arrived at 6 PM. Weather very fine. Strength – At training Officers 8 OR 18 Employed " 11 " 362 19 " 380

2353 Wt. W2544/1454 700,000 5/15 D. D. & L. A.D.S.S./Forms/C. 2118.

Instructions regarding War Diaries and Intelligence Summaries are contained in F. S. Regs., Part II. and the Staff Manual respectively. Title pages will be prepared in manuscript.

WAR DIARY
or
~~INTELLIGENCE SUMMARY.~~

2nd REGT. SOUTH AFRICAN INFANTRY.

(Erase heading not required.)

Army Form C. 2118.

Place	Date	Hour	Summary of Events and Information	Remarks and references to Appendices
MONCHY-BRETON.	8.5.17		Inspection of DRAFT by MAJOR C.R. HEENAN. Tempy commanding 2nd S.A.I. 9.30-12.30 regiment at training MONCHY-BRETON training ground. 2-4.30 PM draft at training. Weather dull, small showers during morning. Strength Officers 19. O.R. 442.	
	9.5.17		Regiment at training at MONCHY-BRETON training ground from 9.30 AM to 12.30 PM. Bathing at 9th DIVISION BATHS, ROCOURT during afternoon. Weather fine. Strength 19 Officers. 442. O.R.	
	10.5.17		Regiment at training during morning. Recreational training in the afternoon. Three O.R. left for BOULOGNE REST CAMP. One N.C.O. and eight men from duty at Prisoner of War Cage, ARRAS. Weather fine.	
	11.5.17		Regiment at training during morning. Recreational training in the afternoon. Weather fine. Strength 19 Officers 439 O.R.	

2353 Wt. W2544/1454 700,000 5/15 D. D. & L. A.D.S.S./Forms/C. 2118.

Instructions regarding War Diaries and Intelligence Summaries are contained in F. S. Regs., Part II. and the Staff Manual respectively. Title pages will be prepared in manuscript.

2ND RGT. SOUTH AFRICAN INFANTRY

INTELLIGENCE SUMMARY.

(Erase heading not required.)

Place	Date	Hour	Summary of Events and Information	Remarks and references to Appendices
MONCHY-BRETON	12.5.17		Regiment moved to ORLENCOURT. Recreational training in afternoon. Weather fine. Strength 19 Officers 438 O.R.	App. I O.O. No 68 attached. Sheet 36B 1/40000. K.4.T.6.
ORLENCOURT	13.5.17		1ST SOUTH AFRICAN INFANTRY BRIGADE paraded at 10.30 AM on MONCHY-BRETON training ground and was inspected by GENERAL SIR EDMUND ALLENBY K.C.B. who, after the inspection spoke congratulating all ranks on the fine work done during the battle of ARRAS. Weather fine during day, thunder showers at night 13/14th. Strength 19 Officers 438 O.R. CAPT R.N. JENKINS, 2ND LT P.C. LILBURN and 2ND LT A.B. Cooper returned from base and taken on strength	App. II O.O. No 69
ORLENCOURT.	14.5.17		Regiment moved to L'ABBAYE DE NEUVILLE FARM. Composite company returned at 2.45 P.M. Casualties – 1 man killed, 1 man wounded. The Brigadier General Commanding has been asked by GENERAL SIR EDMUND ALLENBY KCB 3RD Army Commander, to convey to O.C. Units his appreciation of the smart and clean turnout of the men of the S.A. BRIGADE at his inspection on the 13th inst.	SHEET 36B 1/40000 N.3.4.a. App. II A. O.O. No 70 App. III Diary Composite Company. App. IV Diary Comp. [illegible]

Instructions regarding War Diaries and Intelligence Summaries are contained in F. S. Regs., Part II. and the Staff Manual respectively. Title pages will be prepared in manuscript.

WAR DIARY

2ND REGT. SOUTH AFRICAN INFANTRY.

~~INTELLIGENCE SUMMARY.~~

(Erase heading not required.)

Army Form C. 2118.

Place	Date	Hour	Summary of Events and Information	Remarks and references to Appendices
L'ABBAYE DE NEUVILLE FARM	15.5.17		Regiment at training under company arrangements. During the absence on leave of LT.COL. W.E.C.TANNER C.M.G., MAJOR C.R.HEENAN takes command of the Regiment (from date). MILITARY MEDAL awarded to the following NCOs and men of the Regiment :- No 3479 SGT CLARK MILLER.	
			8451 CPL GEORGE WILLIAM FOADEN.	App I
			7785 PTE PATRICK WILLIAM HEALY.	
			3821 PTE FRANK CLEVERLEY.	
			4618 PTE CECIL ERNEST ADLAM.	
			Authority B.R.O. No 110 d/15/5/17.	
			LT and QMR W PYMM having been evacuated to ENGLAND is struck off the strength of the Regiment with effect from 29.4.17. Strength :- 22 Officers 436 O.R. Weather fine. LT Col W.E.C.TANNER CMG and LT G.G. GREEN. MC granted leave to ENGLAND for period 16th - 26th APRIL 1917.	
	16.5.17		Regiment at training under company arrangements. Recreational training in afternoon. Weather, overcast, showery. Strength 21 Officers 436 men	

2353 Wt. W2544/1454 700,000 5/15 D. D. & L. A.D.S.S./Forms/C. 2118.

Instructions regarding War Diaries and Intelligence Summaries are contained in F. S. Regs., Part II. and the Staff Manual respectively. Title pages will be prepared in manuscript.

WAR DIARY

2nd REGT. SOUTH AFRICAN INFANTRY.

~~INTELLIGENCE SUMMARY.~~

(Erase heading not required.)

Army Form C. 2118.

Place	Date	Hour	Summary of Events and Information	Remarks and references to Appendices
L'ABBAYE DE NEUVILLE FARM	17.5.17		Regiment at training in billets. LEWIS GUN instruction. Weather overcast, showery. Strength 21 Officers 436 OR	
	18.5.17		Regiment at training under company arrangement. Lt.Col. E. CHRISTIAN taken on the strength of Regiment from the 25.4.17 and will be detached under Corps Employ. 2nd Lt E.J. BROOK granted three days special leave to ROUEN, 18th to 21st May 1917. Weather fine, overcast. Strength 22 Officers 436 O.R.	
	19.5.17		Regiment paraded at 9.30 AM for route march, till 12 AM. BATHING at 9th DIVISION BATHS, ROCOURT in afternoon. Weather fine overcast. Strength 22 Officers 435 O.R. Under authority of XVIII Corps telegram No 1221 the Brigadier-General Commanding has appointed on probation to temporary commissioned rank as temporary 2nd Lieutenants from this day 19th May the following:- (over)	

2353 Wt. W2544/1454 700,000 5/15 D. D. & L. A.D.S.S./Forms/C. 2118.

WAR DIARY
2ND SOUTH AFRICAN INFANTRY
INTELLIGENCE SUMMARY.

(Erase heading not required.)

Instructions regarding War Diaries and Intelligence Summaries are contained in F. S. Regs., Part II. and the Staff Manual respectively. Title pages will be prepared in manuscript.

Place	Date	Hour	Summary of Events and Information
L'ABBAYE DE NEUVILLE FARM	19.5.17	(Continued)	2ND REGIMENT S.A.I.
			No 2194 Sgt C.N. ROBERTS D Coy — No 2379 L/Cpl K.S. DICKERSON
			No 7688 Sgt F.E. MILLS D Coy — No 1615 L/Cpl S.G. PHILLIPS
			No 3153 L/Sgt H.G. PRITCHARD B Coy — No 7697 Pte D.F. BELL
			No 6953 Cpl J.C.A. TOOKE B Coy — No 10316 Pte E.D. BIRRELL
			The Army Commander has awarded the MILITARY MEDAL to No 7032 Cpl. R. PAGE. D Coy. 2ND S.A.I.
	20.5.17		Regiment at training. Weather overcast, showery. Strength [illegible] 430 O.R.
	21.5.17		Regiment at training. Lt E.C. BRYANT promoted to rank of [illegible] In the three Open Events in the DIVISIONAL 1ST LINE TRANSPORT COMPETITION at BELLE EGLISE, the 2ND REGT TRANSPORT took two [illegible] PRIZES and a consolation prize. Weather overcast and [illegible] Strength 30 Officers 430 O.R.

File

Copy No. 2

War Diary

ORDER NO: 70. App II A

Reference
Sheet 36B. S.W.

In the Field,
12.5.17.

1. **INTENTION.**
It is the intention of the C.O. to march to L'ABBAYE de NEUVILLE FARM to-morrow at 10.a.m.

2. **DISTRIBUTION.**
~~The head of the Battalion~~ will pass the starting point at 10.a.m. Companies will parade in full marching order as follows:-
Drums, Headquarters, "D" Coy. "C" Coy. "B" Coy. "A" Coy.

3. **STARTING POINT.**
Battalion Orderly Room.

4. **ROUTE.**
From ORLENCOURT NORTH towards LA THEUILOYE, thence EAST by SOUTH to destination.

5. **BILLETS.**
All men to be clear of Billets by 9.15. a.m. The second in command and Medical Officer will inspect billets at 9.30 a.m.
Usual certificates to be rendered.

6. **BAGGAGE.**
All Lewis Guns, Company Stores and Officers Kits will be piled outside Company Orderly Rooms by 9.a.m. Two men per company will be detailed to load stores under supervision of an N.C.O.

7. **STATES.**
Marching in states will be handed in immediately on arrival at billets.

8. **BLANKETS.**
Blankets will be carried on pack.

9. **REPORTS.**
Reports to Head of the column.

R. Beasley
Captain & A/Adjutant,
2nd S.A.I.

Issued at 9.30 p.m.

Nos. 1,2 & 3.	Retained.	
No. 4.	"A" Coy.	By orderly.
No. 5.	"B" Coy.	do.
No. 6.	"C" Coy.	do.
No. 7.	"D" Coy.	do.
No. 8.	Transport Officer.	do
No. 9.	O.C. Headquarters Detachment.	do

Instructions regarding War Diaries and Intelligence Summaries are contained in F. S. Regs., Part II. and the Staff Manual respectively. Title pages will be prepared in manuscript.

WAR DIARY
or
INTELLIGENCE SUMMARY.
(*Erase heading not required.*)

2nd REGT SOUTH AFRICAN INFANTRY.

Army Form C. 2118.

Place	Date	Hour	Summary of Events and Information	Remarks and references to Appendices
L'ABBAYE DE NEUVILLE FARM	22.5.17		Regiment at training and instruction in billets. 2nd Lt E. J. BREW returned from SPECIAL LEAVE to ROUEN. 2nd Lt L. EGAN and 1 O.R. proceeded on ten days leave to ENGLAND. Weather cloudy, showery. Strength :— With Unit 22 Officers 341 O.R. Not with Unit 7 Do 43 O.R. Detached 1 Do 46 O.R. 30 Officers. 430 O.R.	
	23.5.17		Regiment at training in field south of L'ABBAYE DE NEUVILLE FARM. Recreational training in afternoon. Weather fine.	
	24.5.17		Regiment at training on MONCHY-BRETON training ground: all ranks fired grouping practice on range there. 9.30 PM to 10.30 PM night operations in vicinity of FARM. Congratulatory messages received from 3rd Army Commander and 17th Corps Commander for those awarded Honours in the recent fighting.	

2353 Wt. W2544/1454 700,000 5/15 D. D. & L. A.D.S.S./Forms/C. 2118

Instructions regarding War Diaries and Intelligence Summaries are contained in F. S. Regs., Part II. and the Staff Manual respectively. Title pages will be prepared in manuscript.

WAR DIARY

2nd REGT SOUTH AFRICAN INFANTRY.

~~INTELLIGENCE SUMMARY.~~

(Erase heading not required.)

Army Form C. 2118.

Place	Date	Hour	Summary of Events and Information	Remarks and references to Appendices
L'ABBAYE DE NEUVILLE FARM	24.5.17		Honours:-	
			Lt G.G.GREEN. M.C. awarded bar to MILITARY CROSS.	
			Lt N.THORBURN awarded the MILITARY CROSS.	App. D
			#2658 Sgt G.S.FERNIE. awarded DISTINGUISHED CONDUCT MEDAL.	
			Draft of fortyone other ranks arrived from base.	
			Weather fine. Strength 30 Officers 430 O.R.	
	25.5.17		Regiment out on ROUTE MARCH in the morning. Recreational training in afternoon. Night operations from 10 PM to 11 PM. Three O.R. returned from duty with at 9th DIVISION BATHS ROCOURT. Weather fine. Strength Officers O.R.	
			BRIGADE BOXING COMPETITION at LA THIEULOYE. The entries from the 2nd REGT. were:- FEATHER WEIGHT #8213 Pte TINKLER. B.	
			LIGHT Do 8218 Pte TOWNSEND. N.H.	
			MIDDLE Do 3403 Pte LEWIS. J.	
			HEAVY Do 7187 Pte SWART. H.J	(contd)

2353 Wt. W2544/1454 700,000 5/15 D. D. & L. A.D.S.S./Forms/C. 2118.

Instructions regarding War Diaries and Intelligence Summaries are contained in F. S. Regs., Part II. and the Staff Manual respectively. Title pages will be prepared in manuscript.

WAR DIARY

2ND REGT. SOUTH AFRICAN INFANTRY.

~~INTELLIGENCE SUMMARY~~

(Erase heading not required.)

Army Form C. 2118.

Place	Date	Hour	Summary of Events and Information	Remarks and references to Appendices
L'ABBAYE DE NEUVILLE FARM	25.5.17		PTE TINKLER was beaten by the eventual winner of the FEATHER WEIGHT.	
			PTE TOWNSEND won the LIGHT WEIGHT COMPETITION.	
			PTE LEWIS was second in MIDDLE WEIGHT	
			PTE SWART was second in the HEAVY.	
			Strength 50 Officers 471 O.R.	
	26.5.17		Regiment paraded in fighting order at 9.15 AM and marched to MONCHY-BRETON training ground where athletic sports were indulged in: they were the SOUTH AFRICAN INFANTRY BRIGADE SPORTS. A track had be laid out and all arrangements made to enable the attached programme of events to be carried out. The weather was very fine and a most interesting day spent by all ranks. The following of this regiment secured prizes:—	App VII

Instructions regarding War Diaries and Intelligence Summaries are contained in F. S. Regs., Part II. and the Staff Manual respectively. Title pages will be prepared in manuscript.

WAR DIARY

2ND REGT SOUTH AFRICAN INFANTRY.

~~INTELLIGENCE SUMMARY.~~

(Erase heading not required.)

Army Form C. 2118.

Place	Date	Hour	Summary of Events and Information	Remarks and references to Appendices
L'ABBAYE DE NEUVILLE FARM	26.5.17		1ST PRIZE HIGH JUMP — No 6679 PTE LUCAS J.G.	
			3RD PRIZE SACK RACE — No 4642 PTE REDWOOD C.H.	
			1ST PRIZE OFFICERS FLAT RACE 440 YDS — 2ND LT C.H. ROBERTS.	
			3RD PRIZE Do Do — 2ND LT V.S. DICKERSON.	
			1ST PRIZE BOLSTER BAR — No 10568 PTE PHIPSON. C.	
			2ND PRIZE ALL RANKS RELAY RACE — "A" COMPANY.	
			3RD PRIZE LONG JUMP. — No 6679 PTE LUCAS J.G.	
			1ST PRIZE MULE RACE — No 3226 PTE LEHMKUHL. N.J.	
			2ND LT P.C. LILBORN detached for duty with BRIGADE HEADQUARTERS as BRIGADE INTELLIGENCE OFFICER. No 2825 PTE C.F. LAREDO proceeded on ten days leave to ENGLAND. Strength 30 Officers 468 O.R.	
	27.5.17		Usual church services. Weather very fine. Strength 30 Officers 466 O.R.	

Instructions regarding War Diaries and Intelligence Summaries are contained in F. S. Regs., Part II. and the Staff Manual respectively. Title pages will be prepared in manuscript.

WAR DIARY

2nd REGT. SOUTH AFRICAN INFANTRY.

(Erase heading not required.)

Army Form C. 2118.

Place	Date	Hour	Summary of Events and Information	Remarks and references to Appendices
L'ABBAYE DE NEUVILLE FARM	28.5.17		Regiment at training under company arrangement. Each company had one hours special bayonet fighting under Divisional Instructor. MAJOR C.R. HEENEN relinquishes command of Regiment. LIEUT. COL. W.E.C. TANNER. CMG, having returned off leave, assumes command of the Regiment. The following men proceeded on ten days leave to ENGLAND :- No 2752 Pte G.B. LeROUX. No 3064 Pte A.N. AYRES. Weather fine. Strength of Regiment 30 Officers 466 O.R.	
	29.5.17		Route March by Platoons combining map reading practice for Junior Officers and Senior N.C.O.s. Lecture by commanding officer to Officers on "Discipline and Trench Warfare". Weather fine. Strength 30. Officers 466. O.R. No 7071 Pte J.B. STEPHENS. 2nd S.A.I. awarded the FRENCH decoration MEDAILLE MILITAIRE.	App VIII
	30.5.17		Regiment marched to MONCHY-BRETON training ground for the presentation of RIBBONS by LIEUT. GENL. CHARLES FERGUSSON. Bt. K.C.B. M.V.O. D.S.O. Weather fine. Strength 30 Officers 465 O.R.	

Army Form C. 2118

WAR DIARY

2nd REGT. SOUTH AFRICAN INFANTRY.

~~INTELLIGENCE SUMMARY.~~

(Erase heading not required.)

Instructions regarding War Diaries and Intelligence Summaries are contained in F. S. Regs., Part II. and the Staff Manual respectively. Title pages will be prepared in manuscript.

Place	Date	Hour	Summary of Events and Information	Remarks and references to Appendices
L'ABBAYE DE NEUVILLE FARM	31/5/17		Regiment at general training, special attention being paid to Musketry Instruction. Capt R.N. JENKINS appointed Town Major of MONCHY-BRETON and therefore detached from regiment. Weather fine. Strength:- With Unit 20 Officers 371 OR Not with Unit 7 " 50 " Detached 3 " 44 " TOTAL 30 Officers 465 OR	

W. Tanner Lt. Col.
Commanding 2nd S.A.I.

War Diary 1 R

Copy No. 1

ORDER NO. 68.

IN THE FIELD,
12.5.17.

Map Reference
LENS 11.

No. 1. INTENTION. It is the intention of the C.O. to march to ORLENCOURT ~~xxxxxxxx~~ at 12. noon. to-day.

No. 2. DISTRIBUTION. Companies will march independently, passing the starting point in the following order at 2 minutes interval, commencing at 12. noon.

"C" Company.
"A" Company.
"B" Company.
"D" Company.
Headquarters.

Transport will follow in rear of the Battalion.

No. 3. STARTING POINT. Lane opposite Transport Lines.

No. 4. ROUTE. Main Road from MONCHY BRETON to ORLENCOURT.

No. 5. BILLETS. All men to be clear of billets by 11.15. a.m. The Second in Command and Medical Officer will inspect billets at 11.15. a.m. Usual certificates to be handed in by 11.15. a.m.

No. 6. BAGGAGE. All lewis guns, Company Stores and Officers kits will be piled outside Company Orderly Rooms by 11a.m. Two men per company will be detailed to load limbers under supervision of an N.C.O.

No. 7. STATES. Marching in states will be handed in immediately on arrival at billets.

No. 8. REPORTS. Reports to Battalion Headquarters.

Issued at Orderly Room 6.a.m. 12.5.17.

R Beverley
Captain & A/Adjutant,
2nd Regiment S. A. Infantry.

Copy No. 1. War Diary.
No. 2. File.
No. 3. Major Heenan, by orderly.
No. 4. to 7. Companies, by orderly.
No. 8. Transport Officer.

Copy No..2....

ORDER NO: 69.

IN THE FIELD,
12.5.17.

1. The Battalion will parade for inspection by the Army Commander to-morrow.

2. Companies will parade as strong as possible in front of the Headquarter mess at 10.10. a.m. Officers servants and Headquarter details will parade with their companies. Signalling class will report to Companies at 9.a.m.
Companies will parade in the following order:-
Drums, "A" Coy. "B" Coy. "C" Coy. "D" Coy.

3. Companies will be equalised and sized on parade.

4. Markers as detailed by the R.S.M. will report at the Orderly Room at 9.45 a.m.

5. DRESS. Fighting order, steel helmets, box respirators and P.H.Helmets will be worn. Officers will wear gloves, no canes will be carried.

6. The Battalion will form up on the Brigade parade ground in close column of companies at 12 paces distance.

7. The Battalion will be prepared to march past in column of route.

8. Parade states, also shewing distribution of men in billets will be handed to Orderly Room by 8.a.m. to-morrow.

R Beverley

Captain & A/Adjutant,
2nd S.A.I.

Issued 10.p.m.

Copy Nos. 1,2,3.	Retained.
Copy No. 4.	"A" Coy.
Copy No. 5.	"B" Coy.
Copy No. 6.	"C" Coy.
Copy No. 7.	"D" Coy.
Copy No. 8.	Transport Officer
Copy No. 9.	O/C. Headquarter Detachment

Instructions regarding War Diaries and Intelligence Summaries are contained in F. S. Regs., Part II. and the Staff Manual respectively. Title pages will be prepared in manuscript.

9

WAR DIARY
2ND REGT SOUTH AFRICAN INFANTRY
~~INTELLIGENCE SUMMARY.~~
(Erase heading not required.)

Army Form C. 2118.

2 S A Infy Bn
Vol 15

Place	Date	Hour	Summary of Events and Information	Remarks and references to Appendices
L'ABBAYE DE NEUVILLE FARM	1.6.17		Regiment marched via OSTREVILLE and MARQUAY to LIGNY ST FLOCHEL station then entrained and thus proceeded to ARRAS. The transport proceeded to ARRAS by road. One O.R. granted ten days leave to ENGLAND. Weather fine. Strength 30 Officers 465 OR.	App^dx I. O.O. No 72.
ARRAS	2.6.17		Kit, equipment etc inspected under company arrangement. One OR proceeded on ten days leave to ENGLAND. Weather fine. Strength 30 Officers 465 OR	
	3.6.17		Church Parade at 9.30 AM. Attack practice by companies at 10 AM on training ground at G.19 a and b. CAPT R.N. JENKINS, having returned from employment as TOWN MAJOR, MONCHY-BRETON assumes command of D Company from date. CAPT R.C. KNIGHT 2ND LTS V. BEETON J.C. CRAGG and J.G. PRITCHARD with 115 O.R. proceeded on working party at 6.30 AM to DINGWALL CAMP, G 18. b 4.4. Weather fine. Strength 30 Officers 465 OR. 2ND LT V.S. DICKERSON and 1 O.R. proceeded to HAUTE-AVESNES on XVII CORPS General Course.	Map Ref. 51B NW Edition 5A 1/20000. App^dx II OO No 73

Instructions regarding War Diaries and Intelligence Summaries are contained in F. S. Regs., Part II. and the Staff Manual respectively. Title pages will be prepared in manuscript.

WAR DIARY

2ND REGT SOUTH AFRICAN INFANTRY

~~INTELLIGENCE SUMMARY.~~

(Erase heading not required.)

Army Form C. 2118.

Place	Date	Hour	Summary of Events and Information	Remarks and references to Appendices
ARRAS	4.6.17.		Bathing at COLLEGE COMMUNAL. ARRAS in the morning: afternoon Bayonet fighting and Physical Training. Weather fine. Strength 30 Officers 464 O.R. 2ND LT J.C.A. TOOKE proceeded to LE-TOUQUET on LEWIS GUN Course	
Do	5.6.17		Inspection and training under company arrangement. Training gas N.C.O^s by Divisional Gas N.C.O. 2-3 PM Lecture on GAS to N.C.O^s by Divisional Gas N.C.O. Bathing at COLLEGE COMMUNAL. Weather fine. Strength 30 Officers 464 O.R. 2ND LT D.F. BELL and 30 O.R. proceeded to DINGWALL CAMP, approximately G.18.c.5.5. Composite Battalion formed; Commanded by LT COL McLEOD. D.S.O. 4TH S.A.I., consisting of 2ND REGT. 6 Officers 130 O.R. {5 Officers 100. O.R. went up on 3rd inst as working party; 1 Officer 30. O.R. went up to-day} 4TH REGT. 8 Officers 270 O.R. 4TH REGT. H.Q. Staff. LT C.J. STEIN AND W.L. KING having arrived from ENGLAND are taken on strength. The following men proceeded on ten days leave to ENGLAND:- 2738 PTE H.J. BROWN, 3053 PTE J.L. WITHERSPOON and 812 PTE G.P. MARITZ.	

Instructions regarding War Diaries and Intelligence Summaries are contained in F. S. Regs., Part II. and the Staff Manual respectively. Title pages will be prepared in manuscript.

WAR DIARY

2nd REGT. SOUTH AFRICAN INFANTRY.

~~INTELLIGENCE SUMMARY.~~

(Erase heading not required.)

Army Form C. 2118.

Place	Date	Hour	Summary of Events and Information	Remarks and references to Appendices
ARRAS.	6.6.17.		Battalion, less detached parties, at training: Bayonet fighting and close order drill. Gas instruction for N.C.O's in the morning and Gas lecture for all ranks, from 2-3 PM; both by DIVISIONAL GAS N.C.O.. 3367 Cpl H.D. STANTON proceeded to ENGLAND as candidate for commissioned rank. 2724 R.S.M. PAGET. W.A. proceeded to ENGLAND to attend a course at CHELSEA SCHOOL. Lt D.F. BELL and 34 O.R. rejoined unit from composite battalion. Fine during day, thunder showers during evening. Strength 32 Officers 463 O.R.	
Do.	7.6.17.		Battalion less working party at Bayonet fighting and Musketry. Gas instruction to all ranks by DIVISIONAL GAS N.C.O. Five "other ranks" proceeded to BOULOGNE for fourteen days rest at camp there. Weather, warm, thundershowers during day. Strength 32 Officers and 462 O.R.	

Instructions regarding War Diaries and Intelligence Summaries are contained in F. S. Regs., Part II. and the Staff Manual respectively. Title pages will be prepared in manuscript.

Army Form C. 2118.

WAR DIARY
2ND REGT SOUTH AFRICAN INFANTRY
or INTELLIGENCE SUMMARY.
(Erase heading not required.)

Place	Date	Hour	Summary of Events and Information	Remarks and references to Appendices
ARRAS	8.6.17		Regiment at training, including musketry on range at FREDS WOOD, BLANGY, first aid lecture for stretcher bearers. Lewis Gun instruction during afternoon. Bathing from 3-5 PM at DIVISIONAL SWIMMING BATHS. 4592 PTE J. MILLS proceeded to ENGLAND on ten days leave. SIR DOUGLAS HAIG'S Despatch of 9th April, submitting names deserving of special mention, published in the London Gazette of Tuesday 15 May 1917, contains:-	
			HILL. TEMP. LIEUT. N.J., 2ND S.A.I.	
			TATHAM. TEMP. 2ND LIEUT. E.V., 2ND S.A.I.	
			Weather warm, cloudy. Strength - 32 Officers, 462 O.R.	
Do.	9.6.17		Regiment at Musketry Practice on range at FREDS WOOD, BLANGY. Bathing during afternoon. Weather warm, some showers. Strength 32 Officers 458. O.R.	

Instructions regarding War Diaries and Intelligence Summaries are contained in F. S. Regs., Part II. and the Staff Manual respectively. Title pages will be prepared in manuscript.

WAR DIARY
2nd REGT SOUTH AFRICAN INFANTRY.
or
INTELLIGENCE SUMMARY.
(Erase heading not required.)

Army Form C. 2118.

Place	Date	Hour	Summary of Events and Information	Remarks and references to Appendices
ARRAS	10.6.17		Church Parade in the morning. Composite Company consisting of 4 Officers and 100. O.R. with three companies of the 4th S.A.I. moved at 6.45 PM to STIRLING CAMP, approximately H.13 a 8.9. and on arrival there came under the orders of the G.O.C. 26th Infantry Brigade, as the Battalion in Brigade Reserve during operations of the 10/11 June. Regiment (less Composite Company and Working Party moved via the ARRAS - St POL road to "Y" HUTMENTS Map Ref. L.1.6.7.2. Weather fine. Strength 32 Officers 455 O.R.	APPx III O.O. 74 APPx IV O.O. 75 Map FRANCE 51C 1st Edition 1/40000.
"Y" HUTS	11.6.17		General inspection of arms and equipment. Lewis guns cleaned and inspected. Composite Company returned. Draft consisting of 25 O.R. arrived from base and taken on strength. The following NCO and men awarded the MILITARY MEDAL :- 8334 Pte COLE H.J. 7062 " ELLWOOD H.M.B. 6619 " PRINGLE G.G. 2175 " FORBES J. 7814 SGT. MOORE C.V.	APPx V

2353 Wt. W2544/1454 700,000 5/15 D. D. & L. A.D.S.S./Forms/C. 2118.

Instructions regarding War Diaries and Intelligence Summaries are contained in F. S. Regs., Part II. and the Staff Manual respectively. Title pages will be prepared in manuscript.

WAR DIARY

Army Form C. 2118.

2nd SOUTH AFRICAN INFANTRY.

~~INTELLIGENCE SUMMARY~~

(Erase heading not required.)

Place	Date	Hour	Summary of Events and Information	Remarks and references to Appendices
"Y" HUTS.	12.6.17		Regiment at training on parade ground adjoining "Y" HUTS. Gas lecture by Divisional Gas NCO in the afternoon. 1 Officer and two Lewis Gun teams supplied as anti-aircraft guards on the dumps at LARESSETTE.	
			"1607 Pte G.G. TANNER. 2nd S.A.I. awarded the DISTINGUISHED CONDUCT MEDAL.	APPx VI
			Weather fine. Strength - With Unit 17 257 Not with Unit 13 183 detached 2 39 32 Off. 479 OR.	
			CAPT. R.C. KNIGHT granted ten days leave to ENGLAND. 12th-22nd June.	
'Y' HUTS.	13.6.17		Regiment at training including Lewis Gun instruction. Bathing at XVII Corps Baths DUISANS. Weather fine. Strength 32 Officers 479 OR.	
'Y' HUTS	14.6.17		Regiment at general training in the morning. Regiment moved to huts at LARASSET. Lt R.D.W. KIRK returned from hospital taken	APPx VII

Instructions regarding War Diaries and Intelligence Summaries are contained in F. S. Regs., Part II. and the Staff Manual respectively. Title pages will be prepared in manuscript.

WAR DIARY

2nd REGT SOUTH or AFRICAN INFANTRY

~~INTELLIGENCE SUMMARY~~

(Erase heading not required.)

Army Form C. 2118.

Place	Date	Hour	Summary of Events and Information	Remarks and references to Appendices
			Contd.	
	14.6.17		taken on the effective strength of the Regiment. DRAFT of two Officers, CAPT T. H. SYMONS and 2nd Lt C.D. CONNOCK, and 103 O.R. arrived from base and taken on strength. Weather very fine. Strength 32 Officers 478 O.R.	
LARASSET	15.6.17		New draft on cleaning equipment and adjusting buttons, helmets etc to regimental pattern. Battalion less new draft on general fatigues. Lewis Gun instruction for all from 2-4 P.M. 2nd Lt B.P. HENNESSY 2nd S.A.I. awarded the MILITARY CROSS. Weather very fine. Strength 34 Officers 581 O.R.	Appdx VIII
Do	16.6.17		New draft paraded for training and inspection by the Commanding Officer. Regiment at training on parade ground in vicinity of HUTMENTS, LARASSET. Actg Capt E.C. BRYANT relinquishes rank of acting Captain on ceasing to command a company with effect from 14.6.17. One other rank proceeded on ten days leave to ENGLAND. Weather fine. Strength 34 Officers. 581 O.R.	

Instructions regarding War Diaries and Intelligence Summaries are contained in F. S. Regs., Part II. and the Staff Manual respectively. Title pages will be prepared in manuscript.

WAR DIARY

2nd Regt SOUTH AFRICAN INFANTRY.

[redacted]

(Erase heading not required.)

Army Form C. 2118.

Place	Date	Hour	Summary of Events and Information	Remarks and references to Appendices
LARASSET	17.6.17		The Battalion, less Roman Catholics, paraded for DIVINE SERVICE. The working party under Lt C.O. STEIN returned from BALMORAL CAMP ARRAS. Weather hot, cloudy: some thunder showers. Strength 34 Officers 579 O.R. 2nd Lt J.C.A. TOOKE was drowned while bathing at LE-TOUQUET.	
Do	18.6.17		Regiment, less working party from ARRAS, at training on XVII Corps training area. 2nd Lt J.C.A. TOOKE having been accidently drowned at LE TOUQUET, ETAPLES, on the 17th June 1917 is struck off the strength of the Regiment. 3832 Pte W.H. ROBSON granted ten days leave to ENGLAND. Weather overcast, some thunder showers. Strength 34 Officers 576 OR.	
Do	19.6.17		Regiment at general training. Bathing at XI Corps baths DUISANS. 2nd Lt J.N. HARVEY, having arrived from base is taken on strength. Weather hot, some showers. Strength 33 Officers 576 O.R.	

2353 Wt. W2544/1454 700,000 5/15 D. D. & L. A.D.S.S./Forms/C. 2118.

Instructions regarding War Diaries and Intelligence Summaries are contained in F. S. Regs., Part II. and the Staff Manual respectively. Title pages will be prepared in manuscript.

WAR DIARY

Army Form C. 2118.

2ND SOUTH AFRICAN INFANTRY.

(Erase heading not required.)

Place	Date	Hour	Summary of Events and Information	Remarks and references to Appendices
LARASSET	20.6.17		Regiment at general training. Lt E.C. BRYANT returned from Lewis Gun Course at LE TOUQUET. Weather, showery. Strength 34 Officers 576 O.R.	
Do	21.6.17		Regiment at general training, including Attack Practice. Lt H.L. KING and CSM. DEWAR NR. proceeded to AUXI-LE-CHATEAU to attend a general course at III ARMY SCHOOL. 3457 Pte O'BRIEN. NR proceeded on ten days leave to ENGLAND. Weather cloudy, some showers. Strength of Regiment:- With Unit 25 Officers 480 O.R. / Not with Unit 6 Do 40 Do / Detached 3 Do 56 Do / TOTAL 34 Do 576 Do	
Do	22.6.17		Regiment at general training, including Attack Practice and Reconnaissance march. Draft of 1 Officer, 2nd Lt F.L. MARILLIER, and 25 O.R. arrived from base. No 3457 Pte N. O'BRIEN. "C" Coy granted 10 day leave.	

A6945 Wt. W11422/M1160 350,000 12/16 D. D. & L. Forms/C./2118/14.

Instructions regarding War Diaries and Intelligence Summaries are contained in F. S. Regs., Part II. and the Staff Manual respectively. Title pages will be prepared in manuscript.

WAR DIARY

Army Form C. 2118.

2ND SOUTH AFRICAN INFANTRY

(Erase heading not required.)

Place	Date	Hour	Summary of Events and Information	Remarks and references to Appendices
LARASSET.	22.6.17		(Contd). 2ND LT. MEWHELAN awarded the MILITARY CROSS.	App-dix IX
			Weather cloudy, some showers. Strength 35 Officers 601 O.R.	
Do	23.6.17		Regiment at general training including firing on ETRUN range.	
			CAPT R.C. KNIGHT returned from special leave to ENGLAND.	
			2ND LTS T BANCROFT and G.E. MARSHALL arrived from ENGLAND and taken on strength of regiment. One officer and fifty two	
			other Ranks proceeded on fatigue to XVII Corps School	
			HAUTE-AVESNES. Weather fine. Strength 35 Officers 599 O.R.	
Do	24.6.17		Church Parade for all denominations. Weather fine. Strength of Regiment 37 Officers and 598 O.R.	
Do	25.6.17		Regiment at general training including attack practise.	
			Bathing at VI Corps Baths DUISANS. Weather fine. Strength 37 Officers 597 O.R.	

A6945 Wt. W11422/M1160 350,000 12/16 D. D. & L. Forms/C./2118/14.

Instructions regarding War Diaries and Intelligence Summaries are contained in F. S. Regs., Part II. and the Staff Manual respectively. Title pages will be prepared in manuscript.

WAR DIARY

Army Form C. 2118.

2nd REGT, SOUTH AFRICAN INFANTRY.
[redacted]
(Erase heading not required.)

Place	Date	Hour	Summary of Events and Information	Remarks and references to Appendices
LARASSET	26.6.17		Regiment at General Training including Attack Practice. Demonstration of Attack Practice by A and D companies on XVII Corps training ground HAUTE-AVESNES. Grouping and application practices fired on range at ETRUN. DRAFT of 11 OR arrived from base. Weather fine. Strength 37 Officers 596 OR	
Do	27.6.17		Regiment at General Training. No 2462 Cpl CHITTENDEN H and No 4444 Pte HASTINGS A. proceeded on ten days leave to ENGLAND. Weather fine. Strength 37 Officers 605 OR	
Do	28.6.17		Regiment at General Training. Bathing at II Corps Baths DUISANS. Weather fine till evening then heavy storm. Strength 37 Officers 605 OR	

A6945 Wt. W11422/M1160 350,000 12/16 D. D. & L. Forms/C./2118/14.

Army Form C. 2118.

Instructions regarding War Diaries and Intelligence Summaries are contained in F. S. Regs., Part II. and the Staff Manual respectively. Title pages will be prepared in manuscript.

WAR DIARY

2nd SOUTH AFRICAN INFANTRY.

(Erase heading not required.)

Place	Date	Hour	Summary of Events and Information	Remarks and references to Appendices
LARASSET	29.6.17		Regiment at General Training. 4 OR transferred to Light Trench Mortar Battery. Draft consisting of 11 OR arrived from base. Weather fine. Strength 37 Officers 605 O.R.	
Do	30.6.17		Regiment at General Training. 2nd Lts V.S. DICKERSON and D.J. BELL returned from course at XVII Corps School, HAUTE-AVESNES. Weather cool, cloudy, some rain.	
			Strength of Regiment :- With Unit 28 Officers 529 O.R.	
			Not With Unit 6 " 20 "	
			Detached 3 " 52 "	
			TOTAL 37 Officers 601 O.R.	

[illegible] Lt Col.
Commanding 2nd S.A.I.

A6945 Wt. W11422/M1160 350,000 12/16 D. D. & L. Forms/C./2118/14.

8. **STATES.** (a) Marching out states will be handed to the Adjutant at 6.a.m.
(b) Marching in states will be handed to Orderly Room on arrival in Billets at ARRAS.

9. All Transport will march to Transport lines at ARRAS at G.17.a. and will report to Lieut. STUCKEY for instructions.

10. **REPORTS.** Reports to the head of the Battalion.

Issued at 12. noon.

R Beverley
Captain & A/Adjutant,
2nd S. A. Infantry.

Copy No. 1. to Capt. Bryant, personally.
Copy No. 2. to 2/Lt. Brook "
Copy No. 3. to Capt. Knight "
Copy No. 4. to Lieut. Pearse. "
Copy No. 5. to Transport Officer. "
Copies Nos. 6 - 7 retained.

---

app I

Copy No. 7

ORDER No: 72.

Reference
Sheet LENS II
1/100000.

In the Field,
31. 5. 17.

1. INFORMATION. The 1st South African Infantry Brigade will move to ARRAS on June 1st. On completion of move the Brigade will be in Divisional Reserve.

2. INTENTION. The C.O. intends to march to LIGNY ST. FLOCHEL to-morrow for the purpose of entraining there and proceeding by rail to ARRAS, whilst the Transport will march by road to ARRAS.

3. DISTRIBUTION. The Battalion, less Transport, will parade in full marching order in the Avenue facing NORTH WEST at 6.30. a.m. in the following order,- from the right:-
Drums, Headquarters, "A" "B" "C" "D" Companies.
The Transport will parade in column of route in the Avenue at 6.a.m.

4. STARTING POINT. (a) Starting Point, the end of the Avenue EAST of Billets. The head of the Battalion will pass the starting point at 6.40. a.m.
(b) The head of the Transport will pass the Starting Point at 6.5. a.m.

5. ROUTE. (a) The Battalion, less Transport, will march from L'ABBAYE DE NEUVILLE FARM via OSTREVILLE and MARQUAY to LIGNY ST. FLOCHEL Station.
(b) The Transport will proceed via ORLENCOURT, CHELERS to TINCQUES, at which latter place the Transport Officer will report at 8.20. a.m. to Lieut. JOHNSTONE of the 4th S.A.Infantry for instructions regarding the remaining portion of the march.

6. LEWIS GUNS. Lewis Guns, which are to be loaded on limbers by 5.p.m. will be transported to LIGNY ST. FLOCHEL at 7.30. p.m. to-day, and be loaded on the train the following day.
"A" Company will detail one Sergeant, and each company one lewis gunner to accompany guns as a guard to these at LIGNY ST. FLOCHEL Station.
2nd Lieut. MERRIMAN will post this guard at the Station at a point to be indicated by Brigade Billeting Officer, 2nd Lieut. LILBURN.

7. BAGGAGE. (a) Officers Kit will be piled outside the main gate at 5.30. a.m.
(b) Company Stores will be placed outside the NORTH SIDE of billets at 8.p.m. to-night for loading.
(c) All baggage and kit will be loaded under instructions of the Transport Officer.

app II

Copy No. 3.

ORDER No. 75.

Reference
SHEET 51b N.W.3.
1/20,000

In the Field.
5/6/1917.

No. 1.
INFORMATION.

The Brigade will form two composite Battalions for DIVISIONAL RESERVE in connection with forthcoming operations.

No. 2.
INTENTION.

The O.C. intends to furnish the undermentioned parties for attachment to "B" Battalion (Lieut. Colonel MACLEOD).
 (a) 1 Platoon, ("B" Company)
 (b) Working Party under command of Captain KNIGHT ("C" and "D" Companies).

No. 3.
DISTRIBUTION.

Units will report to the Adjutant, 4th S.A.Infantry as follows:-
(a) Officer in Command of "B" Coy. Platoon (2/Lieut BELL) will report with his unit to the Adjutant, 4th S.A.I. at 6.15 p.m. to-night for in the PLACE ST CROIX.

(b) Senior officer in charge of Working Party (Captain KNIGHT) will report to Adjutant, 4th S.A.I. at BALMORAL CAMP at 6.30. p.m. to-night for instructions.

No. 4.
DRESS.

Dress - Fighting Order, rations for 6th instant will be carried.

No. 5.
LEWIS GUNS.

In addition to the Lewis Gun on platoon establishment "B" Company platoon will furnish 1 Lewis Gun and ammunition complete.

Issued at 6.45 p.m.

(sgd) R.Beverley

Captain & A/Adjutant
2nd Regiment, S,A.Infantry.

Copy No. 1. to 2/Lieut Brook personally
No. 2 to Capt. Knight by cyclist orderly.
Copies Nos. 3 & 4 Retained.

Copy No.....2

ORDER NO: 75.

Reference
Sheet LENS II
1/100000.
Sheet ARRAS 1/10000
Sheet 51C 1/40000.

In the Field,
10th June, 1917.

App IV

1. INFORMATION.

(a) The 9th Division, less artillery, will be relieved by the 4th Division, less artillery, in the right sector of the XVII Corps front on the night June 11/12th and 12/13th.

(b) The 1st South African Brigade, less 4th S.A.I. and detached parties, will proceed by march route to "Y" HUTS to-day.

2. INTENTION.

The C.O. intends to march to "Y" HUTS at 2.45.p.m. to-day.

3. DISTRIBUTION.

The Battalion, less working party and composite company and baggage guard, will parade in full marching order at 2.40. p.m. to-day at the Convent for the purpose of marching to "Y" Huts. Transport will follow in rear of Battalion.

4. ROUTE.

Through ARRAS, via the PORTE de BAUDIMONT, which place the head of the Battalion will pass at 3.15. p.m, by the main ARRAS - ST.POL ROAD to "Y" HUTS.

5. BAGGAGE.

(a) All baggage will be stacked ready for loading outside billets by 1.30. p.m. "A" and "B" Companies will provide a fatigue party of 1 N.C.O. and 6 men each for the purpose of loading baggage under the direction of the Transport Officer.
(b) "A" and "B" Companies will detail one Lewis Gunner each as Lewis Gun Guard, this guard will march behind lewis gun limbers with Transport.
(c) Baggage for which transport is not available will be stacked in yard at CONVENT under a guard of 1 N.C.O. and 6 men to await return of necessary waggons. 2nd Lieut. ROBERTS will be in charge of this party.

6. BILLETS.

Men will be clear of billets by 2.p.m., at which hour the usual inspection will take place. Clearance certificates will be handed to Orderly Room by 2.p.m.

7. STATES.

Marching out states will be handed to Orderly Room at 2.p.m.
Marching in states will be handed to Orderly Room on arrival at Billets at "Y" Huts.

8. DETACHMENTS.

(a) The Composite Company (Captain JENKINS) will on completion of its allotted duty march under instruction of O.C. 4th S.A.Infantry and join Battalion at "Y" Huts.
(b) The working party under A.D. Signals, XVII Corps, will be attached to 4th S.A.Infantry for discipline and rations from the 11th instant.

Copy No....1...

ORDER NO: 74.

Reference
Sheet PLOUVAIN,1/10000.
" ARRAS. 1/10000.

In the Field,
10th June,1917.

app III

1. INFORMATION.

(a) The 27th Infantry Brigade during the night of 9th/10th June will establish and consolidate a firing line from the ARRAS - DOUAI Railway at a point I.14.a.7.6. Northwards to COD trench at L.8.c.2.5. This line will be continued NORTHWARDS along COD and CUTBERT trenches by 34th Division. It will be connected by communication trenches to the CUPID, CURLY and CHARLES LINE.

(b) The 1st South African Infantry Brigade will furnish one composite Battalion (Lieut.Col. McLEOD) of 400 rifles composed of 4th S.A.I. and 1 company, 2nd S.A.I.

(c) This Battalion will be at the disposal of G.O.C. 26th Infantry Brigade, and will be the Battalion in Brigade reserve during the above mentioned operation. The Composite Battalion will be located at STIRLING CAMP (H.13.d.6.6.)

2. INTENTION.

The C. O. intends to furnish a composite company for attachment to the 4th S.A.Infantry.

3. ORGANIXATION.

The Composite Company (Captain R.N.JENKINS) will consist of 4 officers and 103 other ranks, organized into 3 platoons and Company Headquarters, (including 4 Stretcher Bearers) "A" Company will supply 2 officers and 43 other ranks and "B" Company 1 officer and 29 other ranks. The Brigade Signalling Class will furnish 27 other ranks. Two runners and two signallers will be supplied by Battalion Headquarters. Three lewis guns and mobilization equipment will be supplied by the respective companies concerned.

4. DISTRIBUTION.

The Composite Company will parade in Fighting Order and the officer in command (Captain R.N. JENKINS) will report with his company to Adjutant, 4th S.A.Infantry at the OIL WORKS, PLACE ST. CROIX at 6.30. p.m. to-day.

5. RATIONS.

Rations will be carried for one day. The Company will be rationed subsequently by the 4th S.A.Infantry.

Issued at 6.30. a.m.

Captain & A/Adjutant,
2nd Regiment S.A.Infantry.

Copies Nos.1 & 2. Retained.
Copy No. 3. Captain Jenkins.
Copy No. 4. O.C. "A" Coy. Capt. Bryant.
Copy No. 5. O.C. "B" Coy. Lieut. Stein.

----

9. **ADVANCE PARTY.** Lieut. PEARSE and billeting party will report to 2nd Lieut. SWEENEY at Town Major's Office, "Y" HUTS at 12. noon. to-day.

Issued at 8.a.m.

R Bromley
Captain & A/Adjutant,
2nd S.A.I.

Copies Nos. 1 & 2. retained.
Copy No. 3. O.C. "A" Coy. to Capt. Bryant personally.
" No. 4. O.C. "B" Coy. to Lieut.Stein "
" No. 5. O.C. "C" Coy. to Lt. Pearse "
" No. 6. O.C. "D" Coy. to Capt. Jenkins "
" No. 7. O.C. Working Party by cyclist orderly. (Capt Kimpton)
" No. 8. Transport Officer. personally

----

app V

To. Whom Awarded.	Act for which Recommended	Nature of Award	Authority
No 7062 Private William. Bertram. Miller. Ellwood.	For conspicuous devotion to duty when employed as runner during operations from April 9th to 12th 1917. He was constantly employed running with messages under heavy shell ~~fire~~ and machine gun fire between Company and Battalion Headquarters and although suffering severely from exhaustion he refused on several occasions to be relieved from his duties until severely wounded. He set a fine example of pluck and dash.	Military Medal.	Divisional Routine Order Dated. 10-6-17
No 8334. Private Harold. James. Cole.	For conspicuous devotion to duty whilst employed as company runner during operations between 9th and 12th April 1917. He showed great courage in the execution of his duties, on several occasions he carried messages between Company and Battalion Headquarters under heavy shell and machine gun fire. On the 12th April at the attack near Fampoux he dressed the wounds of his Company Commander and a Sergeant under heavy fire, and when the attack had been held up he assisted the company Commander, who was severely wounded to a place of safety. In the Fampoux attack when the company Commander was wounded he wrote a message at the dictation ~~and~~ of this officer and delivered it at Battalion Headquarters, where he was also able to supply further clear details of the situation.	Military Medal	Divisional Routine Order Dated 10. 6. 1917

To Whom Awarded	Act for which Recommended	Nature of Award	Authority
No. 7814 Sergeant Victor Clifford Moore.	For conspicuous gallantry and good leadership during operations on April 9th 1917. Throughout the day this N.C.O was particularly noticeable for his dash and coolness under fire. He inspired all his command by his fearless bearing and his good leadership. He has always been conspicuous for his devotion to duty.	Military Medal	9th Divisional Routine Order Dated 10-6-1917
No. 6617. Private Gideon George Pringle	For conspicuous gallantry in action near Fampoux on April 12th 1917. When the Platoon officer and all the N.C.Os of his platoon had become casualties he took the initiative and lead the Platoon in the advance. He continued to do so until he and practically all the platoon had been killed or wounded. He showed great coolness and courage at all times during operations.	Military Medal	Divisional Routine Order Dated 10-6-1917
No 2175 Private John Forbes	For conspicuous gallantry and devotion to duty whilst employed as company runner on the 12th April 1917 at Fampoux. Although severely wounded he continued in the execution of his duties, until compelled by exhaustion and loss of blood, to give in. He has at all times in the past shewn conspicuous courage in the execution of his duty.	Military Medal	Divisional Routine Order Dated 10-6-1917

To Whom Awarded	Act for Which Recommended.	Award	Authority.
No 1607. Privite George Garnet Tanner.	This soldier during the operations in Delville Wood, showed great courage and determination under very exceptional circumstances. He had been sent back by his company commander at a critical moment to explain the serious position the company was placed in, as the greater majority had been killed or wounded. To carry out his instructions he had to penetrate a devastating barrage, and unflinchingly faced it and although successful in making the report to Battalion Headquarters, it was seen that he was badly shell-shocked having been blown up. In spite of this Privite Tanner although suffering considerably and very badly shaken, insisted upon returning with the reply. I did not consider he was in a fit state to make the attempt, but no other man was available and he was permitted to go, although I recognised he had been given and accepted a most dangerous task owing to the terrible fire of all discriptions. This instance of this mans conduct has often been brought up, but not knowing his name, it was only the other day that I met him and recognised Privite Tanner as a man whose conduct was outstanding in Delville Wood on July 19th 1916.	Distinguished Conduct Medal.	London Gazette Part. 2. Orders from Base

There in new lines will be
similarly taken over.
Receipts will be forwarded to
Batt HQ by 10 AM 9th inst

All orders taken over from
1st SAI will be obeyed

1st SAI have arranged to
leave 1 Officer & 1 Signaller
to hand over stores orders
& telephones to companies in
their new lines.

On relief Batt HQ will be
in DIVISIONAL RESERVE
LINE

Completion of relief will be reported
to Batt HQ by code word RAIN.

Issued at 2 PM

R Bromley
Capt Adjt

Copy No 1 OC A Coy
2 - B Coy
3 C -
4 - D -
5 1st SAI
6 File
7 8 War diary

A + B Companies commencing
at 4.45 PM
D + C Companies commencing
at 6.45 PM

Order of relief A B D C Coys
which will be relieved by opposite
companies of 1st SAI.

6(a) 1 Guide per platoon and 1 guide
for each Coy H.Q. will
report at Batt H.Q. at
3.30 PM Each guide will
be in possession of a ticket
showing number + Company

b) 1st SAI will supply a
similar number of guides
to guide companies to lines
indicated in Para 3

c) B Coy will obtain fresh guides
also provided by 1st SAI on
Sunken road at present Batt
H.Q to guide them to their
lines.

7 All trench stores, defence
orders and telephones will be
handed over and receipts
obtained.

Copy No. 2

ORDER NO: 76. app. VII

Reference
Sheet 51C.
1/40,000.

In the Field,
14th June, 1917.

1. INFORMATION. There will be a redistribution of the Units of the 1st South African Infantry Brigade within the Brigade area.

2. INTENTION. The O.C. intends to march to LARASSET at 3.p.m. to-day.

3. DISTRIBUTION. The Battalion, less working parties, will parade in line, in full marching order, at 2.45. p.m. to-day in the following order:-
Drums, Headquarters, "A" Coy. "B" Coy. "C" Coy. "D" Coy.
Transport will march in rear of the Battalion.
The head of the column will pass the starting point at 3.p.m.

4. STARTING POINT. Starting point, the junction of the camp road and the main road.

5. ROUTE. From "Y" HUTS to LARASSET, via the HERMAVILLE road.

6. BILLETS. All men will be clear of billets at 2.30. p.m. at which time the usual inspection will take place. Billet certificates will be handed to Orderly Room at 2.30. p.m.

7. BAGGAGE. (a) All Baggage and lewis guns will be piled near the track NORTH WEST of the camp ready for loading at 2.p.m. Each company will detail 1 N.C.O. and 5. men for loading.
(b) 1 Lewis Gunner per company will accompany guns with transport.
(c) All baggage will be loaded under the supervision of the Transport Officer.

8. STATES. Marching states will be handed to Orderly Room at 2.0. p.m. and on arrival at LARRSSET billets, respectively.

9. ADVANCE PARTY. 1 N.C.O. per company will report to 2nd Lieut. RICHES at LARASSET huts at 2.30. p.m. to-day.

10. REPORTS. Reports to the head of the column.

Issued at 10.30. a.m.

A Bamsley
Captain & A/Adjutant,
2nd S. A. I.

Copies Nos. 1 & 2.	Retained.
Copy No. 3.	O/C. "A" Coy. personally.
Copy No. 4.	O/C. "B" Coy. personally.
Copy No. 5.	O/C. "C" Coy. personally.
Copy No. 6.	O/C. "D" Coy. do.
Copy No. 7.	Transport Officer.

App VIII

To Whom Awarded	Act for Which Recommended	Award	Authority
2nd Lieutenant Brian Pope Hennessy	For conspicuous and fearless leadership on the 12th April at Fampoux. After his company Commander and a large number of men had become casualties, he immediately collected and organized all available men and pushed on the advance under heavy shell and machine gun fire until he himself was severely wounded. By his fearless example he inspired all with confidence.	Military Cross	Brigade Routine Order No 135 Dated 15-6-17.

app IV

To Whom Awarded	Act for Which Recommended	Award	Authority
2nd Lieutenant Maurice Esmond Whelan	For conspicuous gallantry and good leadership during the attack on April 9th 1917. This officer throughout the day was particularly noticeable for his dash and splendid example of utter disregard of personal danger. He was eventually very seriously wounded by our barrage when gallantly leading close on the heels of the barrage. Even when very seriously wounded he continued to push on until completely exhausted. His example was beyond praise.	Military Cross	Brigade Routine Order 22-6-1917.

Instructions regarding War Diaries and Intelligence Summaries are contained in F. S. Regs., Part II. and the Staff Manual respectively. Title pages will be prepared in manuscript.

WAR DIARY

2nd SOUTH AFRICAN INFANTRY

~~INTELLIGENCE SUMMARY~~

(Erase heading not required.)

Army Form C. 2118.

Place	Date	Hour	Summary of Events and Information	Remarks and references to Appendices
LARESSET	1.7.17		Church Parades for all denominations. Weather fine. Strength 37 Officers 610 O.R.	
Do	2.7.17		Regiment at general training including company and platoon attack practice. Lt G.G.GREEN M.C. having been evacuated to ENGLAND is struck off the strength of the regiment. DRAFT of 29 O.R. arrived from Base taken on strength. *2707 Pte RAWLINGS J. granted ten days leave to ENGLAND. Weather fine. Strength 57 Officers 610 O.R.	
Do	3.7.17		Regiment at general training. Weather fine. Strength 36 Officers 637 O.R. 2nd Lt A.B.COOPER and 1 NCO proceeded on General Course at XVII Corps Infantry School, HAUTE-AVESNES.	
Do	4.7.17		Regiment at general training. *6388 L/Cpl PHIPSON W.W. granted ten days leave to ENGLAND. Weather raining till midday then fair. Strength 36 Officers 637 O.R.	

A6945 Wt. W11422 M1160 350,000 12/16 D. D. & L. Forms C. 2118/14.

Instructions regarding War Diaries and Intelligence Summaries are contained in F. S. Regs., Part II. and the Staff Manual respectively. Title pages will be prepared in manuscript.

WAR DIARY

2nd REGT SOUTH AFRICAN INFANTRY

~~INTELLIGENCE SUMMARY~~

(*Erase heading not required.*)

Army Form C. 2118.

Place	Date	Hour	Summary of Events and Information	Remarks and references to Appendices
LARESSET	5.7.17		Regiment at General Training. Lt D.E. LUCAS rejoined from leave. 2nd Lt A.D. COOPER and 1 O.R. proceeded to HAUTE-AVESNES for General Course at XVII Corps School. Weather fine. Strength 36 Officers 636 O.R.	
	6.7.17		Regiment moved to SIMENCOURT. Map Ref. G.10.6. A DRAFT [illegible] of 18 O.R. arrived from Base. *1622 Pte D.J. BENNETT and 2nd [illegible]. Pte H.J.S. PLEASS granted 10 days leave to ENGLAND. Weather fine. Strength 35 Officers 655 O.R. MAJOR [illegible] left for a three months course (Senior Officers) [illegible] in ENGLAND.	App I [illegible]
SIMENCOURT.	7.7.17		Regimental Route March in the morning. Company drill in afternoon. Recruits under R.S.M. for training. Weather fine. Strength:- With unit 28 Officers 581 O.R.; Not with Unit 7 " 72 "; TOTAL 35 Officers 653 O.R.	

Instructions regarding War Diaries and Intelligence Summaries are contained in F. S. Regs., Part II. and the Staff Manual respectively. Title pages will be prepared in manuscript.

WAR DIARY
2nd REGT. SOUTH AFRICAN INFANTRY.
INTELLIGENCE SUMMARY.
(Erase heading not required.)

Army Form C. 2118.

Place	Date	Hour	Summary of Events and Information	Remarks and references to Appendices
SIMENCOURT	11.7.17		ten days leave to ENGLAND. Weather fine. Strength 36 Officers 677 O.R. 2nd Lt F.L. MARILLIER invalided to ENGLAND.	
Do	12.7.17		Regiment at training on XVIII Corps training ground near WAILLY. No 4725 L/Cpl SEDDON L.J. and Pte WAGNER A.G. (No 4686) granted ten days leave to ENGLAND. Weather fine. Strength 36 Officers 671 OR	
Do	13.7.17		Regiment at general training. 2nd Lt F.L. MARILLIER invalided to ENGLAND. Weather fine. Strength 35 Officers 669 O.R.	
Do	14.7.17		Regiment at general training. 6 men sent to base as unfit for duty in front line. No 3006 Sgt. FRITCHLEY J.R. and No 3707 Pte SMITH J.N. granted ten days leave to ENGLAND. 2nd Lt J.N. HARVEY left for Lewis Gun Course at XVIII Corps School HAUTE-AVESNES. Strength 35 Officers 669 O.R. 2 O.R. granted 10 days leave to ENGLAND.	

A6945 Wt. W11422/M1160 350,000 12/16 D. D. & L. Forms/C./2118/14.

Instructions regarding War Diaries and Intelligence Summaries are contained in F. S. Regs., Part II. and the Staff Manual respectively. Title pages will be prepared in manuscript.

WAR DIARY

~~INTELLIGENCE SUMMARY~~

2ND REGT. SOUTH AFRICAN INFANTRY.

(Erase heading not required.)

Army Form C. 2118.

Place	Date	Hour	Summary of Events and Information	Remarks and references to Appendices
SIMENCOURT	15.7.17		Church parades for all denominations. CAPT L.M. JACOBS and 2ND LT WYLIE with a draft of 171 OR arrived from base. 2ND LT L.EGAN returned from Brigade Signalling Class. 2ND LT C.O. CONNOCK proceeded to BERNEVILLE on Brigade Physical Training and Bayonet Fighting Class; 2ND LT C.H. ROBERTS returned from this Class. LT DE LUCAS proceeded to 3RD ARMY Musketry School at ALBERT. Weather showery. Strength 35 Officers 663 O.R. Two OR proceeded, on 10 days leave, to ENGLAND	
Do	16.7.17		Regiment at General Training. CAPT R. BEVERLEY. M.C. and 2ND LT G.V. MERRIMAN granted 10 days leave to ENGLAND. CAPT R.C. KNIGHT appointed acting Adjutant during the absence of CAPT R BEVERLEY M.C. on leave. Weather fine.	
			Strength:- With Unit — OFFICERS 27, O.R. 748	
			Not with Unit — OFFICERS 10, O.R. 84	
			TOTAL — OFFICERS 37, O.R. 832	

Army Form C. 2118.

Instructions regarding War Diaries and Intelligence Summaries are contained in F. S. Regs., Part II. and the Staff Manual respectively. Title pages will be prepared in manuscript.

WAR DIARY
2nd REGT. SOUTH AFRICAN INF.
or
INTELLIGENCE SUMMARY.
(Erase heading not required.)

Place	Date	Hour	Summary of Events and Information	Remarks and references to Appendices
SIMENCOURT	8.7.17		Church Parades for all denominations. 2510 L/Cpl KIRBY S.A. and 2821 Pte SHACKELTON R.H. granted 10 days leave to ENGLAND. 2nd Lt C.H. ROBERTS and 4 NCOs joined Brigade Physical and Bayonet Fighting Class at BERNEVILLE. Weather cloudy, some showers. Strength 35 Officers 653 OR. 1 NCO proceeded on SNIPING COURSE at IIIrd Army Scouting School	
Do	9.7.17		Regiment at General training. DRAFT consisting of Capt F.A. LAGERWALL and 12 O.R. arrived from base. Weather cloudy, some showers. Strength 35 Officers 653 O.R.	
Do	10.7.17		Regiment at General training on training area in vicinity of WAILLY. DRAFT of 14 O.R. arrived from base. Weather fine. Strength 36 Officers 663 O.R	
Do	11.7.17		Regiment at General training. 2nd Lt F.E. MILLS, Sgt THOMSON W.G., Pte 971 BRUKEKSHA S.R. and 2773 Pte TIERNEY G. granted ten days	

Instructions regarding War Diaries and Intelligence Summaries are contained in F. S. Regs., Part II. and the Staff Manual respectively. Title pages will be prepared in manuscript.

WAR DIARY
2nd REGT. SOUTH AFRICAN INFANTRY
or ~~INTELLIGENCE SUMMARY~~

(Erase heading not required.)

Army Form C. 2118.

Place	Date	Hour	Summary of Events and Information	Remarks and references to Appendices
SIMENCOURT	17.7.17		Regiment at attack practice at training area WAILLY. No. 1095 Cpl BONES N.V., No. 5563 Pte ALLSOPP L.V. and No. 1100 Pte BOCK G.C. granted ten day leave to ENGLAND. Weather showery. Strength 37 Officers 831 O.R.	
Do	18.7.17		Regiment marched to training area WAILLY and took part in Brigade Attack scheme. No. 1102 Pte C A BARRETT and 3824 Pte E A ASHWORTH granted ten days leave to ENGLAND. Weather showery. Strength 37 Officers 828 O.R.	
Do	19.9.17		Regiment at Advance Guard practice on training area, WAILLY. No. 1102 Pte A.E. DOVEY and No. 4490 Pte G.V. DAWSON proceeded on ten days leave to ENGLAND. Weather cloudy, fine. Strength 37 Officers 828 O.R. 16 Stretcher Bearers proceeded to AVESNES-LE-COMTE for training course with S.A.F.A.	

A6945 Wt. W11422/M1160 350,000 12/16 D. D. & L. Forms/C./2118/14.

Instructions regarding War Diaries and Intelligence Summaries are contained in F. S. Regs., Part II. and the Staff Manual respectively. Title pages will be prepared in manuscript.

WAR DIARY

Army Form C. 2118.

2ND SOUTH AFRICAN INFANTRY.

~~INTELLIGENCE SUMMARY.~~

(Erase heading not required.)

Place	Date	Hour	Summary of Events and Information	Remarks and references to Appendices
SIMENCOURT	20.7.17		Regiment at general training. Bathing at Baths SIMENCOURT. Swimming at ponds BERNEVILLE. 2726 PTE GRIFFITHS granted ten days leave to ENGLAND. Weather fine. Strength 37 Officers 843 O.R.	

Instructions regarding War Diaries and Intelligence Summaries are contained in F. S. Regs., Part II. and the Staff Manual respectively. Title pages will be prepared in manuscript.

WAR DIARY

2nd REGT. SOUTH AFRICAN INFANTRY.

(Erase heading not required.)

Army Form C. 2118.

Place	Date	Hour	Summary of Events and Information	Remarks and references to Appendices
SIMENCOURT.	23.7.17		Regiment practicing Advance Guard work at training area WAILLY. Extracts from Supplement to the London Gazette dated 11th and 17th July 1917:-	
			SOUTH AFRICAN INFANTRY.	
			The undermentioned to be 2nd LIEUTENANTS :-	
			No 3660 Cpl. H. PERRY.	
			No 4654 Cpl. F.H.F. HATCHARD.	
			No 2734 L/Cpl. F.A. BARNETT.	
			No 4602 Pte. F.A. AULD.	
			9th DIVISIONAL CINEMA showed on 2nd REGT. Parade Ground, SIMENCOURT.	
			Weather fine. Strength 37 Officers 837 O.R.	
Do	24.7.17		Regiment at general training. New draft on range SIMENCOURT practicing grouping and application. Night Operations carried out between 9 and 11 P.M.	

A6945 Wt. W11422/M1160 350,000 12/16 D. D. & L. Forms/C./2118/14.

Army Form C. 2118.

Instructions regarding War Diaries and Intelligence Summaries are contained in F. S. Regs., Part II. and the Staff Manual respectively. Title pages will be prepared in manuscript.

WAR DIARY
2ND REGT. SOUTH ~~or~~ AFRICAN INFANTRY
~~INTELLIGENCE SUMMARY.~~
(Erase heading not required.)

Place	Date	Hour	Summary of Events and Information	Remarks and references to Appendices
SIMENCOURT.	21.7.17		Regiment at general training. DRAFT of 17 O.R. arrived from base taken on strength with effect from 19.7.17. In the final Rugby Football match for Major General Lukin's Cup, the 1st REGT SAI beat the 2nd REGT S.A.I 18pts-8. Weather fine. Strength 37 Officers 842 O.R. "3821 Pte CLEVERLEY proceeded to ENGLAND on ten days leave.	
Do	22.7.17		Church Parades for all denominations. 7944 L/Cpl WILLARD. W.F. proceded to ENGLAND on a Cadet Course. "3171 Pte MAY J proceeded to ENGLAND on ten days leave. 2nd Lt J.C. CRAGG rejoined regiment from Hospital. Weather fine. Strength :-	

	Officers	OR
With Unit	23	567
Not with Unit	14	275
TOTAL	37	842

Instructions regarding War Diaries and Intelligence Summaries are contained in F. S. Regs., Part II. and the Staff Manual respectively. Title pages will be prepared in manuscript.

WAR DIARY

2nd REGT. SOUTH AFRICAN INF or ~~INTELLIGENCE SUMMARY.~~

(Erase heading not required.)

Army Form C.

Place	Date	Hour	Summary of Events and Information	Remarks and references to Appendices
SIMENCOURT	24.7.17		(Contd) Medical Officer inspected every man in camp. The following NCO and MAN granted ten days leave to ENGLAND :- 2400 L/Cpl F. METH from 24/7/17, 4453 Pte GEERCKE. J. Weather fine. Strength 37 Officers 837 OR. 2nd Lt E. LEWELL arrived from base, and a draft of 32 O.R.	
Do	25.7.17		Regiment at General Training.	
Do	26.7.17		Regiment at SIMENCOURT. General fatigues and camp cleaning. Kit inspection under company arrangements. Transport details and advance party left at 8pm for SAULTY to entrain for BAPAUME, remainder of	
Do	[illegible]		Transport left 8.30 AM by March route for NEUVILLE BOURJONVAL. General preparations for move tomorrow to new area.	

Instructions regarding War Diaries and Intelligence Summaries are contained in F. S. Regs., Part II. and the Staff Manual respectively. Title pages will be prepared in manuscript.

WAR DIARY
or
INTELLIGENCE SUMMARY.
(Erase heading not required.)

Army Form C. 2118.

Place	Date	Hour	Summary of Events and Information	Remarks and references to Appendices
SYMENCOURT	27.7.17		2/Lt ROBERTS and 6 ORs on 10 days leave to England. 9th Division moves to IV Corps. Regiment moves in accordance with ORDER No 78 to new AREA and billets at NEUVILLE BOURJONVAL. Ref. Sheet 57 C Ed 2 1/40000 P 22. Arrived at destination 8 pm.	App. I ORDER 78 Ref. 57c 1/40000
NEUVILLE BOURJONVAL	28.7.17		Battalion moves into the line to take over TRESCAULT sub-section (left) of Centre section of right sector - taken over from 58th Division - moves in accordance with Order No 79. Batt. takes over from 2/8th London Regt on night of 28th/29th. Three ORs sent to Base. 11 ORs Town Majors of BARASTRE and LECHELLE. Two ORs to S A Bde as observers.	App. I ORDER 79 Ref 57c 1/40000
TRESCAULT TRENCHES	29.7.17		Battalion settled down in trenches - TRESCAULT SECTION left Battalion - Patrols out at night. Casualties 1 OR Killed, 2/Lt BIRREL & 1 OR wounded in encounter with enemy. - Quiet line no enemy activity. Capt BEVERLEY and 2/Lt Merriman returned from leave.	

Instructions regarding War Diaries and Intelligence Summaries are contained in F. S. Regs., Part II. and the Staff Manual respectively. Title pages will be prepared in manuscript.

WAR DIARY
or
INTELLIGENCE SUMMARY.
(*Erase heading not required.*)

Army Form C. 2118.

Place	Date	Hour	Summary of Events and Information	Remarks and references to Appendices
TRESCAULT SECTOIN.	30 7 17		'A' Company reports casualties 1 OR Killed, 1 Off & 1 OR wounded. Names as in yesterday's diary. Quiet day. 20 enemy Heavy Trench Mortars fell in front of left company; no damage done. Weather fair & cloudy. – Capt Cochran J.E. rejoined Battalion from S.A. Brigade. – Supervision of works taken over by Capt Cochrane – Rain in afternoon. Enemy quiet.	
Do.	31-7-17		Nothing particular reported from previous night. Patrols out no enemy encountered. Work continued on trenches & firebays, attention paid to draining. Quiet day. Enemy inactive except for a few HTMs on left company front. Little damage done. Rain afternoon & evening, trenches in bad condition. Work continued but all attempts at drainage nullified by rain. Lt King & 2/Lt Harvey returned from courses – 2/Lt J Addison and 2/Lt J.H.A. Hatchard joined from England. Seven other ranks returned from courses & leave. Strength of Regiment 39 & 858 OR.	

1/8/17

W. [signature] Lt. Colonel
Commanding 2nd S.A.I.

A6945 Wt. W11422/M1160 350,000 12/16 D. D. & L. Forms/C./2118/14.

2nd South African Infantry

War Diary

July 1917

Vol 16

Index to Appendices

I Order No 77
" No 78
" No 79.

II Sketch Map of Trescault Trenches occupied by Battalion.

Appendix 1. Copy No. 2

W.D.

ORDER No. 77

In the Field.
5. 7. 1917.

Reference
Sheet 51C.
1/40000.

---

1. **INFORMATION.** The 1st South African Infantry Brigade will move to-morrow to the SIMENCOURT-BERNEVILLE area. Brigade Headquarters will be at BERNEVILLE.

2. **INTENTION.** The C.O. intends to march to SIMENCOURT at 1.p.m. to-morrow.

3. **DISTRIBUTION.** Companies will pass the starting point in the following order:-

   Drums, Headquarters & "D" Coy,
   "C" Coy. "B" Coy. "A" Coy.

   The leading company will pass the starting point at 1.p.m. Four minutes interval will be maintained between companies during the march.

4. **STARTING POINT.** Starting point the cross roads at the junction of the HAUTE AVESNES - AGNEZ- and HERMAVILLE - "Y" HUTS roads.

5. **ROUTE.** From LARASSET due South to SIMENCOURT through AGNEZ-LEZ-DUISANS and BERNEVILLE.

6. **BILLETS.** All men will be clear of billets by 12.noon, at which time arms and equipment will be piled on company parade grounds. Billets will be then finally cleaned and inspected at 12.30.p.m. The usual certificates will be handed to Orderly Room at 12.30. p.m.

7. **BAGGAGE.** (a) All Company Baggage and Lewis guns will be piled at the NORTH side of Billets ready for loading by 11.30. a.m. Each company will detail 1 N.C.O. and 5 men for loading.
   (b) 1 Lewis gunner per company will accompany guns with transport.
   (c) Officers kits and stores will be loaded on the road outside officers quarters at 12.p.m.
   (d) Quartermaster's stores will be loaded by arrangement with the Transport Officer.
   (e) All baggage will be loaded under the supervision of the Transport Officer.

8. **STATES.** Marching states will be handed to Orderly Room at 12.noon. at LARASSET and on arrival at SIMENCOURT billets respectively.

9. **ADVANCE PARTY.** Advance Billeting party will proceed to SIMENCOURT at 12.30. p.m.

10. **REPORTS.** Reports to the head of the column.

Issued at 7.p.m.

[signature]
Captain & Adjutant,
2nd S. A. Infantry.

/over

Copy No. 2

ORDER NO 78

Reference
Sheet 51 c
1/40,000

25th July 1917.

No. 1
INFORMATION.

(a) The 9th Division will be transferred to the 4th Corps on the 4 31st instant and will relieve the 58th Division in the line.

(b) The S. A. Infantry Brigade will move into the 4th Corps Area on the 27th instant and relieve the 174th Infantry Brigade in the line, the following day.

No. 2.
INTENTION.

The O.C. intends to march to BEAUMETZ at which place the battalion (less transport) will entrain and proceed by rail to BAPAUME, thence by route march to NEUVILLE BOURJONVAL.

No. 3.
DISTRIBUTION

(a) The Battalion will entrain as per attached schedule of trains at SAULTY and BEAUMETZ on the 27th instant.

(b) The transport details for Nos. 1 and 2 OMNIBUS TRAINS will parade at 8 pm on the 26th instant and proceed by march route to SAULTY.

(c) The remainder of the Transport will parade at 8-30 AM on the 26th instant and proceed by march route and under separate instructions to NEUVILLE BOURJONVAL.

(d) The Battalion (less Transport) will parade in marching order at 11.45 am and proceed to BEAUMETZ for entrainment.

(e) Upon arrival at the detraining Station arrangements will be made for the evening meal to be served and the Battalion will then proceed to its destination NEUVILLE BOURJONVAL via Le TRANSLOY, ROCQUIGNY, BUS and YTRES.

(f) The following day Saturday, 28th instant the Battalion will take over a portion of the line, details of which will be communicated to all concerned in a further order.

No. 4.
RATIONS.

All ranks will carry the unexpended portion of to-morrows the 27th rations and rations for the following day.

No. 5.
MARCH DISCIPLINE.

During the March from BAPAUME to NEUVILLE BOURJONVAL a distance of 100 yards will be maintained between Companies.

Issued at 8 pm on the 25th July 1917.

[signature]
Captain & A/Adjutant
2nd Regt. S.A.Infantry.

Copies Nos. 1 & 2		Retained.		
Copy No. 3	Handed	to Lieut.	Bryant	"A" Coy.
Copy No. 4	"	" Capt.	Davis	"B" Coy.
Copy No. 5	"	" Lieut.	Pearse	"C" Coy.
Copy No. 6	"	" Capt.	Jenkins	"D" Coy.
Copy No. 7.	"	" 2/Lt.	Arnold, Transport Off.	
Copy No. 8	"	"	Adjutant	
Copy No. 9				

Copy No. 2

ORDER No. 79

Map Reference
Sheets 57c N.E.
57c S.E.

28th July 1917.

No. 1 RELIEF. The Battalion will relieve the 2/8th Battalion London Regiment on the night of the 28/29th July in the LEFT Sub-sector of Centre Sector.

No. 2. DISTRIBUTION. Headquarters S.A.I. will relieve Headquarters 2/8 London Regiment

"A" Company	S.A.I relieves	"C"	Company	London Regt.	(Lef
"D" Company	" "	"A"	"	"	"(right)
"B" Company	" "	"B"	"	"	"(centre
"C" Company	" "	"D"	"	"	"(suppor

No. 3. ROUTE. By train from P.22.c.2.5 to Q.9.d.2.6. in accordance with attached train table.

No. 4. PARADE. Companies will be ready to march off at 7.45 p.m. shar
The order of march will be Headquarters "A" "[illegible]" "D" "B" "C" Companies.

No. 5. GUIDES. One guide per platoon will meet companies at Detrainin point and lead them to their position in the line.

No. 6. DRESS. Full marching order and mobilisation equipment to be carried on person.

No. 7. LEWIS GUNS. Lewis Guns with all drums, ammunition and accessories will be carried to entraining point by teams and taken along in trucks by them.

No. 8. LOG BOOKS. Companies will take over Log Books, maps, defence scheme, etc from the outgoing Regiment.

No. 9 TRENCH STORES. These will be takenmover and receipts in duplicate forwarded to Battalion Headquarters by 9 a.m. 29th instant.

No. 10 WORKING PARTIES. Work taken over will be continued.

No. 11 SIGNALS. O.C. Companies will be responsible that all their Officers and N.C.O.s understand the 2 light signals.

No. 12. TELEPHONES. In accordance with orders in force regarding the use of telephones no message whatever will be sent over t line regarding relief except the code word reporting it.

No. 13. COMPLETION OF RELIEF This will be reported by telephone to Battalion Headquarters by using the code word "GIN.

No. 14 GAS ALERT. The Box respirators will be worn in the alert positio and P.H. worn over the left shoulder and hanging unde the arm.

No. 15 BAGGAGE, COY STORES. OFFICERS MESS BOXES ETC. Everything required to be taken to the line will be dumped at R.Q.M.S.'s stores by 6 p.m. and will be carried up by transport to Battalion Headquarters to-night. The remainder will be dumped at the same pl and time but in a separate heap and will be taken to Transport Lines for storage.

No. 16 RATIONS AND COOKS To-morrow's rations will be carried on person if issu in time, otherwise will be brought up by Transport Company cooks will accompany limbers bringing up cooking utensils.

Issued at 3.30. p.m. 28th July 1917.

R.C. Kranjou[?]

Captain & A/Adjutant
2nd Regt. S.A.Infy.

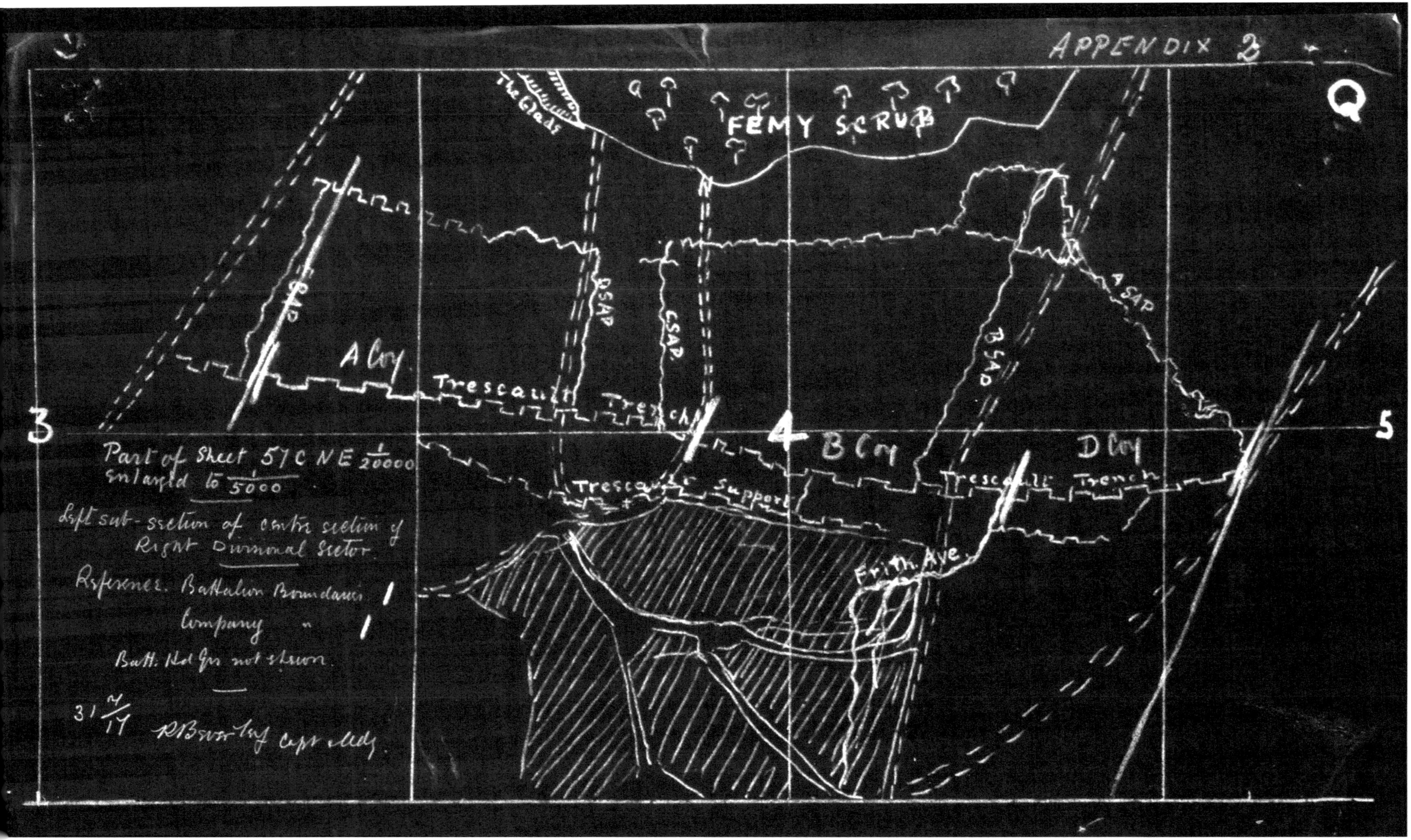
APPENDIX 2
Q
FEMY SCRUB
The Glade
A Coy
B Coy
D Coy
A SAP
B SAP
C SAP
D SAP
E SAP
Trescault Trench
Trescault Support
Frith Ave.
3
4
5
Part of Sheet 57C NE 1/20000
enlarged to 1/5000
Left sub-section of centre section of
Right Divisional Sector
Reference. Battalion Boundaries
Company "
Batt. Hd Qrs not shewn
31/7/17

ENTRAINING TABLE

ENTRAINING TABLE.

28th July 1917.

Entraining Point P.22.c.2.5.

Detraining Point About Q.9.d.2.6.

Time of Entraining 8.30. PM

Train	Occupants	No. of Trucks.	Capacity per truck	Total per train
1st	Headquarters & "A" Company	7	26	182
2nd	"D" Company	7	26	182
3rd	"B" Company	7	26	182
4th	"C" Company	7	26	182
	Total capacity, 4 Trains			728

The trains will be numbered from FRONT to REAR and it is very essential that the above order be adhered to.

R C Knight

Captain & A/Adjutant
2nd Regt. S.A. Infantry.

Instructions regarding War Diaries and Intelligence Summaries are contained in F. S. Regs., Part II. and the Staff Manual respectively. Title pages will be prepared in manuscript.

WAR DIARY

2nd S. A. Infantry

[redacted].

(Erase heading not required.)

Army Form C. 2118.

Place	Date	Hour	Summary of Events and Information	Remarks and references to Appendices
TRESCAULT SECTION	1/8/17		Wet morning. Trenches muddy & wet. Work nullified by rain. Enemy quiet except slight artillery activity in afternoon. No damage done. Explosions heard in village of HAVRINCOURT - not due to gun fire. Our artillery active retaliating 3 or 4 shells to enemy's one. Seven other ranks on leave to England entraining at new railhead BAPAUME. Weather cleared up in the afternoon. 3 Officers 4th S.A.I. arrived for instruction. Usual work proceeding, horse being needed for officers. General Dawson called at office in the afternoon. Lt. G. G. Green M.C. returned from England off sick leave 10 p.m. Fine moonlight evening. C.O. & Lt Green M.C. up to D Coy. 10.45 p.m. Special attention is being paid to salvage of arms S.A.A., rum jars &c, left by previous units. Strength of Regiment In Trenches 23 Off 668 O.R. Total strength 40 Off. 858 O.R.	Sheet 57C N.E. 27-28
do	2/8/17		Usual Trench routine. - Very wet day - Work continued in cleaning, draining & constructing Trenches. Enemy quiet; a few light enemy shells sent over. Nothing serious. Patrols out at night.	

Instructions regarding War Diaries and Intelligence Summaries are contained in F. S. Regs., Part II. and the Staff Manual respectively. Title pages will be prepared in manuscript.

WAR DIARY
or
INTELLIGENCE SUMMARY.
(Erase heading not required.)

Army Form C. 2118.

Place	Date	Hour	Summary of Events and Information	Remarks and references to Appendices
TRUSCAULT SECTION.	3/8/17		Patrol up to B Coy, Sgt Wilson EC 224 & No. 12963 Pte Wright wounded whilst out on patrol. Enemy fired a burst on patrol & then rapidly retired. Relief orders received — Batt: relieved by 4th SAI ORDER No 80 by Lt/Col Tanner CMG attached. Relief effected by 11 PM Batt: proceeded by DECAUVILLE Trains to Billets at YTRES. Arrived 2pm — Rain. Men very tired.	Appendix I. Batt Order No 80.
YTRES Camp	4/8/17		In billets at YTRES — Comfortable & a fair amount of room. Working party to Town Major 1 NCO & 12 men daily also 1 limber. — 3 NCO 20 — 258th Tunnelling Coy at NEUVILLE Bourjonval for work for a fortnight — Sgt MILLS A. Coy in charge. Various duties detailed for tomorrow. Guard also found for billets vacated by 9th Scottish Rifles at YTRES. — Rained intermittently all day — Draft 174 other ranks arrived at 11am. Good quality of men, but undisciplined. Capt Symons returned from Hospital — 2/Lt Cooper returned from 5 week Course.	Sheet 57c P.20.c

A6945 Wt. W11422/M1160 350,000 12/16 D. D. & L. Forms/C./2118/14.

Instructions regarding War Diaries and Intelligence Summaries are contained in F. S. Regs., Part II. and the Staff Manual respectively. Title pages will be prepared in manuscript.

WAR DIARY
or
INTELLIGENCE SUMMARY.
(Erase heading not required.)

Army Form C. 2118.

Place	Date	Hour	Summary of Events and Information	Remarks and references to Appendices
YTRES	5/8/17		Sunday – Weather cleared up – Church parade – C & D Coys on working parties at HAVRINCOURT WOOD all day. Proceed to work by Train. 29 OR ranks on courses – 1 officer & 7 other ranks to Army rest camp at ST VALERY-SUR-SOMME. Draft of 14 O.R. arrived 2pm – C.O inspected draft of 175 which arrived on 4th inst. at 5 p.m. Orders received for Corps Commander's inspection tomorrow.	
"	6/8/17		Weather warm & fine – Corps Commander's parade cancelled. General training carried out, special attention paid to new draft – Capt. Lapwall returned from course. 5 other ranks left on leave. – M/General Lukin CB &c. called at camp in the morning. – Orders received for Corps Commander's inspection tomorrow.	

A6945 Wt. W11422/M1160 350,000 12/16 D. D. & L. Forms/C./2118/14.

Instructions regarding War Diaries and Intelligence Summaries are contained in F. S. Regs., Part II. and the Staff Manual respectively. Title pages will be prepared in manuscript.

WAR DIARY
or
INTELLIGENCE SUMMARY.
(Erase heading not required.)

Army Form C. 2118.

Place	Date	Hour	Summary of Events and Information	Remarks and references to Appendices
YTRES	7/8/17		Fine but dull morning, no rain. Battalion inspected by Corps Commander IVth Corps Lt General Sir C.L. WOOLLCOMBE. K.C.B. – Parade a success, a really smart turnout. 27 Officers & 746 O R including transport on parade. – Afternoon, training as usual. – C.O. Capt Davis, Lt Green visited Delville Wood. Lt Bryant & 2/Lt Marshall to Hospital.	
"	8/8/17		Battalion at training all day nothing unusual happened	
"	9/8/17		Training in the morning, and preparing for move. Battalion less 1 platoon per company will relieve 4th S A I in the left sub-section of TRESCAULT SECTION tonight. – Details & 1st line Transport 5 off & 267 OR move to NEUVILLE BOURJONVAL and EQUANCOURT respectively at 2pm. Heavy rain in the afternoon – Lt Col Tanner CMG to Brigade to take temporary command at 7pm. Battalion moves into line by Decauville Tram, entraining at 8 pm	Sheet 57C

A6945 Wt. W11422/M1160 350,000 12/16 D. D. & L. Forms/C./2118/14.

Army Form C. 2118.

Instructions regarding War Diaries and Intelligence Summaries are contained in F. S. Regs., Part II. and the Staff Manual respectively. Title pages will be prepared in manuscript.

WAR DIARY
or
INTELLIGENCE SUMMARY.
(Erase heading not required.)

Place	Date	Hour	Summary of Events and Information	Remarks and references to Appendices
	9/8/17		at Canteen Siding at YTRES. Major Cochran in command. Quiet in trenches relief completed 12.30 midnight. – Promotions notified in BRO 174 Capt. F E COCHRAN to be Major – 2/Lt E C BRYANT to be Captain – 2/Lt J. ADDISON to be Lieut. Strength 39 off: 1043 OR	ORDER No 81
TRESCAULT SECTION LEFT SUB SECTION	10/8/17		Quiet night. Gas projectors should have been discharged from the Brigade section on our left; postponed three times & finally cancelled. Fine weather. Trenches drying up. Our Artillery 18lb guns Battery 51 D very active up to 12.30 am firing at back areas behind HAVRINCOURT. Our machine guns 28th MG Coy also active up to 11 30 PM. Enemy machine guns fired a few bursts on the roads in & leading to TRESCAULT village. Usual work wiring &c done during the night. Gas projectors again notified as last night & cancelled about 9 pm. Very fine clear evening. 2/Lt Craggs patrol found all quiet on enemy wire.	

A6945 Wt. W11422/M1160 350,000 12/16 D. D. & L. Forms/C./2118/14.

WAR DIARY
or
~~INTELLIGENCE SUMMARY~~.
(Erase heading not required.)

Instructions regarding War Diaries and Intelligence Summaries are contained in F. S. Regs., Part II. and the Staff Manual respectively. Title pages will be prepared in manuscript.

Army Form C. 2118.

Place	Date	Hour	Summary of Events and Information	Remarks and references to Appendices
TRESCAULT SECTION LEFT SUB SECTION	11/8/17		No activity early morning. Very fine bright day, warm. Enemy sent a few 10 CM Howitzer shells and a few gas shells on support line. No casualties. RE officer O/C 64th Coy R.E. called re work. Lt Col Tanner CMG acting Brigadier went round the lines. Brigade recall all rifle Grenades except Mill 23 an SOS - SOS grenades recalled (made between 1-9 July) - Quiet night. 1 Casualty No 12110 Pte Davis AS wounded. Expected discharge of gas cylinders from left Brigade front expected, postponed & finally cancelled. Weather showery but generally fine. Work on Trenches continuing, wire being strengthened &c.	
	12/8/17		Fine day inclined to be showery. No activity. 10th A&SH relieved 8 RH on our left front. Enemy machine guns fairly active at night. Slight artillery activity on both sides. Night cloudy with slight rain. Company dumps established by working party from 4th SAI. Usual patrols report little enemy activity at night except work in FEMY SCRUB.	51C K34 central

A6945 Wt. W11422/M1160 350,000 12/16 D. D. & L. Forms/C./2118/14.

Instructions regarding War Diaries and Intelligence Summaries are contained in F. S. Regs., Part II. and the Staff Manual respectively. Title pages will be prepared in manuscript.

WAR DIARY
or
INTELLIGENCE SUMMARY.
(Erase heading not required.)

Army Form C. 2118.

Place	Date	Hour	Summary of Events and Information	Remarks and references to Appendices
TRESCAULT LEFT SUBSECTION	13/8/17		Very quiet day. Intermittent rain but warm. Usual work proceeding. Bath house complete. Kitchens started. S.A. L.T.M.B. registered on certain points in enemy outpost line, they were covered by 51st Bde R.F.A. Registration successful. Usual reconnaissance patrols out. No contact with the enemy. Quiet night. Usual patrols	
	14/8/17		Fine day. A little rain later. L.T.Mortars and Field guns shelled outpost line at FEMY WOOD and HAVRINCOURT. Work on trenches improving. Kitchen excavation going well ahead. Our artillery was fairly active at night. Enemy sent over 10 H.T.M. shells (Minnenwerfer) at about 5-6 pm. 3 slight casualties, Trench of Left Company blown in. Rain at night. Usual reconnaissance patrols - no enemy encountered	

Instructions regarding War Diaries and Intelligence Summaries are contained in F. S. Regs., Part II. and the Staff Manual respectively. Title pages will be prepared in manuscript.

WAR DIARY
or
INTELLIGENCE SUMMARY.
(Erase heading not required.)

Army Form C. 2118.

Place	Date	Hour	Summary of Events and Information	Remarks and references to Appendices
TRESCAULT SECTION LEFT SUBSECTION	15/8/17		Intermittent rain all day. Enemy activity nil, one of the quietest days since relief. Our artillery fired a few shells during the day. Greater activity at night, when enemy back areas were shelled. Work in trenches proceeding. General improvement to firebays, and sap heads progressing. Excavation for Kitchen commenced in Fifth Avenue. Work commenced on H.T.M. emplacement in TRESCAULT. Preparations being made for Raid on enemy lines.	
	16/8/17		Preparations continuing for raid. Intermittent rain all day. 2/Lt Mills made a reconnaissance of wire at point to be raided, before dawn. Raiding party withdrawn to ~~[illegible]~~ HAVRINCOURT WOOD to rest for the day. Fine weather. One shower of rain in afternoon. Working parties withdrawn from the line on account of raid. Preparations for raid complete by 11 P.M. 2/Lt Mills and 32 O.R. detailed for this operation.	

Army Form C. 2118.

Instructions regarding War Diaries and Intelligence Summaries are contained in F. S. Regs., Part II. and the Staff Manual respectively. Title pages will be prepared in manuscript.

WAR DIARY

or

(Erase heading not required.)

Place	Date	Hour	Summary of Events and Information	Remarks and references to Appendices
TRESCAULT SECTION LEFT SUBSECTION	17/8/17	1am	Raiding party in B sap ready to go over. Party reached wire in safety. Three systems of wire were found. Party failed to penetrate 3rd system and were forced to return. All arms co-operated in raid as follows. 50th & 51st Bde of field artillery including Field Howitzer Batteries. H.T.Mortars 1 Gun. S.A.L.T.M. Battery (Capt Featherstone) 28th M.G. Company. For full details of Raid vide Appendices 2 & 3. Party returned and mustered at Batt Hd Qrs at 3 AM No casualties. Very fine clear dawn and warm day. Four enemy Aeroplanes over our lines 4.45 am. They flew through A.A. Barrage but made off north on appearance of 4 of our planes. Preparing for relief by 4th SAI tonight. Batt relieved by 4th SAI vide order No 83. Relief completed & Batt moved into billets at METZ (51 C 1/40000). Move completed by 4 am.	Appendix 2 Op Order 82 Instructions re above. Reports on raid by Major Cochran & 2/Lt Mills Appendix 3 AREA Map. TRESCAULT SECTION
METZ	18/8/17		Battalion in Brigade reserve at METZ. Fine day. Day spent in settling down in Billets. 3 officers & 104 O.R. working for IV Corps Signals, digging cable trench, all night between Right & Left Batts. in TRESCAULT SECTION.	

A6945 Wt. W11422/M1160 350,000 12/16 D. D. & L. Forms/C./2118/14.

Army Form C. 2118.

Instructions regarding War Diaries and Intelligence Summaries are contained in F. S. Regs., Part II. and the Staff Manual respectively. Title pages will be prepared in manuscript.

WAR DIARY
or
INTELLIGENCE SUMMARY.
(Erase heading not required.)

Place	Date	Hour	Summary of Events and Information	Remarks and references to Appendices
~~[illegible]~~ METZ	19/8/17		Sunday. Men on working parties paraded 12 noon for inspection. Church parades. C of E 2.30 pm + 4.15 pm. – Wesleyan etc 3 pm. RC 12 noon. Night working parties, 7 officers and 383 OR, on working parties in trenches. Beautifully fine weather. Strength of Battalion. 41 off. 1072 OR – with unit 23 off. ~~625 OR~~ 787 OR, not with unit 18 off 285 OR.	
	20/8/17		Training in morning and afternoon for all available men. Working parties at night. 9 officers 18 Sgts 435 OR. Fine weather. Batt. supplied firing party for 2/Lt McMillan & 1 Sgt's funeral of 4th SAI. Certain officers & platoons redistributed amongst billets. 2 OR on leave. 15 OR to rest camp at St Valery sur Somme. Several German aeroplanes hovered with impunity over METZ despite our AA gun fire.	

Army Form C. 2118.

WAR DIARY

or

~~INTELLIGENCE SUMMARY~~.

(Erase heading not required.)

Instructions regarding War Diaries and Intelligence Summaries are contained in F. S. Regs., Part II. and the Staff Manual respectively. Title pages will be prepared in manuscript.

Place	Date	Hour	Summary of Events and Information	Remarks and references to Appendices
METZ	21/8/17		Fine day not too warm. Training carried on as far as possible, but interfered with by working party etc. Bomb throwing in the afternoon by recruits. German aeroplanes over METZ despite of AA guns shooting. Working parties 9 Officers, 8 Sgts 440 O R ranks working for R.E.s, & Divisional Signal Company. 2 O.R on leave.	
"	22/8/17		Fine day; Training as usual. Bomb practice with live Bombs completed by recruits. Nothing unusual occurred. Inter company football in afternoon	
	23/8/17		Training at METZ. Fine day. C O R M O & Company commanders went to BUS to attend a day's instructional course at Divisional Gas school. – Football in afternoon. Lt Lucas & 1 O R on leave.	

Army Form C. 2118.

WAR DIARY
or
~~INTELLIGENCE SUMMARY~~.
(Erase heading not required.)

Instructions regarding War Diaries and Intelligence Summaries are contained in F. S. Regs., Part II. and the Staff Manual respectively. Title pages will be prepared in manuscript.

Place	Date	Hour	Summary of Events and Information	Remarks and references to Appendices
METZ	24/8/17		Usual training. Football in afternoon. Slight rain. Usual working parties. 2/Lt Cooper & 1 OR on leave.	
	25/8/17		Training as usual. Football in afternoon. Working parties. 9 officers and 440 OR variously distributed working in front area in TRESCAULT SECTION. Weather fine but somewhat colder. 2 OR on leave - 1 officer 4 OR on courses. Strength of unit - With unit 24 off. 827 OR. Not with unit 18 off 236 OR. 42 1063.	
	26/8/17		Church parades in morning + afternoon. Enemy shelled artillery position all day with 10 cm shells. No shells in village. Weather cold. 2 OR on leave. Working parties reduced owing to anticipated move. 2 officers 58 OR on working parties under 63rd Coy RE. — Heavy rain for 1 hour in evening.	

Army Form C. 2118.

WAR DIARY

or

~~INTELLIGENCE SUMMARY.~~

(Erase heading not required.)

Instructions regarding War Diaries and Intelligence Summaries are contained in F. S. Regs., Part II. and the Staff Manual respectively. Title pages will be prepared in manuscript.

Place	Date	Hour	Summary of Events and Information	Remarks and references to Appendices
METZ	27/8/17		Training during the morning. Afternoon camp cleaning & general fatigues preparatory to move. Rain in afternoon. Col Tanner returned from Brigade in the evening. Rain again at night. All working parties cancelled for the night.	
	28/8/17		Lt-Col Tanner & 2/Lt DICKERSON on leave to England. Battalion moved out of METZ billets at 5.30 AM en route for ACHIET LE PETIT. Route via BERTINCOURT - VELU - ACHIET LE GRAND to destination vide Order No 84. Arrived in Billets at ACHIET LE PETIT 2.30 PM. Accommodation entirely inadequate. Endeavours are being made to obtain more tents. Afternoon spent in camp cleaning and digging drains. Camp very dirty. Regt. relieved 1st R.I.F. High wind and intermittent rain all day.	Reference 57C/40000 Vide Appendix

A6945 Wt. W11422/M1160 350,000 12/16 D. D. & L. Forms/C./2118/14.

Army Form

Instructions regarding War Diaries and Intelligence Summaries are contained in F. S. Regs., Part II. and the Staff Manual respectively. Title pages will be prepared in manuscript.

WAR DIARY
or
INTELLIGENCE SUMMARY.
(Erase heading not required.)

Place	Date	Hour	Summary of Events and Information	Remarks and references to Appendices
ACHIET LE PETIT	29/8/17		Training all day and re adjusting the camp. New shelters and Bivouacs erected. Intermittent rain & high wind all day. 2 O.R. on leave, detained owing to Port of Boulogne being closed.	
"	30/8/17		Training all day. Brigadier General visited camp. Training ground reconnoitred by officers. Intermittent rain all day. 3 O.R. on leave.	
"	31/8/17		Warmer but showery. Training all day. Lt Pease on leave. Football match 2nd v 4th S.A.I., latter won 3 goals to nil. Weather clear, fine & cold at night.	
			State:— With unit 25 Off. 931 O.R.	
			Not with unit 17 Off. 127 O.R. Total 42 Off. 1058 O.R.	
			[illegible] Capt & Adjt for Major Temp Commanding 2nd S.A.I.	

A6945 Wt. W11422/M1160 350,000 12/16 D. D. & L. Forms/C./2118/14.

2nd REGIMENT SOUTH AFRICAN INFANTRY.

WAR DIARY.

AUGUST 1917.

Appendices:-

No. 1. Operation Orders 80, 81, 83, 84.

II Orders, Instructions, etc. re Raid on FEMY SCRUB.

III Sketch Map of Trescault Section, 1/5000, part of sheet 57C enlarged.

War diary. APPENDIX No I

2

ORDER NO: 80.

Copy No.....

Reference
Sheet 57c N.E.
Sheet 57c S.E.
1/20000.

In the Field,
3. - 8. - 17.

1. INFORMATION.

(a) The 4th S.A.I. will relieve the 2nd S.A.I. in the left sub-section of the TRESCAULT SECTION during the night of 3rd/4th inst.

(b) On completion of relief the 2nd S.A.I. will become the Battalion in Divisional Reserve.

(c) The Relieving Battalion will be less one company.

(d) The distribution of the relieving Battalion will be as follows:-

R IGHT COMPANY. - Two Platoons in "A" Sap, one platoon in TRESCAULT TRENCH and one platoon in support in COSY COPSE.

CENTRE COMPANY. - One platoon in "B" Sap, Two platoons in TRESCAULT TRENCH and one platoon in support at COSY COPSE.

LEFT COMPANY. One platoon each in "C" and "D" Saps and two platoons in TRESCAULT TRENCH.

2. INTENTION.

The C.O. intends to proceed by DeCauville trains to YTRES on completion of relief.

3. RELIEF.

The units of the 4th S.A.I. will relieve the units of the 2nd S.A.I. in the following order, commencing at 9.45.p.m.

(a) Headquarters, 4th S.A.I. will relieve Headquarters, 2nd S.A.I.

(b) LEFT COMPANY. "A" Coy. 4th S.A.I. will relieve "A" Coy. 2nd S.A.I. in the following order of platoons-
Left platoon in TRESCAULT TRENCH, Platoon in "D" Sap,
Right platoon in TRESCAULT TRENCH, Platoon in "C" Sap.

(c) RIGHT COMPANY. "C" Company 4th S.A.I. less 1 platoon will relieve "D" Coy. 2nd S.A.I. in the following order of platoons. -
Forward platoon in "A" Sap, rear platoon in "A" Sap,
2 Platoons in TRESCAULT Trench will be relieved by
1 platoon "D" Coy. 4th S.A.I.

(d) CENTRE COMPANY. "B" Company 4th S.A.I. less 1 platoon will relieve "B" Coy. 2nd S.A.I. as follows:-
Platoon in "B" Sap by 1 platoon "B" Coy. 4th S.A.I.
Platoons in TRESCAULT TRENCH will be relieved by 2 platoons "B" Coy. 4th S.A.I. commencing from the right.

(e) SUPPORT COMPANY, COSY COPSE. - 1 platoon "C" Coy. 4th S.A.I. will relieve right platoon "C" Coy. 2nd S.A.I.
1 Platoon "B" Coy. 4th S.A.I. will relieve left platoon of "C" Coy. 2nd S.A.I.

(f) Two platoons of "C" Coy. at Kitchens in HAVRINC OURT WOOD will be relieved by certain details of the 4th S.A.I.

/p4.

4.
ENTRAINING.

(a) On relief each Company will march to the railway siding at Q.9.d. entraining there under direction of Company Commanders.
The first Company relieved will entrain in the last arrived train. Each train will move off when filled.

(b) Number of trains - 4. Number of trucks 7 per train. Each truck carries 26 passengers.

5.
BILLETS.

(a) On arrival at Billets at YTRES Companies will be met by Billeting N.C.Os. and will march direct to their billets.

(b) A Hot meal will be served on arrival at billets.

6.
GUIDES.

(a) Platoon Guides will report at Battalion Headquarters at 8.p.m.

(b) Each guide will be in possession of a ticket shewing order of relief.
Bearer of ticket marked "A" will guide the first platoon of 4th S.A.I., - guides will continue in sequence as each relieving platoon arrives.

7.
BAGGAGE.

All officers kit and baggage will be piled at Battalion Headquarters on ration dump by 9.p.m. to-night.

8.
TRENCH STORES.

(a) Trench Stores will be handed over and duplicate receipts forwarded to Battalion Headquarters as usual.

(b) Maps, aeroplane photos, ~~and~~ defence scheme, etc. will be handed over to the relieving units.

9.
WORKING PARTIES.

All details of working parties will be handed over to the relieving companies.

10.
REPORT.

Completion of relief will be reported in writing to the Orderly Room at YTRES by 8.a.m. to-morrow.

Issued at 3.15. p.m.

R Beasley

Captain & Adjutant,
2nd S.A.I.

Copies Nos. 1 & 2. retained.
No. 3. to O.C. "A" Coy. by orderly.
No. 4. to O.C. "B" Coy. by orderly.
No. 5. to O.C. "C" Coy. by orderly.
No. 6. to O.C. "D" Coy. by orderly.
No. 7. retained for C.O.

Copy No. 1..

ORDER NO: 1.

Reference
Sheet 57C N.E.
Sheet 57C S.E.
1/20000.

In the Field,
9. 8. 1917.

1. IN FORMATION.

The 2nd Regiment South African Infantry less four platoons will relieve the 4th Regiment South African Infantry in the left sub-section of the TRESCAULT SECTION during the night of the 9/10th inst.

2. INTENTION.

The C. O. intends to proceed to the trenches by rail at 8.p.m. to-night.

3. DISTRIBUTION.

(a) "A " Company less 1 platoon and plus 1 platoon of "C" C ompany will relieve "A" Coy. 4th S.A.I. in the left company front.

(b) "D" Company less 1 platoon will relieve "C" Company 4th S.A.I. in the right company front.

(c) "B" Company less 1 platoon will relieve "B" Coy. 2nd S.A.I. in the centre company front.

(d) "C" Company less 2 platoons will relieve "D" Company 4th S.A.I. at COSY COPSE in the support lines.
"C" Company will also provide two posts on "A" Coy. front.
"C" Company will also detail a permanent working party of 1 N.C.O. and tenmen for attachment to Headquarters.

4. ENTRAINING.

The Battalion will entrain at 8.p.m. to-night at the CANTEEN SIDING, P.20.C., in the following order:-
Headquarters Cooks & Working party.
1 platoon of "C" Company.
"A", "D", "B", "C" Coys.
Companies will be ready to entrain at 7.45.p.m.

5. BAGGAGE.

(a) All Company baggage to be taken to the trenches will be piled at Canteen Siding by 7.30.p.m.
Loading parties from each company will be detailed to load immediately trains arrive.
Baggage will accompany units.

(b) Surplus baggage not required in the trenches will be piled outside Quartermaster's stores by 2.p.m.

6. ADVANCE PARTY.

1 officer and 1 N.C.O. per company will report at the Orderly Room at 1.p.m. for the purpose of proceeding to the trenches to take over stores, etc.

7. DETAILS.

1 Platoon per company remaining behind, together with Drums, under-age men, and men awaiting commissions, and all officers detailed to remain at Depot will parade under Captain KNIGHT at 2.p.m. for the purpose of proceeding to NEUVILLE BOURJONVAL.
Rations for 10th instant will be carried, and together with baggage will be loaded on Transport at 1.30.p.m.
Transport Officer will provide necesary vehicles.

(over

8. WORKING PARTIES. — Companies will take over all duties and standing working parties from the companies they relieve.

9. TRENCH STORES. — Trench Stores will be taken over and duplicate receipts rendered to Orderly Room as usual.

10. TRANSPORT. — Transport will move to the Transport lines at EQUANCOURT under orders of the Transport Officer.

11. COOKING. — Cooking will be done in HAVRINCOURT WOOD. All cooks and two mess orderlies per platoon will report to the Sergeant Cook to-night at 7.p.m. in full marching order for instructions. Two mess orderlies per ~~company~~ platoon will remain in the line with companies.

12. REPORTS. — Completion of reliefs will be wired to Headquarters by code word "SNOW".

Completion of relief mentioned in para 7. will be wired to Brigade by code word "HEEP".

Issued at 11.a.m.

Captain & Adjutant,
2nd Regiment S.A.Infantry.

Copies Nos. 1 & 2. Retained.
No. 3. to O.C."A" Coy. Captain Symons personally.
No. 4. to O.C."B" Coy. Capt. Davis do.
No. 5. to O.C."C" Coy. " Jacobs do.
No. 6. to O.C."D" Coy. " Jenkins do.
No. 7. to Transport Officer.
No. 8. Adjutant.

SECRET.

Copy No.....2

ORDER NO. [illegible].

Reference
Sheet 57C. N.E.
" 57C. S.E.
1/20000.

In the Field 16/8/17.

1.
INFORMATION. The 4th S.A.Infantry (less 4 platoons) will relieve the Battalion on the night of 17/18th. On relief the Battalion will be the unit in Brigade Reserve at METZ.

2.
INTENTION. The O.C. intends to march to METZ on completion of relief.

3.
RELIEF. Reliefs will commence about 9.p.m. as follows:-
Hqrs. 4th S.A.I. will relieve Hqrs. 2nd S.A.I..
"C" Coy, 4th S.A.I. will relieve "D" Coy, 2nd S.A.I. in right company sector.
"B" Coy. 4th S.A.I. will relieve "B" Coy, 2nd S.A.I. in centre company sector.
"D" Coy. 4th S.A.I. will relieve "A" Coy. 2nd S.A.I. in left company sector.
"A" Company 4th S.A.I. will relieve "C" Coy. 2nd S.A.I. and 1 platoon on left company front and 2 platoons in support.
An interval of 5 minutes will be maintained between platoons.

4.
WORKING PARTIES. All standing working parties will be handed over to relieving units.

5.
TRENCH STORES & LOG BOOKS. (a) Trench Stores, including Defence Scheme, will be handed over and receipts obtained. Duplicate Trench Stores cards will be handed to Orderly Room at METZ by 9.a.m. the following day.

(b) Log Books will be completed and handed over.

6.
GUIDES. Guides will be at Battalion Headquarters by 8.p.m. They will be in possession of tickets shewing order of relief.

7.
BAGGAGE. All baggage will be at Battalion Headquarters ready for loading by 8.p.m. One man per company will remain with baggage till loading is completed.

8.
TRANSPORT. Transport Officer will arrange for sufficient transport to convey baggage to METZ. Waggons will arrive at Battalion Headquarters at 9.p.m.

9.
DETAILS. Details will move as directed in Brigade Order No. 122. O.C. Details of this Regiment will arrange to take over Billets and Trench Stores at METZ. All guards will be taken over by the details.
O.C. details will arrange for guides to meet relieved units outside METZ.

10.
KITCHENS, COOKING & WATERCARTS.

(a) Field Kitchens will leave the WOOD at 6.p.m. togther with cooks and mess orderlies, and personnel employed at the wood, in charge of Sgt. LE SUEUR. Party will report to Captain KNIGHT on arrival.

(b) A hot meal will be provided on arrival at Billets in METZ.

(c) One water cart will return and one will be handed to 4th S. A. I.

(d) Transport Officer will arrange horses for the above.

11.
COMPLETION OF RELIEF.

Completion of relief will be reported personally by an officer from each company.

12.
REPORTS.

Reports to Battalion Headquarters.

13. ACKNOWLEDGE.

R Bromley

Issued at 9.p.m.

Captain & Adjutant.
2nd Regiment S. A. Infantry.

Copies Nos. 1 & 2.	Retained.	
No. 3.	O.C."A" Coy	by orderly.
No. 4.	"B" "	do.
No. 5.	"C" "	do.
No. 6.	"D" Coy	do
No. 7.	Transport Officer	do.
No. 8.	O.C. Details, Captain KNIGHT	by orderly.

Q Returned

Copy No......

ORDER NO. 84.

Reference
Sheet 51C. 1/40000.
Lens II 1/100000.

In the Field,
27. 8. 17.

------

1. INFORMATION. The 1st South African Infantry Brigade will be relieved by the 107th Infantry Brigade on August 28th 1917 in the TRESCAULT SECTION. On relief the 1st S.A.Infantry Brigade will move to ACHIET LE PETIT.

2. INTENTION. The O.C. intends to proceed to ACHIET LE PETIT by TRAIN + march route entraining at METZ at 6.a.m.

3. ROUTE. The Battalion will entrain at Siding B.W.13. at METZ at 6.a.m. detraining at BERTINCOURT, from thence to YTRES by march route, entraining there for ACHIET LE GRAND, from which latter place the Battalion will march to billets at ACHIET LE PETIT.

4. DISTRIBUTION. Companies will pass the starting point as follows:-

Headquarters.	5.40.a.m.
"D" Company.	5.42. a.m.
"A" Company.	5.44.a.m.
"B" Company.	5.46.a.m.
"C" Company.	5.48.a.m.

Companies will entrain and march in the above order, 100 yards interval being maintained between companies on the march.

5. STARTING POINT. The starting point will be the Ruined Church in METZ.

6. TRAINS.
(a) Eight trains are available for the Battalion.
(b) Each train consists of five trucks.
(c) Each truck holds 25 men in Full marching order.
(D) Captain LAGERWALL is detailed as Entraining Officer. He will report at the Siding B.W.13. at 5.30.a.m. to-morrow. He will be in possession of a state shewing numbers entraining and will proceed by the last train.

7. ADVANCE PARTY. Advance party, already detailed, will meet trains at ACHIET LE GRAND and conduct companies to billets on arrival.

8. LEWIS GUNS.
(a) Lewis Guns and eight magazines per gun will accompany units on march.
(b) Lewis Gun boxes and remainder of magazines will be piled at Battalion Headquarters by 5.p.m. to-day for loading on transport.
(c) Each company will detail one N.C.O. and a loading party.

/over.

9. **BAGGAGE.** (a) Officers kit, mess stores, orderly room boxes and six dixies per company (headquarters 2 only) will be piled at Orderly Room by 5.~~p.m.~~ ~~to-day~~. to-morrow. A.M.

(b) Loading party under ~~2/Lieut. Harvey and 2 men~~ Capt BRYANT & 1 m[illegible] RB per company will remain with baggage and load same on lorry proceeding ~~proceeding~~ with lorry to ACHIET LE PETIT. A cyclist orderly will be attached to this party.

(c) Baggage not immediately required will be piled at Battalion Headquarters by 5.p.m. to-day and loaded on Transport. Each company will provide loading party.

(d) All loading will be done under supervision of Transport N.C.O.

10. **TRENCH STORES.** Trench Stores will be handed over to representatives of relieving units to-day, and trench store cards will be submitted in duplicate by 9.p.m. to-night.

11. **BILLETS.** Usual billet certificates will be handed in at 5.a.m. at which time all men will be clear of billets and Medical Officer and 2nd in Command will make the usual inspection.

12. **STATES.** Marching states shewing distribution on March will be handed in at 5.a.m. and on arrival at billets at ACHIET LE PETIT.

13. **TRANSPORT.** Transport will move under orders of the Brigade Transport Officer.

14. **REPORTS.** Reports to Battalion Headquarters.

Issued at 2.p.m.

Captain & Adjutant,
2nd South African Infantry

C opy No. 1 & 2. Retained.
3. to O.C. "A" Coy. by orderly.
4. to O.C. "B" Coy. do.
5. to O.C. "C" Coy. do.
6. to O.C. "D" Coy. do.
7. to Transport Officer.
8. Quartermaster personally.

CORRECTION TO ORDER NO. 89.

The following correction should be noted -

Section 9. "SIGNAL FOR RETURN" para 3. for "Rockets" read "White Rockets"

Captain & Adjutant.
2nd Regiment S. A. Infantry

Issued to recipients of copies of Order No. 89.
15/8/17.

APPENDIX No II

Raid

Night of 16/17 Augst. 1917.

Order No 82 Copy No 2.

Instructions issued in connection with above.

CO's report.

2/Lt Mills report

SECRET.

ORDER NO. 82. **Copy No. 2**

Reference Map
Area Map
TRESCAULT SECTOR
1/10,000.

In the Field, 14/8/17.

1. INFORMATION.

The enemy are occupying a post in SOUTH-EAST corner of FEMY WOOD at approximately K.34.d.60.10.

2. INTENTION.

The C.O. intends to raid this post for purpose of:
(1) Capturing prisoners.
(2) To obtain identifications.
(3) To do as much harm as possible to the enemy.

3. FORCES.

Raiding party to consist of 2/Lieut. MILLS and 25 other ranks, and 4 stretcher bearers.
Wire party - 3 other ranks.

ARTILLERY. To be arranged by South African Brigade.

TRENCH MORTARS. ~~Three~~ Four guns.

MACHINE GUNS - To be arranged by South African Brigade.

4. MAIN LINES OF ACTION.

The enemy outpost line will be entered at a point approximately Q.4.b.30.95.
Enemy wire opposite point of entrance to be cut by explosion of BANGALORE TORPEDO.
BANGALORE TORPEDO to be placed in position and fired by WIRE PARTY.
Raiding party will then enter gap and work along enemy line to right of gap and attack post at K.34.d.60.10, seizing any enemy and destroying any work.
A party of 1 N.C.O. and 4 men will remain at gap on enemy side of wire and face WEST ready to deal with any enemy attack from that flank.
Stretcher bearers will remain on outside of enemy wire ready to attend to casualties.
A tape will be run out behind Raiding party to connect gap in enemy wire and "B" Sap, as a guide to party returning.

5. ASSEMBLY.

Wire and raiding parties will form up in file clear of wire at head of "B" Sap. in time for Wire Party to reach edge of FEMY WOOD directly in front of point of entry by 1.45. A.M.
Raiding party must be in close touch with wire party.

6. ZERO.

Zero for Artillery, Trench Mortar and Machine gun barrage will be at 1.45.A.M. on 17th inst.
ZERO for raiding party to enter gap will be explosion of BANGALORE TORPEDO.

7.
WIRE CUTTING.

At 1.45.A.M. Wire party will move forward under cover of Artillery action, place BANGALORE TORPEDO in position and fire same.

8.
ADVANCE TO ASSAULT.

As soon as Bangalore Torpedo has exploded Raiding party will enter Gap and proceed as indicated in para. 4.

9.
SIGNAL FOR RETURN.

The signal for return will be repeated long blasts of whistles which will be given by Officer in charge of party or N.C.O's. other than N.C.O. at Gap, when prisoners have been secured and post at K.34.d.60.10 cleared.
In no case will party remain longer than 15 minutes after entering gap, but will return as early as possible taking care to ensure that all enemy at the point indicated have been disposed of or dispersed.
As an extra guide for return of party 3 Rockets will be fired from "B" Sap at the expiration of 15 minutes after explosion of Torpedo. These rockets will be fired at one minute intervals.

10.
RETURN OF PARTY.

On receiving the signal, party will return as quickly as possible to "B" Sap along Tape. passing along "B" Sap to Battalion Headquarters.
In the event of wire at point of entry not being sufficiently cut to allow of raiding party entering, the raiding party will withdraw under support of covering party to be detailed by O.C. "D" Company.

11.
ARTILLERY ACTION.

At 1.45.A.M. the Artillery will put down a Barrage on a line approximately 200 yards North of enemy outpost line in FEMY SCRUB and outpost line EAST of FEMY SCRUB.
Barrage would be along line approximately K.34.c.7.4. - K.34.d.1.3. - K.34.d.4.4. K.34.d.9.3. to K.35.c.20.56.
In addition artillery will engage the following targets:-

Enemy machine guns at	K.34.a.9.4.
" " " "	K.34.b.40.30.
Crater at	K.35.c.20.56.

12.
LIGHT TRENCH MORTAR ACTION.

At 1.45.a.m. Light Trench Mortar Battery will fire on selected targets -
Hollow in Glade.
Chalk Recess.
Enemy post N.W. of Hollow.
On enemy outpost line between the Hollow in Glade and Q.4.b.10.90.

13.
MACHINE GUN

Machine Guns will fire on -
Crater at K.35.c.20.56.
Enemy outpost line East and West of FEMY WOOD.

14.
CEASE FIRE. Artillery, Trench Morters and machine guns will cease fire at 2.30.A.M.

15.
DRESS. Dress as detailed in special order to be issued.

16.
CASUALTIES. Wounded will be evacuated via "B" Sap, TRESCAULT TRENCH and FRITH AVENUE. Regtl. Medical Officer will arrange special bearer parties who will walk the course.

No notice is to be taken by raiding parties of casualties on the way over.

17.
ROLL CALL. Raiding party will return to Battalion Headquarters where names will be checked.

18.
PRISONERS. All prisoners will be conducted to Battalion Headquarters without delay.

19.
SYNCRONIZATION OF WATCHES. Watches will be synchronised at Battalion Headquarters at 6.p.m. on 16th inst.

20.
REPORTS. Reports to Battalion Headquarters.

R Bromley

Issued at.................. Captain & Adjutant.
2nd Regiment S. A. Infantry.

Copies	Nos. 1 & 2	Retained.
Copy	No. 3.	S.A. Brigade.
"	" 4	O/C. "D"Coy.
"	" 5	O/C. "B"Coy.
"	" 6	" "A" "
"	" 7.	2/Lieut.MILLS.
"	" 8.	O/C. S.A.L.T.M.B.
"	" 9.	" 28th M.G.C.
"	" 10.	Artillery.

Ofc B Coy Copy No 2
R

INSTRUCTIONS ISSUED IN CONNECTION WITH ORDER NO. 82

OF THE 14/8/1917.

1.
FORMING UP AND ACTION OF RAIDING PARTY.

As indicated in Order 82. party will be formed up in file in following order:-
Sgt. MORGAN & 2 O.Rs. as wire party to carry Bangalore Torpedo in front.
2nd Lieut. MILLS.

No. 1. Section. Sgt DEWAR & 3 O.R's. "B"Coy.
No. 2 Section. " SHEARER & 3 O.R's."D"Coy.
No. 3 Section. Cpl. POTE & 3 do. "B"CO.
No. 4 Section. Cpl. BULCOCK & 3 O.R's. "D"Coy.
No. 5 Section L/Cpl. LIEDERANDT & 3 O.R's "B" Coy.
No. 6. Section. Sgt.HATTON & 4 O.R.s "B"Coy.
Four stretcher Bearers, two from each "B" and "D" Companies.

SB { Daly Williamson

2 Res SB.

No.6. section will form stop at Gap inside wire, and will deal with any enemy attack from the left flank(WEST).

The remainder of the party after entrance will move rapidly along the wire and determinedly attack the enemy post. As soon as the officer in charge is satisfied that all enemy at post have been disposed of, the signal for return will be given.

Prisoners will be placed inch-arge of nearest man and will be immediately taken back. The men of No.1. and No. 2 sections will pay particular attention to the enemy post, and will not if possible be sent back with prisoners.
No. 3 and 4 sections will be utilized for this duty if necessary. No. 6 section will be the last to leave enemy lines, and will cover retreat of raiding party at this point.

No. 2.
COVERING PARTY.

O. C. "D" Coy. will detail an officer, 10 men and one lewis gun as a covering party. This party will take up a position approximately at Q.4.b.9.8. The action of this party will depend generally upon the situation, but it should be in readiness to deal with any counter-attack or demonstration by the enemy from the right flank, or any enemy target that presents itself particularly on the right flank.
At artillery ZERO the lewis gun will fire to the east of the tip of FEMY SCRUB, using short bursts, but keeping a reserve supply of drums.

No. 3.
SUPPORT PARTY.

A party of 10 men and two lewis guns under Lieut. GREEN, MC. will be held in readiness at the head of "B" Sap. This party will be ready to assist the raiding party in any withdrawal necessary, generally on the lines of a front attack on the direct front of the enemy outpost at the S.E. corner of the wood. One of these lewis guns will open fire into THE TIP OF FEMY SCRUB. for three minutes starting at artillery ZERO.

4. LEWIS GUNS.

Two lewis guns under an officer will be detailed by O.C. "A" Coy. and will be placed at the head of "C" Sap. These guns will open fire at ARTILLERY ZERO on enemy outpost line between WEST SIDE OF SCRUB and a point approximately Q.4.a.9.5.9.5. One lewis gun under an officer will be placed in position in "D" Sap and will open fire at ARTILLERY ZERO on enemy outposts lines between west EDGE OF FEMY SCRUB and HOLLOW.

Great care must be taken not to enfilade the point of wood to be raided, and officers detailed for these duties must reconnoitre positions and place pegs to prevent guns traversing too far to the EAST. Lewis Guns should fire short bursts at frequent intervals but care will be taken to keep a reserve of loaded drums in hand. All available riflemen in these positions should fire down the GLADE and into the HOLLOW, and will not fire into FEMY SCRUB during the raid.

5. ARMS, DRESS AND EQUIPMENT.

All marks of identification will be removed from clothes by members of the raiding party. Section leaders will personally inspect men to ensure that this order is carried out.
Tunics will be provided for the purposes of this Operation. Caps will be worn.
No equipment will be worn.
Bayonets will be fixed but dulled with mud.
All magazines will be full charged, in addition to this men will carry four loose clips of S.A.A. in right side pocket of Tunic.
MILLS GRENADES. Two Mills grenades will be carried by each N.C.O. and man, except personnel of No. 6 Section, who will each carry four grenades.
SECTION LEADERS. The leaders of Nos. 1 & 2 Sections will carry revolvers, with SIX spare Cartridges in pocket of coat. The remainder of section leaders will carry rifle and bayonet. Section leaders with exception of leader of No. 6 section will carry whistles.

6. OFFICER FOR ROCKET FIRING.

2nd Lieut, HATCHARD will act as Forward Observing officer and will be in charge of rockets, and will fire same as directed in Order No. 82.

7. WIRE CUTTERS.

Wire cutters will be carried by wire party and leading file of raiding party.

8. CASUALTIES.

Casualties going over will be attended to by bearer party under instructions of Regimental Medical Officer. Every effort will be made by raiding party to bring back any casualties that may occur after reaching enemy wire, but the safety of the operations will not be endangered by the party remaining after time allotted.

9. **PRISONERS.** A few prisoners are required for purposes of identification and intelligence.

10. **SIGNAL FOR RETURN. &PASSWORD.** All ranks must be thoroughly clear regarding the the signal for return, The word "RETIRE" will not be used. Anyone using it will be treated as hostile.

For purposes of identification the pass-word "SECOND" will be used, and answered by the same word.

11. **TAPE FOR RETURN.** O.C. "B" Coy. will detail 3 men to lay a tape from "B" Sap to point of entry. One man will follow up the raidingparty with a tape which will be let out from a reel in front of "B" Sap. One man will follow with the tape at 100 yards interval. One man will hold tape at a point outside "B" Sap. This tape will be drawn in after return of party, if practicable.

12. **RETURN OF PARTY.** Raiding party will report and give their names in at "B" Coy, headquarters on their way to Battalion Headquarters. Rolls will be checked again at Battalion Headquarters.

13. **TRENCHES.** All trenches along line of evacuation and return of party will be kept clear. Men in saps and trenches will stand on fire steps in order to allow a clear passage.

14. **NOMINAL ROLLS.** Nominal rolls will be handed to Regimental Orderly Room as early as possible on day of Raid. Any alterations in same will be notified immediately.

15. **RAIDING PARTY.** All ranks of raiding party will withdraw to the Kitchens in the wood at XXX 7.a.m. on the morning of the 16th. They will remain there under orders of 2/Lieut, MILLS. They should take all their equipment with them.

R Beasley

Captain & Adjutant.
2nd Regiment South African Infantry.

15/8/17.

C.Os Report

R

SOUTH AFRICAN BRIGADE.

I beg to submit report on Raid carried out on enemy lines at 1.45.a.m. to-day.-

(1) Raiding party left "B" Sap and were formed up inside scrub on edge of wood at 1.40.a.m.

(2) Artillery opened punctually at ZERO.

(3) Raiding party moved up rapdily to wire unobserved by enemy.

(4) First series of wire met with consisted of light trip wires. These were cut by hand cutters. Second series consisted of Concertina Barbed wire securely pegged down at close intervals. After attempting to cut this by hand cutters the Officer in Charge decided to blow this up with Bangalore torpedo, which was done. Third Series consisted of main wire, but there was not sufficient time to allow of this being cut by hand, and 2/Lieut, MILLS decided to withdr his men, which withdrawal was carried out in an excellent manner.

(P.T.O.

(5) The point on wire reached was rather more to West that the original point decided upon.

(6) Enemy machine gun fired from K. 34.d.60.10. during raid but could evidently not be brought to bear on party, or party was not observed at any time as all its fire was directed to the EAST

(7). The Artillery Barrage was excellent and very accurate.

(8) Stokes Mortar Barrage was also excellent and accurate.

(9) Effect of our machine guns could not be observed

(10). Enemy retaliation was very feeble and consisted of four 77mm. shells which fell on the left of this subsection.

(11.) Enemy Signals. Beyond one red rocket and the usual Very lights no other signals were observed. Most of the Very lights appeared to come from Hollow and Glade; some were fired from S. E. Corner of Wood.

(12) No casualties were sustained.

(P.T.O.

S.A. Bde.

I was only yesterday able to find Mr Birrell in hospital & obtain from him the details of his patrol. I, as you will remember, explained to the Divisional Commander what I feared was the case but am glad to say that that appreciation of what occurred was wrong. Mr Birrell is most clear on the point, & states that without any doubt in his mind that the two casualties, other than himself, were distinctly caused by an enemy rifle grenade fired from a point in front of where he was. Upon leaving the two men, who were hit, about to be returned bearing to his right, & came on the party he had left in rear, & was unfortunately wounded himself by one of our own men who mistook him, owing to the direction from which he approached. I attach Mr Birrell's report.

W. Tanner Lt Col
2nd S.A. Inf.

B.E.F.
6th Aug 1917

2/Lt Mills Report

17/8/1917.

COPY.

REPORT ON RAID ON FEMY SCRUB.

I left "B" Sap with 32 N.C.Os. and men at 1.20.a.m. on 17/8/17 for the purpose of raiding the enemy outposts directly in front of this sap. We left the sap onthe extreme left at approximately Q.4.a.80.30 in file, the party of 1 N.C.O. & 2 men carrying Bangalore torpedo.leading.

On reaching the edge of scrub we formed up in close touch with one another and at 1.40.a.m. pushed forward. The barrage opened at 1.45.a.m. and we immediately increased our pace. After finding that our direction was too much to the WEST weturned half right and came across trip wires; these were cut by hand. A series of concertina barbed wire was our next obstacle. This we cut by hand also, but found it firmly pegged to the ground, so I decided to blow the torpedo up under it. This was done.

The next series of wire which is about 5 yards wide was then encountered. I then saw that it was impossible to break through this in the time allowed so ordered the withdrawal, which was carried out in an orderly manner, the whole party being in the sap by 2.20 a.m.

(P.T.O.

3.

(13) Apparently concertina wire has been put in recently and the wiring along the enemy outpost line varies in depth and regularity and forms a difficult obstacle for a short raid.
There appears to be no doubt that the post in S.E. Corner is occupied and includes a machine gun.

I regret that raiding party did not succeed in its mission, but consider that 2/Lieut. MILLS was right in withdrawing under the circumstances. 2/Lieut. MILL'S report is attached.

I would be glad if my thanks can be conveyed to the artillery for their splendid ssupport.

[signature]
Major.
Temp. Commanding 2nd Regiment S. A. Infantry

17/8/1917.

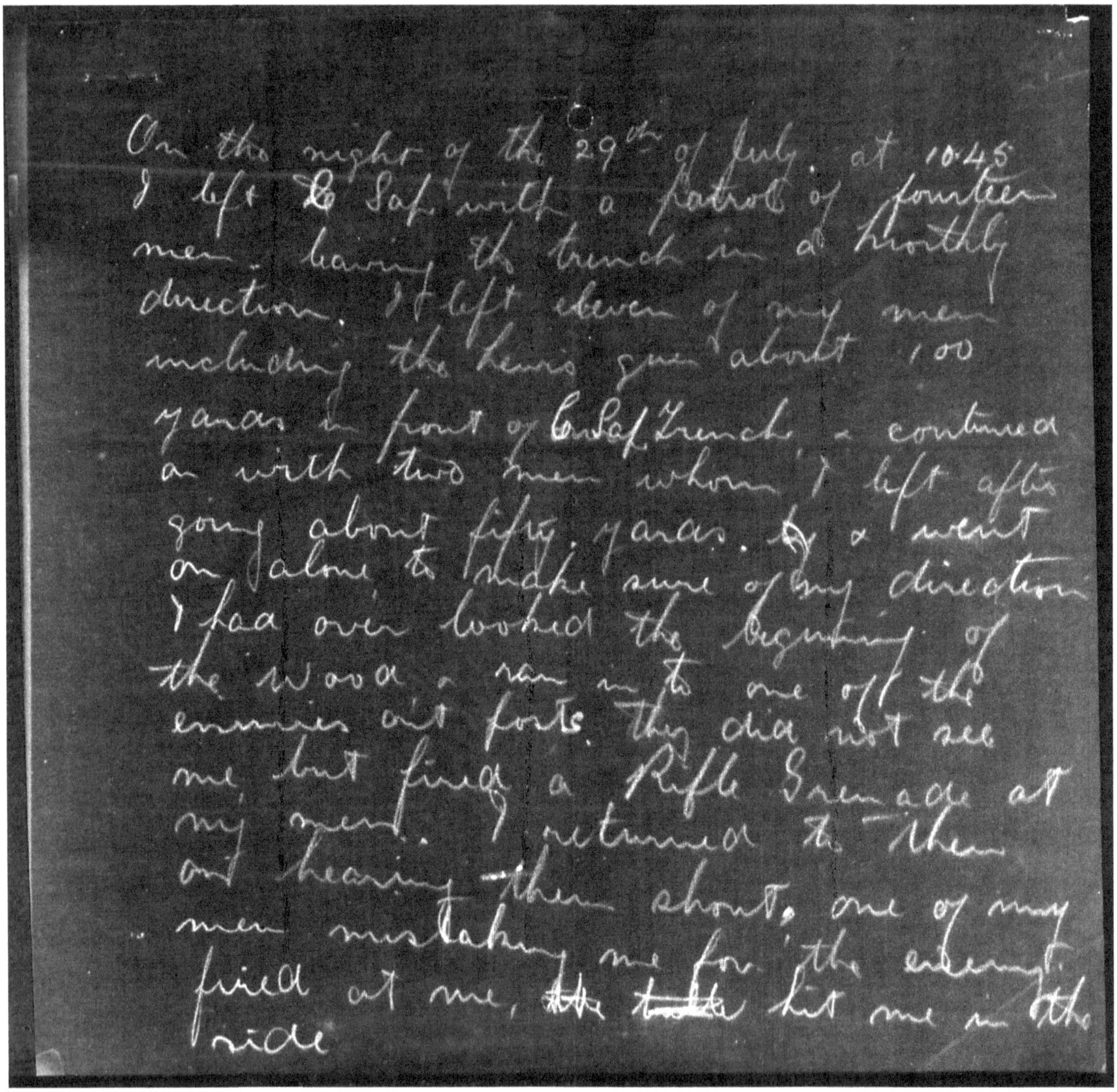
On the night of the 29th of July at 10.45
I left B Sap with a patrol of fourteen
men leaving the trench in a northerly
direction. I left eleven of my men
including the Lewis gun about 100
yards in front of B Sap Trench & continued
on with two men whom I left after
going about fifty yards. & I went
on alone to make sure of my direction
I had over looked the beginning of
the Wood & ran into one of the
enemies out posts they did not see
me but fired a Rifle Grenade at
my men. I returned to them
on hearing them shout, one of my
men mistaking me for the enemy
fired at me, ~~the bullet~~ hit me in the
side

Page [illegible].

There were no Casualties.

I do not consider that the party was observed by the enemy as the locality was overgrown with weeds some 3 feet high. There was no sign of the enemy in the vicinity of our immediate front.

2/Lieut.
2nd S. A. Infantry.

2 SA. Inf Bn July 1917 . X. 8/2706/1 6.8.17. O/27/4

1ST SOUTH AFRICAN INFANTRY BRIGADE.

9TH DIVISION.

Report herewith for the information of the Divisional Commander.

H S Dawson

Brigadier General.

6/8/17 Commanding 1st S,African Inf. Brigade.

G Br

seeing it was no good going on any further as we had been seen I returned to the Sap.

E. H. Birrell 2 Lt.
2nd Sap.

September 1917 — 2 S.A. Inf.

WAR DIARY

Army Form C. 2118.

Instructions regarding War Diaries and Intelligence Summaries are contained in F. S. Regs., Part II. and the Staff Manual respectively. Title pages will be prepared in manuscript.

(Erase heading not required.)

Place	Date	Hour	Summary of Events and Information	Remarks and references to Appendices
ACHIET LE PETIT.	1st		Cold morning & dull. Usual training. 6 am 2 officers and 6 O.R. to AMIENS on one days leave. Entrained at ACHIET LE GRAND. Demonstration by model platoon (B Coy). Football match 1st SAI v 2nd SAI. former won 1 pt - nil. Good game. 3 O.R. on leave. C.O. discussed future operations & training with all officers 6.30 pm. Cold night, inclination to frost.	
	2nd		Cold morning. Leave to Amiens as yesterday. Church parades at 10 AM. all denominations. CO & Lt Owen reconnoitred the Field firing area near camp. Adjutant and Company Commanders visited training area. Foot-ball in afternoon. Intermittent rain during day. No leave. Capt Reid SAMC on leave, relieved by Capt. Liston SAMC as MO.	

Army Form C. 2118.

WAR DIARY

or

~~INTELLIGENCE SUMMARY.~~

(Erase heading not required.)

Instructions regarding War Diaries and Intelligence Summaries are contained in F. S. Regs., Part II. and the Staff Manual respectively. Title pages will be prepared in manuscript.

Place	Date	Hour	Summary of Events and Information	Remarks and references to Appendices
ACHIET LE PETIT	3rd		Battalion marched to Le Sars to visit the BUTTE DE WARLINCOURT. Left camp 8.30 AM returned 4.30 pm. Route via MIRAMONT & COURCELETTE. Competition for Brigade guards. A very smart turn out. No decision given. 2/Lt Pritchard & 1 OR on leave. Usual daily leave to Amiens.	Reference 57c 1/40000
"	4th		Fine warm day. Battalion marched to the Field Firing Area near Camp at 7.30 A.M. Attack scheme carried out with Ball ammunition. Very successful training. 22000 rounds of S.A.A. used. Marched to camp at 12.30 pm. — 2.30 p.m. demonstration by model platoon. Bathing. Football. 2 O.R. on leave. Usual Amiens leave.	

A6945 Wt. W11422/M1160 350,000 12/16 D. D. & L. Forms/C./2118/14.

Instructions regarding War Diaries and Intelligence Summaries are contained in F. S. Regs., Part II. and the Staff Manual respectively. Title pages will be prepared in manuscript.

WAR DIARY

or

~~INTELLIGENCE SUMMARY~~.

(Erase heading not required.)

Army Form C. 2118.

Place	Date	Hour	Summary of Events and Information	Remarks and references to Appendices
ACHIET LE PETIT	5th		Fine warm day. Training. Battalion marched to training area 7.30 AM. Platoon & Company attack practice on training area over old German Trenches near BUCQUOY 2 miles WEST of ACHIET LE PETIT. Sports in the afternoon. 2 OR on leave — 6 all ranks leave to AMIENS.	
	6th		Little rain in morning, otherwise fine. Training all morning. Sports in afternoon, inter-company competitions. Lecture for officers on Machine Gun work at Brigade Headquarters. Thunderstorm in afternoon fine later. 2 officers & 4 OR leave to AMIENS. 2 O.R. leave to England. Lt Lucas returned from leave.	
	7th		Fine day. Training on Trench Area - Battalion Assault practice - Sports in afternoon. No Pte Lefevre accidentally killed in a brawl. 2 O.R to England. 6 OR Amiens leave. 2/Lt Cooper returned from leave.	

Instructions regarding War Diaries and Intelligence Summaries are contained in F. S. Regs., Part II. and the Staff Manual respectively. Title pages will be prepared in manuscript.

WAR DIARY

or

(*Erase heading not required.*)

Army Form C. 2118.

Place	Date	Hour	Summary of Events and Information	Remarks and references to Appendices
ACHIET LE PETIT	8th		Fine day, misty till 11 AM. Training in morning. Lewis gun firing, Rifle bombing &c. Sports in afternoon. Funeral of Pte Le Fevre at ACHIET LE GRAND. Meeting of Officers in evening to discuss future operations	
	9th		Cloudy day, but fine. Church parade S.A. Bde. G.O.C. present at 9.30AM. Brigade Sports all day. 1st S.A.I. won the championship ours were 2nd. Good day's sport. Strength of Regiment 21 officers 886 OR with unit. 21 officers 160 OR not with unit.	
	10th		Cloudy day, fine. Battalion rehearsed Brigade attack ~~of~~ on prepared area. Returned 2 pm Lecture on Machine Guns 5 pm. 2 OR on leave. - 6 OR on leave to AMIENS.	

Instructions regarding War Diaries and Intelligence Summaries are contained in F. S. Regs., Part II. and the Staff Manual respectively. Title pages will be prepared in manuscript.

WAR DIARY
or
INTELLIGENCE SUMMARY.
(Erase heading not required.)

Army Form C. 2118.

Place	Date	Hour	Summary of Events and Information	Remarks and references to Appendices
ACHIET LE PETIT	11th		Fine day. Col. Tanner returned from leave. Brigade assault practice on marked out area. Afternoon camp cleaning and general preparations for move. 2 O.R. on leave to England.	
	12th		Moved to new area under order No 85. Entrained at BAPAUME 2·30 pm. By train via HAZEBROUCK to GODEWAERVELDE. From there to Billets in WATOU AREA No 2.	Appendix I Reference Sheet Lens 11 1/100000 Hazebrouck 5A 1/100000
PEAR TREE CAMP	13th		Arrived at PEAR TREE CAMP 6·30 AM L 8 · C 3.5. Settled down in billets. Good tent accommodation. Inhabitants friendly & willing to supply milk, butter &c. Foot inspection & kit inspection by Companies. Orders received for move tomorrow. 2 OR on leave to England. Weather fine. CAPT PEARCE reported off leave.	Reference Belgium France 2 Sheet 27 1/40000
	14th		Left PEARTREE CAMP 2 pm and marched to ERIE CAMP at BRANDHOEK.	O.O. No 86
ERIE CAMP			G 11.c. Weather fine.	REF SHEET BELGIUM SH.

Instructions regarding War Diaries and Intelligence Summaries are contained in F. S. Regs., Part II. and the Staff Manual respectively. Title pages will be prepared in manuscript.

WAR DIARY
or
INTELLIGENCE SUMMARY.
(Erase heading not required.)

Army Form C. 2118.

Place	Date	Hour	Summary of Events and Information	Remarks and references to Appendices
ERIE CAMP	15TH.		Church Parades. No Training. Capt REID MO returned off leave from SCOTLAND. Weather fine. 2 O.R. on leave.	
	16TH		General preparation for move into line. Bde O.O. received for move. Weather fine.	
	17th.		No training. General Clean up and preparations. Coy Cmdrs, O.C. and INTELLIGENCE OFFICER proceeded at 2AM to reconnoitre line. Weather fine. Regt. moved to support trenches in Left Battalion Support Sub Section at 6pm. 3pm to 5pm All Officers and NCOs viewing model of scene operation. Strength of Regt marching out 21 Officers (MO) 586 O R. At 2pm Transport and details Officers 6 O.R. marched to H.16 (?) where they remain during the operations. Weather fine.	Ref BELGIUM 28 N.W. R.O.D.
			Battalion moved into Trenches east of YPRES in accordance with operation order No 87 of 16th Sept	Appendix I

A6945 Wt. W11422/M1160 350,000 12/16 D. D. & L. Forms/C./2118/14.

Instructions regarding War Diaries and Intelligence Summaries are contained in F. S. Regs., Part II. and the Staff Manual respectively. Title pages will be prepared in manuscript.

WAR DIARY

or

~~INTELLIGENCE SUMMARY.~~

(Erase heading not required.)

Army Form C. 2118.

Place	Date	Hour	Summary of Events and Information	Remarks and references to Appendices
YPRES AREA	17th		The relief was effected without incident. Warm fine night. Batt. HQ at Mill Cot in deep dug out (Ref. Sheet 28 NE 1/20000). Batt. relieved 5th Lanc Fusiliers, did not know much about their own line.	
			Strength of Regt. and distribution.	
			In line 20 Officers 703 Other Ranks (including carriers & Brigade parties)	
			At 1st line Transport 7 " 147 "	
			Detached 15 " 174 (42 Off: 1024 OR)	
	18th		Battalion still in Trenches in Reserve lines. Preparations made in distributing stores &c. At 10 AM the enemy shelled the trenches and caused twenty-three casualties. Transport worked very well eight carts of water being delivered daily to the Battalion. Several other units including Brigade Headquarters appreciated this. Reconnaissances made of the routes to the assembly trenches by night. No specially noteworthy incident. Weather fine.	

A6945 Wt. W11422/M1160 350,000 12/16 D. D. & L. Forms/C./2118/14.

Instructions regarding War Diaries and Intelligence Summaries are contained in F. S. Regs., Part II. and the Staff Manual respectively. Title pages will be prepared in manuscript.

WAR DIARY
or
INTELLIGENCE SUMMARY
(Erase heading not required.)

Army Form C. 2118.

Place	Date	Hour	Summary of Events and Information	Remarks and references to Appendices
YPRES	19th		Preparation for the assembly prior to the assault being completed	
AREA			All stores water and rations issued. The day passed without	
			incident. Order No 88 for the Attack issued at 4 P.M	Appendix I
			Reconnaissance of Routes and marking of assembly area	
			completed vide paras 7 and 8 of REPORT on OPERATIONS	
			by Major J E Cochran - Steady rain during the assembly	Appendix II
"	20th		Assembly completed by 2 20 AM and reported 2.45 AM.	
			Enemy shelled assembly position but only one casualty was	
			sustained. Battalion Headquarters established at LOW	
			FARM reference Sheet L3 1:10,000 Ed 1	Appendix II
			Attack commenced at Zero 5 40 AM	
			Casualties Killed Officers ~~OR~~ 2 OR 44	
			Wounded 8 " 186	
			Missing " 6	

A6945 Wt. W11422/M1160 350,000 12/16 D. D. & L. Forms/C./2118/14.

Instructions regarding War Diaries and Intelligence Summaries are contained in F. S. Regs., Part II. and the Staff Manual respectively. Title pages will be prepared in manuscript.

WAR DIARY
or
INTELLIGENCE SUMMARY.
(Erase heading not required.)

Army Form C. 2118.

Place	Date	Hour	Summary of Events and Information	Remarks and references to Appendices
YPRES AREA	20th		Operations continued successfully. Vide Report.	Appendix II
"	21st		Operations continued. Touch with 55th Div on left maintained. All line fully consolidated & held. Half battalions of 3rd + 4th S A I withdrawn from line. For account of this day's operations, vide report attached.	Appendix II
			Casualties. Killed 1 officer 14 O.R.	
			Wounded 2 " 39 O R	
			Missing — 2 O R.	
			Relief of Battalion commenced at 9 P.M. and continued throughout the night. Artillery of the enemy was active. 7th Batt. Seaforth Highlanders relieved. The night was very black and relief over the shell pitted area was consequently very difficult.	

A6945 Wt. W11422/M1160 350,000 12/16 D. D. & L. Forms/C./2118/14.

Army Form C. 2118.

WAR DIARY
or
INTELLIGENCE SUMMARY.
(Erase heading not required.)

Instructions regarding War Diaries and Intelligence Summaries are contained in F. S. Regs., Part II. and the Staff Manual respectively. Title pages will be prepared in manuscript.

Place	Date	Hour	Summary of Events and Information	Remarks and references to Appendices
EAST of YPRES	22nd		Relief of Battalion completed by 5 A.M. Personal report made to Brigade. Rum and rations issued. Moral of men notwithstanding fatigue, particularly high. Kitchens & hot meal ready. Officers had breakfast at Brigade. Roll call at 12 noon. Casualties to noon. 13 officers 298 O.R.	
			Battalion slept in reserve Trenches NORTH of MILL COT.	
"	23rd		Arrangements being made for withdrawal from the line to staging camp at TORONTO CAMP G 18 A. Details from 1st line Transport at H 16 central also moving to that camp. Move commenced at 10 P.M. and all men were clear of the Trench area by 11·20 P.M.	Sheet 28 1/40000
			ORDER No 89 refers to this move. Night fine.	Appendix I
	24th		Move completed and whole regiment arrived in camp at 1 A.M. Hot meal and rum issued. Preparations for move the following morning to the WINNIZEELE Area made. Order No 90.	Appendix I

Instructions regarding War Diaries and Intelligence Summaries are contained in F. S. Regs., Part II. and the Staff Manual respectively. Title pages will be prepared in manuscript.

WAR DIARY
or
INTELLIGENCE SUMMARY.
(Erase heading not required.)

Army Form C. 2118.

Place	Date	Hour	Summary of Events and Information	Remarks and references to Appendices
~~24~~ WINNE-ZELE	24th		Move completed to WINNEZELE by 3pm. Route through STEENVOORDE by Bus & by march route. Camped in a farm paddock in tents. Comfortable surroundings. 4th S.A.I. who arrived earlier lent their band to play us into camp & invited officers to lunch. 2 O.R. on leave.	Reference Sheet 27 1/40000
"	25th		Still at above place. Training carried out as far as possible. Batt. resting refitting and cleaning up. 2 OR on leave. Strength state. 19 off 608 OR with unit. 11 off 135 OR not with unit	
"	26th		Training and resting at WINNEZEELE. Draft of 2/Lt Middleton & 2/Lt Garstang and 127 O.R. arrived at 2pm inspected by C.O. & posted to companies. A good class of man but one or two coloured men — 2 O.R. on leave. Weather still warm and fine. Orders for move tomorrow.	

A6945 Wt. W11422/M1160 350,000 12/16 D. D. & L. Forms/C./2118/14.

Instructions regarding War Diaries and Intelligence Summaries are contained in F. S. Regs., Part II. and the Staff Manual respectively. Title pages will be prepared in manuscript.

WAR DIARY
or
INTELLIGENCE SUMMARY.
(*Erase heading not required.*)

Army Form C. 2118.

Place	Date	Hour	Summary of Events and Information	Remarks and references to Appendices
WINNEZEELE to ARNEKE	27th		Battalion moved by march route to ARNEKE. Reference sheet 27 Order No 91 refers. Hot day. New recruits suffered in the march owing to lack of condition. Left 10 AM arrived at ARNEKE 2 30 PM, all stragglers reported by 4 PM – Weather still fine – Billet distribution not good. Companies well billeted but too widely scattered in rural areas, Battalion Headquarters in village of ARNEKE. 9th Division also billeted in village. 9 OR to 5th Army rest camp at EQUIHEN	1/40000
ARNEKE	28th		Still at ARNEKE. day spent in bathing and re issue of clothing. CO & Adjutant visited billets. 2 OR on leave. Weather fine	
	29th		Training in company areas. CO visited all companies. Weather very fine. Following officers rejoined 2/Lt Terry, 2/Lt Arnold, 2/Lt Egan. Redistribution of billets and issue of tents. 12 OR reinforcements arrived from Base.	

Army Form C. 2118.

Instructions regarding War Diaries and Intelligence Summaries are contained in F. S. Regs., Part II. and the Staff Manual respectively. Title pages will be prepared in manuscript.

WAR DIARY

or

~~INTELLIGENCE SUMMARY~~

(Erase heading not required.)

Place	Date	Hour	Summary of Events and Information	Remarks and references to Appendices
ARNEKE	30th		Beautiful mild weather = Church parades as usual.	
			Football in afternoon.	
			Strength States With unit 23 officers 750 O.R.	
			Not with unit 9 officers 97 O.R.	
			[illegible] Lt Col	
			Sept. 30th 1917 Commanding 2nd S A Inf	

A6945 Wt. W11422/M1160 350,000 12/16 D. D. & L. Forms/C./2118/14.

Copy No. Spare

ORDER NO: 8[illegible].

In the Field,
11. - 9. 17.

Reference
LENS II. 1/100000.
HAZEBROUCK 5A.
1/10000.

1. **INFORMATION.** The South African Brigade will move from the present area to the WATOU AREA on the 12th instant.

2. **INTENTION.** The C.O. intends to proceed to the WATOU Area by march route and by rail.

3. **ROUTE.** The route will be from ACHIET-LE-PETIT by march route as reconnoitred to BAPAUME WEST, from thence to GODEWAERSVELD by train, and from there by march route to Billets.

4. **STARTING POINT.** Where main ACHIET-LE-PETIT - BUCQUOY ROAD joins main street in ACHIET-LE-PETIT.

5. **DISTRIBUTION.** The battalion will be distributed as follows and will pass the starting point at times mentioned hereunder:-

(a) First line transport, less "B" Company Field Kitchen at	10.a.m.
(b) The Battalion less "B" Coy. and First Line Transport.	11.30.a.m.
(c) "B" Company Field Kitchen.	12.40. p.m.
(d) "B" Company.	2.0. p.m.

6. **ENTRAINING.** The Battalion will entrain as per attached Schedule of trains at BAPAUME WES T.

7. **BAGGAGE, ETC.** Baggage will be piled outside Quartermaster's stores by 8.30.a.m. for loading. Usual loading parties will be detailed.
Lewis Guns should be loaded to-night.
Loading will be ~~done~~ under supervision of Transport Officer.

8. **RATIONS.** Unexpired portion of to-morrow's rations will be carried.

9. **MARCH DISCIPLINE.** In New Area 200 yards will be maintained between Companies.

10. **GUARDS.** Each company will detail a guard of 1 N.C.O. and 4 other ranks to prevent men leaving the train at halts.

11. **ADVANCE OFFICER.** Captain KNIGHT will report to Staff Captain at entraining station four hours before departure of train.

/over.

1.

12. **REPORTS.** Reports to Battalion Headquarters.

Issued at 4.p.m.

Captain & Adjutant,
2nd Regiment South African Infantry

Copies Nos. 1 & 2. Retained.
Copy No. 3. to O.C. "A" Coy. by orderly.
4. to O.C. "B" Coy. by orderly.
5. to O.C. "C" Coy. by orderly.
6. to O.C. "D" Coy. by orderly.
7. to Transport Officer.
8. to Quartermaster.

SCHEDULE OF TRAINS.

Issued in connection with Order No. 88.

Station.	Distribution.	Train number.	Dep.
BAPAUME WEST Siding A 6.	2nd Regt. S.A.Infantry. less 1 company & Field Kitchens.	H.T.6.	5.30.p.m.
Siding A.8.	"B" Company & Field Kitchen.	H.T.9.	6.10. p.m.

INSTRUCTIONS ISSUED IN CONNECTION WITH ORDER No. [illegible].

(1.) Each entraining detachment of the Battalion will send forward an officer to report to Staff Captain 4 hours before trains depart, as under:-

(a) Captain WRIGHT will represent the Battalion less "B" Company.

(b) An officer of "B" Company will proceed with the Battalion in advance of "B" Company.

Each of above officers will be in position of entraining states in duplicate.

(2) A lorry for conveyance of stores will be at Orderly Room of 1st Regiment S.A.Infantry at 8.30.a.m. Quartermaster will detail a guide to meet the lorry. This lorry will convey officers kit to station. "D" Company will detail 1 N.C.O. and two men as guard to the kit. They will report to Quartermaster at 8.30.a.m.

(3) Tents will be left standing. All tentage will be handed over to Area Commandant at 12.noon. 2/Lieut. HATCHARD will hand over these tents and obtain a duplicate receipt for same.

(4) On arrival of Transport at the entraining point all animals will be uncoupled and taken to water at the SUCRIE Water Point. Transport Officer will be directed to water point by Staff Captain. Water buckets will be carried in each horse truck.

(5) Breast ropes for horse-trucks will be provided by the Transport. Lashing ropes for vehicles will be provided by the railway.

(6) (a) Trains consist of 1 officers carriage, 17 flat trucks, and 30 covered trucks.

(b) Each flat truck will take on an average 4 axles. Each covered truck will take 40 men, 6 H.D.Horses or 8 L.D. Horses.

(c) No personnel or stores will be allowed in Brake Vans or on the roofs of trucks. No covered trucks should be used for baggage.

(7) Special attention will be paid to cleanliness of camp. Usual certificates will be handed in by 10.30.a.m.

(6) (d) Trucks are distributed as follows:-

Flat trucks - all vehicles and baggage.
Covered trucks - 9 for horses.
21 for men.

35 men will travel in each truck. On arrival at entraining station the Battalion will be numbered off in parties of thirty-five. Units will be kept together as far as possible. When entraining parties will face the trucks in depth. Each party will be in charge of a sergeant.

R.Beverley

Captain & Adjutant.
2nd Regiment S. A. Infantry

11/9/1917.

MARCH TABLE ISSUED IN CONNECTION WITH ORDER No. 86

Reference.
Sheets 27 & 28
1/40,000.

Date.	No.	Unit in order of March	Starting Point	Time.	Route.	Destination.
Sept. 14th	1	Headquarters and "B" Company	Road Junction at L.8.d.8.8. Sheet 27 1/40,000	1.40. p.m.	Road through L.9, L.10 a and b thence Switch Road N. of POPERINGHE to BRANDHOEK.	BRANDHOEK No. 2. AREA.
do	2.	"A" Company	do	1.43 p.m.	do	do
do.	3.	"D" Company	do	1.46 p.m.	do	do
do	4.	"C" Company	do	1.49 p.m.	do	do.

REMARKS.

Distances of 200 yards will be maintained throughout.

Companies will parade and march out independently.

No. 1 Unit will be on parade ready to march out at 1 p.m.

Copy No. 2.

ORDER No. 60.

Reference
Sheets 27 & 28.
1/40,000.

In the Field.
13th September 1917.

1.
INTENTION.
The 1st South African Infantry Brigade will move from [illegible] No. 3 AREA to [illegible] No. 2 AREA to-morrow 14th instant.

2.
[INTENTION].
The C. O. intends to march to [illegible] No. 2 AREA in accordance with attached march table on the 14th instant.

3.
BAGGAGE.
All baggage will be piled in front of [illegible] by 10.30 a.m. Usual loading parties will be detailed. Transport Officer will supervise loading.

4.
MARCH DISCIPLINE.
100 yards will be maintained between Companies. Usual halts will be made at 10 minutes to the hour.

5.
WATCHES.
Watches will be synchronized at 10 a.m.

6.
REPORTS.
Reports to the head of the column.

[signature]

Issued at 6. p.m.

Captain & Adjutant
2nd Regt. S.A. Infantry.

Copies No. 1 & 2. Retained.
Copy No. 3. to O.C. "A" Coy. by Orderly
4 to O.C. "B" Coy. by Orderly
5 to O.C. "C" Coy. by Orderly
6. to O.C. "D" Coy. by Orderly.
7 to Transport Officer.
8 to Quartermaster.

Copy No.

ORDER NO: 87.

Reference
Sheet ~~ZONNEBEKE~~ 28 N.E.1.
1/10000. and
Sheet 28 N.W. 1/20000.

In the Field,
16th Septr. 1917.

1.(a) **INFORMATION.** The 9th Division will relieve the 42nd Division in the Right Sector of the 5th Corps front on the nights 16/17th and 17/18th September, 1917.

(b) The 1st South African Brigade will relieve the 125th Infantry Brigade in the left sub-sector on the night of 17/18th September 1917.

(c) Brigade Headquarters will be at MILL COT I.5.a.

(d) The 27th Infantry Brigade will be on the right of the South African Brigade.

(e) The Boundary between the Brigades will be a line from D.25.d.3.4. through J.1.a.0.5. to GULLY FARM I.5.d.6.1.

2. (a) **INTENTION.** The O.C. intends to relieve the 5th Lancashire Fusiliers on the night of 17/18th September, 1917. in the left SUPPORT Battalion sub-section, proceeding there by march route and by rail as per March and Train table attached.

(b) Details under command of Captain R.N.JENKINS and first line transport will move to billets and standings in the vicinity of H.16. Central at 2.p.m.

3. **ROUTE.** The Battalion, less First Line Transport and details, will proceed as far as the ASYLUM(H.12.d.) by rail and from thence through YPRES and via the MENIN GATE to destination.

4. **GUIDES.** Guides from the 5th Lnc. Fusiliers will meet the Battalion on arrival at the MENIN GATE:-
2 guides for Battalion Headquarters.
1 " for Company Headquarters.
2 " for each platoon.

5. **TRENCH STORES.** All Trench Stores, Maps, Aeroplane Photos, etc, will be taken over and duplicate receipts forwarded to Battalion Headquarters.

6. **RELIEF.** Completion of relief will be reported to Battalion Headquarters by code word RUM.

7. **MARCH DISCIPLINE.** Distance of 200 yards will be maintained between platoons EAST of ASYLUM.

8. **BATTALION HEADQUARTERS.** Battalion Headquarters will be at MILL COT at I.5.a.

9. **REPORTS.** Reports to Battalion Headquarters.

Issued at 9.p.m.

R Beswitz[?]
Captain & Adjutant,
2nd Regiment S.A.Infantry.

MARCH TABLE

ISSUED WITH ORDER NO: 67.

16th Septr. 1917.

No.	Party.	Starting Point.	Time.	Entraining Station.	Train Departs.	Destination.
1.	"A" & "B" Coys. Battn.Hqrs. less carriers.	Road Junction G.11.c.6.3.	7.5. p.m.	G.11.a.9.9. No.3. Stn.	8.p.m.	ASYLUM H.12.d.
2.	"C" & "D" Coys. Batt. Carriers. under C.S.M. Brickhill.	do.	9.0. p.m.	ditto.	10. p.m.	ditto.

NOTE.

(1) 200 yards will be maintained between companies on line of march to station.

(2) An officer of "A" and "C" Companies respectively will proceed to station half-an-hour before units to arrange entraining.

Copy No. 2

ORDER No. 88

Reference
Marked Sheet
ZONNEBEKE
Edition 6.a.
1/10,000.

In the Field,
18th September 1917.

1. INFORMATION.

(a) i. The enemy in our front is [illegible] strongly posted in shell holes, concrete dug-outs, and concreted ruins.
ii. His front line troops are disposed in depth in mutually supporting posts carefully concealed, to which he persistently clings and on many occasions when these posts have been overlooked in our advance they have become actively offensive in our rear, and inflicted considerable damage.
iii. He is holding the line on a system of Regimental fronts with one Battalion in front line, one battalion in supports, [illegible] and one battalion in immediate reserve.
iv. The supporting battalion is approximately 1,100 yards behind the line, and is employed when required for immediate counter-attacks.
v. The Reserve Battalion in our particular Brigade Front are left behind the PASSCHENDAELE RIDGE, and they are also brought forward under cover for counter-attacks when special vigilance is ordered.

(b) i. The 9th Division in the forthcoming operations will attack with the 27th Infantry Brigade on the right, South African Brigade on the left and the 26th Brigade in Reserve.
ii. An Australian Division will attack on the right of the 9th Division, and the 55th Division on its left.
iii. The South African Brigade will move within the limits of the BLUE Lines shewn on the reference and attack the two objectives marked first by RED and second by GREEN lines.
iv. The South African Brigade will attack in normal form of attack on two battalion frontage, the two leading Battalions will assault the first or Red objective, the remaining two the second or Green objective.
v. The [illegible] 3rd and 4th South African Infantry will attack the first or red objective, with the 3rd S.A. Infantry on the right and the 4th S.A. Infantry on the left.
vi. The 1st and 2nd S. A. Infantry will then pass through the 3rd and 4th S.A. Infantry, on the first [illegible] Red objective, and proceed to the attack of the second or Green objective. The 1st S.A.I. on the right will pass through the 3rd S.A.I. and the 2nd S.A.I. on the left will pass through the 4th S.A.I.

2. INTENTION.

The O.C. intends to form up immediately in rear of the 4th S.A. Infantry, who are occupying our present front line, and at Zero to follow in rear of this Battalion to a position clear of the present front line, and then at the appointed time to pass through the Red objective and proceed to the capture of the Green objective

3.
DISTRIBUTION. (a) The Battalion will attack on a three Company Frontage with the remaining Company in immediate support.

(b) The Boundaries and limits of Company objectives are theses shewn in yellow on the reference.

(c) "D" Company will attack on the right, "C" Company in the centre, "B" Company on the left, and "A" Company in immediate support of the whole.

(d) The supporting Company "A", will provide one platoon to support "D" Company, one platoon to support "B" Company, and deploy the remaining two platoons in rear of "C" Company to be used as the Reserve and employed as may be found necessary in any point or points on the Battalion front in the attack.

4.
ASSEMBLY. Instructions regarding Assembly will be issued under a separate order.

5.
ATTACK. (a) RED OBJECTIVE

(i) At Zero the 4th S.A.Infantry will advance under the protection of the Artillery barrage, which will open 100 yards EAST of the enemy front line and move by lifts of 50 yards.
(ii) The first lift will be at ZERO plus 3 minutes then the barrage will creep forward for 200 yards at the rate of 4 minutes per 100 yards, and from this 200 yards advance to the RED objective at the rate of six minutes per 100 yards.
(iii) The Battalion will advance at ZERO in artillery formation of single file immediately in rear of 4th S. A. Infantry to a position as shown on the reference marked with Green Dots, some 200 yards WEST of the Red objective.
(iv) The capture of the red objective by the 4th S.A.Infantry is timed for ZERO plus 20 minutes, thereafter the barrage will pause in advance of the red line until ZERO plus one hour twenty minutes.

(b) GREEN OBJECTIVE.

(i) The Battalion will halt on the Green dotted line until ZERO plus one hour, when the whole will advance to the first or red objective and closely follows the barrage to the assault of the second or green objective.
(ii) With the exception of the leading line of the front waves, which will deploy into line, the Battalion will advance from the Green dotted line, and thence to the assault of the 2nd or green objective in normal artillery formation of single file. The deployment of the front line will be undertaken during the halt on the green dotted line.
(iii) From the position of the pause in front of the 1st or red objective, barrage will move forward at the rate of 100 yards in eight minutes, commencing at ZERO plus one hour twenty minutes.
(iv) The system as practised of occupying enemy posts etc en route must be most carefully carried out, in order to avoid all chances of over garrisoning these posts, and to ensure this officers and N.C.O.s of the rear waves will see that any surplus men in these posts are brought on.
(v) The object of occupying all enemy posts as they are reached by the leading waves is to ensure that the enemy is is prevented from re-appearing from dug-outs and becoming offensive in our rear.

6
OUTPOSTS. "D", "C", and "B" Company Commanders will be careful to definitely detail one Lewis Gun and section together with six Riflemen from the rear lines of each Company, for the purpose of being immediately pushed out to form the outpost line in front of the second or green objective.

7.
MACHINE GUNS.
(a) One section of the 55th Machine Gun Company will be attached to the Regiment for these operations. During the advance these guns will be disposed of as follows;
(b) One gun immediately in rear of each platoon of "A" Company.
(c) Upon the second or green objective being gained the O.C. 55th Machine Gun Company Section will arrange to dispose of these guns as follows:-
1 Gun at MITCHELL'S FARM.
1 Gun at [illegible] or vicinity.
2 Guns in [illegible] REDOUBT or its vicinity.

8.
BARRAGE.
(a) In addition to the Creeping Field Artillery barrage it will be combined with a Machine Gun Barrage and a heavy bombardment of all known strong points and communications
(b) The Barrage on MITCHELL'S FARM and [illegible] REDOUBT and the immediate vicinities will dwell for an additional lift (four minutes) to enable the troops to pass round the flanks of these positions and thus facilitate the assault of them. The barrage will then lift 100 yards to regain the line of the barrage.

9.
BOMBARDMENT. A continuous bombardment of the enemy position will take place at least 24 hours prior to the attack.

10
CONTACT AEROPLANES.
(a) A contact aeroplane will fly over at the following hours.
ZERO plus one hour
ZERO plus two hours
ZERO plus three hours and thirty minutes
(b) Red flares will be lighted by the leading Infantry when called for by KLAXON HORN or VERY LIGHT.

11
COUNTER-ATTACKS
(a) All Ranks are reminded of the utmost importance of being prepared to meet the immediate and subsequent counter-attacks which are certain to develope on our reaching the objective.
(b) Arrangements have been made for the warning of the Artillery by the Air Service of any probable counter-attacks

12.
MEDICAL.
(a) The Regimental Aid post will be established at SQUARE FARM until the capture of the first or Red line, then at BORRY FARM, and after the capture of the second or green line at MITCHELL'S FARM.
(b) Collecting posts - BAVARIA HOUSE.

13.
PRISONERS OF WAR.
(a) Prisoners captured will be sent to Divisional collecting post at HILL [illegible]. [illegible]
(b) Receipts for prisoners will be obtained.
(c) All officer prisoners are to be searched directly they are captured, and all documents found on them are to be placed in a sand bag and sent with the escort, special attention should be paid to pockets in back skirt of tunics and back of trousers

14. **WATCHES.** Watches will be synchronised at an hour to be notified.

15. **ZERO.** "Z" day and ZERO will be

16 **REPORTS.**
(a) Reports to SQUARE FARM up to ZERO plus 40 minutes then to [illegible] FARM at ZERO plus 2 hours 30 minutes thence to MITCHELL'S FARM.
(b) Company Commanders are reminded of the importance of keeping Battalion headquarters constantly informed of the situation.

[signature]

Issued at 4 p.m.

Captain & Adjutant
2nd Regiment South African Infy

Copy No. 1.	Retained
Copy No. 2.	do personall
" " 3	To Captain Symons, O.C. "A" Coy. "
" " 4.	" Captain Davis O.C. "B" Coy "
" " 5.	" Captain Jacobs O.C. "C" Coy "
" " 6.	" Captain Lagerwall " "D" Coy."
" " 7.	" S.A. Brigade by orderly.
" " 8.	Retained.

ASSEMBLY. Copy No. 1...

1. The Battalion will assembly in rear of the 4th S.A.Infy. and will move by platoons at 5 minutes interval on the night of 19/20th in the following order.

Timeof leaving reserve trenches	No of platoon	Company
11 p.m.	5	"B" Coy.
11.5. p.m.	6	do
11.10 p.m.	7	do
11.15 p.m.	8	do
11.20.p.m.	10	"C" Coy.
11.25.p.m.	9	do
11.30.p.m.	12	do
11.35.p.m.	11	do
11.40.p.m.	15	"D" Coy.
11.45 p.m.	13	do
11.50 p.m.	16	do
11.55 p.m.	14	do
12.0. p.m.	4	"A"Coy.
12.5. p.m.	3	do
12.10.p.m.	2	do
12.15.p.m.	1	do

2. A line of tape will mark the front of each wave of "B" "C" and "D" Companies.
Platoon boards will be placed marking the right flank of each platoon.

3. Each platoon will assemble in line and has a frontage of approximately 80 yards. The normal frontage of two lines per wave will be assumed as the Battalion moves off at ZERO.

4. Machine Guns will accompany their respective platoons of "A" Company which they are to accompany.

5. Nos. 16, 14, and 1 platoons will march to assembly area with their right in front. All other platoons will march with their left in front.

6. Officers and guides as previously ordered will meet Lieut GREEN MC at 9 p.m. to-night at SQUARE FARM.
Guides for each platoon will meet their respective platoons at SQUARE FARM and will lead them into their assembly positions.

7. Sketch plan is attached shewing Assembly position.

8. Route from Reserve Trenches will be in a via "G" Route unless notified to contrary.

9. The GOLDEN value of SILENCE must be clearly impressed on all ranks.

10. Completion of assembly of each Company will be reported to Battalion Headquarters at LOW FARM by code word BED.

R Bentley

Issued at 2 p.m.

Captain & Adjutant
2nd Regt. S.A.Infantry.

Copies No. 1 & 2	Retained.	
Copy No. 3.	O.C. "A" Coy.	Capt.Symons,
4	O.C. "B" Coy.	" Davis
5	O.C. "C" Coy.	" Jacobs.
6	O. C. "D" Coy.	" Lagerwall

Ref: [illegible]
Sheet 28 NW
1/10000

Copy No 2

ORDER No 89

1) The SA Bde will be relieved in the line to night 23/24.

2 The CO intends to march to TORONTO Camp tonight at 10 pm.

3 Route via MENIN GATE through YPRES VLAMERTINGHE by main road.

5 Companies will march out in the following order C. D. B. A. Headquarters will march with C Coy. Leading Coy will pass the starting point at 10 pm.

6 The Battalion will march out by ½ companies till clear of YPRES from there each company will march as a complete company.

7 Guides will meet companies at Cross Roads VLAMERTINGHE H 9 a 8 0 70.

8 200 yds will be maintained between units on the line of march.

9 Lewis Gun limbers will be at the site of Field Kitchens on the main road at 9 pm. Lewis Guns will be loaded on limbers immediately on arrival of the latter.

10. Reports to Batt. H.Q.

Issued at 4.30 pm.

R Beardsley
Capt [illegible]

Copy No 1 & 2 retained
3 OC A Coy
4 OC B Coy
5 OC C Coy
6 OC D Coy

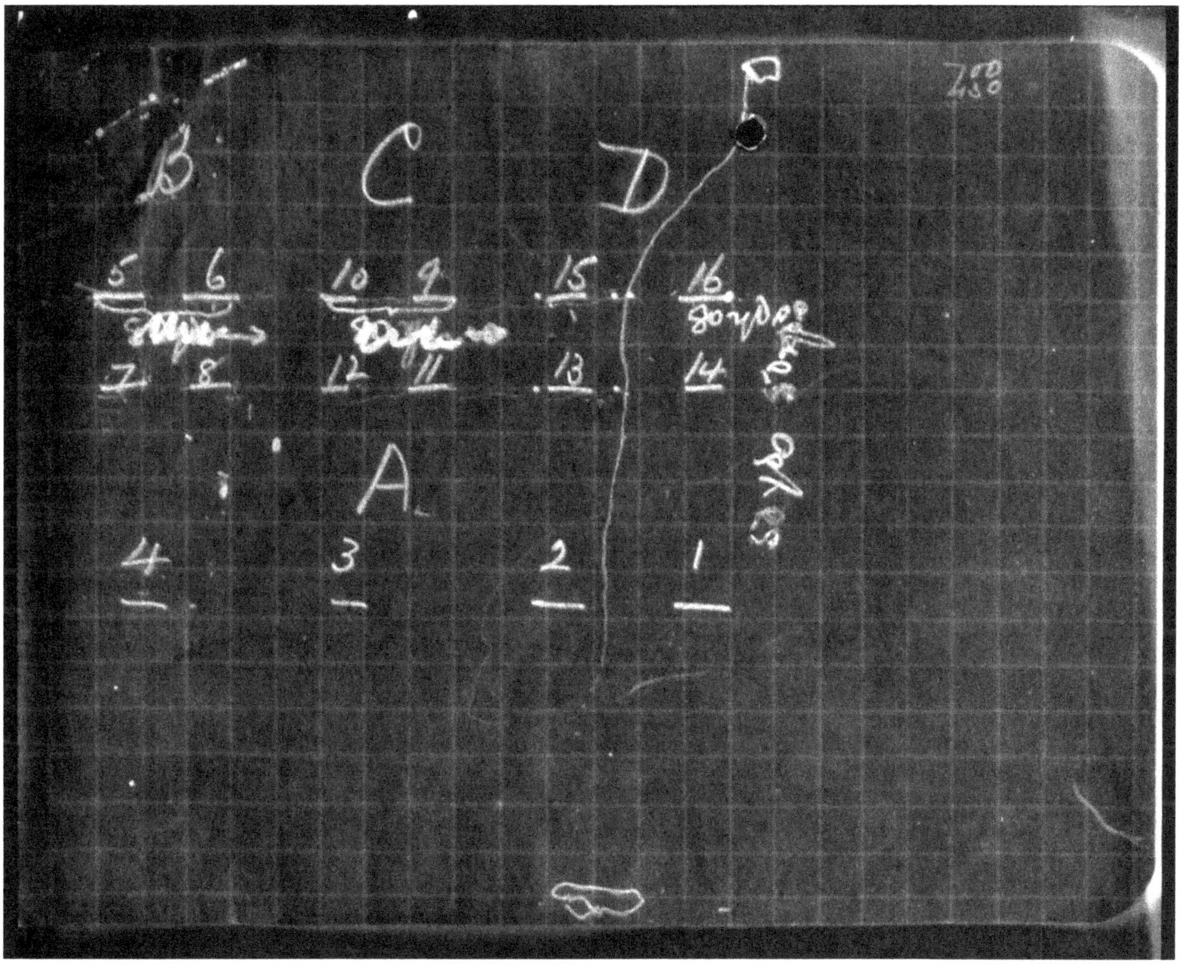

B
C
D
5 6
10 9
15
16
7 8
12 11
13
14
A
4 3 2 1

MARCH TABLE ISSUED WITH ORDER NO: 90.

Unit.	From	To.	Starting Point.	Time of Passing Starting point.
Hqrs. & "A" Coy.	TORONTO CAMP	Embussing Point H.9.a.5.4.	Gate N. of Parade Ground.	12. noon.
"B" Coy.				12.2. p.m.
"C" Coy.	"	"	"	12.4. p.m.
"D" Coy.	"	"	"	12.6.p.m.

REMARKS.

Each Bus holds 25 men.

Officers will travel with their companies.

Captain STEIN will arrange the embussing, which will take place without delay on arrival of companies.at the embussing Point.

Copy No.....

ORDER No. 91.

Reference
Sheet 27.
1/40000.

In the Field,
27th September, 1917.

1. (a) The 9th Division will be transferred from the V Corps to the XIX Corps.

(b) The South African Infantry Brigade will move from the WINNEZEELE AREA to the ARNEKE AREA.

2. The O.C. intends to march to ARNEKE at 9.35.a.m. to-day.

3. The head of the battalion will pass the starting point at 9.35. a.m. in the following distribution:-
Hqrs. "B" - "C" - "D" - "A" Coys. 1st Line Transport.

4. STARTING POINT - The gate on the road N.W. of camp.

5. ROUTE. Through Cross roads at J.11.c.20., and by road passing through J.16. b. & c., J.21. b & c. thence through J.26. & 25 and I.30. to Cross Roads at I.29.b.5.6. thence to ARNEKE via cross roads at I.33.a.6.0.

Track in J.26.a. and J.25.b. is passable for Infantry only. Transport will move via cross roads J.31.b.0.9. and Road Junction J.25.b.4.7.

6. Baggage will be piled outside Quartermaster's stores ready for loading at 8.a.m. Loading will be supervised by Transport Officer.

7. All troops will be clear of billets by 8.30.a.m. at which time the Medical Officer and Second in Command will inspect billets.
Billet certificates will be rendered by this hour.

8. Marching states will be handed to Adjutant by 9.a.m. and immediately after arrival at new billets.

9. Reports to the head of the Battalion.

Issued at 6.a.m. 27th Septr.'17.

[signature]

Captain & Adjutant,
2nd Regiment South African Inf.

Copies 1 & 2.		Retained.
Copy No.	3.	O/C. "A" Coy.
	4.	O/C. "B" Coy.
	5.	O/C. "C" Coy.
	6.	O/C. "D" Coy.
	7.	Transport Officer.
	8.	Quartermaster.

Copy No. 2

ORDER NO.90.

Reference
HAZEBROUCK 5A
1/250000.
Sheets 27 & 28.
1/40000.

In the Field,
24. 9. 17.

1. The South African Brigade will complete the move to the WINNIZELE area to-day.

2. The C.O. intends to proceed to the WINNIZELE area by march route and by bus at 12.noon. to-day, in accordance with attached march table.

3. DISTRIBUTION. First company will pass the starting point at 12. noon.
Headquarters & "A" Company,
"B" Coy. "C" Coy. "D" Coy.
Companies will march to the embussing point with 100 yards intervals.

4. Starting Point - Camp gate NORTH of parade ground.

5. Route - By main road to the embussing point, at H.9.a.5.4.

6. Marching out states will be handed to the Adjutant on parade. Marching-in states immediately on arrival in new area.

7. Reports to the head of the Battalion.

R Beverley

Captain & Adjutant,
2nd Regiment S.A.Infantry.

Issued at 10.45.a.m.

Copy Nos 1 & 2.	Retained.
" No. 3.	O.C."A" Coy.
" No. 4.	O.C."B" Coy.
" No. 5.	O.C. "C" Coy.
" No. 6.	O.C."D" Coy.
" No. 7.	Transport Officer.
" No. 8.	Quartermaster.

99

Addendum to Order No. 91.

1. Delete para. 3. at 9.35. AM. and substitute 10. am.

2. Route - delete para. 5 and substitute -
Cross roads J. 21. b. 6. 3. - WORMHOUDT C 16 - 17 - LEDRINGHEM - I 2 b.

3. Guides will meet the Battn. at Cross roads I. 2 b. 5. 0.

4. Billets will be clean and ready for inspection by 9. am.

R Bentley

Capt. & Adjt.
2nd S. A.

27 - 9 - 1917.

War diary

2nd REGIMENT SOUTH AFRICAN INFANTRY.

REPORT ON OPERATIONS EAST OF YPRES BETWEEN THE 19th and 22nd SEPTEMBER, 1917.

1st SOUTH AFRICAN INFANTRY BRIGADE.

1. I have the honour to submit herewith my report upon operations of the 2nd Regiment South African Infantry during the period 19th to 23rd September, 1917.

2. Upon receipt of the advanced instructions and later the Brigade Operation order everything that could be arranged was done to ensure all ranks being thoroughly instructed in all details appertaining to the particular operation to be taken in hand.

3. Upon the night of the 17th September the Battalion moved from [redacted] Camp by rail to a point about a mile WEST of YPRES Camp and thence by march route to the Reserve trench line some three quarters of a mile EAST of MILL COT.

EYRE

4. At about 10.a.m. on the [illegible]th the enemy shelled the Reserve trench line and caused us twenty three casualties.

5. On the nights of the 17th and 18th the routes from the Reserve trenches to the position of assembly in rear of the 4th Regiment South African Infantry, then in the front line, were thoroughly reconnoitred and arrangements made for the collection of the estimated requirements in white tape to assist in clearly marking the position of assembly and the leads to it from the tracks to be used.

6. On the night of the 18/19th September the limits of the position of assembly were definitely fixed and a reconnaissance of this was carried out by Platoon officers and Platoon guides.

7. On the night of the 19/20th I personally reconnoitred the track known as "H" Track, which was presumed to be outside the area of the enemy usual barrage. This track was not in good condition and I found it necessary to employ "G" Track.

8. Lieut. G.G.GREEN, M.C., with an officer and four guides from each company were despatched early on the evening of the 19th to the position of assembly. The assembly lines and leads from the main track were taped off, and platoon position boards placed.

9. To add to our difficulties it rained steadily during the assembly owing to which the arrival of the troops was much delayed, the first platoon not arriving until 12.30. a.m.

10. The assembly was complete at 2.20. a.m. and reported to Brigade Headquarters at 2.45 a.m. enemy shelling in the vicinity of our position was frequent throughout but only one casualty was sustained then.

11. I consider the success of the assembly was due to the following:-

(a) Early and careful reconnaissance in connection with which an early knowledge of the definite limits of each regimental position of deployment.

(b) The taping out of assembly position with unsoiled tape, for which a large supply should be available.

(c) Careful selection of guides and marking of routes with tape.

(d) Platoon notice boards bearing the number of the platoon and placed on one or other of the platoon flanks.

(e) The assembly was made close up behind the 4th S.A.I in order to get clear of our front line trenches as soon as possible after ZERO and thus avoid the enemy barrage usually placed on our front line when first he is alarmed.

12. When at ZERO the 4th S.A.I. advanced the 2nd S.A.I. closely followed until clear of the enemy barrage zone when the usual attack formation distances were gradually assumed.

13. Just at first the light was not quite sufficient to clearly distinguish the ground, but shortly afterwards points of direction could be easily recognised and a slight adjustment of direction had to be made.

14. At ZERO plus 35 minutes the Battalion halted in rear of the 4th S.A.Infantry on the first objective, where all necessary re-adjustments were made preparatory to the advance to the 2nd objective.

15. Just prior to our advance for the 2nd objective a portion of the 4th S.A.Infantry advanced from the 1st objective through our barrage to Mitchell's Farm, which was then still being heavily shelled according to programme. Owing to this mistake the 4th S.A.Infantry suffered a number of casualties from our own guns.

16. The Battalion was disposed on a three company frontage with one company in support, "D" Company on the right "C" Company in the Centre, "B" Company on the left and "A" Company in support.

17. The barrage apparently rested on MITCHELL'S FARM longer than was anticipated and for this reason the centre Company was some few minutes later than the one on the right in reaching the final objective.

18. After passing MITCHELL'S FARM it was found that the troops on our left, on the NORTH bank of the ZONNEBEKE stream were not moving abreast of us and at the same time my left Company ("B" Company) began to encounter resistance from WATEREND FARM and the high ground in the vicinity of TULIP COTTAGE and HILL 37.

19. In addition to the resistance described in the foregoing paragraph, ZEVENCOTE itself still remained to be dealt with. This latter resistance was speedily undertaken by pressing round the right flank and at the sametime maintaining touch with the troops of the 55th Division on our left.

20. The defences of ZEVENCOTE itself were cleared and occupied from the flank and in WATEREND FARM alone 3 Machine

20.
continued. Guns and seventy prisoners were captured.

21. In the meanwhile at 8.30 a.m. centre and right Companies had gained GREEN LINE Objective, and I was able to report occupation of right portion of objective at 8.48 a.m. (my B/14).
I had previously reported progress of advance at 7.55 am in my B/13.
At 9.13 I was able to report occupation of objective by centre company, who, however, reported they were not in touch with left.
I immediately sent up a small reserve of 17 men to strengthen left flank and to connect with centre who had at this time extended to left and turned their flank down to connect with "B" Company.
I also strengthened left by sending a portion of support company to this point.
As I had not heard directly from left Company I con--cluded that officer casualties had been heavy, so sent my Signalling Officer 2nd Lieut. DICKERSON to take charge of this flank.
Lieut. GREEN MC who was at MITCHELL'S FARM then sent me a situation report as regards the left and I was then satisfied that this flank was adequately held.
During this time no advance had been made by the 55th Division, their line being roughly in front of DELVA FARM and I connected to them through Scottish post at K NORTH.
Our line was then being subjected to sniping and Machine Gun fire from direction of TULIP COTTAGES and ridge on left.

22. At 9.45 a.m. I reported a counter attack massing on left.
This attack was caught in our barrage and rifle fire and crushed before it reached our line.
During the forenoon, I received reports that position was being well consolidated in two lines of detached posts. Rear posts covering gaps in front line. An outpost line of Lewis Guns had also been established.
Reports had also been received stating that casualties continued to occur principally from Machine Gun fire from left and shelling, and that strength in line was diminishing.
As 4th S.A.Infantry could not spare any men at that time I asked the CAMERONS to send me one officer and 30 other ranks, which was done. These were sent to re-inforce "C" Company and left flank near junction with "C" Company and proved most valuable.
At approximately 5.50. p.m. 55th Division started to advance on to ridge running along DITCH TRENCH and TULIP COTTAGES and succeeded in occupying same.
This movement completed line to Left and obviated any necessity for a portion of Flank which had been formed.
The night passed quietly with only moderate shelling on our front principally in vicinity of MITCHELL'S FARM and BORRY FARM.
Our ARTILLERY opened with a bombardment on enemy lines in early morning of 21st.

22. cont. During the morning and up to 3.30. p.m. on 21st very little shelling was indulged in and most of wounded were evacuated and positions further consolidated.
~~[illegible]~~.

23. In compliance with orders from Brigade for withdrawal of half strength of 3rd and 4th S.A.Infantry.
The 3rd S.A.Infantry started to withdraw at about 3.45 p.m.
This movement was undoubtedly noticed by the enemy who put down a heavy bombardment causing a number of casualties and preventing further movement at that time.
This Bombardment continued up to 8 p.m. Front Line being barraged as well as area west of line.
In accordance with Brigade Orders the 7th SEAFORTHS relieved the Battalion and portion of the 4th S.A.Infy. between 12 midnight and 5.30. a.m. Relief being reported at 5.25 a.m. The only incident being the difficulty and time it took to relieve all posts.

__REPORTS__ Re: Frequent reports were sent to Brigade Headquarters, during operations.
The following points and observations were noted.

__ASSEMBLY.__ These are contained in Para. 11.

__ADVANCE.__ On several occasions the advance was maintained by quick movements from shell hole to shell hole, and ~~incidentally~~ undoubtedly this method helped to immune a number of men.
The advantage of a correctly designed model of the country to be crossed on as large a scale as possible being available for troops to study before an advance cannot be over estimated as it is easy then for every one to recognise country and keep a correct direction during the operations.

__BARRAGE.__ Our barrage was extremely good and easy to follow. The addition of smoke shells was a help.
In the shelled pitted area a proportion of the barrage should be shrapnel.
The lifts of the barrage were distinct and it was not considered that the pace was too slow.
Those who attempted to pass through the Barrage suffered heavily, our own troops included.
In reply to S.O.S. our barrage was quickly and correctly put down and on all occasions inflicted heavy casualties on enemy.
The enemy Barrage was in some cases very heavy and was generally put down some 200 yards in rear of front line and extending to some distance in rear, preference being shown to valleys and known strong points or positions.
This Barrage did not contain much shrapnel and shell effect was local. It would appear that when an effort was made by the enemy to engage a wide front his barrage was visibly weaker.
It is considered at all times the enemy barrage formed a serious obstacle to troops.

__MACHINE GUNS.__ The enemy did not employ any machine guns on Barrage work on ground within 1,000 yards of Front line.

__SIGNALS.__ Aeroplanes called for flares by firing Very lights when troops reached objectives. Flares were lit but no report was received that these had been seen.
No other communication with Aeroplanes was made.
Day light lamps were successfully used from Front Line

SIGNALS (Continued).

TO Battalion Headquarters for a short period but unfortunately these lamps were blown up by shell fire and could not be re-placed and practically all messages between companies and Battalion Headquarters had to be sent by runners.

On the night of relief a lamp was placed on each flank of Battalion. These were of greatest value to incoming units.

From Battalion Headquarters to Brigade, Power buzzer and at times telephones were successfully used. Pigeon messages were also sent but I have heard no report if these were reseived.

SUGGESTION. It is considered that for night work a small flash light (electric torch) would be of greatest value, but some system of acknowledging the message should be arranged.

S.O.S. Signals were found in some cases to be defective and did not fire correct light signal. The rifle grenade is a most convenient manner in which to use this signal.

The Line of runner posts would be of the greatest value as guides but were only partially completed before relief.

The Message maps were found to be of great value, and allowed of messages being rapidly written and sent.

PROTECTION OF ARMS. Rifles were protected by breech cover only and a liberal supply of oil and 4" X 2" was issued to each man. This proved sufficiently effective to keep all rifles in good working order.

A waterproof cover was made for lewis guns to easily slip over gun with drum placed in position, and to tie with strap round small of butt.

Although the condition of the country was wet and muddy and guns were continually in contact with the ground, in no cases did mud or wet cause stoppages. After firing gun men in line slipped on these covers and found them of the greatest value. It is considered that these covers might be adopted.

CASUALTIES. Points dealing with casualties are contained in Medical Officer's report attached herewith.

In conclusion I wish to express my appreciation of the gallant conduct of all ranks who were under my command during operations and have much pleasure in forwarding certain recommendations for acts of conspicuous gallantry which came to my notice.

Sgd. F E Cochran
Major

Lieut. Colonel,
Tmp Commanding 2nd Regiment South African Infantry.

In the Field,
26th September, 1917.

Appendix V

1:10,000 L.3. EDITION I. Part of 28 N.E.

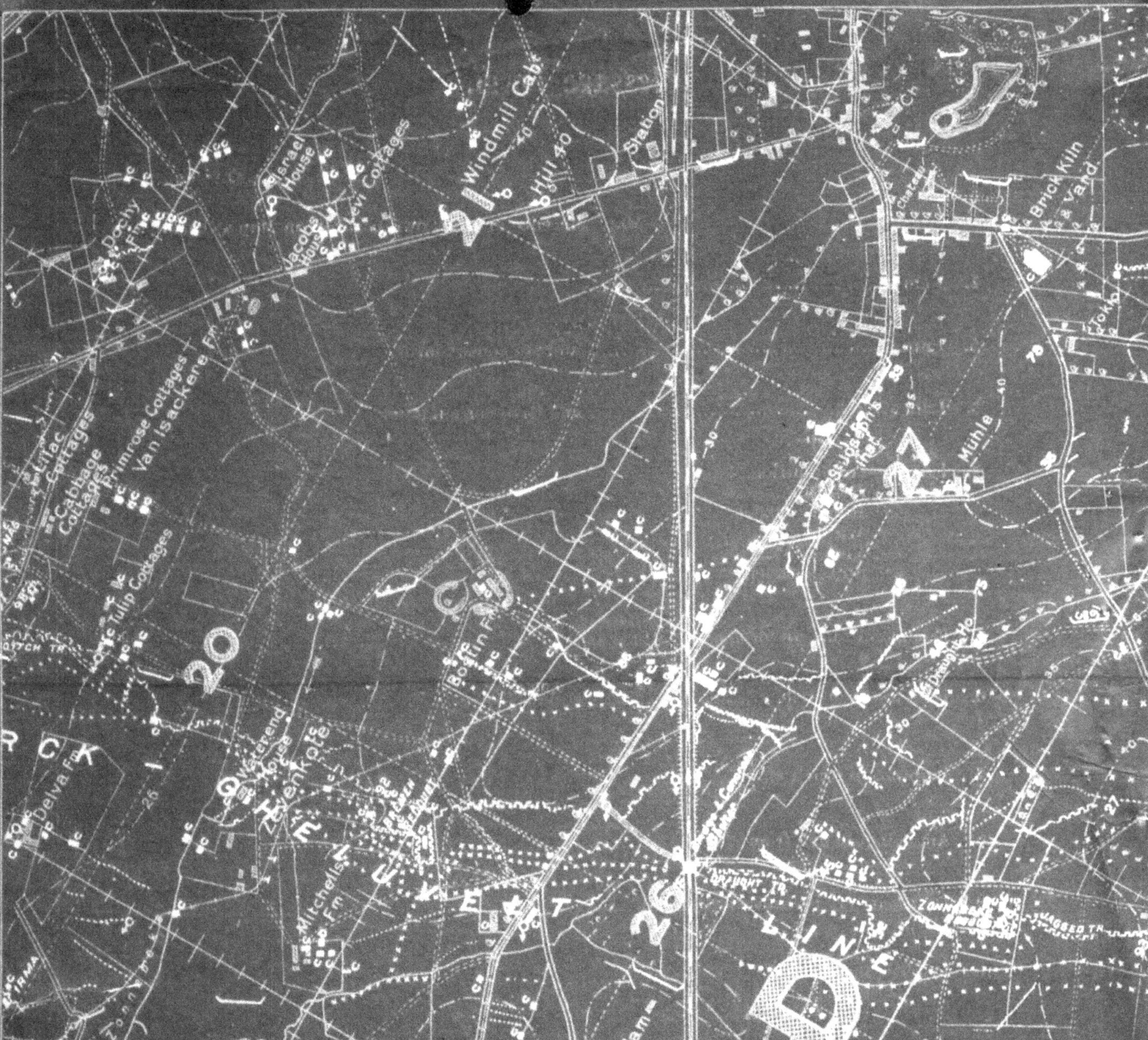

FIELD SURVEY COY, R.E. (2681) 14.9.17

Scale. 1:10,000.

YARDS 500 400 300 200 100 0 500 1,000 YARDS

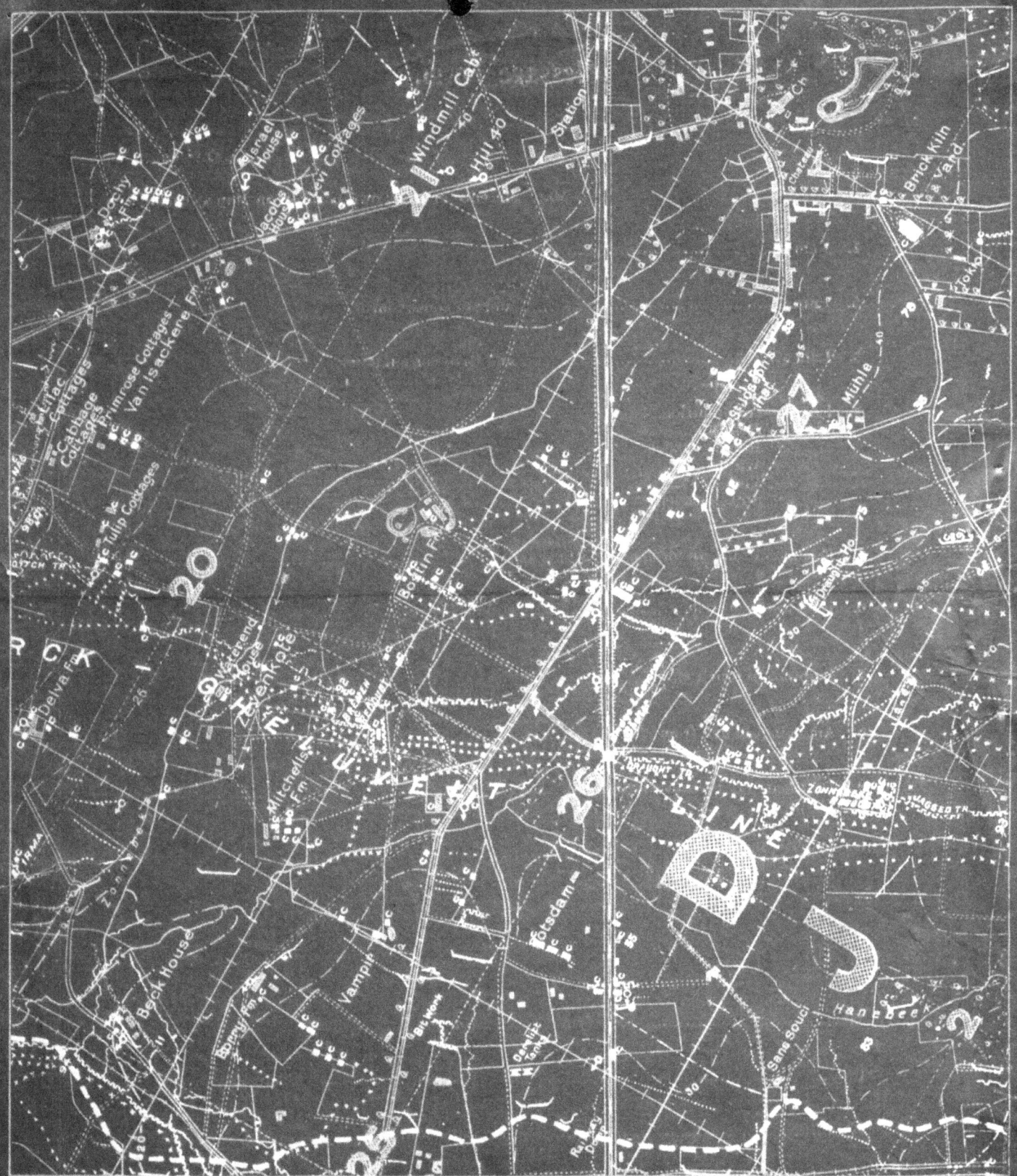

October 1917

2nd South African Infantry

Army Form C. 2118.

WAR DIARY

or

[redacted]

(Erase heading not required.)

Instructions regarding War Diaries and Intelligence Summaries are contained in F. S. Regs., Part II. and the Staff Manual respectively. Title pages will be prepared in manuscript.

Place	Date	Hour	Summary of Events and Information	Remarks and references to Appendices
ARNEKE	1st		Fine warm day. Training as usual – 2/Lt LEWELL rejoined from Base. Strength State. With unit 24 officers 750 O.R. Not with unit 9 officers 102 O.R.	Sheet Hazebrouck 5a
"	2nd		Fine warm day. Training as usual. – Major Heenan returned from senior officers course in England. Company commanders and Lt Green M.C. to VOLKERINCKHOVE on a three days course at XVIIIth Corps School. – Bombs dropped from aeroplanes near ARNEKE. 7 O.R. to sea coast for one days trip under DIVISIONAL arrangements.	
"	3rd		Fine day, cloudy, cool. Training as usual. 8 O.R. to sea side for trips under DIVISIONAL Arrangements – 1 O.R. on leave. 6 O.R. draft arrived from Base. Warning order for move received 7 pm. – 12 midnight no definite order received. Adjutant + Orderly Sgts waiting for orders.	

A6945 Wt. W11422/M1160 350,000 12/16 D. D. & L. Forms/C./2118/14.

Instructions regarding War Diaries and Intelligence Summaries are contained in F. S. Regs., Part II. and the Staff Manual respectively. Title Pages will be prepared in manuscript.

WAR DIARY
or
INTELLIGENCE SUMMARY
(Erase heading not required.)

Army Form C. 2118

Place	Date	Hour	Summary of Events and Information	Remarks and references to Appendices
ARNEKE MOULLE	4th		Battalion marched out of billets at 8.30 AM. – Order No 92 refers – Packs were carried on horses. 14 mile march. Everybody very fit – no stragglers. Arrived at MOULLE 3.30 PM. Billets comfortable but rather scattered. Weather rainy and cold. Major Cochran temporarily appointed to command 3rd S.A. Inf.	Appendix I Sheet HAZEBROUCK 5A 1:100000
MOULLE	5th		Training commenced. 12.30 AM – 6 PM. Rifle & Lewis Gun practice on the range – 5th Army B range – Good shooting. Weather cold but fine.	
"	6th		Training on Training area near MOULLE – Wet day & cold. 2 O.R. on leave.	
	7th		Voluntary services – Training 9 AM – 1 PM – Wet day & cold. Strength state. With Unit 24 439 Not with unit 10 128 34 – 867 9 other ranks attached to 28th Machine Gun Coy. for duty as Carriers for forthcoming operations –	

Instructions regarding War Diaries and Intelligence Summaries are contained in F. S. Regs., Part II. and the Staff Manual respectively. Title Pages will be prepared in manuscript.

WAR DIARY
or
INTELLIGENCE SUMMARY
(Erase heading not required.)

Army Form C. 2118

Place	Date	Hour	Summary of Events and Information	Remarks and references to Appendices
MOULLE	8th		Training 9 AM – 1 PM. Fine morning, wet and cold in afternoon. 26 O.R. returned from Musketry Course. Orders received 9.30 PM. for move of Transport tomorrow.	
MOULLE	9th		Training – Battalion attack practice – 9 am – 12 noon. Firing on range for Indifferent Shots – 12 noon – 3. p.m. – First line Transport, less cookers, mess cart and riders, proceeded at 1. pm. by road to New Area. –	ORDER 93.
MOULLE	10th	A.M. 4.30	Regiment, less 1st line transport and details, marched to WATTEN, – entrained at 9. am. and proceeded to DIRTY BUCKET CORNER, and marched to destination – BRAKE CAMP (Sheet 28 (Belgium –	ORDER 94.
BRAKE CAMP		4. PM	A. 30.) Cookers and details of 1st line transport entrained at ST. OMER, and proceeded to VLAMERTINGHE by Omnibus train, marching from there to BRAKE CAMP, arriving about an hour after the Regiment. – Transport which travelled by road arrived later in the evening. – 1 other rank on leave. Weather – cold and showery all day. –	
			Strength State: With Unit — Off 23 . O/Ranks 763	
			Not with Unit — 11 . 104	
			Total: 34 . 867	

1875 W: W593/826 1,000,000 4/15 J.B.C. & A. A.D.S.S./Forms/C. 2118.

Instructions regarding War Diaries and Intelligence Summaries are contained in F. S. Regs., Part II. and the Staff Manual respectively. Title pages will be prepared in manuscript.

WAR DIARY
or
~~INTELLIGENCE SUMMARY.~~
(Erase heading not required.)

Army Form C. 2118.

Place	Date	Hour	Summary of Events and Information	Remarks and references to Appendices
BRAKE CAMP.	11th	AM. 9.0.	Personnel remaining out of action – 1 off. (CAPT L. M. JACOBS) and 60 other ranks proceeded by march route to HOUTKERQUE 1 other rank on Musketry Course Cameirs, – 4 other ranks to Divisional Dump for duty. –	
REIGERS-BERG.		10 am	Regiment, less 1st line transport and administrative details ordered to proceed to forward area – marched to REIGERS-BERG Camp* (Order 95.) Fighting Strength – 19 off. 540. other ranks plus Medical Officer attached. – 1st line transport and details at BRAKE CAMP. – Cloudy weather – rain threatening. –	Order No 95. * Sheet 28 H 6 a
Do.	12th	6 am	Regiment moved by march route to CANAL BANK. – arriving there at 7 30 AM – Dugouts were allotted on EAST side of CANAL BANK* – Day was occupied in drawing shovels – bombs &c, for expected attack – Good accommodation – Wether wet and cold.	Order 96. * Sheet 28 H 2 5 d

D. D. & L., London, E.C.
(A7853) Wt. W809/M1672 350,000 4/17 Sch. 52a Forms/C/2118/14

Instructions regarding War Diaries and Intelligence Summaries are contained in F. S. Regs., Part II. and the Staff Manual respectively. Title pages will be prepared in manuscript.

WAR DIARY
or
~~INTELLIGENCE SUMMARY~~
(*Erase heading not required.*)

Army Form C. 2118.

Place	Date	Hour	Summary of Events and Information	Remarks and references to Appendices
YPRES CANAL BANK	13th		Still uncertain as to future operations – Issue of rations & stores completed – 1pm warning order received that the regiment will take over & hold the trenches occupied at present by a mixture of units of 26th & 27th I. Bde which were rather disorganised after a not too successful attack on 12th inst. Lt Col. Tanner CMG & 5 Officers proceeded to reconnoitre positions. 2pm 1 officer and 88 OR including 8 sick were returned to the detail camp at MARSH FARM.* 4 PM Battalion under command of the Adjutant proceeded to the line to relieve units of 26th & 27th Bdes. Vide order No 97. – Guides met parties as arranged. Owing to darkness, mud and lack of knowledge on the part of the guides reliefs were not completed that night. Casualties 2 OR Killed 1 off. Capt. Pearse wounded 6 O.R. wounded. A fair amount of hostile shelling, principally directed at duckboard tracks leading to front line. Weather wet & cold. Dispositions vide map Appendix 2. Part of 28 NE & 20 SE 1:10000	Order 97 App. I * Sheet 28 H 4 a

D. D. & L., London, E.C. (A7823) Wt. W809/M1672 350,000 4/17 Sch. 52a Forms/C/2118/14

Instructions regarding War Diaries and Intelligence Summaries are contained in F. S. Regs., Part II. and the Staff Manual respectively. Title pages will be prepared in manuscript.

WAR DIARY
or
INTELLIGENCE SUMMARY.
(Erase heading not required.)

Army Form C. 2118.

Place	Date	Hour	Summary of Events and Information	Remarks and references to Appendices
YPRES FRONT	14th		Batt: HQ established at a concrete shelter near ALBATROSS FARM 10 AM company reliefs reported complete & connected with 2nd NZR Bde on right and 24th S.A.T. on the left. – Weather finer but cold. Intermittent shelling all day. Concentrated shelling on Batt H.Q. 12 midnight onwards.	
do	15th		Shelling on front line & Batt H.Q. very heavy 1 PM – 3 PM. Casualties at Batt. H.Q. 1 killed 4 wounded. – Companies several casualties. General Dawson CMG. visited H.Q. and front line about 8 A.M. Day occupied in improving H.Q. running rations &c. 63rd Coy R.E. built splinter proof shelter under good cover at Batt. H.Q. Fine but cold – Enemy aerial activity great – several bombs dropped in the Battalion Sector. Shelling less during the day but increased at night.	

D. D. & L. London, E.C. (A7883) Wt W893/M1672 350,000 4/17 Sch. 52a Forms/C2118/14

Instructions regarding War Diaries and Intelligence Summaries are contained in F. S. Regs., Part II. and the Staff Manual respectively. Title pages will be prepared in manuscript.

WAR DIARY
or
INTELLIGENCE SUMMARY.
(Erase heading not required.)

Army Form C. 2118.

Place	Date	Hour	Summary of Events and Information	Remarks and references to Appendices
YPRES FRONT	16th		1 AM onwards to dawn enemy shelling fairly heavy. 7 AM Maj-Gen. LUKIN CMG DSO CB & B-Gen DAWSON CMG arrived and inspected the front line. – Lt Col Tanner CMG relieved by Major Heenan left the line to proceed to 8th Bde. to the command of which he has been promoted – Quiet day – fine & cold – little shelling – enemy aeroplanes active. – Hostile artillery more active at night.	
"	17th		1 AM to dawn hostile artillery active. A few casualties occurred during the night. Relief expected. Heavy hostile shelling on front & support lines – quiet after dark. Relief commenced by 3rd S.A.I. at 7 PM and was completed by 10 PM when regiment moved to Tents camp at IRISH FARM*. All Battalion in by 12 midnight. Fine weather – All very tired. – Hot meals were and rum was issued –	ORDER 99 App I. * Sheet 28 NW 27 a. 25·65

D. D. & L., London, E.C. (A6133) Wt. W593/M1672 350,000 4/17 Sch. 52a Forms/C2118/14

Army Form C. 2118.

WAR DIARY
or
INTELLIGENCE SUMMARY.
(Erase heading not required.)

Instructions regarding War Diaries and Intelligence Summaries are contained in F. S. Regs., Part II. and the Staff Manual respectively. Title pages will be prepared in manuscript.

Place	Date	Hour	Summary of Events and Information	Remarks and references to Appendices
IRISH FARM.	18th		At IRISH FARM all day – Casualty rolls since 17th inst. completed. 1 officer wounded – 17 OR killed. 1 OR Died of wounds, 48 OR wounded – Day spent in cleaning up. Three cases only of "Trench feet" despite the fact that whale oil was not available. Much rain.	
do	19th		Resting – Fine weather but cold – Enemy aeroplanes very active on CANAL and region of IRISH FARM – several bombs dropped, a few casualties on canal.	
do	20th		Moved to REIGERSBURG CAMP. 2nd Lt MANDY & HENNESSY arrived with regimental police & sanitary squad. 4 officers 200 men on working party to forward area. Rain & cold.	ORDER No 100 App I

D. D. & L., London, E.C.
(A7883) Wt. W809/M1672 350,000 4/17 Sch. 52a Forms/C/2118/14

Instructions regarding War Diaries and Intelligence Summaries are contained in F. S. Regs., Part II. and the Staff Manual respectively. Title pages will be prepared in manuscript.

WAR DIARY
or
INTELLIGENCE SUMMARY.
(Erase heading not required.)

Army Form C. 2118.

Place	Date	Hour	Summary of Events and Information	Remarks and references to Appendices
REIGERSBURG CAMP.	21st		Rain – 300 with usual officers & Sgts on working parties to front line.	
	22nd		Rain. 400 men with usual officers & Sgts on working parties to the front line.	
„	23rd		The Brigade is relieved by a Brigade of the 63rd (Naval) Division.	
			Battalion move by Buses to NOUVEAU MONDE* ORDER 101. Buses were late and the destination was not reached till 8 P.M. – Men did not settle down till 12 midnight. – Billets were scattered and intercommunication difficult.	Appendix I * Sheet 27 D 21
			Move order for tomorrow received 12 midnight.	

Instructions regarding War Diaries and Intelligence Summaries are contained in F. S. Regs., Part II. and the Staff Manual respectively. Title pages will be prepared in manuscript.

WAR DIARY
or
INTELLIGENCE SUMMARY.
(Erase heading not required.)

Army Form C. 2118.

Place	Date	Hour	Summary of Events and Information	Remarks and references to Appendices
NOUVEAU MONDE to WORMHOUDT	24th		Battalion marched to WORMHOUDT* - 3 miles - at 10 - 30 AM in accordance with Order No 102. Billeted in WORMHOUDT. - Lt COOPER & 25 O.R arrived from base as reinforcements. 2/Lt HENNESSY & 2/Lt MIDDLETON arrived with 80 O.R. from working party. Casualties on working parties 12 O R wounded. Total Casualties Period 13th - 23rd Oct 1917. Killed 17 OR. - Missing NIL - Wounded 1 Officer (Capt T.F. PEARSE.) and 60 OR - Wounded, at duty, 10 O R. Total 1 officer & 88 O R.	Sheet 27 C.10
do	25th		Marched to DUNKERQUE area - PETIT SYNTHE - Order No 103 - 13 miles march - packs carried in lorries - men all fit - arrived 3 pm. Good billets well arranged - AREA Commandant most helpful.	Sheet 19 Appendix I

D. D. & L., London, E.C. (A7883) Wt. W809/M1672 350,000 4/17 Sch. 52a Forms/C/2118/14

Army Form C. 2118.

Instructions regarding War Diaries and Intelligence Summaries are contained in F. S. Regs., Part II. and the Staff Manual respectively. Title pages will be prepared in manuscript.

WAR DIARY
or
INTELLIGENCE SUMMARY.
(Erase heading not required.)

Place	Date	Hour	Summary of Events and Information	Remarks and references to Appendices
PETIT SYNTHE	26th		Day occupied in cleaning up. re-issuing equipment and adjusting billets. Everybody is very comfortably billetted — Weather fine & not cold.	
"	27th		Company parades & inspection. CAPT THERON of U.D.F. staff attached to regiment for instruction. 1 O.R. on leave.	
	28th		Church parades. Warning order for move tomorrow to forward area	

D. D. & L., London, E.C. (A7883) Wt. W809/M1674 350,000 4/17 Sch. 52a Forms/C/2118/14

Instructions regarding War Diaries and Intelligence Summaries are contained in F. S. Regs., Part II. and the Staff Manual respectively. Title pages will be prepared in manuscript.

WAR DIARY

or

(Erase heading not required.)

Army Form C. 2118.

Place	Date	Hour	Summary of Events and Information	Remarks and references to Appendices
PETITE SYNTHE	29th		1 AH Bde O. Order NO 141 received re move to-day. Batt: moved out at 9 AM under O.Order N104 - Regiment entrained at ST. POL for COXYDE BAINS and moved off at 10 AM. Quick comfortable journey — Arrived at destination 2 pm - Relieved 11th Royal West Kents in centre Sub-sector of COXYDE SECTION * of Coast Defence System. - Relief completed 4 P.M.	App I. *Sheet DUNKERQUE 10 2 H 55 50
COXYDE LES BAINS	"		Companies comfortably settled down mostly in houses. Strength of Regiment with unit 22 Officers 711 O R. not with unit 11 " 75 " — 33 786.	
"	30th		At COXYDE LES BAINS - Very cold, stormy & wet. Enemy shelled the village with HV Guns. Direct hit on Bde HQ - casualties in other units. 2/Lt Terry at o/c D Coy reports case of suspected Espionage i.e. Signalling from house at ST. IDELSBALD. Reports to Brigade & Division APM enquiring.	~~[illegible]~~

D. D. & L., London, E.C. (A7883) Wt. W809/M1672 350,000 4/17 Sch. 52a Forms/C/2118/14

Army Form C. 2118.

Instructions regarding War Diaries and Intelligence Summaries are contained in F. S. Regs., Part II. and the Staff Manual respectively. Title pages will be prepared in manuscript.

WAR DIARY

or

(Erase heading not required.)

Place	Date	Hour	Summary of Events and Information	Remarks and references to Appendices
COXYDE LES BAINS	31st		Fine weather and warm. – Front line companies and part of reserve companies employed on works in front line e.g. clearing trenches, revetting Lewis Gun emplacements, building shelters &c. Details from reserve companies at Training 110 O.R. – 138 O.R. draft arrived from XVth Corps reinforcement camp GHYVELDE Sheet DUNKERQUE 1a 3G 3.7 120 new men and 18 returned BEF men. Enemy aeroplanes over COXYDE LES BAINS at night no bombing.	
			Strength state. With unit 19 officers 851 O.R.	
			not with unit 14 " 74 "	
			Map shewing disposition of Battalion in the centre subsector of the Coast defence area will be put up next month.	
			2 Officers & 2 O.R. on leave.	
			C R Heenan Major	
			Temp Commanding 2nd S.A.I.	

D. D. & L., London, E.C. (A7883) Wt. W809/M1672 350,000 4/17 Sch. 52a Forms/C/2118/14

2nd REGIMENT SOUTH AFRICAN INFANTRY.

WAR DIARY.

OCTOBER, 1917.

INDEX TO APPENDICES

MARCH TABLE ISSUED IN ACCORDANCE WITH ORDER NO: 92.

4. 10. 1917.

Unit.	From	To.	Starting POINT	Time	Route
Hqrs. "A" "C" "D" Transport	BILLETS	HOULLE.	Railway Gates ARNEKE, WEST SIDE of LINE.	8.15.a.m.	ARNEKE – le MENEGAT. – BALEMBERG. – LEDERZEELE. – ST. MOMELIN – LE BAS. – SERQUES.
"B"	"	"	"	8.30.a.m.	"

NOTE. "B" Company will fall in behind "D" Company in the column and in front of 1st line transport. The Company should be ready in column of fours in road leading from billets to main road, to join Battalion as it passes at 8.30.a.m.

INSTRUCTIONS ISSUED IN CONNECTION WITH ORDER NO: 92.

1. 2nd Lieut. EGAN and Billeting N.C.Os. will report at Orderly Room at 7.30.a.m. with bicycles. They will meet Staff Captain at Area Commandant's office, HOULLE, at 10.30.a.m. to-day.

2. G.S.Waggons will report at Companies as under for officers kit and mess stores. –

   1 G.S.Waggon. "A" "C" and "D" Companies.
   1 do. HQrs. Quartermaster stores & "B" Coy.

   Baggage to be ready by 6.30.a.m.

3. Lorries will be distributed as follows:–

   1 Hqrs. and Quartermaster Stores.
   1 "B" and "A" Companies.
   1 "C" and "D" Companies.

   Lorries will be at Orderly Room at 12. noon.
   1 guide per company will meet lorries.

4. Men's packs and any stores not already loaded will be loaded on lorries. 1 N.C.O. and 2 men per company will remain behind as loading party.
   All packs will be stacked in roads outside Company billets by 12. noon. Headquarter packs at Orderly Room and Quartermaster's stores.
   2nd Lieut. LOWELL will be in charge of this rear party and will report to Adjutant at 8.a.m. to-day.

5. A list of all tents handed over to be forwarded to Battalion Headquarters as early as possible after arrival in new area. The number of Billet and owner's name to be given in each case.

6. Billets will be thoroughly cleaned and the usual certificates handed to Adjutant.

7. DRESS will be fighting order. Mess tins and haversack rations to be carried.

[signature]
Captain & Adjutant.

ADDENDA TO INSTRUCTIONS ISSUED WITH ORDER NO. 92.

9a. TENTS at present in use in the area to be struck, packed and handed over to owner of Billets who should be requested toe look after them until collected by Area Commandant.

R Brinsley

Captain & Adjt.
2nd S.R.I.

4. 10. 17.

Copy No. 2

ORDER NO. 92.

Reference
Sheet 27 1/40000.
HAZEBROUCK 5A.
1/100000.

In the Field.
4. 10. 17.

------

1. **INFORMATION.** The South African Brigade will move to the MOULLE area to-day.

2. **INTENTION.** The C.O. intends to march to MOULLE in accordance with attached march table at 8.3[illegible] a.m. this morning.

3. **DISTRIBUTION.** The order of march will be as follows:- Headquarters, "A" Coy. "C" Coy. "D" Coy. "B" Coy. 1st Line Transport.

4. **MARCH DISCIPLINE.** Halts will be taken by the clock hour. There will be 1 hours halt at mid-day.
Marching-

5. **STATES.** States will be handed to the adjutant at the starting point and on arrival at new area.
Usual certificates will be rendered.

6. **REPORTS.** Reports to the head of the Battalion.

R B[illegible]
Captain & Adjutant,
2nd S.A.I.

Issued at 5.a.m.

Copies Nos. 1 & 2.		Retained.	
3.	O/C.	"A" Coy.	by orderly.
4.		"B"	do.
5.		"C"	do.
6.		"D"	do
7.		Transport Officer.	
8.		Quartermaster.	

Copy No..

ORDER NO: 93.

Reference
HAZEBROUCK 5A.
1/100,000.
and Sheet 28,
1/40000.

In the Field,
9 - 10. 1917.

------

1. Transport of South African Brigade less certain details, will proceed by road to BRAKE CAMP - A.30. - to-day.

2. Regimental first line transport, less 4 cookers, 2 water carts, 1 medical cart, 1 mess cart, 18 chargers and pack animals will proceed by road to BRAKE CAMP to-day.

3. ROUTE - Via SERQUES - ST. MOMELIN - RUBROUK - LEDRINGHAM to Destination.

4. Starting point - Cross Roads MOULLE opposite Hospital 59.

5. Head of the transport will pass the starting point at 1.5.p.m. to-day.

6. The Staging area will be at LEDRINGHAM.

7. Billets at staging area will be arranged by 2nd Lieut. J. ESTILL, 3rd S.A.Infantry, who will meet transport at railway crossing on main RUBROUK - WORMHOUDT ROAD.

8. 2nd Lieut. H.B.CROFT, 3rd S.A.I. will be in command of the column.

Issued at 6.30.a.m.

Captain & Adjutant,
2nd Regiment South African Infy

Copies Nos. 1 & 2.	Retained.	
3.	O/C. "A" Coy.	by orderly.
4.	"B" Coy.	do.
5.	"C" Coy.	do.
6.	"D" Coy.	do.
7.	Transport Officer.	
8.	Quartermaster.	

INSTRUCTIONS ISSUED IN CONNECTION WITH ORDER NO: 93.

1. As much baggage as possible will be loaded in transport to-day.

2. Limbers will call at Company Orderly Rooms for Lewis guns at 11.a.m. All magazines and boxes will be ready for loading at that time. Guns will be loaded as soon as companies return from training.

3. Company stores and orderly room boxes, etc. should be ready for loading at 9.a.m. - details not at training will provide loading parties.

4. Hand boxes, signalling equipment and pioneer's tools not required at training to-day will be piled at Orderly Room by 5.p.m. Headquarter details not at training will supply loading parties.

5. Quartermaster's stores will be loaded on transport as far as possible.

6. Officers kits/and mess stores will be loaded on lorry on the 10th inst.

7. Transport Officer will superintend loading.

8. One lorry will be available for one journey only on 10th inst. - it is therefore essential that as much kit, stores, etc. as possible should be sent by road.

Captain & Adjutant,
2nd S.A.I.

9.10.17.

Copy No. 1

ORDER NO. 94.

Reference
SHEET HAZEBROUCK 5A.
1/100000.
and SHEET 28
1/40000.

In the Field,
9. 10. 1917.

1. INFORMATION. (a) The 9th Division will concentrate in the XVIII Corps forward area.

(b) The South African Infantry Brigade will proceed by march route and by rail to BRAKE CAMP (Sheet 28 - A.30) to-morrow.

2. INTENTION. The Battalion, less 1st line transport which proceeded by road to-day, will move to BRAKE CAMP by march route and by rail to-morrow.

3. DISTRIBUTION. (a) Companies will pass the starting point in the following order of march at 4.30.a.m. -
Headquarters, "D" Co. "C" Co. "B" Co. "A" Co.

(b) First Line transport details will march at 5.a.m.

4. STARTING POINT. Starting point - Junction of MOULLE Road and main ST. OMER road.

5. ROUTE. (a) Battalion less 1st line transport details will march from MOULLE via SERQUES to entraining point at WATTEN, thence by rail to detraining point at DIRTY BUCKET CORNER, and from there to BRAKE CAMP by march route.

(b) Transport details will march to ST. OMER via ST. MARTIN au LAERT entraining there for VLAMERTINGHE and from thence will proceed by road to BRAKE CAMP.

6. ENTRAINING. The Battalion will entrain in accordance with entraining table attached.

7. STATES. Marching-in states will be furnished on arrival at BRAKE CAMP.

~~10.~~
9. REPORTS. Reports to the Head of the Battalion.

R Brunsky

Issued at 11.20. p.m.

Captain & Adjutant,
2nd Regiment South African Infy.

Copies Nos. 1& 2.	Retained.		
3.	O/C. "A" Co.	by orderly.	
4.	"B" Co.	do.	
5.	"C" Co.	do.	
6.	"D" Co.	do.	
7.	a/Quartermaster	do.	
8.	Transport	do.	

ENTRAINING TABLE.

Issued in connection with Order No. 94.

10. 10. 1917.

COACHING STOCK TRAIN - Serial letter I.
Time of departure - 8.a.m.

Unit - BATTALION, less transport details.

Entraining Station - WATTEN.

Time of departure. - 8. a. m.

Detraining Station - DIRTY BUCKET CORNER.

Lieut. G.G.GREEN, M.C. will report to Brigade Representative at WA TTEN at 5.30. a.m. and will be in possession of entraining state in duplicate.
Lieut. HALLACK, M.C. 1st S.A.I., is the Brigade representative.

OMNIBUS TRAIN. Serial letter J.

Unit. - Transport Details.

Entraining station. ST. OMER.

Time of departure. 9.10. a.m.

Detraining station - VLAMERTINGHE.

Transport details will arrive at Entraining station by 7.30.a.m.

Corpl. BOWEN will report to 2nd Lieut. LILBURN, 2nd S.A.I., at the entraining station at 6.30.a.m. - he will be in possession of entraining state in duplicate.

R Beverley

Captain & Adjutant,
2nd Regiment South African Infantry.

PRELIMINARY INSTRUCTIONS ISSUED IN CONNECTION WITH

MOVE ON 10/10/1917.

---

1. Rouse. 2.30.a.m.

2. TEA will be prepared by 2.45. a.m. There will be no time to cook breakfast. Haversack rations for two meals will be carried and water bottles filled.

3. The Battalion starting point will be the Junction of the MOULLE road and the main CALAIS - ST. OMER road.

4. Companies will pass the starting point as follows:-
Headquarters, "D", "C", "B" "A", Coys.
commencing at 4.30.a.m.

5. Marching-out states and billet certificates will be handed to the Adjutant at the starting point.

6. Kitchens will be cleaned and ready tp pull out by 3.30.a.m. Camp kettles of Headquarters and "D" Company will be loaded on the kitchens.
Two cooks only per company and the Sergeant Cook will accompany the kitchens with transport.

7. Officers kit and Mess Kit will be conveyed to destination by lorry, which will arrive about 9.30.a.m. Three baggage dumps will be established.
   (a) "D" Company Orderly Room, for "C" and "D" Company Baggage.
   (b) BATTALION ORDERLY ROOM, for Headquarter Officers' baggage and Orderly Room boxes.
   (c) QUARTERMASTER'S STORES - for "A" and "B" Companies, and for baggage of officers billeted in the vicinity.

8. Each company will detail one man only to remain with baggage and assist loading party. One Headquarter orderly will meet lorry at Brigade Headquarters at 9.a.m. and guide same to Baggage dumps, commencing with Quartermaster's stores.

9. LEWIS GUNS and MAGAZINES will be carried by the troops.

10. The Sergeant cook will arrange to have a hot meal ready on arrival at new camp.

11. MESS CART and MALTESE CART will be loaded at 3.30.a.m. One officer's mess man and one medical orderly will accompany these vehicles.

12. Confirmatory and detailed orders will be issued later.

R B Beverley(?) Capt

Captain & Adjutant.
2nd Regiment S.A.Infantry

Issued at 10.p.m.
to Company Commanders,
R.S.M. Quartermaster
and Transport N.C.O.

Copy No. 2.

ORDER NO: 95.

Reference
Sheet 28 NW. 1/20000.
and 28 1/40,000.

In the Field,
11. 10. 1917.

1. The South African Brigade, less 1 Battalion and Brigade Headquarters will move to forward area to-day.

2. The 2nd Regiment South African Infantry will march to REIGERSBERG to-day at 10.a.m.

3. Companies will march in the following order, with 10 minutes interval between companies:-

"A" Company.
"B" Company.
"C" Company.
"D" Company.

3a The leading company will pass the starting point at 10.a.m.

4. STARTING POINT - Dirty Bucket Corner. A.30.d.1.9.

5. ROUTE - Dirty Bucket Corner - HOSPITAL FARM - BRIDGE JUNCTION - SIEGE JUNCTION, - DAWSON'S CORNER - BRIELEN to destination.

6. Three field kitchens, water cart, mess cart and maltese cart will accompany the Battalion.
Lewis Guns and officers kits will be loaded on limbers.

7. Marching-in states and nominal rolls will be handed in on arrival.

8. Reports to the head of the Battalion.

Issued at 9.30.a.m.

Captain & Adjutant,
2nd Regiment S.A.Infantry

Copies Nos. 1 & 2. Retained.
3. O/C. "A" Coy.
4. " "B" Coy.
5. "C" Coy.
6. "D" Coy.
7. Transport Officer.

PRELIMINARY INSTRUCTIONS IN CONNECTION WITH MOVE - 28.10.1917.

The Battalion will be moved to the new area in lorries. The Battalion will move at about 9.a.m. to-morrow morning in Full [illegible] Marching order. Instruction re transport and kits will be issued later.
Usual billeting N.C.Os. will be warned and ready to parade in full marching order by 6.a.m. to-morrow morning.
2nd Lieut. EGAN will be advance Billeting Officer.

All kit will probably be loaded at an early hour. Orders will be issued later when received from Brigade.

2nd Lieut. Marshall will be in charge of loading party.

Captain & Adjt.
2nd S.A.I.

Issued to all recipients of Operation Orders.
28.10.17.

INSTRUCTIONS IN REFERENCE TO MOVE TO-MORROW.

1. The Battalion will probably move at 9.a.m. to-morrow.

2. BAGGAGE. All baggage must be ready for loading by 7.a.m. Loading points and actual times of loading will be notified later.

3. BILLETING. Billeting Parties will be in readiness to report to Orderly Room by 6.a.m.

4. All billets will be thoroughly cleaned by 7.a.m.

5. 2/Lieuts. MARSHALL AND HENNESSY, and one man per company will report at the Orderly Room at 8.a.m. to-morrow in full marching order. They will leave their equipment at the Orderly Room and then proceed with billet wardens to hand over billets.

6. No instructions or operation order has yet been received from the Brigade, but these will be issued as soon as possible. In the meantime companies will act on orders as issued.

Captain & Adjutant,
2nd S.A.I.

11.30.p.m.
28.11.17.

Copy to each recipient of O.Orders.

Instructions issued in
connection with Order No 96

(1) The Battalion will move in accordance with
order No 96 at 6 AM tomorrow.

(2) Reveille will be at 4.30 AM.

(3) Breakfast 5 A.M.

(4) Lewis guns, mobilisation Equip except as
will be carried by troops

(5) Cooks & Kitchens will remain at present site
till further orders. Sgt Cook will see that
camp & Kitchens sites are thoroughly
cleaned.

(6) 1 NCO. per Company will report to Lt Green M.C
at 5 ~~AM~~ 30 AM as advance party.

(7) Grease for greasing feet will be obtained
from the Sgt-Cook & carried to
next Camp. R.S.M. will arrange.

(8) Feet will be well greased & rubbed on
arrival next Camp.

(9) Officers Kits will be piled at Kitchens
D Coy will detail 1 man as a guard to them

ORDER No 96 Copy No 2

Reference In the Field
Sheet 28 1:40000 11-10-17

1 The Battalion will move to CANAL BANK at 6 A.M tomorrow.

2 Companies will march at 10 minutes interval commencing at 6 AM in the following order B Co, C Co, D Co, A Co.

3 Route – from Reigersburg camp to CANAL BANK via SALVATION CORNER.

4 Advance party under LT GREEN MC will proceed to AREA Commandant CANAL BANK at 5.30 AM to arrange accommodation

5 Reports to the head of the Battalion

Issued at 8 PM. [illegible]
Capt & Adjt.

Dictated to orderly Sergeants.

Instructions issued in Connection with Order 99.

1 Blankets & Socks will be available at IRISH FARM.

2. All dirty socks will be collected by 12 noon on 17th inst. for removal.

3. Hot food & rum will be issued on arrival at IRISH FARM.

4. A.C. B Coy will hand over 1 LEWIS GUN to B Coy 3rd Regiment.

5 Every endeavour should be made to complete each mans equipment & SAA before leaving the line

16/10/17.

R Bromley
Capt & Adjt.
2. S.A.I.

(6) Seventeen tins of water will be issued to each company to be carried with the line.

(7) Feet will be rubbed & dry socks put on before leaving. It is hoped that a further supply of whale oil will arrive.

(8) Two days rations will be issued & carried by all ranks.

13/10/17

R Bromley
Capt & Adj.

Order 97 — Copy No 2

Reference — In the Field
Map 28 S.N.W. — 13-10-17
1:20000

1/ The 1st S.A.I. Bde will relieve the 26 & 27th Bde in the line during the night of 13/14th October.

2 The Battalion will relieve units in the right subsector and will march out at 4 p.m. today.

3 Companies will march out in the following order H Qrs, A Coy C Coy B Coy D Coy. 50 yds distance will be maintained between platoons.

4/ The route will be MOUSE TRAP Track as reconnoitred by Officers today. ADMIRALS ROAD will not be crossed before 5 P.M.

5 Guides of 26th & 27th I. Bdes. will meet the Battalion at 7.30 P.M. at HUBNER FARM D.I.C 5.8 [?]

6 SOS signals will be a rifle Grenade bursting into four red rockets.

7 Completion of relief & report will be sent to Batt H.Q.

8 Batt HQ will be at a place to be notified later.

Issued at 3.30 pm. — R B Smith [?]
Capt & Adjt

Copies 1 OC A Coy
2 OC B Coy
3 – C Coy
4 – D Coy
5 retained.

Instructions issued in connection with Move to Trenches 13-10-17

(1) The Batt. will move to the trenches today.

(2) Each Company twenty men including 1 NCO. This number may be altered later, but companies will be prepared to hand out the above.

(3) This party will be under command of 2/Lt BEVIS, who will arrange that all kits & equipment that are left are safely removed to 1st Line Transport Lines. This party will clean huts & collect all Rum Jars, salvage etc & remove same to salvage dumps near DIV H.Q.

(4) Flares & Smoke Grenade No 27 will not be carried. These will be collected & placed together ready to be sent to salvage. As many Very Lights as possible will be taken.

(5) All water bottles will be filled before proceeding to the line.

Order Nº 99. Copy Nº 2

1. The 2nd & 4th S.A.I will be relieved in the line tonight by the 3rd & 1st S.A.I.
2. The Battalion will be relieved in the right Subsector by the 3rd S.A.I.
3. The relief will commence at about 8 p.m. Companies will be relieved in the following order
   C Coy – A Coy – D Coy – B Coy –

4. Four guides per company will report to Lt GREEN M.C. at Batt. H.Q. via support Coys. at 5.30 p.m. punctually
   Guides will meet their corresponding companies of the 3rd S.A.I at junction of X track at St JULIEN Road under direction of Lt GREEN at 7 p.m.

5. A & C Coys will shew red lights as guides to the reliefs – B & D Coys will shew Orange lights – Lights must be shewn at short intervals from 7.30 p.m. till relief is effected

6. On relief Companies will proceed via X track MOUSETRAP TRACK to IRISH FARM on BOUNDARY RD. where they will be met by guides to conduct them to their camps.

7. Completion of relief will be reported to Batt. H.Q. by runner as each company passes Batt H.Q. by code word "FINISH".

8. The relief will be effected via X Track, RAP & Support Coys – Incoming Coys will not pass Batt H.Q. – Out going Companies will proceed by route selected at discretion of Coy Commanders

Issued at 1 p.m.
17-10-17

1 Copy O/C A Coy.
2 " " B "
3 " " C "
4 " " D "

Capt [illegible]
2nd S.A.I.

Copy No. 2

ORDER No 100

Ref. Sheet 28 N W 1/20000

In the Field
20-10-17

1 The 1st S A Inf. Bde will be relieved by the 27th Inf. Bde. in the line on the night of 20/21st October 1917

2 The 2nd S A Inf. will be relieved by the 12th Royal Scots on the afternoon of today.
On relief the Battalion will move to REIGERSBURG CAMP.

3. Companies, less working party already detailed, will move out at 10 minutes interval in the following order commencing at 2.30 p m
Headquarters and A Coy.
B Coy.
C Coy.
D Coy.

4 Guides will meet companies at I 1 C 1·5 and conduct them to billets.

5 The route will be the ordinary march route via SALVATION CORNER to REIGERSBURG CAMP.

6 Baggage will be packed in accordance with instructions issued.

7 Reports to Batt. H Qrs on arrival at REIGERSBURG CAMP.

20-10-17

R Beverley
Capt & Adjt
2nd S A I

Dictated to Company Commanders & RSM at 12.15 P.M.

2nd S.A.I.

Instructions issued in connection with move 20-10-17

1 The Battalion less working parties will move to REIGERSBURG CAMP at about 2 PM today.
2 Men will march light packs & blankets will be carried on Transport
3 All blankets will be rolled tightly in bundles of 10 ready for loading by 11 AM. The articles of equipment is to be used for rolling blankets
4 Mens valises, officers kits etc and all rum jars will be loaded at 2 pm
5 Lewis guns & Magazines will be ready for loading by 2 PM.
6 2 men per company will accompany baggage waggons. Sick men will be chosen for this work
7 1 Lewis gunner per company will accompany Lewis gun limbers.
8 Camp will be thoroughly cleaned & usual certificates handed in by 1 PM
9 Distribution states will be handed in by 1 PM. [illegible]

from Transport lines will be shewn with their companies.

[illegible]
Capt & Adjt

Dictated to Coy Commanders & RSM at 10 AM.

ORDER NO 101. Copy No 2

Reference
Sheet 28 N.W. 1:20000
HAZEBRUCK 5a 1:100000
Sheet 27 1:40000

In the Field
23.10.17.

1 (a) The 9th division less artillery will be transferred from the 5th Army XVIII Corps to 4th Army XV Corps on 24th 25th + 26th inst.
(b) The S.A. Bde will move to the new area on the above dates
2 The Battalion less working parties will move to NOUVEAU MONDE at 1 p.m. today by march route + by Bus
3 Companies will march out at 200 yds interval in the following order
Headquarters + A Coy.
B Coy, C Coy, D Coy.
4 Embussing point will be on the road at H.4.a.1.0.

Route

(a) via BRIELEN Road to road junction at B 29 C 8 9 then S.W. to embussing point

(b) by Bus route to destination

6 The head of the column will be bus ... on the road D 10 C 6 6

7 Billets will be inspected at 12 noon at which time certificates of clean... will be rendered.

8 Marching in States will be ... immediately on arrival at bi...

9 Reports to Battalion Headquar...

Capt ...

Dictated to Company Comman...

at 10 A M.

Instructions issued with Order No 101.

1 Battalion will move at 1 P.M.
2 Rations will be retained for lunch
3 Kitchens will be ready to pull out at 8.30 a.m.
4 All officers kit will be ready to load at 8.30 A.M. Any other company baggage will be loaded at this time
5. Men unable to march will parade ... police tent at 8.30. A.M. in full ... order
6 Battalion will march out in Full March... Order.
7 The working party already detailed ... move under separate order.
8 Marching out states will be rendered by 10 A.M. shewing officers & other ranks marching with
(a) Battalion
(b) Transport

23.10.17.

Capt & adjt
2nd S.A.I.

ORDER No 102.

Copy No 2

In the field

24.10.17.

Reference
HAZEBROUCK 5a. 1.200000
Sheet 27 1.40000.

1 The S.A. Bde will move to the WORMHOUDT AREA today

2 The Battalion will march to billets in the WORMHOUDT AREA in the vicinity of St JOSEPH C.4.d.

3 The head of the Battalion will pass the starting point at 10.30. a.m.

4 The starting point will be the Cross Roads 300 yds S.W of the Batt. ORDERLEY Room D 2 5 b 2 0 4 5

5 Companies will pass the starting point in the following order B. C D A. Coy Head quarters will join the Battalion en route
Transport will follow in rear of A Compa...

6. Route – from starting point through WORMHOUDT thence N.W by the BERGUES main road to Billets.

7. Billeting parties will proceed under separate order and guides will meet companies N.W. of WORMHOUDT.

8. Marching in states shewing distribution of all ranks will be rendered immediately on arrival at Billets

9. Reports to the head of the Battalion

Issued at 5. A.M.

Capt & adjt.
2nd S.A.I.

Copies No 1 & 2 retained
3-6 O/c A.B.C.D. Coys.
7 Transport Officer
8. C.O.

Instructions issued with Order No 102

1. Billeting N.C.O's report to Capt Knight as already ordered

2. Dress Full Marching Order

3. Blankets will be carried on Transport and piled as follows – for loading
A Coy outside A Coys billets
B.C.D. Coys at Q.M. Stores
all blankets to be piled by 9 A.M. and rolled in bundles of 10.

4. Officers kits will be piled as above and at the same time

5. G.S. Waggons as now loaded will pull out at 7 A.M. and will return to collect blankets & Kits

6. Men unable to march will parade with Kit dumps & will be carried on waggons
Number of men per Coy. unable to march should be communicated

ORDER No 103

Copy No 1

Reference
Sheets 27 & 19
1/40000

In the Field
24th - 10 - 17

1. The 1st S.A.I. Bde will move to the SYNTHE area tomorrow

2. The Battalion will march to SYNTHE tomorrow

3. The Battalion will pass the starting point at 8.20 AM in the following order of Companies
Hd Qrs & Drafts, A Coy, C Coy, D Coy, B Coy. 1st Line Transport will follow in rear of B Coy and will pull out as that company passes the Transport lines – Companies will march in file

4. Starting point – Battalion Headquarters

5. Main road via BERGUES to SYNTHE

6. Clock hour halts will be observed – 1 hour halt at 12 30 pm

7. Marching in states will be rendered immediately on arrival at billets

8. Reports to the head of Battalion

Issued at 10 30 pm
Copies 1 & 2 retained
3-6 O/Cs Coys
7 Transport officer
8 CO

R Beverley
Capt Adjt
2nd S.A.I.

Instructions issued with Order 103.

1. Billeting –
Lt Knight & 3 OR will proceed as billeting party tomorrow. The 3 OR will be detailed by Batt H Q.
Party will rendezvous at Brigade H Q at [illegible] 30 am 25th inst – Dress full marching order.
Billeting party will meet the [illegible] at CANAL BRIDGE 1 Kilometre NORTH of GOUDEKERQUE BRANCHE.
Staff Captain will indicate locality to guides.

2. Men unable to march –
Men marked unable to march by MO at to-days sick parade will parade in the Square under Lt GREEN MC at 8 am.
These men must carry their full packs & equipment & blankets in order that there may be sufficient room on transport for mens packs.
Motor conveyances will transport this party to the New Area.
Party should be mustered in the square ready to parade at 7.45 AM.

3. Routine
Reveille 5 am Breakfast 6.30 AM

4. Kitchens –
Kitchens must be ready to harness up by 7.30 am.
Two cooks will accompany each kitchen. Tea will be made en route.

5. Rations will be carried on kitchens.

6. Baggage loading. All mens packs will be at Batt HQ by 6 AM. [illegible] men per Coy will be [illegible] to load.
Packs will be as squarely and solidly packed as possible.
Officers mess stores which must be absolutely reduced to a minimum and officers kits will be ready for loading as follows –
C & D Coys by 7 AM for 2M Stores
A & B at Batt HQ by 6.30 AM

7. Packs of Headquarters will be taken to transport lines by 7 am to be loaded on limbers. A Sergeant will be in charge of the party and will report to the Transport Officer punctually.

This party will have breakfast [illegible] before going to transport and will be dressed in fighting order.

D Coy will supply 1 NCO & [illegible] men as 2M Stores fatigue at 7 AM.

Times must be strictly adhered to and dinner will be 1 hour [illegible] if necessary.

7. Dress for march. fighting order.

8. Nominal roll of men unable to march will accompany each party.

25-10-17

R Bromley [illegible]
Capt & Adjt
2nd [illegible]

9. Mess cart will report at 7.30 AM at [illegible]
G.S. waggons report to 2M [illegible] 7 am.
Officers horses & usual company horses will be packed [illegible]

ORDER NO: 1?4. R Copy No. 1.

Reference -
Sheet Dunkerque 1a,1/10000.
Sheets 11,12.20. 1/40,000.

In the Field,
October 29th 1917.

1. INFORMATION. (a) The 9th Division will relieve the 41st Division on 28th and 29th October, 1917.

(b) The 1st South African Infantry Brigade will relieve the 122nd Inf. Brigade in the COXYDE BAINS Coast Defence sector on 29th instant.

(c) On relief Brigade Headquarters will be at COXYDE BAINS.

2. INTENTION. The C.O. intends to move to the COXYDE BAINS AREA in accordance with march table attached.

3. STARTING POINT Starting Point - Cross road at Battalion Headquarters.

4. DISTRIBUTION. (a) The head of the Battalion will pass the starting point at 9.a.m. in the following order of companies:- Drums, Headquarters, "A" "B" "C" "D" Coys.

(b) Transport will move with Brigade Transport column.

(c) On the road in new area 200 yards distance will be maintained between companies.

5. ROUTE. From Petite Synthe via DUNKERQUE - ADINKERKE - LA PANNE - to COXYDE BAINS.

6. ADVANCE PARTY. Advance parties will proceed by lorry at 7.a.m. reporting at Orderly Room at 6.a.m. for instructions.

7. GUIDES. Guides will meet the Battalion on Road at W.6.a.4.c.

9. STATES. Usual states and reports will be rendered.

10. COMPLETION OF RELIEF will be reported by code word SEA.

11. Battalion Headquarters on completion of relief will be at COXYDE BAINS. W.6.a.5.4.

12. REPORTS to Battalion Headquarters.

R Beasley

Captain & Adjutant.
2nd Regiment S.A.Infantry.

Issued at 5.a.m.

Usual recipients.

MARCH TABLE ISSUED WITH ORDER NO: 104.

29/10/17.

BATTALION, LESS TRANSPORT.

Starting Point.	Time.	Embussing Point.	Time.	Debussing point.
Cross Roads Battalion Headquarters.	9.a.m.	H.3.a.9.3. DUNKERQUE, Petite Synthe Road.	9.45.a.m.	COXYDE BAINS AREA.

		TRANSPORT. Route.	Destination.
H.5.c.2.4. Sheet 19.	10.25.a.m.	DUNKERQUE - ADINKERKE - LA PANNE - to Destination.	To be notified later.

Brigade Transport Officer will issue further instructions en route.
Distances of 200 yards will be maintained between sections of transport of equal road space to a company.

INSTRUCTIONS ISSUED IN CONNECTION WITH ORDER NO.104.

1.
BAGGAGE.

Officers kits, mess stores, etc. will be loaded at Orderly Room on lorry at 7.30.a.m. Not more than two men per company will be detailed to load. These will parade in full marching order.

Company Stores, orderly Room boxes, etc. will be collected by G.S.Waggons at 7.a.m. 1 waggon for "C" and "D" and one for "A" and "B". This baggage will be rdady for loading at "C" Company and "A" Company billets respectively at 7.a.m.

Band Boxes and spare instruments on G.S. waggons. To be at "A" Company billet at 6.45.a.m. and to be loaded before company stores.

Quartermaster's stores.- One lorry will report to Quartermaster's stores at about 7.30.a.m. Part of G.S. waggons will also be available for Quartermaster's stores.

Orderly Room boxes on lorry at Battalion Headquarters.

Quartermaster will supervise loading as far as possible.

2.
BILLETING

Billeting party will report at Orderly Room at 6.a.m. for orders.

3. Billets will be handed over as directed in previous instructions.

4. 2nd Lieut. Marshall will be responsible that all men and baggage are clear of billets.

5. Captain STEIN will act as embussing officer and will report at Battalion Headquarters at 8.a.m. for instructions.

R.Bromley

Captain & Adjutant,
2nd S.A.I.

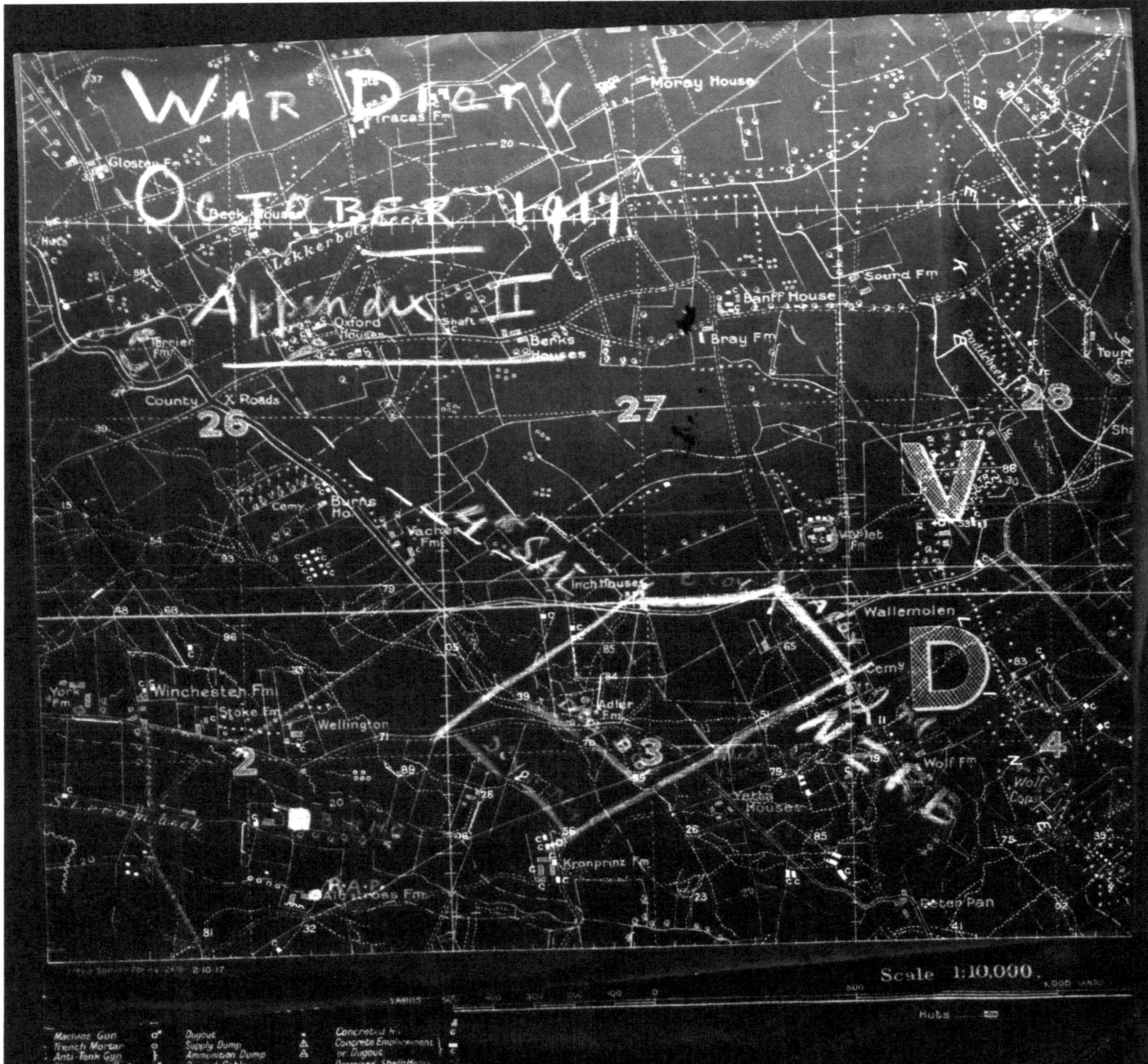
War Diary
October 1917
Appendix II
Moray House
Fracas Fm
Glosten Fm
Beek House
Lekkerboterbeek
Oxford Houses
Shaft
Berks Houses
Banff House
Bray Fm
Sound Fm
Terrier Fm
County X Roads
26
27
28
V
Burns Ho
Cemy
Vacher Fm
Inch Houses
Wallemolen
D
Winchester Fm
Stoke Fm
Wellington
York Fm
Adler Fm
Kronprinz Fm
Yetta Houses
Wolf Fm
Wolf Copse
Albatross Fm
Peter Pan
2
3
4
Scale 1:10,000
Huts
Machine Gun
Trench Mortar
Anti-Tank Gun
Observation Post
Dugout
Supply Dump
Ammunition Dump
Buried Cable
Concreted Pit
Concrete Emplacement or Dugout
Organised Shell Holes

November 1917

Instructions regarding War Diaries and Intelligence Summaries are contained in F. S. Regs., Part II. and the Staff Manual respectively. Title pages will be prepared in manuscript.

WAR DIARY

or

(Erase heading not required.)

2nd S.A. Inf.

Army Form C. 2118.

Place	Date	Hour	Summary of Events and Information	Remarks and references to Appendices
COXYDE LES BAINS	1st		Weather warm and fine – 138 OR who arrived from base last night posted to Companies. 2/Lt Marshall i/c, 2 Officers 139 OR proceeded to ST IDESBALDE to report to the 2nd Australian Tunnelling Company for attachment for 3 mo. – 300 men bathed – clean clothes – at ST IDESBALDE Baths. – Lewis gun instruction in billets. C.O. inspected draft at 2 p.m. – A good class of men and well trained. No shelling. Enemy Aeroplanes passed over at night en route for DUNKIRK	Sheet 11 & 19. DUNKERQUE 1a.
	2nd		Dull day – Capts. Jenkins & Bryant reported having returned from leave last night – Leave cancelled for three days – 200 O.R. at Baths. Draft and details from reserve companies at Training. 2 Men from leave – 4 details from hospital &c. Warm mild night.	
	3rd		Bright day. Fairly warm. Training & working parties as usual. No enemy activity by day. A few bombs dropped at COXYDE about 11 PM.	

D. D. & L., London, E.C. (A7853) Wt W593/M1612 350,000 4/17 Sch. 52a Forms/C2118/14

Instructions regarding War Diaries and Intelligence Summaries are contained in F. S. Regs., Part II. and the Staff Manual respectively. Title pages will be prepared in manuscript.

WAR DIARY
or
~~INTELLIGENCE SUMMARY.~~
(Erase heading not required.)

Army Form C. 2118.

Place	Date	Hour	Summary of Events and Information	Remarks and references to Appendices
COXYDE LES BAINS	4th		Sunday Fine day - slightly colder. No enemy activity during day. Church parades. 300 men bathed at baths at YORKSHIRE CAMP at X3a.9.1 Sheet 11. Lt GREEN returned from Hospital.	
	5th		Fine day somewhat colder. Training and working parties as usual. Most of the Battalion attending Trench foot preventative treatment under 4th Army Orders. Draft of 19 O.R. arrived from Base	
	6th		Training, working parties, and foot treatment at South African Field Ambulance. Enemy sent 4 H.V. 10 c.M shells in our lines, no casualties. Nieuport, Tractor Triplane fell on the beach opposite No 3 post. Guard posted and Brigade informed. Fine day, but cold.	

D. D. & L., London, E.C.
(A7859) Wt W809/M1672 350,000 4/17 Sch. 52a Forms/C/2118/14

WAR DIARY
or
~~INTELLIGENCE SUMMARY~~.
(*Erase heading not required.*)

Instructions regarding War Diaries and Intelligence Summaries are contained in F. S. Regs., Part II. and the Staff Manual respectively. Title pages will be prepared in manuscript.

Place	Date	Hour	Summary of Events and Information	Remarks and references to Appendices
COXYDE LES BAINS	7th		Rain & cold - Parades & Training cancelled. - B-Gen TUDOR C.M.G. act- G.O.C. 9th DIV. inspected transport and expressed appreciation at condition of horses. O.C 7th Seaforths. came to reconnoitre lines with a view to taking over on 10th inst. - 2Lts BENNETT and AULDS arrived from base. - Cold night - no enemy activity.	
"	8th		Fine & cold. Training & working parties. 7 O.R. on leave. No enemy activity. 4 O.R. arrived from Base.	
"	9th		Fine & cold. Training & working parties. Preparation for move to morrow. Flight of enemy aeroplanes passed over COXYDE LES BAINS about 2 P.M. They were dispersed by A.A. gun fire. Slight enemy shelling on beach 4 - 5 P.M. Rain at night.	

Instructions regarding War Diaries and Intelligence Summaries are contained in F. S. Regs., Part II. and the Staff Manual respectively. Title pages will be prepared in manuscript.

WAR DIARY

or

[redacted]

(Erase heading not required.)

Army Form C. 2118.

2 S.A.I.

Place	Date	Hour	Summary of Events and Information	Remarks and references to Appendices
COXYDE	10th		Battalion relieved by 9th Seaforth Hgrs. 10 – 12 noon, and, on relief	
LES			marched to YORKSHIRE CAMP X 3 a. vide Order NO 105.	Sheet 11
BAINS			Arrived at YORKSHIRE CAMP 1.30 PM – Accommodation in	
			huts & dug outs amongst the sand dunes.	
			Strength state with unit 22 Officers 601 OR.	
			not " " 12 " 338 "	
			34 " 939 "	
			Cold Raining day & night. Enemy shelled vicinity of camp	
			with 5.9 shells about 8 – 9 P.M. No damage.	
YORKSHIRE CAMP.	11th		Cold & rain. Church parade in church hut. Duties' parade 2 p.m.	
			Company commanders & party of B & D Coys to reconnoitre the	
			front lines 2 pm, returned 7 p.m. Slight shelling in	
			vicinity of camp.	

Instructions regarding War Diaries and Intelligence Summaries are contained in F. S. Regs., Part II. and the Staff Manual respectively. Title pages will be prepared in manuscript.

WAR DIARY

or

[redacted]

(Erase heading not required.)

Army Form C. 2118.

2 S.A.I

Place	Date	Hour	Summary of Events and Information	Remarks and references to Appendices
YORKSHIRE CAMP	12th		Bright day - Fairly Warm. Training and Duties as usual. Slight enemy shelling South of the Camp and in Transport Lines - 1 man (Transport) slightly wounded. 5 men proceeded on leave to England. - 11 O.R. Reinforcements and 2 Details from leave arrived. Slight shelling in the evening also.	
	13th		Bright day and warm. Training and Duties as usual. Flight of enemy aeroplanes passed over about 11 a.m. but were dispersed by A.A. Gun fire. Considerable aerial activity and intermittent shelling throughout the day	
	14th		Dull day and cold - slight drizzle. Training and Duties as usual. 5 O.R. proceeded on leave to England. Enemy sent 5 light H.E. Shells into the Camp about 1.30 p.m. and 3 more about 2.45 p.m. Intermittent shelling during the night. No casualties.	

D. D. & L., London, E.C. (A7839) Wt. W1080/M1672 350,000 4/17 Sch. 52a Forms/C2118/14

Army Form C. 2118.

WAR DIARY
or
~~INTELLIGENCE SUMMARY~~.
(Erase heading not required.)

Instructions regarding War Diaries and Intelligence Summaries are contained in F. S. Regs., Part II. and the Staff Manual respectively. Title pages will be prepared in manuscript.

Place	Date	Hour	Summary of Events and Information	Remarks and references to Appendices
YORKSHIRE CAMP	15th		Fine day but cold. Training and Duties as usual. No enemy activity. 3 Details returned from leave and hospital.	
	16th		Battalion relieved by 2nd Batt. 141st Regiment of the French Army about 4 p.m. after a delay of about 5 hours occasioned by non-arrival of the French troops, and as relieved, marched off by Companies to FURNES CAMP, LA PANNE (W.22.b.5.5) vide Order 106. Arrived at destination about 6 p.m. - Good accommodation in large bungalows. Officers billetted in the town of LA PANNE. 2/Lt Marshall i/c 2 Officers and 130 O.R. reported back from 2nd Australian Tunnelling Company R.E. arriving FURNES CAMP 12.30 p.m. 4 Details returned from leave and hospital. Battalion Hqrs at JOLLEMONT VILLA - LA PANNE. Transport lines at W.14.c.75.80. Orderly Room at FURNES CAMP. Weather Dull and Cold	

D. D. & L., London, E.C.
(A7883) Wt. W809/M1672 350,000 4/17 Sch. 52a Forms/C/2118/14

Instructions regarding War Diaries and Intelligence Summaries are contained in F. S. Regs., Part II. and the Staff Manual respectively. Title pages will be prepared in manuscript.

WAR DIARY

or

~~INTELLIGENCE SUMMARY.~~

(Erase heading not required.)

Army Form C. 2118.

Place	Date	Hour	Summary of Events and Information	Remarks and references to Appendices
FURNES CAMP	17th		Dull day and cold. Training and Duties as usual.	
			2/Lts Riches E. J. and Craig C. returned from leave	
			Strength State With Unit 24 Officers 838 O.R.	
			not " " 10 " 96 "	
			34 " 934 "	
	18th		Dull day and cold. Church Parade in Company Bungalows	
			3 O.R. reported from Base and leave. 9 O.R. went on leave	
			to England. Preparations for move tomorrow	
	19th		Fine day and cold. Battalion moved by march route	
			to GHYVELDE (DUNKERQUE (A.) 8G 3065) Time of departure - Head starting	
			[illegible] LA PANNE (cross roads) at 1.0 p.m. Arrived at destination	
			H Camp, GHYVELDE 3.45 p.m. - see order No 107.	
			Billets in huts and tents. 2 Rebuts reported sick.	

D. D. & L. London E.C.

Instructions regarding War Diaries and Intelligence Summaries are contained in F. S. Regs., Part II. and the Staff Manual respectively. Title pages will be prepared in manuscript.

WAR DIARY

or

~~INTELLIGENCE SUMMARY.~~

(Erase heading not required.)

Army Form C. 2118.

Place	Date	Hour	Summary of Events and Information	Remarks and references to Appendices
GHYVELDE	20th		Dull day and fairly cold. Battalion marched to TETEGHEM SOUTH and GOUDEKERQUE via route order No 108 – March table A. Time of departure 10-30 a.m. and arrived at destination at 12-30 p.m. A Coy at GOUDEKERQUE ref HAZEBROUCK 5A 1E 99 95. Headquarters, B C & D Coys at [struck through] TETEGHEM SOUTH ref DUNKERQUE 1A 3F 30 55. Capt Skeen & 3 OR proceeded on leave to England. 3 NCOs candidates for Cadet Course left for England.	DUNKERQUE 1A 1/100000 and HAZEBROUCK 5A 1/100,000
TETEGHEM SOUTH and GOUDEKERQUE	21st		Dull day and rain during the afternoon and evening. Battalion marched to WORMHOUDT via order 108 – March table B. Time of departure 8 a.m. and arrived 1 p.m. at WORMHOUDT 9.F 60 60	HAZEBROUCK 5A 1/100000
WORMHOUDT	22nd		6 OR proceeded on leave to England, and 1 OR on duty [illegible]. Battalion marched to ZERMAZEELE 9.F 40 90 vide order 108, March table C. Time of departure 8.30 a.m. and arrived 10.45 a.m. Dull day and drizzle in the afternoon.	do

Instructions regarding War Diaries and Intelligence Summaries are contained in F. S. Regs., Part II. and the Staff Manual respectively. Title pages will be prepared in manuscript.

WAR DIARY
or
~~INTELLIGENCE SUMMARY~~
(Erase heading not required.)

Army Form C. 2118.

Place	Date	Hour	Summary of Events and Information	Remarks and references to Appendices
ZERMEZEELE	23rd		9 O.R. on leave for England. Fine day and fairly warm. Battalion marched to COUBRONNE area 4.D.60.26 vide order 108 March table D. Time of departure 9 a.m. – arrived COUBRONNE 4 p.m. Distance covered 16 miles in full marching order. Extraordinary good marching on the part of all ranks – Morale excellent, no one falling out, and the Battalion finishing the march in as good order as the start.	HAZEBROUCK 5a 1/100,000
COUBRONNE	24th		Stormy day – Strong wind and drizzle. Battalion marched to AVROULT vide order 108 March table E. Time of departure 9 AM but delayed 1 hour by instructions from Brigade which arrived after Battalion had moved off, to the effect that column must not enter main road at X roads 5.C.05.75 before 1 p.m. Arrived AVROULT 1.30 p.m. 3 O.R. reported back from leave.	do.

D. D. & L., London, E.C.
(A7823) Wt. W809/M1672 350,000 4/17 Sch. 52a Forms/C2118/14

Instructions regarding War Diaries and Intelligence Summaries are contained in F. S. Regs., Part II. and the Staff Manual respectively. Title pages will be prepared in manuscript.

WAR DIARY

or

~~INTELLIGENCE SUMMARY~~.

(Erase heading not required.)

Army Form C. 2118.

Place	Date	Hour	Summary of Events and Information	Remarks and references to Appendices
AVROULT	26th		Bright, cold morning with strong wind - Blizzard during afternoon but fine night. Battalion marched to BOURTHES - CATELET - LE LOT area 5.F.2.2. marching out from AVROULT at 12 noon. arrived BOURTHES 4.30 p.m. - Billetting accommodation very poor.	CALAIS 1/100.000 Sheet 13.
			Strength State - with Unit 23 Officers 813 O.R.	
			not " " 11 " 111 "	
			Total 34 " 924 "	
			Lieut Col. E. Christian having arrived assumes command of the Battalion with effect from 26/11/1917. A draft of 1 Officer (2/Lieut Gooding) and 68 other ranks arrived from Base and is taken on strength from date.	
BOURTHES	26th		Fine day but cold. 2 Details reported back from Base. 2 O.R. proceeded to England on leave. Rifle inspection parade for all Companies & H.Qrs. & new draft inspected by C.O. and posted to Companies. Duties mount at Rivailles. Guard 4 p.m. 3 O.R. reported back from leave.	

D. D. & L., London, E.C. (A7833) W1 W803/M1072 350,000 4/17 Sch. 52a Forms/C2118/14

Army Form C. 2118.

WAR DIARY
or
~~INTELLIGENCE SUMMARY~~.
(Erase heading not required.)

Instructions regarding War Diaries and Intelligence Summaries are contained in F. S. Regs., Part II. and the Staff Manual respectively. Title pages will be prepared in manuscript.

Place	Date	Hour	Summary of Events and Information	Remarks and references to Appendices
BOURTHES	27th		Dull day rain and snow in the evening. Parades under Company arrangements. Duties as usual. 15 O.R evacuated are struck off the strength.	
	28th		Dull day but fine. Training as per programme and duties as usual. Lieut. Terry and 6 O.R proceeded to England on leave. 5 O.R being evacuated are struck off the strength. 7 O.R arrived from Base.	
	29th		Fine day & cold. Training as per programme and duties as usual. The Commanding Officer inspected the Battalion in the morning. 1 O.R evacuated.	
	30th		Dull day and rain. Training as per programme and duties as usual. 6 O.R proceeded on leave to England and 1 O.R to Base. 2/Lt. D.E. Bell reported back from leave. 1 O.R evacuated.	

D. D. & L. London, E.C.
(A7883) Wt. W593/M1672 350,000 4/17 Sch. 52a Forms/C2118/14

Instructions regarding War Diaries and Intelligence Summaries are contained in F. S. Regs., Part II. and the Staff Manual respectively. Title pages will be prepared in manuscript.

WAR DIARY
or
INTELLIGENCE SUMMARY.
(Erase heading not required.)

Army Form C. 2118.

Place	Date	Hour	Summary of Events and Information	Remarks and references to Appendices
BOURTHES	30th		Strength State With Unit 26 Officers 888 O.R.	
			Not " " 9 " 100 "	
			35 " 988 "	
			Preparations for move to-morrow.	

SOUTH AFRICAN 2ND S.A. INFANTRY 30-11-17 OVERSEAS EXPEDITIONARY FORCE

Iwane Christian
Lt-Col
Commanding 2nd S.A.I.

War diary

R

Copy No. 7.

ORDER NO: 105.

Reference
Sheet 11 S.E.
1/20000.
Sheet 12 S.W.
1/20000.

In the Field,
9th November, 1917.

1. **INFORMATION**

(a) The 1st S.A.Infantry Brigade will relieve the 26th Infantry Brigade in the NIEUPORT BAINS sector, and the latter will take over the Coast Defences presently held by the 1st S. A. Infantry Brigade.

(b) On completion of relief the dispositions of Battalions of the 1st S.A.I. Brigade will be as follows:-

1st Regiment S.A.I.	Right sub-sector.
3rd Regiment S.A.I.	Left sub-sector.
4th Regiment S.A.I.	SUPPORT, at Middlesex camp, R. 32.d.5.9.
2nd Regiment S.A.I.	Reserve, at YORKSHIRE FARM, X.3.a.9.1.

(c) The 7th Seaforth Highlanders will relieve the Battalion in the COXYDE BAINS Section of the Coast Defence Sector, on the morning of the 10th instant.

(d) Lewis Gun Posts at YORKSHIRE Camp will continue to be held by the 8th Black Watch until completion of relief.

2. **INTENTION.**

On completion of relief by the 7th Seaforth Highlanders the Battalion, less working parties, will move to YORKSHIRE CAMP and relieve the A.A. Lewis Gun Posts of the 8th BLACK WATCH.

3. **INSTRUCTIONS FOR RELIEF.**

(a) The relief will be effected by companies in the following order, C. B. D. A. Hqrs.

"B" Co.	7th Seaforth	Highlanders	will relieve	"C" Coy.	2nd S.A.I.
"D" Co.	do.	do.	will relieve	"B" Co.	2nd S.A.I.
"C" Coy.	do.	do.	ditto	"D" Co.	do.
"A" Coy.	do.	do.	ditto	"A" Co.	do.

(b) On relief each company will march to billets at YORKSHIRE CAMP.

(c) Signallers of the 7th Seaforth Highlanders will take over signal stations, commencing with Headquarters at 10.30.a.m.

(d) No post held by the Battalion will be vacated until relieved.

4. **GUIDES.**

Guides as detailed hereunder will meet ~~the incoming~~ relieving companies at the Cross Roads, COXYDE LES BAINS. W.6.a.95.65., at 10.30.a.m.

"C" and "D" Coys.	1 guide per platoon, & 1 per coy H.Q.
"A" and "B" Coys.	1 guide per coy. & 1 per coy. H.Q.
Headquarters.	2 guides.

5. **ADVANCED PARTIES.**

Advanced parties as hereunder detailed will parade at 8.a.m. for the purpose of proceeding to YORKSHIRE CAMP to take over huts, stores, etc.

Lieut. GREEN, M.C. Hqrs.- 1 N.C.O. and 2 signallers.
Each company - 1 N.C.O. and 4 men.

/over.

6. **TRENCH STORES.**	All Defence Schemes, Sector Maps, Trench Stores, etc. will be handed over to the relieving Battalion, and receipts forwarded to Battalion Headquarters.
7. **BAGGAGE.**	Baggage will be loaded in accordance with separate instructions issued.
8. **STATES.**	Usual states and certificates will be rendered.
9. **BATTALION HEADQUARTERS.**	Battalion Headquarters will open on arrival at YORKSHIRE CAMP.
10. **REPORTS.**	Completion of relief and move will be reported in writing by orderly to Battalion Headquarters.

R.Bssons Capt.

Issued at 9.a.m.

Captain & Adjutant,
2nd Regiment S.A.Infantry.

Copy No.1.	O.C. "A" Coy.	By orderly.
2.	O.C. "B" Coy.	do.
3.	O.C. "C" Coy.	do.
4.	O.C. "D" Coy	do.
5.	Transport Officer.	do.
6.	O/C. 7th Seaforth Highlanders.	
7/8	War Diary and file.	

SECRET. Copy No. 8.

ORDER No. 108.

Reference
Sheet 11.
1/10,000.

In the Field,
15. 11. 17.

1. INFORMATION. The Battalion will be relieved to-morrow by a unit of the French Army. Relief to be completed by 12. noon.

2. INTENTION. On relief the Battalion, less certain detached details, will move to LA PANNE and take over FURNES CAMP.

3. DISTRIBUTION. (a) The relief will be effected by companies in the following order:-

"D" Coy. "C" Coy. "B" Coy. "A" Coy. Hqrs.

(b) On relief each company will march to Billets at LA PANNE.

4. ROUTE. From camp to OOST DUNKERKE – COXYDE ROAD, thence N.W. through COXYDE to LA PANNE.

5. GUIDES. Guides will meet companies on the LA PANNE road.

6. BATTALION HEADQUARTERS. Battalion Headquarters will be established at JOLLEMONT VILLA, LA PANNE.

7. DETAILS. Details employed at Rear Brigade Headquarters, party with Tunnelling Company and Brigade Signalling Class will rejoin the Regiment ~~before~~ on the relief to-morrow.

8. REPORTS. Usual reports, states, etc. will be rendered to Battalion Headquarters immediately on arrival at LA PANNE.

Issued at 9.30. p.m.

Captain & Adjutant,
2nd Regiment S. A. Infantry.

Copy No.	1.	"A" Coy.
	2.	"B" Coy.
	3.	"C" Coy.
	4.	"D" Coy.
	5.	2/Lt. G.W. Marshall, attached Australian Tunnelling Coy.
	6/7/8	File and War Diary.

SECRET.

Copy No..8...

ORDER No: 107.

Reference
Sheet DUNKERQUE
1a. 1/10000.

In the Field,
18. - 11. - 17.

------

1. **INTENTION.**	The Battalion will move by march route to GHYVELDE to-morrow.
2. **DISTRIBUTION.**	(a) Companies will pass the starting point in the following order of march, commencing at 9.a.m. Headquarters and "A" Coy. "B" Company. "C" Company. "D" Company. First line transport. (b) 200 yards distance will be maintained between companies and sections of Transport of equivalent road space during the march.
3. **STARTING POINT.**	Starting Point - Cross roads by GRAND HOTEL DES ARCADES.
4. **ROUTE.**	From LA PANNE via ADINKERKE thence by main road to cross roads at 3.G.3.6. thence south to GHYVELDE.
5. **BAGGAGE.**	Baggage will be loaded as per instructions issued.
6. **STATES.**	Usual states and certificates will be rendered.
7. **REPORTS.**	Reports to head of Battalion.

Issued at 12.noon.

Captain & Adjutant,
2nd Regiment S.A.Infantry.

Copy No. 3. "A" Coy.
4. "B" Coy.
5. "C" Coy.
6. "D" Coy.
7. Transport Officer.
1. File.
2. War Diary.

Copy No. [illegible]

SECRET.

ORDER No. [illegible]

In the Field,
19. 11. 1917.

Reference
Sheet 19. 1/40000.
DUNKERQUE 1a. 1/100000.
HAZEBROUCK 5a. 1/100000.

---

1. INFORMATION. (a) The 9th Division is transferred from the XV Corps to the X Corps.
(b) The 1st South African Infantry Brigade will move from present area to FRUGES area.

2. INTENTION. The Battalion will move to the FRUGES area in accordance with march table to be issued daily.

3. HALTS. Clock hour halts will be observed on the march.

4. PROTECTION. In event of hostile aeroplanes flying over the march area, all movement will immediately cease.

5. STATES. Usual states and certificates will be rendered daily.

6. REPORTS. Reports to the head of the Battalion.

[illegible signature]

Captain & Adjutant,
2nd Regiment South African Infy.

Copy No. 1. "A" Coy.
2. "B" Coy.
3. "C" Coy.
4. "D" Coy.
5. Transport Officer.
6. File.
7/8. War Diary.

MARCH TABLE "A" ISSUED IN CONNECTION WITH ORDER: 108. Copy No 8

20-11-17

ITEM	UNIT	FROM	TO	STARTING POINT	TIME OF PASSING S.P.	ROUTE
1.	Hqr	GHYVELDE	GOURCH	church GHYVELDE.	10.40. a.m.	From Ghyvelde S.W. - UXEM - WAGHEM - BROUGGHE to Destination
2.	"C" Coy	Do	TETEGHEM SOUTH		10.42 a.m.	
3.	"B" Coy	Do	Do		10.44. a.m.	
4.	"D" Coy	Do	Do		10.46 a.m.	
5.	Transport	Do	Do		10.48. a.m	

REMARKS.

(a) 200 yards distance between Companies and section of transport of equivalent road space.

(b) Clock hour halts.

(c) Hqr will halt at TETEGHEM.

(Sgd) R.Beverley
Captain & Adjutant
2nd Regt S.A.Inf.

Issued to resipients
of Order 108.

Copy No 8
R

MARCH TABLE "B" ORDER 108.

Item.	Unit.	From	To	Starting Point.	Time of passing S.P.	ROUTE.
1.	Hqrs. XXXXXX	TETEGHEM SOUTH.	WORMHOUDT "A"	Branch Rd. I.22.a.30.55 (Sheet 19)	7.55. a.m.	via H.D. des MOERES - HOYMILLE - EAST OF BERGUES to WORMHOUDT.
2.	"D" Co.	do.	do.	H.D. des MOERES.	8.35. a.m.	ditto.
3.	"B" Co.	do.	do.	do.	8.37 a.m.	ditto.
4.	"C" Co.	do.	do.	do.	8.39 a.m.	ditto.
5.	"A" Co.	GOUDEKERQUE	do.	South end of Goudekerque village.	8.30. a.m.	via FORT LAPIN Road Junction at O.9.c.2.4. east of BERGUES to Wormhoudt.
6.	Transport.	TETEGHEM SOUTH.	do.	as for Item 1.	8.10. a.m.	as for item 1.

REMARKS.

(a) When the Battalion passes BERGUES the order of march will be the serial order of Items.

(b) 200 yards between companies and equivalent sections of Transport.

(c) Clock hour halts.

(d) Headquarters at WORMHOUDT - Steenvoorde Road - C.17.a.8.6. (Sheet 19) - 2.F.7.6. (Sheet Hazebrouck 5a).

(e) Halt from 10.50.a.m. to 12 noon.

R.Beverley [signature]

Captain & Adjutant,
2nd Regiment S.A.Infantry.

Issued to all recipients of order 108.

3.p.m. 20/11/1917.

Copy No 8

R

MARCH TABLE "C" ORDER 108.

Item.	Unit.	From	To	Starting Point.	Time of passing S.P.	Route.
1.	Hqrs.	WORMHOUDT.	ZERMEZEELE	Corner of Market Place Wormhoudt	8.25.a.m.	via RIETVELD S.W. by 3rd Class road to 2nd class road, then S.E. to Zermezeele.
2.	"C" Coy.	do.	do.	Cross Roads Rietveld.	9.8.a.m.	ditto.
3.	"D" Coy.	do.	do.	do.	9.9.a.m.	ditto.
4.	"A" Coy.	do.	do.	do.	9.10.a.m.	ditto.
5.	"B" Coy.	do.	do.	do.	9.11.a.m.	ditto.
6.	Transport.	do.	do.	do.	9.12.a.m.	ditto.

REMARKS.

(a) Distances 100 yards between companies and transport.

(b) Clock hour halts.

(c) Headquarters opposite church in ZERMEZEELE.

R Beviltof

Captain & Adjutant,
2nd Regiment S.A.Infantry.

Issued to all recipients
of Order 108.

8.p.m. 21/11/1917.

R

MARCH TABLE "D" ORDER 108.

Item.	Unit.	From.	To	Starting Point.	Time of passing S.P.	Route.
1.	Hqrs. & "B" Coy.	[illegible]	[illegible] Sheet 5a. 4.D.6.2.	H.Q. Mess	9.a.m.	Wemaers Cappel - Zuytpeene - X Roads Les Trois Rois - Ebblinghem.- X roads at Belle Croix to destination.
2.	"D" Coy.	do.		600 yds South of Zermezeele Church.	9.1.a.m.	
3.	"A" Coy.	do.	do.		9.2.a.m.	
4.	"C" Coy.	do.	do.	do.	9.3.a.m.	
5.	Transport	do.	do.	do.	9.4.a.m.	do.

REMARKS.

(a) 100 yards between companies and transport.

(b) Clock hour halts.

(c) Baggage waggons and cookers will travel with companies.

(d) Mid-day halt - 11.50.a.m. - 1.p.m.

R. Bamley [signature]

Captain & Adjutant,
2nd Regiment S.A.Infantry.

Issued to all recipients
of order 108.

7.p.m. 22.11.1917.

MARCH TABLE "B" - ORDER 108.

24.11.1917.

Item	Unit.	From	To	Starting Point.	Time of Passing S.P.	Route.
1.	Hqrs. & "A" Co.	COUBRONNE [illegible].	AVROULT	Battalion Headquarters	8.50.a.m.	ECQUES - East to X roads then South to Y roads opposite C of CLARQUES - [illegible] to Destination.
2.	"C" Co.	do.	do.	do.	8.51.a.m.	
3.	"D" Co.	do.	do.	EASTERN X Roads of ECQUES.	9.13.a.m.	
4.	"B" Coy.	do.	do.	do	9.16.a.m.	do.
5.	Transport	do.	do.	do.	9.17.a.m.	do.

REMARKS.

(a) 100 yards between companies and Transport.

(b) Clock hour halts.

R.B. Beverley(?)

Captain & Adjutant,
2nd Regiment S. A. Infantry.

Issued to all recipients of Order 108.

8.p.m. 23.11.1917.

MARCH TABLE "?" [illegible].

Day of March - [illegible].11.1917.

Reference - Sheets [illegible] 17.

Unit:- 2nd REGIMENT SOUTH AFRICAN INFANTRY.

From:- A V R O U L T.

To:- [illegible] - [illegible] - [illegible] AREA.

Order of March:- Headquarters; "?" Co. "?" Co. "?" Co. "?" Co. Transport.

Starting Point:- Branch Roads S. of AVROULT - [illegible] ST. in ST. [illegible].

Time. 12 noon.

Route:- AVROULT - FAUQUEMBERGUES - then west to CAMPAGNE - to destination.

Remarks:- (a) Clock hour halts.

(b) The Battalion will be drawn up in column of route ready to move at 12 noon.

[illegible signature]

Captain & Adjutant.
2nd Regiment South African Infantry.

Issued to all recipients of Order [illegible].

?.p.m. 24/11/17.

December 1917 — 2nd Regt: South African Infantry

Army Form C. 2118.

WAR DIARY
or
[redacted]
(Erase heading not required.)

Instructions regarding War Diaries and Intelligence Summaries are contained in F. S. Regs., Part II. and the Staff Manual respectively. Title pages will be prepared in manuscript.

Place	Date	Hour	Summary of Events and Information	Remarks and references to Appendices
BOURTHES	1st		At 6AM orders received from Brigade to move to forward area. Batt: marched out at 9.30 AM – ORDER No 109 – Majority of baggage left behind to come on with horses. Marched to VERCHIN via FRUGES. Arrived 5PM. horses for baggage did not report. Baggage left behind with 2/Lt EGAN & MARSHALL and 12 O.R. Weather cold & rainy. Billetted at VERCHIN for the night. 15 miles march. Strength of Regt: 35 Off: 988 O.R.	Appendix No 1
VERCHIN	2nd		Marched out at 11 AM. to entraining station at ANVIN en route for Peronne. Arrived ANVIN 2PM. – meal served and regiment bivouaced till 6 pm – Entrained 6 PM. Train left at 10 PM. Truck accomodation only. Cold & frosty. – Order No 110 refers	Appendix No 1
	3rd		Arrived at PERONNE 6 AM. Had breakfast on station and marched to MOISLAINS at 10 AM arrived 2 pm – Arranged camp. Many men footsore owing to lack of good boots. Received orders that the Battalion will probably go into action tomorrow on the GOUZEAUCOURT front	

D. D. & L., London, E.C.
(A7883) Wt. W809/M1672 350,000 4/17 Sch. 52a Forms/C/2118/14

Instructions regarding War Diaries and Intelligence Summaries are contained in F. S. Regs., Part II. and the Staff Manual respectively. Title pages will be prepared in manuscript.

WAR DIARY

or

[redacted]

(Erase heading not required.)

Army Form C. 2118.

Place	Date	Hour	Summary of Events and Information	Remarks and references to Appendices
MOISLAINS	3rd		Preparations for move tomorrow - Companies organised at fighting strength & carriers &c detailed	
MOISLAINS	4th		Brigade Order No 147 received. Battalion marched out to FINS to rendezvous ~~for~~ and await for orders to relief the 2nd Brigade Guards Division. C.O and advance parties proceeded ahead to reconnoitre. Battalion under Adjutant marched to FINS and then after meal & rest proceeded to the trenches at GOUZEAUCOURT to relief of Guards viz 3rd Coldstream & 1st Scots Guards Order No 111 refers. — Relief completed by 11 PM. Batt H.Q situated in dugout in sunken road W 6 b central Sheet GOUZEAUCOURT 1:20000. 5 OR. wounded during relief.	
GOUZEAUCOURT	5th		Fairly quiet day. Reconnaissance of area made by C.O. & Adjutant. Several dead buried. Enemy artillery fairly active. Work at night on line. Front line in-accessible by day and trench very shallow with no fire steps. - Usual patrol sent out along front. 6 O.R. wounded	

D. D. & L., London, E.C.
(A7883) Wt. W809/M1672 350,000 4/17 Sch. 52a Forms/C/2118/14

Instructions regarding War Diaries and Intelligence Summaries are contained in F. S. Regs., Part II. and the Staff Manual respectively. Title pages will be prepared in manuscript.

WAR DIARY

or

[redacted]

(Erase heading not required.)

Army Form C. 2118.

Place	Date	Hour	Summary of Events and Information	Remarks and references to Appendices
GOUZEAUCOURT Trenches	6th		Usual trench routine. Improvements being made. No R.E. material available except what can be salvaged. C.O. & Adjutant round trenches at different times during the night. 3 O.R. killed. Enemy artillery fairly active. Disposition of companies in line as follows. Right front Coy B Coy – Left front Coy C Coy. Right support Coy A Coy – Left support Coy C Coy. Stores, S.A.A. Grenades &c gradually being collected & battalion & company dumps being formed. A large amount of salvage lying about left by our troops after retreat and by enemy after being driven back by counter attack.	
do	7th		Usual trench routine. Enemy artillery fairly active. Work on trenches at night. Left company deepening. Right company wiring & blocking saps. Enemy artillery quieter at night.	
do	8th		Enemy shelled front line & valley round support line fairly heavily with all calibres. The following officer casualties occurred early in the	

D. D. & L., London, E.C. (A7883) Wt. W809/M1672 350,000 4/17 Sch. 52a Forms/C/2118/14

Instructions regarding War Diaries and Intelligence Summaries are contained in F. S. Regs., Part II. and the Staff Manual respectively. Title pages will be prepared in manuscript.

WAR DIARY
or
INTELLIGENCE SUMMARY.
(*Erase heading not required.*)

Army Form C. 2118.

Place	Date	Hour	Summary of Events and Information	Remarks and references to Appendices
	8th		morning Killed Capt E C Bryant, 2/Lt Dickson, 2/Lt Mandy – wounded 2 Lt Hennessy 2/Lt Arnold. – Capt Stein and three other officers arrived to replace casualties. Battalion relieved by 1st S.A.I. 6 pm – 9 pm Order No 112. On relief Battalion withdrew to support lines with one company in reserve line. Wet muddy night enemy artillery fairly quiet.	Appendix I
	9th		In reserve & support line. Work done improving & cleaning lines & arranging ration dump. Enemy sent a few shells over to support lines no casualties.	
	10th		In reserve line. Work done in clean & improving reserve trenches. SAA Bombs & R.E. Stores collected. One company withdrawn from support trenches & placed in left of reserve line. Capt Jacobs of C Coy. commands reserve line which is garrisoned by B & C Coys, about 400 yds WEST of GOUZEAUCOURT. Permanent store of SAA water & formed.	

D. D. & L., London, E.C.
(A7883) Wt W809/M1672 350,000 4/17 Sch. 52a Forms/C/2118/14

Instructions regarding War Diaries and Intelligence Summaries are contained in F. S. Regs., Part II. and the Staff Manual respectively. Title pages will be prepared in manuscript.

WAR DIARY
or
INTELLIGENCE SUMMARY.
(*Erase heading not required.*)

Army Form C. 2118.

Place	Date	Hour	Summary of Events and Information	Remarks and references to Appendices
GOUZEAUCOURT	10th		Rain & cold. Four cases of Trench Feet evacuated.	
"	11th		Wet cold day. Orders for relief received. Preparations made to move into the line to relieve 1st SAI. Brigade order 151 refers. Battalion Order No 114 lost in trenches. Slight enemy shelling on reserve lines 2 O.R. wounded. 1st SAI relieved by Battalion by 11 PM. Relief passed off well little enemy shelling.	
"	12th		Fine day. Enemy artillery fairly active. No casualties. Several men suffering from bad feet. Kitchens arranged & hot food sent into the line 3 times per night.	
	13th		A little rain. Usual trench routine. - Patrols out - nothing to report - Work being done in improving front line & communications. A little wire put up. No supplies of wire. All wire used has been salved by regiment	

D. D. & L., London, E.C.
(A7883) Wt. W809/M1672 350,000 4/17 Sch. 52a Forms/C/2118/14

Instructions regarding War Diaries and Intelligence Summaries are contained in F. S. Regs., Part II. and the Staff Manual respectively. Title pages will be prepared in manuscript.

WAR DIARY
or
INTELLIGENCE SUMMARY.
(Erase heading not required.)

Army Form C. 2118.

Place	Date	Hour	Summary of Events and Information	Remarks and references to Appendices
GOUZEACOURT	14th		Quiet day - Usual patrols & work - Communication trench being dug to front line from support system. Clear day. Enemy air craft patrols active.	
"	15th		Quiet morning - Fairly fine and cold. Preparations for relief. At about 2 pm the enemy shelled the front line & new trenches heavily with 77 mm and 10 cm shells. Casualties 3 OR killed 11 wounded. The relief was timed to take place at 6.30 P.M. This was postponed to 8.30 PM owing to Artillery shoot on enemy lines at 7.30 PM. Enemy however anticipated our shoot and shelled our lines intermittently to 8 PM. Relief was eventually effected and completed by 11 PM. The Battalion on relief moved to huts at W.c.3 sheet 57C. Men served with hot meal & rum & sent to bed	

D. D. & L., London, E.C. (A7883) Wt. W809/M1672 350,000 4/17 Sch. 52a Forms/C/2118/14

Instructions regarding War Diaries and Intelligence Summaries are contained in F. S. Regs., Part II. and the Staff Manual respectively. Title pages will be prepared in manuscript.

WAR DIARY

or

~~INTELLIGENCE~~ ~~SUMMARY~~.

(*Erase heading not required.*)

Army Form C. 2118.

Place	Date	Hour	Summary of Events and Information	Remarks and references to Appendices
Reserve Camp WC 3.	16th		Resting all day. Large number of sick and two hospital cases. Three cases of desertion for C.O. All remanded for Court Martial. Two cases of self inflicted wounds reported to Brigade. – Issue of clothing.	
do	17th		All men bathed at HEUDICOURT baths. – Foot treatment at 27th F.A. Foot depot. Reinforcements from detail camp arrive to replace casualties. Reorganisation & reequipment. No incident of note to report.	
do.	18th		A few details sent to baths. Remainder of men sent to 27th F.A. Foot depot for foot treatment. Issue of boots. Enemy artillery fairly active on our guns in front of camp. 5 O.R. on leave. – R.S.M. Wells appointed acting Quartermaster.	

D. D. & L., London, E.C.
(A7883) Wt. W809/M1672 350,000 4/17 Sch. 52a Forms/C/2118/14

Instructions regarding War Diaries and Intelligence Summaries are contained in F. S. Regs., Part II, and the Staff Manual respectively. Title pages will be prepared in manuscript.

WAR DIARY
or
INTELLIGENCE SUMMARY.
(*Erase heading not required.*)

Army Form C. 2118.

Place	Date	Hour	Summary of Events and Information	Remarks and references to Appendices
Ronm Camp W.C.3.	19th		Cold frosty morning - Preparations made for move. Order No 116 issued for move to the trenches to relieve 1st S.A.I. - Nine sick men to hospital - 2 trench feet, 1 E.T. + P.U.O. - Regiment marched out by platoon at 4-30 P.M. Quiet relief. The 105 c/m shells sent over, one of which caught No 3 platoon killing 2 & wounding 5 other ranks. Otherwise quiet - relief completed 9 P.M. C.O. + intelligence officer up the line at 11 P.M.	
GOUZEAUCOURT	20th		Cold frosty morning. Adjutant round line 5 AM - 7 AM. - C.O. round line 10 AM - 12 noon. Slight shelling during morning. Wiring by day owing to bad visibility on account of mist. Two heavy bursts of shelling 77 mm 4.30 PM + 5.30 PM on support system - 3 O.R. wounded. - Rations up as usual. Full rum issue. C.O. + intelligence officer to line 10 PM. returned 12 midnight - Very quiet night	

D. D. & L., London, E.C.
(A7883) Wt. W809/M1672 350,000 4/17 Sch. 52a Forms/C/2118/14

Instructions regarding War Diaries and Intelligence Summaries are contained in F. S. Regs., Part II. and the Staff Manual respectively. Title pages will be prepared in manuscript.

WAR DIARY

or

(Erase heading not required.)

Army Form C. 2118.

Place	Date	Hour	Summary of Events and Information	Remarks and references to Appendices
GOUZEAUCOURT TRENCHES	21st		Cold frosty morning; fairly misty. Adjutant went round line 5 AM - 7 AM. Enemy artillery fairly active 4.30 AM. - 7 AM - 77 mm & 10.5 mm shells searching the valley near support lines. Adjutant round line 10 AM - 12 NOON - C.O. round line 12 noon - 2 pm. Slight artillery activity 4 P.M. 2 O.R. Killed in support Trench. Transport officer called 5 PM. Arrangements made for bringing supplies up on pack animals. Mist cleared at night. 5.30 PM & 6.45 p.m. our artillery put down intense harrassing fire for five minutes on enemy supports & approaches, a relief being suspected. C.O. & intelligence officer to front line 10.30 P.M.	
	22nd		Cold & frost all day and fairly clear - Adjutant went round the line 5 a.m. to 7 a.m. Enemy artillery somewhat active intermittently shelling left company area, also immediate support area. The C.O. made his round between 10 a.m. and 12 noon. Much enemy activity observed behind GONNELIEU and VILLERS GUSLAINS apparently	

Instructions regarding War Diaries and Intelligence Summaries are contained in F. S. Regs., Part II. and the Staff Manual respectively. Title pages will be prepared in manuscript.

WAR DIARY

~~or~~

~~INTELLIGENCE SUMMARY.~~

(*Erase heading not required.*)

Army Form C. 2118.

Place	Date	Hour	Summary of Events and Information	Remarks and references to Appendices
GOUZEAUCOURT TRENCHES	22nd.		continuing RESERVE LINE. ENEMY planes most active, flying low apparently taking photographs of trench system and co-operating with their artillery. Patrol sent out during the night to try to discover enemy outposts but although voices heard no definite locations were possible. Two O.R. killed by shell fire and one O.R. received a self inflicted wound.	
	23rd.		Weather still cold, though mild thaw apparently impending. Sun shone greater part of day and snow rapidly disappearing. Enemy artillery still active, maintaining ~~ha~~ harassing fire on our left company position and immediate supports, ~~and~~ intensity increasing in afternoon to slight barrage. Trench mortars of "granatenwerfer" type fired at right company sector from direction of VILLERS GUSLAINS. Adjutant went round 5 am to 7 am and C.O. visited all companies between 11 am and 1 pm. Enemy planes continued active, flying low over our lines; one observation plane was shot down by one of our planes and fell some 500 to 1000 yards in front of our sector well in the enemy lines; one man was seen to run from the machine about five minutes later and was fired at by a Lewis gunner but apparently	

D. D. & L., London, E.C.
(A7883) Wt W809/M1672 350,000 4/17 Sch. 52a Forms/C/2118/14

Instructions regarding War Diaries and Intelligence Summaries are contained in F. S. Regs., Part II. and the Staff Manual respectively. Title pages will be prepared in manuscript.

WAR DIARY
or
~~INTELLIGENCE SUMMARY.~~
(Erase heading not required.)

Army Form C. 2118.

Place	Date	Hour	Summary of Events and Information	Remarks and references to Appendices
GOUZEAUCOURT			escaped, although it was most improbable that he was one of the crew and	
TRENCHES	23rd.		probably only crept up to investigate. Another enemy machine was also shot down	
			and fell well behind our lines, in the direction of GOUZEAUCOURT. One O.R. a Camn,	
			was killed by shell fire and six O.R. wounded. The Battalion was relieved between	
			8.30 pm, and 9.30 pm. by the 1st S.A.I. and occupied the Support trench system	
			with two companies and the reserve system with the remaining two, vide order 107.	
	24th.		weather continues cold, slight frost over night, tendency for thaw to set in	
			continues. Sky fairly clear, sun-shine at intervals. Companies in Support Line	
			Hut Dispositions further back in line with reserve companies and put towards	
			an Immediate Support System, (vide order 108).	
	25th		weather still cold although last of snow has disappeared overnight.	
			Shelling continued by both sides intermittently during day. Several enemy	
			planes over during morning. Snow started falling towards noon and	
			slight falls continued in afternoon and evening, increasing to steady fall	
			during night. Enemy shell exploded in Elephant hut killing three men	
			and wounding four others. No work done under orders from Brigadier.	

Instructions regarding War Diaries and Intelligence Summaries are contained in F. S. Regs., Part II, and the Staff Manual respectively. Title pages will be prepared in manuscript.

WAR DIARY

~~INTELLIGENCE SUMMARY~~.

(Erase heading not required.)

Army Form C. 2118.

Place	Date	Hour	Summary of Events and Information	Remarks and references to Appendices
GOUZEAUCOURT TRENCHES	26th		weather extremely cold, whole area covered with snow, sun shone almost whole day. Several enemy planes over. Our and enemy artillery activity continued, GOUZEAUCOURT and road still receiving constant attention.	
	27th		Weather continues cold and frosty. Enemy plane reported downed to rear of Reserve line 8 a.m. Intermittent shelling all day of Gouzeaucourt and Fins Road. Two shells crashed at about 6.30 p.m. on road near Battn Headquarters, one man of 2nd Regiment wounded and mule killed. The Regiment moved up to Right subsection of Centre Section at 8.30 p.m. relieving the 1st S.A.I. (see order 109.) Relief very successfully carried out.	
	28th		Weather still cold and frosty and ground snow clad. Two patrols left Right subsection during night but did not come into contact with enemy. Adjutant made rounds 5 am to 7 am. Divisional Commander and Brigadier visited front and Immediate support line during morning, the Commanding Officer conducted the party. Major Heenan and Warrant Officer	

D. D. & L., London, E.C. (A7883) Wt. W809/M1672 350,000 4/17 Sch. 52a Forms/C/2118/14

Instructions regarding War Diaries and Intelligence Summaries are contained in F. S. Regs., Part II. and the Staff Manual respectively. Title pages will be prepared in manuscript.

WAR DIARY
or
~~INTELLIGENCE SUMMARY.~~
(Erase heading not required.)

Army Form C. 2118.

Place	Date	Hour	Summary of Events and Information	Remarks and references to Appendices
	28th (continued)			
GOUZEAUCOURT TRENCHES			visited trenches and initiated works programme for the four days occupation. An enemy plane shot down by one of our aviators above Gouzeaucourt about 11.30 a.m. engine came down in flames, wings and other parts continuing to float in air for some minutes. Enemy artillery and machine gun activity normal. One O.R. wounded by bullet wound in arm. Visibility at night very clear owing to moon and snow.	
	29th.		Our Patrols again encountered no enemy reconnaissances. Weather still cold and frosty and ground snow clad. Enemy appeared to be working on Cemetery road, carrying parties being seen, some activity being observed behind BONNOLIEU and VILLERS GUSLAINS, his artillery somewhat quiet during day. The Adjutant, Commanding Officer and Works Officer made usual rounds. Enemy planes continued active but our aircraft still remains in evidence, driving enemy planes away.	
	30th.		Our usual night patrols reported no enemy activity. Signs of	

D. D. & L., London, E.C.
(A7883) Wt W809/M1672 350,000 4/17 Sch. 52a Forms/C/2118/14

Instructions regarding War Diaries and Intelligence Summaries are contained in F. S. Regs., Part II. and the Staff Manual respectively. Title pages will be prepared in manuscript.

WAR DIARY
or
INTELLIGENCE SUMMARY.
(Erase heading not required.)

Army Form C. 2118.

Place	Date	Hour	Summary of Events and Information	Remarks and references to Appendices
	30th (continued)			
GOUZEAUCOURT TRENCHES			imminent thaw, and trenches muddy. Heavy enemy barrage directed against Brigade on left sector between 6.30 and 7 am, our front quiet. Enemy violently shelled immediate back areas between 8 am and 9 am. The C.O., Adjutant and W arks officer made usual rounds and Brigadier also visited Battalion front. Slight enemy activity observed. another Enemy plane brought down behind our lines by our vigilant aviators. ~~R~~ Deserted Ruins of Gouzeaucourt again fitfully shelled by enemy during the day. One O.R. wounded in hand (S. I.) whilst cleaning rifle, xxxth case in present unprecedented epidemic in Regiment.	
	31st		Weather cold and misty. Slight enemy artillery and machine gun activity on our front. Adjutant visited Companies from 5 a.m. 7 am. and C.O. made his usual ~~xxxx~~ round between 10 am and 12.30 pm. Two O.R. wounded by shell fire. Enemy working party about 200 strong observed at R.32.c.5.5. 3 of our batteries opened fire at 10.15 am. dispersing party. Regiment was relieved by the First S.A.I. at 5 pm. and moved into hutments on Fins Road. (See Operation order 120).	

C R Heenan MAJOR
Commanding 2nd S.A.I.

D. D. & L., London, E.C.
(A7883) Wt. W809/M1672 350,000 4/17 Sch. 52a Forms/C/2118/14

2nd REGIMENT SOUTH AFRICAN INFANTRY.

W A R D I A R Y: & APPENDICES.

for

DECEMBER, 1917

SECRET **MOVEMENT TABLE ISSUED IN CONNECTION WITH ORDER 109.**

Unit.	From	To	Starting Point.	Time	Route	Remarks
Hqrs.	BOURHTES	VERCHIN.	X roads south of BOURTHES.	9.15. a.m.	ERGNY VERCHOCQ	
"C" Co.	do.	do.	do.	9.16	RUMILLY FRUGES to	
"B" Co.	do.	do.	Last House in LA CATELET.	9.45.	Destination.	
"A"	do.	do.	do.	9.46		
"D" Co.	do.	do.	do.	9.47.		

NOTE.

(a) 100 yards between companies : Transport 100 yards in rear of last company.

(b) CLOCK hours halts.

(c) Notification of midday halts will be given.

(SD.) R.Beverley,
Captain & Adjutant,
2nd S.A.I.

Issued at 8.a.m. to
all recipients of
Order No. 109.

ORDER NO: 109. Copy No...

Dec. 1st 1917.

Reference
Sheet 13
" 5a.
" 11.

1. (a) The 9th Division is transferred from X Corps to VII Corps.

(b) The 1st South African Infantry Brigade will move to New area by march route and by rail to-day.

2. The Battalion will move to-day to New Area in accordance with movement table attached.

3. Usual certificates and states will be rendered.

4. Baggage will be loaded in accordance with instructions issued.

5. 2/Lieut. Marshall and two men per company will remain behind as clearing party.

6. Reports to head of Battalion.

(SD.) R.BEVERLEY,
Captain & Adjutant,
2nd S.A.I.

Issued at 8.a.m.

INSTRUCTIONS issued with order No. 109.

(1) All Company baggage will be dumped outside COMPANY ORDERLY ROOMS.

(2) Two men per company will remain as guard and loading party.

(3) All blankets will be rolled in bundles of TEN.

(4) Lorries will collect all baggage.

(5) 2/Lieut. MARSHALL will be responsible that all men and baggage are cleared from billets.

(6) Training ~~xxxxx~~ stores will be handed to the MAYOR for safe keeping and receipts obtained. 2/Lt. MARSHALL will arrange.

(SD.) R.BEVERLEY,
Captain & Adjutant,
2nd S.A.I.

Issued to recipients of
Order No.109.

SECRET. ORDER NO: 111. Copy No.

In the Field. 4.12.17.

Ref. Sheet 57c 1/40000.
62c 1/40000.

---

1. (a) The South African Brigade will relieve the 2nd Brigade Guards Division on the night of 4/5th inst.

(b) The South African Brigade will move by march route and rendezvous near FINS on the morning of 4th.

2. The 2nd S.A.Infantry will relieve a Battalion of the 2d Brigade Guards to-night and will proceed to rendezvous at FINS marching at 11.30.a.m. to-day.

3. Details of relief to-night will be notified later.

4. (a) The Battalion will pass the starting point in the following order of march.-
Hqrs. "B" Co. "C" Co. "D" Co. "A" Co. 1st Line transport, commencing at 11.30.a.m.

(b) Distance of 50 yards will be maintained between platoons and 100 yards between Units and Transport.

5. (a) Starting point cross roads MOISLAINS near church.

(b) Route - via NURLU.

6. (a) Fighting personnel only will proceed to FINS.
(b) 1st line transport and Q.M.Stores will be located at FINS.

7. Details not going into the line will be located at YORK Camp and will move there under separate orders.

8. Usual states and reports will be rendered on arrival at FINS.

9. Reports to Battalion Headquarters.

(SD.) R.Beverley,
Captain & Adjutant,
2nd Regiment S.A.Infantry.

Issued at 8.30.a.m.

Copy No.1. "A" Co.
2. "B" Co.
3. "C" Co.
4.5 "D" Co.
5. Transport Officer.
6. Major Heenan O/C. Details.
7. Medical Officer.
8. File.
9 & 10 War Diary.

2ND S.A.I

Ref
LENS.11.

In the Field
2[illegible]·12·17.

ORDER No 110[B]

1. B Company 2ND S.A.I. will move to PERONNE in accordance with instructions detailed below.

2. ENTRAINING STATION ANVIN.
DETRAINING STATION PERONNE.
Train departs 1-20 AM 3rd inst.

3. Cookers will report at station 3 hours before departure of train.
Personnel will report at station 1½ hours before departure of train.
One officer will report to Staff Captain at R T O's office at ANVIN 3½ hours before departure of train.

4. O.C. B Coy will arrange time and details of move to station.

Issued at 10 A.M.

(Sd) R. Beverley
Capt & Adjt
2nd S.A.I.

2nd Regiment South African Infantry

Ref.
LENS. 11.
1/100000

In the Field
2-12-1917

ORDER No 110A

1. The Battalion less B Coy, one Cooker and team will move to PERONNE today by march route and by rail.

2. The Battalion will pass the starting point as hereunder detailed
   a. 1st Line Transport less 1 Cooker and team 11·30 A.M.
   b. H.Q. A Coy, C Coy, D Coy in order of march named 12·30 P.M.

3. Starting Point – Church in VERCHIN.

4. a. Hot tea will be served at 10·45 A.M.
   b. Kitchens will be ready to pull out at 11 A.M.
   c. If possible hot meal will be prepared at station to await arrival of troops.
   d. All baggage will be loaded by 11 A.M.

5. Entraining Station ANVIN. Time Dep. 4·20 pm
   Detraining Station PERONNE.

6. 2/Lt AULDS will report to Staff Capt (Capt Morrison M.C.) at R.T.Os Office ANVIN at 12-45 P.M. He will be in possession of entraining states.

7. Marching States will be handed to Adjutant at entraining station.

8. Reports to Battalion Headquarters.

Issued at 9·30 A.M.

Copy No 1 A Coy
2 B Coy
3 C Coy
4 D Coy
5 Transport Officer
6 File.

(Sgd) R Beverley
Capt & Adjutant
2nd S.A.I.

ADMINISTRATION INSTRUCTIONS ISSUED WITH ORDER 111.

1. All personnel remaining behind will be billeted in YORK CAMP 15.a.6.2. MOISLAINS at present occupied by 1st S.A.I.

2. Heavy baggage will be left at YORK CAMP.

3. Q.M.Stores will go forward to FINS with Transport.

4. A lorry will be available for transport of Officers Kits and Blankets to FINS.

5. TWO blankets per man of personnel going into the line will be rolled ready for loading by 9.30.a.m.

6. One field kitchen will remain behind with details, "A" Company kitchen is detailed for this duty.

7. Remaining Field Kitchens will cook for personnel going forward. A/Sgt. Cook will arrange all details in regard to this.

8. Officers will take necessary kits to FINS remainder of officers kits will be left at Detail Camp.

9. DRESS for the march will be full marching order.

(SD.) R.BEVERLEY,
Captain & Adjutant,
2nd Regiment S.A.Infantry.

4.12.17.

Copy No

ORDER No 112

Reference
Sheet GOUZEAUCOURT
1:20000

In the Field
8 - 12 - 17

1 The 1st S A I will relieve the 2nd S A I in the Right Sub-sector of the Brigade Front on the night of 8/9 Dec 1917

2 On relief the Battalion will become the Battalion in Brigade support

3 Companies on relief will occupy lines as follows:–
<u>A & C Companies</u> in Trench running from Approx Q 36 d 5 4 to Q 36 d 2 3 to W 6 b 6 4 to W 6 d 5 9.
Joint Coy head quarters in dug out in Trench at W 6 b central
<u>D Coy</u> in Trench EAST of GOUZEAUCOURT approx R 31 c 1 6 to R 31 a 5 3
<u>B Coy</u> will occupy the DIVISIONAL RESERVE LINE from approx Q 35 d 1 1 to W 5 b 8 0.

4. Reliefs will be effected by platoons at 5 minutes interval

ORDER NO. 113.

Copy No...

In the Field.
10.12.17.

Reference
GOUZEACOURT
1/20000.

1. "C" Company 2nd S.A.I. will relieve two companies of 4th S.A.I. in the Divisional Reserve line between points Q.35.d.1.1. and Q.35.b.0.0. approximately in accordance with Order B.86 previously issued.

2. On completion of relief "C" & "B" Companies will comprise the garrison of reserve line.

3. "C" and "B" Companies will be under the command of O.C. "C" Coy. (Capt. L.M.JACOBS) and will come under Brigade Headquarters for orders. These companies will not move without orders from Brigade,

4. Stores in reserve line will be taken over and receipts forwarded to Battalion Hqrs. by 11.a.m. to-morrow.

5. Completion of relief will be reported to Battalion Headquarters by code word "BACON".

6. Acknowledge

(SD.) R.Beverley,
Captain & Adjutant,
2nd S.A.I.

Issued 4.30.p.m.
Copy No.1 O.C. "B" Co.
2. " "C" Co.
3. File.
4-5 - War Diary.

ORDER NO: 115. Copy No...

In the Field,
15.12.17.

Reference
GOUZEAUCOURT 1/20000
and Sheet 57C.

1. The 1st S.A.I. will relieve the 2nd S.A.I. in the right Batt. sub-sector to-night 15/16th.

2. On completion of relief the Battalion will move to Huts at Camp in W.3.c. near cross roads on GOUZEAUCOURT-FINS road.

3.(a) The relief will be effected by platoons at 5 minutes interval commencing at about 8.30.p.m.

~~4~~.(b) Companies will be relieved by corresponding companies of 1st ~~S~~.A.I. in the following order -
"A" Co. "C" Co. "B" Co. "D" Co.

~~5~~ 4. The relief of the Battalion will be completed by 11.30.p.m.

5. Advance parties of the 1st S.A.I. will arrive to take over stores etc. before relief.

6. All stores telephones, etc. will be handed over and receipts forwarded as usual.

7. Details of work in hand, working parties and proposed work will be handed over.

8.(a) Guides are not required by the relieving Battalion.
(b) Guides will meet outgoing companies at cross roads near camp.

9. Completion of relief and move will be reported to Battalion Headquarters immediately on arrival at camp.

Issued at 2.p.m.

(SD.) R.Beverley,
Captain & Adjutant,
2nd S.A.I.

Copies 1 - 4 A.B.C.D. Coys.
5. File.
6-7 War Diary.

Reference
GOUZEAUCOURT
1/20000.

ORDER NO: 116.

Copy No....

In the Field.
19.22. 17.

1. The 2nd S.A.I. will relieve the 1st S.A.I. on the night of 19/20th December 1917.

2. The relief will be effected by platoons at 5 minutes interval in the following order of companies:-
"B" Co. "D" Co. "A" Co. "C" Co.

3. The leading platoon of "B" Coy. will march out of camp at 4.30.p.m.

4.

"B" Co. 2nd SAI.	will relieve	"A" Co. 1st SAI.	in the Right Front Coy. sector.	
"D" Co.	ditto	"C" Co. "	in the Left	ditto
"A" Co.	ditto	"B" Co. "	Right support line	
"C" Co.	ditto	"D" Co. "	Left	ditto.

5.(a) Advance parties consisting of 1 officer and 1 other rank of each company will proceed to the line at 3.p.m. for the purpose of taking over stores.

(b) Observers will proceed to the line under 2/Lt. CRAGG at 2.p.m.

6. All stores orders etc. will be taken over and receipts forwarded to Battalion H.Q. by 12 midnight.

7. Details of work in hand will be taken over.

8. Completion of relief will be reported by wiring the name of company Commanders concerned to Headquarters.

Issued at 9.a.m.

(sd.) R.Beverley,
Captain & Adjutant,
2nd S.A.I.

Copies 1 - 4 A.B.C.D. Coys.
5. File.
6. 1st S.A.I
7 - 8 War Diary.

Operation Order No 117

2nd Regiment South African Infantry

In the Field. 22/12/17.

No 1
RELIEF

The 1st S.A.I. will relieve the 2nd S.A.I. in right Sub: section to-morrow night 23/24th inst. The order of relief will be B.D.C.A. Companies moving off on completion of relief; Relief not to commence before 8.30 pm. After relief disposition of companies will be as follows:

N2.
DISTRIBUTION.

B - right reserve Company.
D - left " "

and will become the Garrison of reserve line under the command of Captain Jenkins.

C. - left support Company
A - right " "

and will become Battalion in support.

3.
Advance PARTY

One Officer and 1 NCO per company will proceed in Advance under Company arrangements and will take over all Trench Stores etc. This Officer will obtain particulars of all work in hand and Company Commanders will ensure that same is continued.

4
TRENCH STORE CARDS

To be submitted to Orderly Room by 8 AM 24th inst.

5
WATER & RATIONS

Water and Rations will be drawn immediately on completion of relief

6.
STATES

Usual States will be rendered.
Marching Out State by 5.pm 23rd inst

7
COMPLETION OF RELIEF

To be reported by wiring the Surname of Company Commander

(Sd) H. Perry
2/Lt & Act. Adjt.
2nd. S.A.I.

22-12-17.

2nd Regt: South African Infantry.
Operation Order No ~~[illegible]~~ 118

MAP REF
GOUZEAUCOURT 1/20,000

In the Field
24/12/17

1 Intention	The following alteration in disposition of Brigade will be effected on the night of 24/25th December 17 A & C Companies of 2nd South African Infantry occupying support line will withdraw from that line to following positions:- "A" Coy to position in bank Approx. W5b 50 HD to W5b 80.90 H Qrs at W5b. 70.80 "C" Coy to position in SUNKEN ROADS at Q35 b 80.10 and Q35.b.20.80. H.Qrs at Q35. b 90.10. The counter attack Company of 3rd SAI will occupy portion of Support Line vacated by C. Coy 2nd SAI. The counter attack Company of 1st SAI will occupy portion of Support Line vacated by A Coy 2nd SAI.
2 Advance Parties	Small reconnoitring parties from respective Support Companies to report to Staff Captain as indicated in Warning Order. Advance Parties from Counter Attack Companies will be sent to take over Stores in Support Line
3. Movement	Movement will be by Platoons at 5 minutes interval starting at 4.45 pm and may be simultaneous from both A & C Coy
4. States	Usual states will be rendered.
5 Completion Movement	Completion of Movement and occupation of New positions will be reported to Battalion HQrs by Wiring name of Company Commander.
6 Work	On completion of movement A & C Coy will become available for Work in forward Area.

(Sd) H. Perry
2/Lieut & Act. Adj.
2nd S.A.I.

24-12-17

MAP REF: GOUZEAUCOURT 1/20000

2nd Regt South African Infantry

Operation Order No. 119

26.12.1917

1. Relief: The 2nd South African Infantry will relieve the 1st South African Infantry in the right Sub Section on the night 27/28th December 1917.
The order of relief will be A.C.D.B. Coys the leading Companies moving off at 8 pm. intervals of 5 minutes will be observed between Platoons.-

2. Distribution: After relief disposition of Companies will be as follows:-

A right Coy – Front Line
C left " – " "
D Immediate Support Company
B Counter Attack Coy in Support line

3. Advance Parties: Consisting of 1 Officer and 1 NCO per Company will proceed in advance under Company arrangements will take over all Trench Stores etc.

4. Work: All Orders with regard to all Work in hand, and Working Parties to be found will be taken over from out-going Companies.

5. Blankets: All Blankets with the exception of 1 Blanket per man in B & D Coy to be rolled in bundles of 10 and stacked at Battalion Hqrs by 6PM. These Blankets to be handed over to Corpl Fitzpatrick.

6. Trench Store Cards: To be submitted to Orderly Room by 9 AM, 28th inst

7. Water & Rations: Water and Rations will be drawn immediately on completion of relief

8. States: Usual States will be rendered, marching Out state by 5 pm 27th inst

9. Completion of Relief: To be reported by wiring names of company Commanders

(Sd) H. Perry
2/Lt & Act Adj
2nd S.A.I.

2nd Regiment South African Infantry

Operation Order No. 120

Copy No.

Reference GOUZEAUCOURT. 1/20000

30th December 1917

1. Relief. The 1st S.A.I. will relieve 2nd S.A.I. in the right sub-section on the night 31st Decr 1917/1st January 1918. The order of relief will be A. C. D. B. Coys. moving off on relief in Platoons, at 200 yards interval. Relief to be completed by 8.30 p.m.

2. Destination After the relief the 2nd S.A.I. will be billeted in Hutments at W.3.c. and will become the Battalion in reserve. –

3. Advance Parties 1 N.C.O per Coy and 1 from Headquarters will report to Capt Theron at Battalion Headquarters at 1-45 pm and will proceed to Hutments to take over all stores Etc. Full marching Order.

4. Work. All orders with regard to work in hand and working parties to be found will be handed over to relieving Units.

5. Blankets and Cooking Utensils All Blankets will be rolled in bundles of 10. Cooking Utensils Etc will be stacked at Ration Dump by 4 P.M. Transport will be available to convey same to destination.

6. Trench Store Cards. To be submitted to Orderly Room at 9 A.M. 1st January 1918.

7. Water & Rations. Will be issued immediately on arrival at destination.

8. States. Usual States will be rendered.

9. Completion of Relief To be reported by wiring names of Company Commanders.

ISSUED. AT.

Copy No. 1. to. A Coy.
2 to B Coy
3 to C Coy
4 to D Coy
5 Transport Officer
6 File
7/8 War Diary

[signature]

2/Lt & Asst Adjutant
2nd Regt S.A.I.

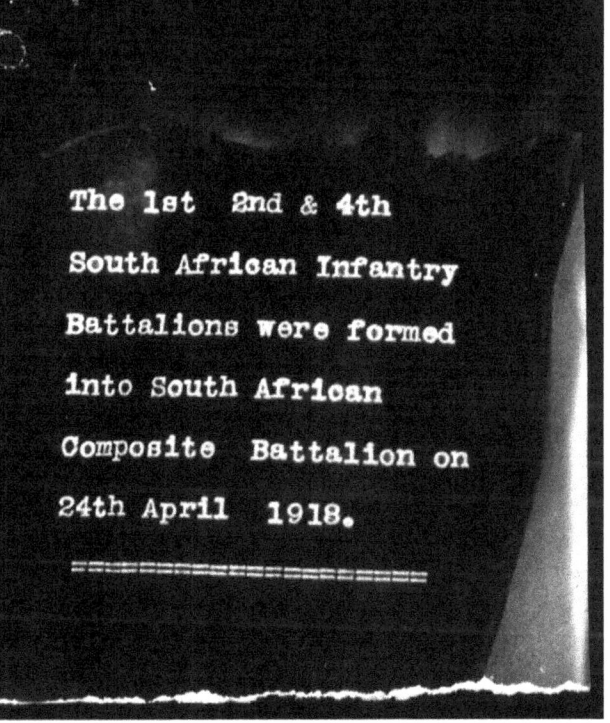

The 1st 2nd & 4th
South African Infantry
Battalions were formed
into South African
Composite Battalion on
24th April 1918.

======================

Instructions regarding War Diaries and Intelligence Summaries are contained in F. S. Regs., Part II. and the Staff Manual respectively. Title pages will be prepared in manuscript.

WAR DIARY

or

~~INTELLIGENCE SUMMARY.~~

(Erase heading not required.)

Army Form C. 2118.

Place	Date	Hour	Summary of Events and Information	Remarks and references to Appendices
GOUZEAUCOURT TRENCHES	1.1.18.		Weather cold but clear. Several enemy aeroplanes reconnoitred back areas and were fired at by A.A. guns and Lewis guns. Regiment was given Christmas dinner and all huts were visited by C.O. during dinner hour and short address given. The Regiment moved to Shelters at Fins at 4 pm as hutments at W.3.c. were considered dangerous having been shelled thrice during occupancy of First Regiment.	
	2.1.18.		Weather continues cold and clear. A working party sent to trenches north of W.C.3. Men started bathing. Draft of one officer and 64 O.R. joined Regiment. The C.O. appears in New Year Honours list D.S.O.	
	3.1.18.		Weather still clear and frosty. Large sick parades, most men being affected in feet. Similar working party sent out and bathing of men continued. Large number of Gothas flew over lines and dropped bombs on camps on left of FINS.	
	4.1.18.		Weather continues clear and frosty. The Regiment moved from	

D. D. & L., London, E.C.
(A7883) Wt. W809/M1672 350,000 4/17 Sch. 52a Forms/C/2118/14

Instructions regarding War Diaries and Intelligence Summaries are contained in F. S. Regs., Part II. and the Staff Manual respectively. Title pages will be prepared in manuscript.

WAR DIARY

~~or~~

~~INTELLIGENCE SUMMARY.~~

(Erase heading not required.)

Army Form C. 2118.

Place	Date	Hour	Summary of Events and Information	Remarks and references to Appendices
GOUZEAUCOURT TRENCHES	4/1/18		Left camp at FINS at 4 pm. and relieved the 1st S A I. in the front line, (vide Operation Order 121). The relief successfully carried out.	Order 121
	5/1/18		No change in the weather. Very little enemy activity. Usual work continued in trenches, removal of frozen snow from bays and traverses entails much trouble. The adjutant and C.O. made usual rounds.	
	6/1		Weather still cold and frosty. Slight enemy activity, small working parties seen, and slight artillery activity. The adjutant and C.O. visited all companies in the morning and afternoon inspecting. The usual patrols were sent out during the night but encountered no hostile parties. Rain started falling during night and thaw commenced.	
	7/1		Rain continued in early morning, thaw becoming serious, nearly all the snow having disappeared; and trenches gradually became worse as melted snow and ice trickled in and with the loose earth formed a slush several inches deep; all available men had to be employed on cleaning trenches during day. The C.O. and adjutant made their usual round. Patrol overnight discovered no enemy activity. One OR. wounded	

D. D. & L., London, E.C.
(A7883) Wt W809/M1672 350,000 4/17 Sch. 52a Forms/C/2118/14

Army Form C. 2118.

WAR DIARY

~~INTELLIGENCE SUMMARY.~~

(Erase heading not required.)

Instructions regarding War Diaries and Intelligence Summaries are contained in F. S. Regs., Part II. and the Staff Manual respectively. Title pages will be prepared in manuscript.

Place	Date	Hour	Summary of Events and Information	Remarks and references to Appendices
	JAN. 1918.			
GOUZEAUCOURT TRENCHES	8.		Weather again cold, heavy frost having taken place overnight. Snow started falling later in morning and after cessation, cold north wind continued to blow loose snow into trenches necessitating all men being put on to keep them clear. The B.G.C. visited Bn. H.Q. and was conducted round by C.O. In the evening the Battn. was relieved by the 1st S.A.I. and moved to Support Line at W & X. (vide Operation Order 122). The Regiment suffered 3 casualties during the relief 1 officer & 1 O.R. killed and 1 O.R. wounded. (2/Lieut. F.A. Archer killed) 2/Lieut. Harrison reported back from Div. Wing.	Order 122
GOUZEAUCOURT SUPPORT TRENCHES.	9.		Weather clear and frosty in morning. Enemy artillery continued intermittent activity. Snow and blizzard in afternoon. Two working parties of 1 N.C.O. and 12 men, and 1 officer + 40 men respectively, supplied for work under R.E's. 1 O.R. wounded. Capt. Knight left from Corps Details	
	10		Camp on leave for England – leave cancelled later, and Capt. Knight sent on special duty to England. Lieut. Cooper slightly wounded but remaining on duty	
	10		Thaw and rain – Billets poor and very muddy and much work entailed in improving same and building them up. Intermittent	

D. D. & L., London, E.C. (A7883) Wt. W809/M1672 350,000 4/17 Sch. 52a Forms/C/2118/14

Instructions regarding War Diaries and Intelligence Summaries are contained in F. S. Regs., Part II. and the Staff Manual respectively. Title pages will be prepared in manuscript.

WAR DIARY
or
~~INTELLIGENCE SUMMARY~~.
(*Erase heading not required.*)

Army Form C. 2118.

Place	Date	Hour	Summary of Events and Information	Remarks and references to Appendices
GOUZEAUCOURT SUPPORT TRENCHES	10		enemy artillery activity throughout the day. Working parties as yesterday increased to 1 Off + 30 men and 1 Off + 60 O.R. respectively. Brig. General visited the line and was conducted round by the C.O. during the morning.	
	11		Thaw continues, and conditions in the trenches extraordinarily bad. Brig General round during the morning. Work in progress improving accommodation for the men - Party from A Coy sent over to assist B Coy with their Shelters. 4 Working parties for the line under R.E. supervision supplied during the afternoon. ~~[illegible]~~ Marked decrease in enemy artillery activity to-day and situation generally quiet - 2/Lieut Skeith for leave to England vice Capt Knight leave cancelled. 4 O.R. despatched on special duty to England.	
	12		Slight frost in the morning but thaw continues during the day. All our positions in W5b shelled by enemy artillery with increasing intensity from 1 p.m to 5 p.m and intermittently throughout the night - 1 O.R. wounded in afternoon. Capt Theron reported to Brigade for duty	

D. D. & L., London, E.C.
(A7883) Wt. W809/M1672 350,000 4/17 Sch. 52a Forms/C/2118/14

Instructions regarding War Diaries and Intelligence Summaries are contained in F. S. Regs., Part II. and the Staff Manual respectively. Title pages will be prepared in manuscript.

WAR DIARY
or
~~INTELLIGENCE SUMMARY.~~
(Erase heading not required.)

Army Form C. 2118.

Place	Date	Hour	Summary of Events and Information	Remarks and references to Appendices
GOUZEAUCOURT SUPPORT	12		Div Commander and Brig General round the line during the morning. Two working parties each 2 Offs and 60 O.R's supplied in the evening. One to work under R.E's GOUZEAUCOURT, and one on C.T in left sub section.	
	13		Enemy activity throughout the day with artillery. The weather changed again to frost. Two enemy aeroplanes came over W.S.G observing, one being brought down while returning to German lines.	
			Two Companies "B" and "D" proceeded to Rest Billets in HEUDECOURT at 5 P.M. "D" Coy. being relieved by 1st A & S.H. No working parties were ordered.	Order 123.
	14.		At 9 A.M the remaining two Companies, "A" and "C" proceeded to Rest Billets in HEUDICOURT. Head Qrs. followed at 10-30 A.M. Situation was abnormally quiet. Weather was fine, but not so cold as previous day. On arrival at billets, the same were found very	

D. D. & L., London, E.C.
(A7883) Wt. W809/M1672 350,000 4/17 Sch. 52a Forms/C/2118/14

Army Form C. 2118.

Instructions regarding War Diaries and Intelligence Summaries are contained in F. S. Regs., Part II. and the Staff Manual respectively. Title pages will be prepared in manuscript.

WAR DIARY
or
INTELLIGENCE SUMMARY.
(Erase heading not required.)

Place	Date	Hour	Summary of Events and Information	Remarks and references to Appendices
HEUDICOURT	14		poor, and a great deal of work had to be done. Brigadier General Dawson and Major Cochrane visited the camp at noon. Major-General Sir H. T. Lukin K.C.B. C.M.G. D.S.O. visited the camp in evening. Rain set in about 9 P.M.	
	15		Rain fell heavily during the night, and much work had to be done as hut was leaking. Tarred felt was obtained, and men were employed all day in roofing the huts. Two working parties were called for, 50 men in one, 150 in the other. The smaller party was working under R.E. supervision on Heudicourt defences, but were informed that sufficient men were already there, so returned at 12 noon. The larger party working on Corps Line, with 9th Seaforth Pion[rs] returned at 2.30. Baths were allotted to the Regt. for the day, which operation was carried out. Rain continued all day in heavy showers.	

D. D. & L., London, E.C.
(A7683) Wt. W809/M1672 350,000 4/17 Sch. 52a Forms/C/2118/14

Instructions regarding War Diaries and Intelligence Summaries are contained in F. S. Regs., Part II. and the Staff Manual respectively. Title pages will be prepared in manuscript.

WAR DIARY

or

~~INTELLIGENCE SUMMARY.~~

(Erase heading not required.)

Army Form C. 2118.

Place	Date	Hour	Summary of Events and Information	Remarks and references to Appendices
HEUDECOURT	16		Rain still ~~continues~~ continues. No working parties ordered for today, except one party of 20 to work on Transport Lines, barricading and revetting. The D.M.S. came round in the morning, and inspected the camp. Improvements were continued with on and around the huts.	
	17		Rain still continues. Working party of 200 O. Ranks and four officers ordered to work under 9th Seaforth Pion[rs]. Task work was allotted on Corps Line, and all the party were home by lunch. Major Gen. Sir H.T. Lukin K.C.B. C.M.G. D.S.O. visited camp, also Brigadier Gen. Dawson C.M.G. [illegible] and Major Cochrane.	
SOREL-LE-GRAND.	18		The Regiment moved at 2 p.m. to a new camp at Sorel-le-Grand, which was formerly occupied by 9th Division H'd Qrs. All ranks were in new	Order 1238.

D. D. & L., London, E.C.
(A7883) Wt. W809/M1672 350,000 4/17 Sch. 52a Forms/C/2118/14

Army Form C. 2118.

Instructions regarding War Diaries and Intelligence Summaries are contained in F. S. Regs., Part II. and the Staff Manual respectively. Title pages will be prepared in manuscript.

WAR DIARY
or
~~INTELLIGENCE SUMMARY.~~
(*Erase heading not required.*)

Place	Date	Hour	Summary of Events and Information	Remarks and references to Appendices
Sorel-le-Grand	18		Camp by 4 p.m. Lt G. Green M.C. rejoined the Regiment after a months leave. Usual working party of 4 off. 200 ORs. worked on Corps line in morning. No rain in morning, but very overcast and windy. Rain fell during afternoon.	
	19		Weather improving. Fine all day. Working party of 3 officers & 150 ORs. working just South of Cemetery by Camp, on sites for new Camp. Major Herman & Lt Green rode over to Bde. Hd. Qrs. to see General Furze—but same could not come till 5 p.m. Training was carried out after the Commanding Officers inspection for rest of the morning. Capt Theron visited camp in afternoon.	
	20		Working party on sites for huts as usual. New draft of 53 ORs. joined Regiment. Inspection by the Commanding Officer in morning. Training carried out under Company arrangements. Lt Col	

D. D. & L., London, E.C.
(A7883) Wt. W809/M1672 350,000 4/17 Sch. 52a Forms/C/2118/14

Instructions regarding War Diaries and Intelligence Summaries are contained in F. S. Regs., Part II. and the Staff Manual respectively. Title pages will be prepared in manuscript.

WAR DIARY
or
~~INTELLIGENCE~~ SUMMARY.
(Erase heading not required.)

Army Form C. 2118.

Place	Date	Hour	Summary of Events and Information	Remarks and references to Appendices
Sorrel.	20		Lt Col Christian D.S.O. returned from leave. Weather conditions good.	
	21		Working parties as usual. Light rain fell during day. Major Cochrane M.C. and Capt. Thom came to lunch.	
	22		Major C.R. Herman, the Adjutant, Lt Tilney, Lt Green, and 2/Lt Egan reconnoitred the line which we take over tomorrow from the 5th Camerons. Got back at 2-30 p.m. Col Christian to Brigade Hd Qrs for lunch. Rain in evening. Working parties as usual.	
	23		The 2nd Reg. left Sorrel to relieve the 5th Cameron Highlanders in the left sub section. "A" Company moved out of camp at 3-30 p.m. Hd Qrs left camp at 4-30 p.m. The relief was complete by 8 p.m. Lt Col Christian to Brigade. Major C.R. Herman assumes	Order 124.

D. D. & L., London, E.C.
(A7883) Wt. W809/M1672 350,000 4/17 Sch. 52a Forms/C/2118/14

Instructions regarding War Diaries and Intelligence Summaries are contained in F. S. Regs., Part II. and the Staff Manual respectively. Title pages will be prepared in manuscript.

WAR DIARY
or
~~INTELLIGENCE~~ SUMMARY.
(Erase heading not required.)

Army Form C. 2118.

Place	Date	Hour	Summary of Events and Information	Remarks and references to Appendices
SORREL.	23		Temporary Command of the Regiment.	
GOUZEAUCOURT TRENCHES.	24.		"A" & "C" Companies in front line Trenches. Trenches in a bad state but 9th Seaforth Pioneers working on them, & have got dry standing room for the posts. Brigadier General Dawson visited Trenches in morning, with Lt Col. Christian who joined Regt & assumed Command from date. No work could be done by day. Weather fine, and visibility good.	
	25.		Carrying parties all night carrying up R.E. material to front line. Remaining men available working on C.T. in Flag Ravine. Weather fine. Enemy shelled Gouzeaucourt intermittently. Major Hewan [?] to Details.	
	26		Same parties carrying up material to front line, and deepening trench in Flag Ravine. Nothing of interest happened during day. Usual shelling of Gouzeaucourt and [illegible] Guard's Trench. "B" & "D" Coys relieved front line Companies last night.	

D. D. & L., London, E.C.
(A7883) Wt. W809/M1672 350,000 4/17 Sch. 52a Forms/C/2118/14

Instructions regarding War Diaries and Intelligence Summaries are contained in F. S. Regs., Part II. and the Staff Manual respectively. Title pages will be prepared in manuscript.

WAR DIARY
or
~~INTELLIGENCE~~ SUMMARY.
(Erase heading not required.)

Army Form C. 2118.

Place	Date	Hour	Summary of Events and Information	Remarks and references to Appendices
Gouzeaucourt Trenches	27.		Telegram came for Lt. Col. Christian to proceed to Brigade assume temporary command of same. Brigadier General Dawson to England on duty. Major C.R. Hunt assumes temporary command of Regiment from date. Working parties as usual. The Reg. is relieved by 1st S.A.I. Relief complete by 8-30 P.M. One slight casualty. 2 Reg. billeted in hutments at W.2.C. Arrived there about 11 P.M.	Order 125
Hutments W.2.C. Nr Fins	28.		Beautiful day. Party of 1 Officer and 40 O.R. working party for 3rd Reg. Back in camp at 10 P.M. Whole day devoted to cleaning up. Rifle and foot inspections. Aerial activity at about 8 P.M. Bombs dropped by E.A. about a mile away. Very clear moonlight night.	
	29.		Morning working party for Signalling Officer. The same as usual. No party in evening.	

D. D. & L., London, E.C.
(A7683) Wt. W809/M1672 350,000 4/17 Sch. 52a Forms/C/2118/14

WAR DIARY
or
INTELLIGENCE SUMMARY
(Erase heading not required.)

Instructions regarding War Diaries and Intelligence Summaries are contained in F. S. Regs., Part II. and the Staff Manual respectively. Title Pages will be prepared in manuscript.

Place	Date	Hour	Summary of Events and Information	Remarks and references to Appendices
~~SORREL LE GRAND~~ HUTMENTS W.2.c. Nr FINS.	29.		Weather fine. Frosty night but warm during day. Enemy air-craft came over. Lt.Col. Christian & Capt Thro came from Brigade in afternoon.	
	30.		Frosty night. Beautifully fine during day & warm. Regiment had baths allotted in afternoon. Usual working party for Signals in morning. Enemy aeroplane over for some considerable time in morning. Our planes went over & made enemy pull down an observation balloon. Clear night. 2/Lieut F.G. Gibbs reported back from leave.	
	31		Frosty & clear in early morning – Enemy aeroplanes came over and dropped bombs in neighbourhood of SOREL LE GRAND about 2 a.m. Later mist developed, and weather misty and very cold for the rest of the day. The Regiment relieved in position of Brigade Reserve by 1/1 Herts Regt. in accordance with Operation Order No 126, and moved to billets in SOREL LE GRAND for accommodation for the night. – Movement commenced about 2.30pm. – Details re-joined the Regiment on arrival at SOREL. Night frosty and still misty.	[illegible] 126

C.R. Neeman Major.
Comm'g [illegible]

2449 Wt. W14957/M90 750,000 1/16 J.B.C. & A. Forms/C.2118/12.

SECRET. ORDER NO: 121. Copy No..9..

Reference GOUZEACOURT I/2000.

In the Field, 3rd January, 1918.

I. INTENTION. The 2nd S.A.I. will relieve the Ist S.A.I. inxt the right sub-section to-morrow night 4/5th January 1918. Order of relief will be "B" "D" "C" "A", leadingcompany moving off at 3.30.p.m with 5 minutes intervals between platoons.

2. DISTRIBUTION. After relief disposition of companies will be as follows:

"B" right front company.
"D" left front company.
"C" immediate support company.
"A" Counter attack company in Sunken Road.

3. ROUTE. The route to front line will be via immediate support and C.T. on left of sub section will not be used by troops of this Brigade for any purpose.

4. ADVANCE PARTIES. Consisting of I Officer and I N.C.O. per company and Headquarters will proceed in advance under company arrangements and take over all trench stores etc.

5. WORK. All work in hand, etc. will be taken over from outgoing companies.

6. WATER AND RATIONS. Will be issued on arrival at destination.

7. TRENCH STORES CARDS. To be handed in to Orderley Room by 9.am. 5th inst.

8. STATES. Usual states and certificates will be xxxxx rendered.

9. COMPLETION OF RELIEF. To be reported by wiring surname of Company Commander.

Signed. H. PERRY.

2nd Lieut.& A/Adjutant,
2nd Regiment S.A.Infantry.

Issued at ....

Copies I 4- "A" "B" "C" "D" Coys.
5 Hqrs.
6 Transport Officer.
7 O/C. Details.
8 File.
9/10 War Diary.

INSTRUCTIONS ISSUED WITH ORDER NO: 121.

In the Field,
3rd January, 1917.

I. BAGGAGE. All officers kits and men's blankets, with the exception of I blanket per man in "C" and "A" Companies will be stacked out side Orderley Rom by II. a.m. Blankets to be rolled in bundles of IO.

2. LEWIS GUNS & AMMUNITION. To be carried by Platoons ammunition to be distributied throughout platoon. Gun boxes a and ammunition boxes will be stacked with blankets, etc outside Orderley Room by II.am.

3. COOCKING UTENSILS. All cooking utensils, stores, etc, required for the line will be dumped in court at Battalion Headquarters by 3.p.m. Limber will be available to convey these to the line.

Travelling kitchens will be packed ready to pull out at this hour for return to transport lines.

(SD.) H.Perry, 2/Lieut. & A/Adjt.,
2nd Regiment South African Inf

[illegible]
[illegible] Reference
GOUZEAUCOURT
1/40,000

Order No 124 ....

Copy No 8

In the field
7th January 1918

No 1 Intention

The 1st S.A.I. will relieve the 2nd S.A.I. in the right Sub-Sector tomorrow night 8th January 1918
Order of relief will be B.D.C.A. Companies moving off by Platoons at [illegible] minutes intervals on completion of Company relief.
"A" Coy 2nd S.A.I. will be relieved by "C" Coy 1st S.A.I
"C" " " " " " " " "A" " "

No 2

Relief will be completed by 7.30 pm

Distribution

After relief disposition of Companies will be as follows.
"B" Coy right reserve Company
"D" " left " "
and will become Garrison of Reserve Line
"C" Coy left Support Company at G.35.b.
"A" " right " " " W.5.b.
and will become Battalion in support

3. Advance Parties

1 Officer and 1 N.C.O. per Company will proceed in advance under Company arrangements and will take over all trench stores etc.
This officer will obtain particulars of all work in hand and Company Commanders will ensure that same is continued.

4. Work

All orders in regard to work in hand and working parties to be found will be handed over to relieving units.

5. Trench Store Cards

To be submitted to Orderly Room by 8 am 9th inst

10. Water & Rations

Water, Rations and Blankets will be drawn immediately on completion of relief

11. States

Ration States will be rendered

12. Completion of Relief

To be reported by wiring the Surname of the Company Commander.

Copies No 1 to 4 to Companies
5 Transport Officer
6 O.C. Details
7 [illegible]
8/9 War Diary

[illegible signature]
[illegible]
[illegible]

Secret

Reference
GOUCHE WOOD Special
SHEET 1/10,000
57c 1/40000.

Operation Order No 123

Copy No. 7

1 Information — The South African Infantry Brigade is being ~~relieved~~ withdrawn from the line on nights 12/13th and 13/14th into rest in FINS and HEUDECOURT.

2 Intention (a) D Coy 2nd SAI will be relieved by one company of 10th A&S Highlanders in reserve line between FINS-GOUZEACOURT METZ-GOUZEACOURT roads on night of 13/14th January - relief to commence about 6pm. On relief this company will be billeted in Billets at HEUDECOURT.

(b) 2nd South African Infantry less D Coy will withdraw from Support Position to Billets at HEUDECOURT on morning of 14th January 1918.
Order of relief will be B.A.C. - commencing 9am companies will move off in parties of not more than 10 at 100 yards intervals.

3 Route — Route will be via Decauville Rly to junction with HEUDECOURT-QUEENS CROSS road at aprox W3a 9.6.

4 Billetting Parties — 1 NCO per company and HQrs will report to 2/Lieut L. Cooper at Battalion HQrs, full marching order, at a time to be notified later.

5 Baggage — Two limbers will be available to convey D Coy blankets on the evening of 13th inst. Blankets will be stacked in readiness by 5pm under company arrangements.
All cooking utensils and food containers for all companies will be stacked at Ration Dump by 5.30 am on the 14th.
BAC Companies and HQ Blankets will be stacked at Ration Dump by 8am on the 14th. These will be handed over to Corpl Fitzpatrick who will arrange for a guard and loading party of 1 NCO and 12 men to remain with them. These Blankets will be transported to HEUDECOURT on the evening of 14th inst.

6. Trench Stores — All trench stores with the exception of Gum Boots and food containers will be handed over to 27th Inf Brigade on the 13th instant and receipts obtained in duplicate. These will be handed in to Batt Orderly Room by 4pm on the 14th inst.
All Aerial photos, Maps and trench names Boards will be handed over. South African Brigade Defence scheme will not be handed over, but will be destroyed.

7. Rations — Will be issued on arrival at destination on the 14th inst.

"OVER"

8 States — Usual States and certificates will be rendered. Marching out States will be handed in to Orderly Room by 9 am 11th inst

9 Completion of Relief — "D" Coy will report completion of relief in usual manner.

Issued at —

Copy No 1 to 4 to Companies
5 to H.Qrs.
6 to Transport Officer
7 to O.C. Details
8 to File
9/10 War Diary

(Signed)
Act Adjutant
2nd S.A.I.

Operation Order No 123 B. COPYNO........7...

In the Field January 18th 1918.

No.1. INTENTION. The 2nd Seuth African Infantry will meve frem HEUDECOURT te SOREL - LE GRAND en the afterneen ef the 18th inst.and will eccupy the camp at present eccupied by Divisienal H.Qrs.

No.2. DISTRIBUTION Mevement will be made by Companies in the fellewing erder starting at 2.p.m. Usual interval te be maintained .-

A.Coy. B.Coy. C.Coy. D.Coy.-

No.3. ROUTE Frem Camp te square by HEUDECOURT Baths,thence S.W. te Serel le Grand.

No.4. GUIDES. Guides will meet Companies en read eutside Serel le Grand.

No.5. ADVANCE PARTY 1 N.C.O. and 6 men will preceed at 11.a.m. te Serel le Grand to act as Guard and eff leading party. This party te be detailed frem Duty Company.

No. 6. BAGGAGE. All Pailiasses te be cellected and stacked by the read near the Guard Reem by 10.a.m.-1 G.S.Wagen will be available te cenvey same te new camp,by 10.30.a.m. All remaining baggage steres etc te be stacked by 1.pm

No.7. TRANSPORT Transpert will repert at 1.30.p.m. fer baggage as under

1 Limber per cempany.fer Lewis Guns,Coy Orderly Reem and Mess kit.-

2 Limbers fer Officers Kits.-

1 Limber fer Battalien Orderly Reem and Canteen.-

Maltese Cart fer Medical Steres.-

Mess Cart fer Headquarters.-

No.8. KITCHENS. Kitchens will meve eff en arrival ef their respective teams.-

No.9. REPORTS. Usual reperts States etc will be rendered te Battalien Orderly Reem immediately en arrival at Billets.-

No.10. AERIAL ACTIVITY. Necessary precautiens regarding aerial ebservatien will be taken.-

Issued at 9pm 17/1/18

Cåepy No 1 te 4 te Companies
5 te Transpert Officer
6 te O.C.Details
7 File
8/9 War Diary.

2/Lieut
and Act Adjutant
2nd Regt S.A.Infantry

Copy No. 9.

ORDER NO: 124

In the field.
22nd January 1918.

Reference
Sheet 57c
and Gouche
Wood. 1/10000

1.
INTENTION

The 1st South African Infantry Brigade willrelieve the 26th Infantry Brigade in the Left Brigade Section on the night 23/24th and 24/25th January 1918.

2
RELIEF

The 2nd South African Infantry will relieve 5th Cameron Highlanders in the left Sub-section on night 23/24th.

Order of relief.-

Companies will move off in following order:-

"A" "C" "B" "D".

Leading Company will move off at 3.30P.M. Platoons at 200 Yards interval.

3.
DISTRIBUTION

"A" Company - right front Company
"C" Company - left front Company
"B" Company - Support and Counter attack Company
"D" Company - Reserve Company.-

4.
ROUTE

Route will be from Sorel to W.2.c.2.0. thence along FINS - GOUZEACOURT road to TYKE Dump. Guides will direct from that Point.

5
GUIDES

Guides from 5th Camerons will meet platoons at TYKE Dump at 5.p.m.

6
ADVANCE PARTY

"B" and "D" Companies will sent an advance party of 1 Officer and 1 N.C.O. per Company at 3.p.m. to take over trench stores of their respective Companies "A" and "C" Companies will take over on arival.Sergt FUGE will proceed with advance party of "B" and "D" Companies and take over stores at H.QRS.-

7
TRENCH STORE CARDS

Trench store cards will be rendered to Battalion Orderly Room together with usual states by 12 noon. 25th inst.

8
WATER

All water bottles to be filled before starting.

9
COMPLETION OF RELIEF.

Will be reported in usual manner.

(Sgd) G.V.Merriman.
2nd Lieut & A/ Adjutant
2nd Regt S.A.Infantry

Issued at 11.15am

Map Reference.
Gauche Wood 1/10000
Sheet 57 C. 1/40000

Order No 125

Copy No. 8

26 January 1918.

No 1
Information.

The 1st South African Infantry will relieve the 2nd S.A. Infantry in the left sub-section on the night of the 27/28th January 1918
The 2nd S.A. Infantry on relief will become the Battalion in Brigade reserve and will be Billeted in Hutments W.2.C.
The relief will be complete if possible by 8.30pm

2
Relief

The relief will take place in the following manner
"A" Coy 1st S.A. Infantry will relieve "B" Coy 2nd S.A.I.
"C" " " " " " "D" " " "
"B" " " " " " "A" " " "
"D" " " " " " "C" " " "

Companies on relief will immediately proceed by March route to W.2.C.

3.
Formation

Platoons at 200 yards intervals
Relief to be reported to this office in the usual manner

4
Advance Party.

Officer. J. Egan and billeting N.C.O. from A & C Coys will proceed to W.2.C. at 2 pm.
1. N.C.O. from "A" & "C" Coys. will accompany this party for purpose of Billeting "B" & "D" Coys

5
Advance Party.

An advance party from 1st S.A.I. consisting of Intelligence officer, observers, and two N.C.Os per company will take over stores from corresponding formation from 2nd S.A.I. during the afternoon

6.
Trench Stores

Trench Stores will be handed over and duplicate receipts forwarded to this office by 10 pm. 27th inst

7
Defence Schemes

Defence scheme and all orders relating to Working Parties will be handed over to relieving units.

8
States

The usual states will be submitted to this office by 10pm 27th inst

9
Guides

"A & C" Coys will supply 3 guides and H.Qrs will supply 1 guide to be at junction of road Q.35.c.5.0 at 5.5 pm. to meet relieving unit.
Distribution of H.Qrs guides will be as follows
3 men to report to "A" Coy 1st S.A.I.
3 " " " " "C" " " "
1 man " " " H.Qrs " "

Over

The above men will be detailed by
R S M.

Cooks. Cpl Forde and 1 Cook per Company and
3 Mess orderlies per company will proceed
to W.R.C. at 3 pm

10 Baggage. All cooking utensils, company mess kit and
surplus L.G. Magazines etc, will be at
Ration Dump by 6 pm.
Companies will carry 16 Magazines per
gun.
"B" & "D" Coys will bring surplus ammunition
to Dump at Dusk.

(Sgd) G T Merriman
2/Lieut & A/Adj
2nd S A Infantry

Reference
Sheet 57c.
1/40000.-
AMIENS, 17.

ORDER NO: 126.

Copy 9

In the Field, 30/1/1918.

1. **INFORMATION.** The 9th Division will be relieved in its present sector by 39th Division and will be withdrawn into G.H.Q. reserve in the BRAY AREA.

The 1st South African Infantry Brigade will be relieved by 118 Infantry Brigade in the line on the night of 31st January / 1st February, 1918.

The 2nd S.A.I. will be relieved by 1/1st Herts. Regiment in Brigade Reserve.

2. **INTENTION.** (a) The 2nd S.A.I. intend to move to Sorel-le-Grand in accordance with March Table "A" attached, and will move to PERONNE on 1st February in accordance with attached Train Table "B".

(b) All Details and Working Parties will rejoin their units at entraining station on 1st February.

3. **INSTRUCTIONS.** Companies will march out in the following order:-
"A" "B" "C" "D" HQrs. by platoons at 200 yards interval, by shortest route.

4. **BILLETING PARTY.** Billeting party of 1 N.C.O. per company and 1 from Headquarters will report to 2/Lieut. L. EGAN at Orderly Room at 8.15.a.m. to-morrow 31st, to proceed to Transport lines where lorries will convey party to new area.

5. **CAMP STORES.** All Camp Stores. Defence Schemes, Maps and all documents relating to sector will be handed over and receipts taken. Receipts (in duplicate) of stores handed over will be rendered to Orderly Room.

6. **BAGGAGE.** (a) Blankets (in bundles of ten) and officers kits will be stacked at edge of road by "A" Coy's. cook house by 10.45.a.m., to be conveyed to SOREL-le - Grand. Duty Company will detail 1 N.C.O. and 10 men for loading party, who will accompany waggons to unload.

(b) Transport will call at 1.30.p.m. for all Lewis Guns and ammunition, except the guns that are mounted in the camp.
These posts will be taken over by incoming Unit.

7. **FIELD KITCHENS.** (a) Kitchens will pull out at 1.30.p.m. and will proceed direct to new camp at SOREL-le-GRAND, where they should be ready to pull out again at 5.p.m. to proceed to PERONNE, reporting to Capt. JACOBS, who will select sites for same.

(b) Hot food will be provided for Units on detraining.

(c) These kitchens will join 1st line transport as it moves through Peronne at about 1.30.p.m. on 1st February, and proceed to final destination.

(d) The Sergeant cook will arrange to keep back sufficient Utensils for breakfast on morning of 1st prox. and will have same carried to Quartermaster's Stores at Transport Lines by 7.30.a.m. Fatigue party will be provided.

xx (e) 1 cook per company will march with field kitchens to Peronne.

/over.

NOTE. Futher instructions as to Baggage on 1st February will be issued later.

8. **STATES AND CERTIFICATES.** Usual states and certificates will be rendered. Billets to be left in a clean and sanitary condition, and certificates to that effedt will be submitted to Orderly Room prior to leaving the camp.

Issued at 9..p.m.

2/Lieut. & A/Adjutant,
2nd Regiment South African Inf.

Copies 1/4 - O.C's. Companies.
5. - Headquarters.
6. - Transport Officer.
7 - Quartermaster.
8/10. - File.

MARCH TABLE "A".

Date.	Unit.	From	To	Route.	ime.	Remarks.
31.1.18	2nd S.A.I.	Hutments W.2.c.	SOREL-le-GRAND.	Any route.	2.p.m.	Platoons at 200 yards intervals.

TRAIN TABLE "B"

Date.	Unit.	Type of train.	Station of Entrainment.	Station of Detrainment.	Hours of Departure.
1.2.18.	2nd S.A.I.	Decauville.	A.X. 13. (V.18.a.1.2.)	A.X. 2.	8.30.a.m.
1.2.18.	do.	C.S. Train.	PERONNE FLAMICOURT.	La PLATEAU.	2.0. p.m.

ADMINISTRATIVE INSTRUCTION NO: 1. ISSUED WITH ORDER No. 126.

No. 1. Orderly Officer. 2/Lieut. F.A.BARRETT.
Duty Company. "A" Company.

No. 2. Rouse. 5.a.m.
Breakfast. 5.30.a.m.

No. 3. All kits, mess stores, and blankets (in bundles of TEN) must be stacked by Guard Room at 6.30.a.m.

"A" Company will detail a loading party of 1 ~~Sergt.~~ cpl. and 8 men, who will proceed by lorry to destination.

DIXIES. Loading party will carry dixies from this camp to the Quartermaster's stores immediately breakfast is over.

One of the loading party will remain at Quartermaster's stores until arrival of lorries there at 7.30.a.m. and will conduct TWO lorries to this camp.

No. 4. 2/Lieut. H. LEWIS is detailed as entraining officer., and will report to Orderly Room to-night for orders.

No. 5. Companies will be ready to move off at 7.0.a.m. The Regiment will move off ~~xx~~ by companies at 200 yards interval to A.X.12. entraining station.

No. 6. On arrival at billets a guide from Headquarters will be detailed to be at Western entrance of CAMP to guide transport to Regimental Transport lines.

[signature]
2/Lieut. & A/Adjutant.
2nd Regiment S.A. Infantry.

21.1.18.

Issued to all recipients

INSTRUCTIONS ISSUED WITH ORDER NO: 12[illegible]

22-1-18.

1
BILLETS

Company Commanders will render a certificate to this office by 2.30.p.m. 23rd inst. Certifying that billets have been left in a clean and sanitary condition.

2
BLANKETS

All Blankets will be stacked in guard room by 11.a.m. rolled in bundles of TEN

Duty Company ("B") will supply guard of 1 N.C.O. and 10 men, which will also act as loading party.

3.
BAGGAGE

All baggage to be ready and stacked by 2.p.m. next to Guard Room.

(Sgd) G.V.Merriman

2/Lieut & A/ Adjutant

2nd Regt S.A.Infantry

Scale 1 : 20,000. GOUZEAUCOURT. Ed. 2 D Special Sheet. Parts of 57c N.E., S.E. and 57b N.W., S.W.

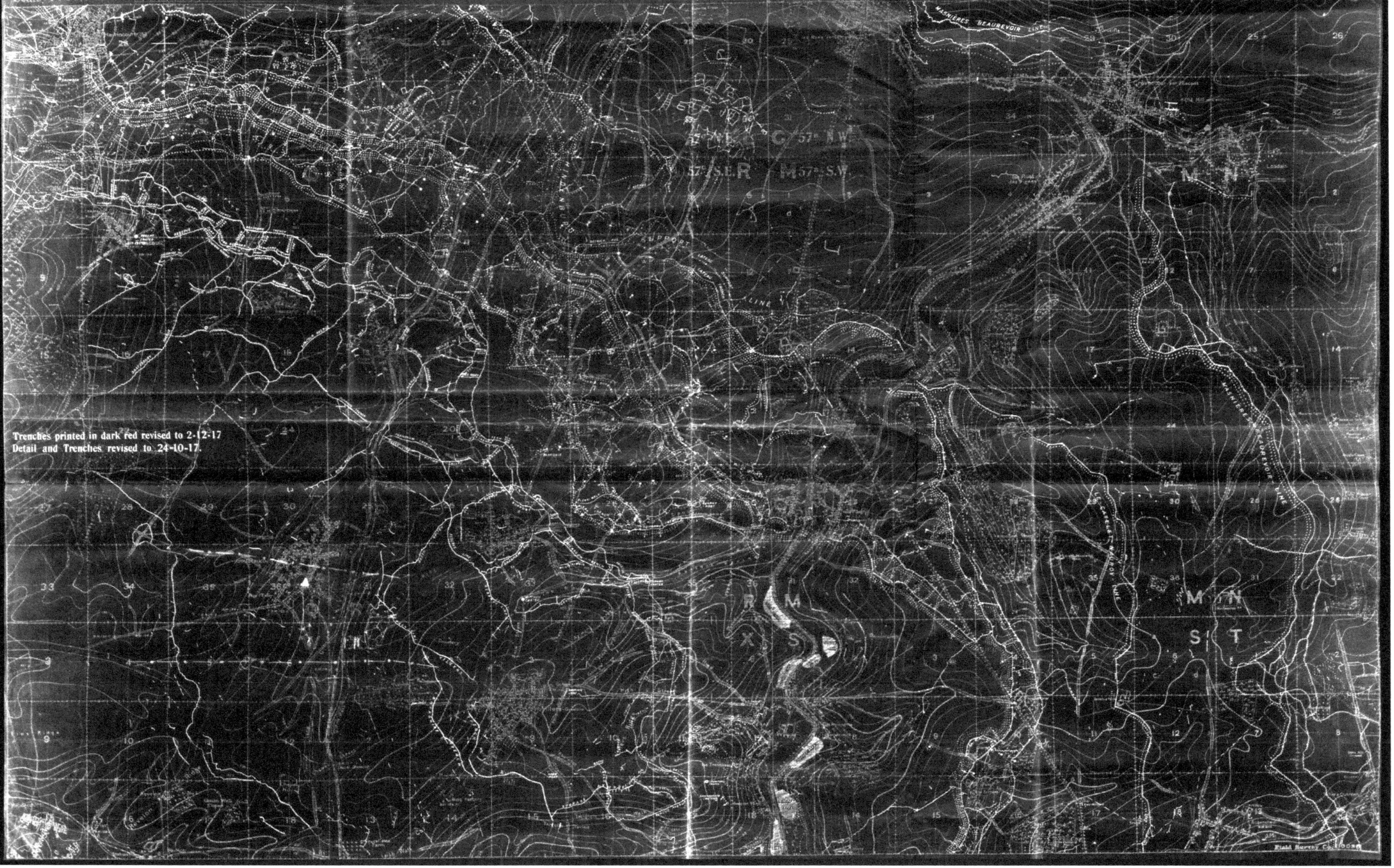

2

Instructions regarding War Diaries and Intelligence Summaries are contained in F. S. Regs., Part II. and the Staff Manual respectively. Title Pages will be prepared in manuscript.

WAR DIARY
or
INTELLIGENCE SUMMARY
(Erase heading not required.)

Army Form C. 2118.

Place	Date	Hour	Summary of Events and Information	Remarks and references to Appendices
SUZANNE	7.2.18		Same working parties as usual:- Assault course - bunking and erecting of Officers hut. Weather changed to a light rain - still very mild. Commanding Officer witnessed a Tank Demonstration in morning. Rugby football match v 2nd Reg. Officers postponed.	
	8.2.18		Working parties as yesterday. Weather very changeable. Heavy rain in morning - still very mild. Firing did not commence on Range today as trench in butts had to be deepened.	
	9.2.18		Working parties as usual. Bunking finished this morning. B and C Companies started firing on Range, application and grouping. Weather fine.	
	10.2.18		Working parties as usual. Bunking etc. 'A' & 'C' Coys on the Range. Church Parade for B & D Coys. The Brigadier visited H.Q. in afternoon, & brought Major Guy, ? U.S. army to stay with us. Weather very fine.	

2440 Wt. W14957/M90 750,000 1/16 J.B.C. & A. Forms/C.2118/12.

Instructions regarding War Diaries and Intelligence Summaries are contained in F. S. Regs., Part II. and the Staff Manual respectively. Title Pages will be prepared in manuscript.

WAR DIARY
or
INTELLIGENCE SUMMARY
(Erase heading not required.)

Army Form C. 2118.

Place	Date	Hour	Summary of Events and Information	Remarks and references to Appendices
SUZANNE.	11-2-18.		Working parties as usual. Weather very fine. 'B' & 'D' Coys. on Range. Major Grey left before lunch. [illegible] Rugby Team played against Brigade H. Qrs. resulted in favour of 2nd S.A.I. Commanding Officer entertained Coy. Commanders at dinner. 2/Lt Hagg back from Musketry course.	
"	12-2-18		Working parties as usual. Misty in morning, but fine & clear by noon. A & C Coys on the Range. B & D training. Brigadier General Tanner D.S.O. came to lunch & stayed the afternoon. Regimental Concert in evening.	
"	13-2-18		A slight misty rain in morning. Damp atmosphere all day. Showery in evening. Adjutant rode out with Staff Captain in morning to select a parade ground for inspection by C in C. 'B' & 'D' Coys practised field firing by platoons in accordance with scheme - most good - considering the little practice that has been done in such work. [illegible] finished in Company lines.	

Instructions regarding War Diaries and Intelligence Summaries are contained in F. S. Regs., Part II. and the Staff Manual respectively. Title Pages will be prepared in manuscript.

WAR DIARY
or
INTELLIGENCE SUMMARY
(Erase heading not required.)

Army Form C. 2118.

Place	Date	Hour	Summary of Events and Information	Remarks and references to Appendices
SUZANNE	14-2-18.		A & C Coys group firing by Platoons. B & D Coys Training. Weather starting to change has been misty all day.	
	15-2-18.		9th Company competition preliminary in Coy. own 3 Companies as follows: "B" 559.4. "D" 511.6. "A" 500.5. "C" 466. 5 Officers & 150 O.R. joined from 3rd Reg. Weather changed. Very cold night, & frost. Cold all day.	
	16-2-18.		Very cold night. Cold all day. Companies reorganisation all morning. 3rd Reg. posted to Reg. as "C" Coy. Baths at Bray allotted to "A" "B" & "C" Companies. 2nd Reg. versus S.A.H.A. rugby at Cappy 2-30 P.M. Resulted in win for 2nd S.A.H.	
	17-2-18.		The Unit marched to Delville Wood for a Brigade memorial service. Two hours march - arriving back to Camp at 4-30 P.M. After service the Divisional Commander presented decorations. General Tanner was present at the service. Weather very cold, but fine - very successful march.	

Instructions regarding War Diaries and Intelligence Summaries are contained in F. S. Regs., Part II. and the Staff Manual respectively. Title Pages will be prepared in manuscript.

WAR DIARY
or
INTELLIGENCE SUMMARY
(Erase heading not required.)

Army Form C. 2118.

Place	Date	Hour	Summary of Events and Information	Remarks and references to Appendices
SUZANNE	18-2-18		Weather improved & beautifully fine. Companies practising A.R.A. competition, won by A Coy, No 1 Platoon who will compete against the 2nd S.A.I. in the final. Companies carrying on with the completing of bomb proof barricades.	
"	19-2-18.		Weather still holds fine. B & D Companies on Range, C Company firing A.R.A. competition under Coy. arrangements. A Company training. F.G.C.M. assembled in 2nd S.A.I. lines.	
"	20-2-18.		Weather changed, rain began to fall slightly in afternoon but increased later on at night. The Brigadier inspected Transport in afternoon – very satisfactory. New Tarrant hut arrived for Officers mess. All Companies training in morning. B on Range, C on Range.	

2449 Wt. W14957/M90 750,000 1/16 J.B.C. & A. Forms/C.2118/12.

Instructions regarding War Diaries and Intelligence Summaries are contained in F. S. Regs., Part II. and the Staff Manual respectively. Title Pages will be prepared in manuscript.

WAR DIARY
or
INTELLIGENCE SUMMARY
(Erase heading not required.)

Army Form C. 2118.

Place	Date	Hour	Summary of Events and Information	Remarks and references to Appendices
SUZANNE.	21-2-18.		Weather improving. All Coys training till 11 A.M. Batt. parade at 11 A.M. practising deployment from Column of Route. The Brigadier General witnessed operations & seemed very pleased. Final of Rugby Lukin Cup in afternoon. 2nd Reg versus first. Resulted in win for 1st Reg. Divisional Commander & staff came to watch the match and afterwards to Hd. Qr. Mess.	
	22-2-18.		Slight misty rain in morning, which came down harder at mid-day. A + C Companies practised an attack scheme on a two company front, with machine gun & stokes mortar accompanying. Final of A.R.A. competition against 4th S.A.I. which was won by 4th S.A.I. by 50 points.	
	23-2-18.		Baths allotted to the Reg. Drying room in working order, also all men having their hair cut short. B. Company on the Range till noon. Weather improving. Finals of Boxing matches in evening in Cinema Hall Suzanne.	

Instructions regarding War Diaries and Intelligence Summaries are contained in F. S. Regs., Part II. and Staff Manual respectively. Title Pages will be prepared in manuscript.

Army Form C. 2118.

WAR DIARY
or
INTELLIGENCE SUMMARY

(Erase heading not required.)

Place	Date	Hour	Summary of Events and Information	Remarks and references to Appendices
SUZANNE	24-2-18.		Weather mild. Baths allotted to this unit all day. All Companies completed their C. Church Parades. Lt Col. Young attached to this Unit. Warning Order for moving.	
	25-2-18.		Weather changed - rain in morning. C. Company practising platoon attacks, Vickers gun in company, remaining companies training on foot-ball field. Inefficient shots firing in afternoon. Sports meeting in afternoon, President Major D. Macdougall.	
	26-2-18.		Weather changed to a beautiful warm day, but chilly towards evening. Brigade field day in morning, which was carried out successfully, all ranks taking a keen interest in the same. Divisional Commander was present, and gave a short talk to all officers after the operations. Scheme attached. Inter Company 5-a-side foot-ball matches in afternoon.	

2449 Wt. W14957/M90 750,000 1/16 J.B.C. & A. Forms/C.2118/12.

Instructions regarding War Diaries and Intelligence Summaries are contained in F. S. Regs., Part II. and the Staff Manual respectively. Title pages will be prepared in manuscript.

Army Form C. 2118.

WAR DIARY
or
INTELLIGENCE SUMMARY.
(*Erase heading not required.*)

Place	Date	Hour	Summary of Events and Information	Remarks and references to Appendices
SUZANNE	27-2-18.		D Company practising platoon attacks in morning. – "A" and "C" Companies carrying out training. B. Company having all mens hair cut and clothes ironed. Weather fine but cold wind. Rain towards evening. Brigadier General visited the training. Five-a-side football in afternoon. Concert given by 4th and 2nd S.A.I. in evening.	
do.	28-2-18		Battalion attack practice. – Battalion paraded at 8.30 am. when the Commanding Officer presented the Military Medal and Parchment to 7785 Pte. P W HEALY and Parchments to 14333 Pte. PATTEN L.V. and 1893 Pte. FAQUHAR S. – Battalion then carried out attack practice. – Weather fair with light showers of rain. – Orders received for the move of the Regiment to HAUTE ALLAINES on 1st March.	
			Strength – With Unit. 25 Off. 947 O.R's Detached. 14. " 133. do. 39 1080	

Edward Christian
Lieut. Colonel
Commanding 2nd Regt S.A.I.

D. D. & L., London, E.C.
(A7683) Wt. W809/M1672 350,000 4/17 Sch. 52a Forms/C2118/14

ORDER.

Reference Sheet 62c.N W. 1/20000.

1. Enemy attacked at 5.a.m. this morning and penetrated our line. His front line now runs approximately Southern edge of VAUX WOOD to G.3.c.5.7. to 'L' Copse to 'K' Copse to 'F' Copse to Northern edge of Billon Wood.

2. 2nd and 4th will attack and capture our old front line.
2nd on Right.
4th on Left.

3. Battalions will move off Parade Ground at 9.20.a.m. by river road through G.9.c. and G.15.b. taking care to keep out of sight of Vaux Wood, and will commence to deploy at 9.50.a.m. The advance will continue at 10.a.m.; track through G.9.c.a.d. to G.10.c. to old shaft.: left of battalion will direct. "A" Company will tell off an officer for this purpose.

4. VAUX WOOD will be heavily bombarded until 10.15.a.m. and smoke and gas bombs will be used on southern slope of Vaux Wood from 9.50 to 10.15.a.m.

5. Battalion will attack - "C" and "A" Companies in front line ("C" on right) "D" and "B" Companies in reserve ("D" on right).

6. The left boundary of the Battalion to be the line from Track junction at G.9.d.8.3. inclusive to bend in road at A.27.b. 8.2.

7. Right company frontage on deployment will be from old shaft to track junction and G 10.c.4.2. exclusive; left company frontage from track junction at G 10.c.4.2. inclusive and track junction at G.9.d.8.3. inclusive.

8. First objective will be a line from road junction G.4.a.9.3. to S.E.point of encampment in G 3.b.7.8.

9. 4th S.A.I. will not advance beyond this first objective.

10. The final objective will be a line from Southern edge of Spur Wood and SUZANNE-MARICOURT Road A.27.b.8.2.
On arrival at first objectives "D" and "B" Companies will leap-frog leading companies and advance on final objective at 11.a.m. supported by "A" Company who will pay special attention to left flank as advance progresses.
"C" Company will consolidate VAUX WOOD, immediately the second advance commences and will pay special attention to road over river from VAUX VILLAGE. Final objective will be consolidated immediately is is reached.

Battalion Headquarters at present Orderly Room till the first objective is reached when they will be established at G.10.a.2.7. R.A.P. - present position.

(Sd.) G.V.Merriman, 2/Lieut.
& A/Adjutant.
2nd Regiment S.A.Infantry

Issued to Company Commanders at 8.37.a.m.

2

APPENDIX

No III

DIARY OF

COMPOSITE COMPANY.

5th to 14th MAY

by.

CAPT. E.C. BRYANT.

O/commndg Composite Company

2 SAI

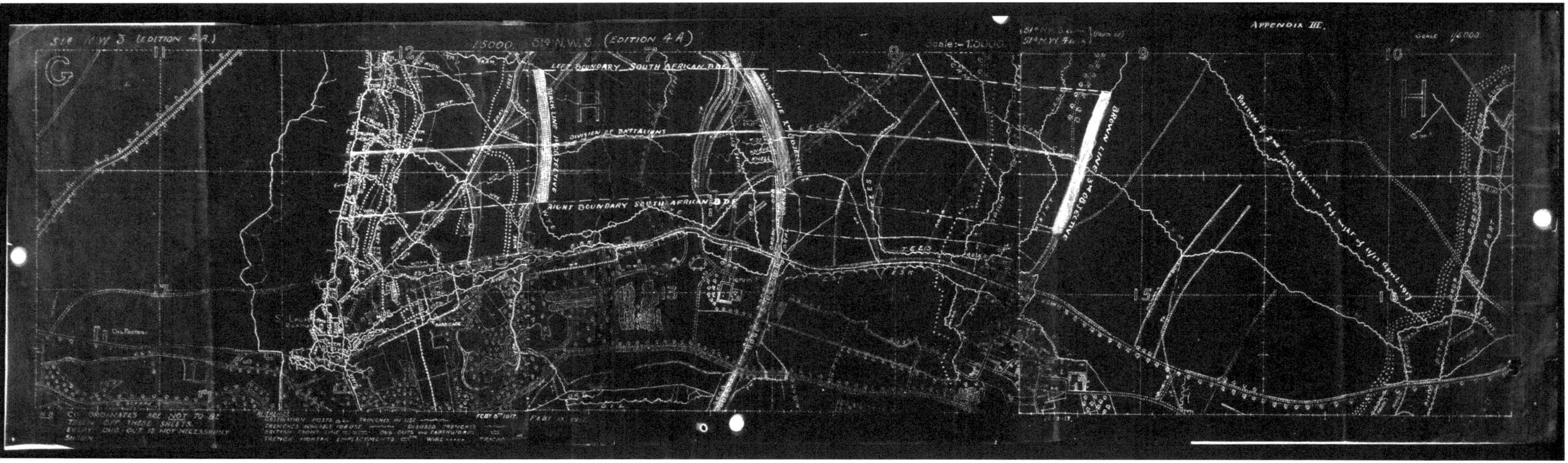

APPENDIX III.
Scale 1/5000
51B N.W. 3 (EDITION 4A)
1:5000 51B N.W. 3 (EDITION 4A)
LEFT BOUNDARY SOUTH AFRICAN BDE
RIGHT BOUNDARY SOUTH AFRICAN BDE
DIVISION OF BATTALIONS
BLACK LINE 1st OBJECTIVE
BLUE LINE 2nd OBJECTIVE
BROWN LINE 3rd OBJECTIVE
Position of 2nd South African Inf. night of 11/12 April 1917
COORDINATES ARE NOT TO BE TAKEN OFF THESE SHEETS.

SHEETS 57c N.E. & S.E. (Parts of) SECRET. On no account to fall in hands of enemy. Scale 1:10,000
Buildings blown up recently
Havrincourt
28
29
H.Q.
Pigeon loft and Sig Stn.
Snowden
Field Kitchen
Wall
Reported Coy
Important Centre
Triangle Wood
80
90
33
35
Femy Wood
Occupied by Enemy
M.G. T.M.
At night
Hostile line of Outposts
Observers frequently seen here
100
Ruined Hut
Recess in bank
Occupied at night by Enemy with M.G.
Wood wired
Havrincourt Wood
Huts destroyed
Boar Cop
Trescault
9
10
11
110
120
Special Area Photo
No 2 Shewn
No 3 Shewn
15
16
17
Corps Topo. Section. Map No 62.
Corrected to 13-3-17

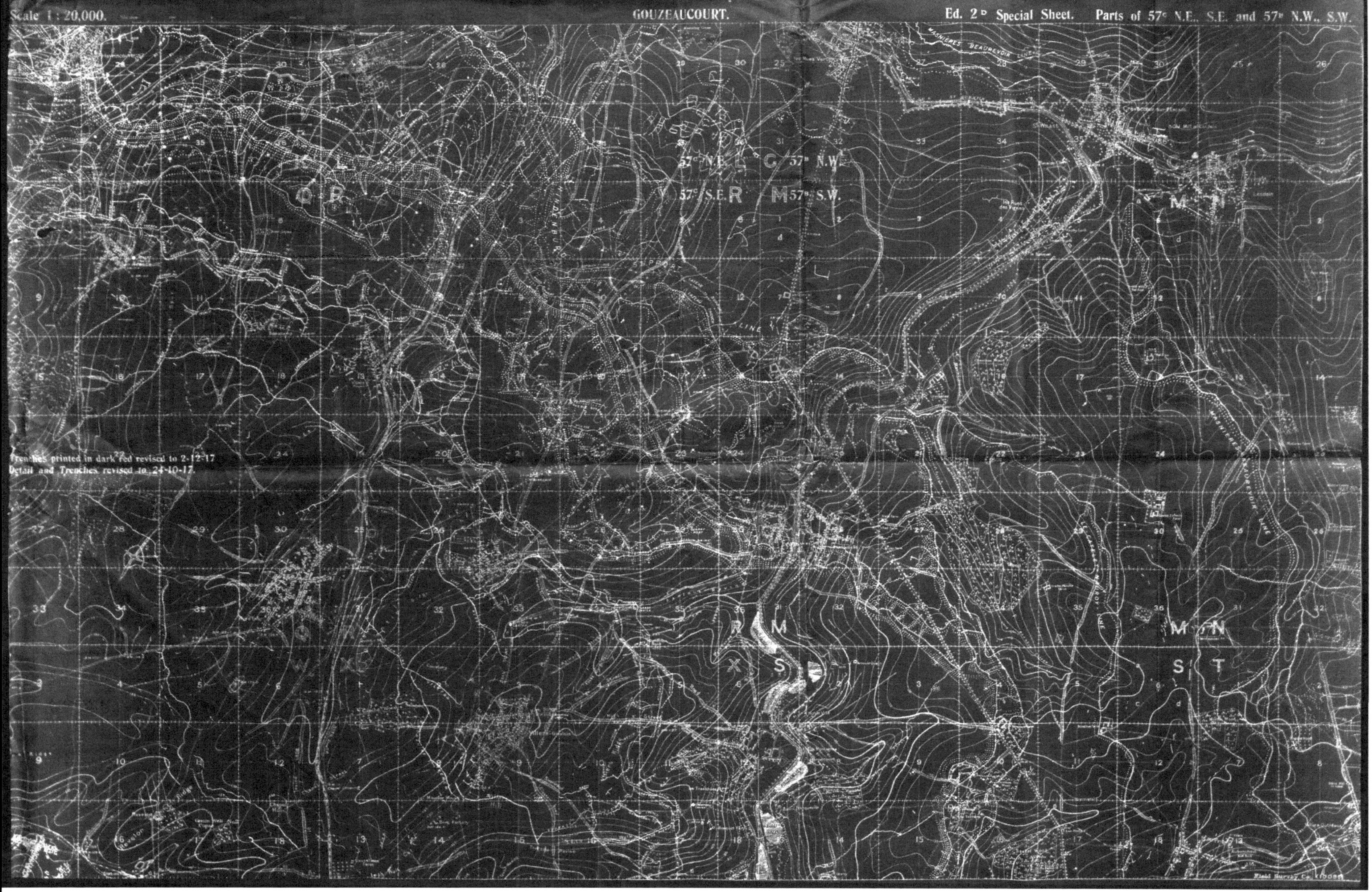

Scale 1 : 20,000.
GOUZEAUCOURT.
Ed. 2 D Special Sheet. Parts of 57c N.E., S.E. and 57B N.W., S.W.
57c N.E.
57B N.W.
57c S.E.
57B S.W.
Trenches printed in dark red revised to 2-12-17
Detail and Trenches revised to 24-10-17.

51B N.W 3 (EDITION 4 A.)
C 1
1:5000.
G
12
17
OIL FACTORY
ST LAURENT BLANGY
FEBY 8TH 1917
R. SCARPE
BARRICADE
AVON
TREE
TRAM
TROT.
TRAY
TRASH
WYE
WIT
WIND
WILD
WING
WINE
WIG
WINK
WORM
WRY
WISE
WISH
ESK
VIEW
VIM
VISIT
VOW
WICK
WAX
WAG
WAIL
TUFT
TRUTH
TRUSS
TWIST
TUSK
TUBE
TRIP
T.M.
N.B. CO-ORDINATES ARE NOT TO BE TAKEN OFF THESE SHEETS.
EVERY DUG-OUT IS NOT NECESSARILY SHOWN.
REFERENCE
OBSERVATION POSTS
TRENCHES IN USE
TRENCHES AVAILABLE FOR USE
DISUSED TRENCHES
BRITISH FRONT LINE
DUG OUTS AND EARTHWORKS
TRENCH MORTAR EMPLACEMENTS
WIRE
TRACKS

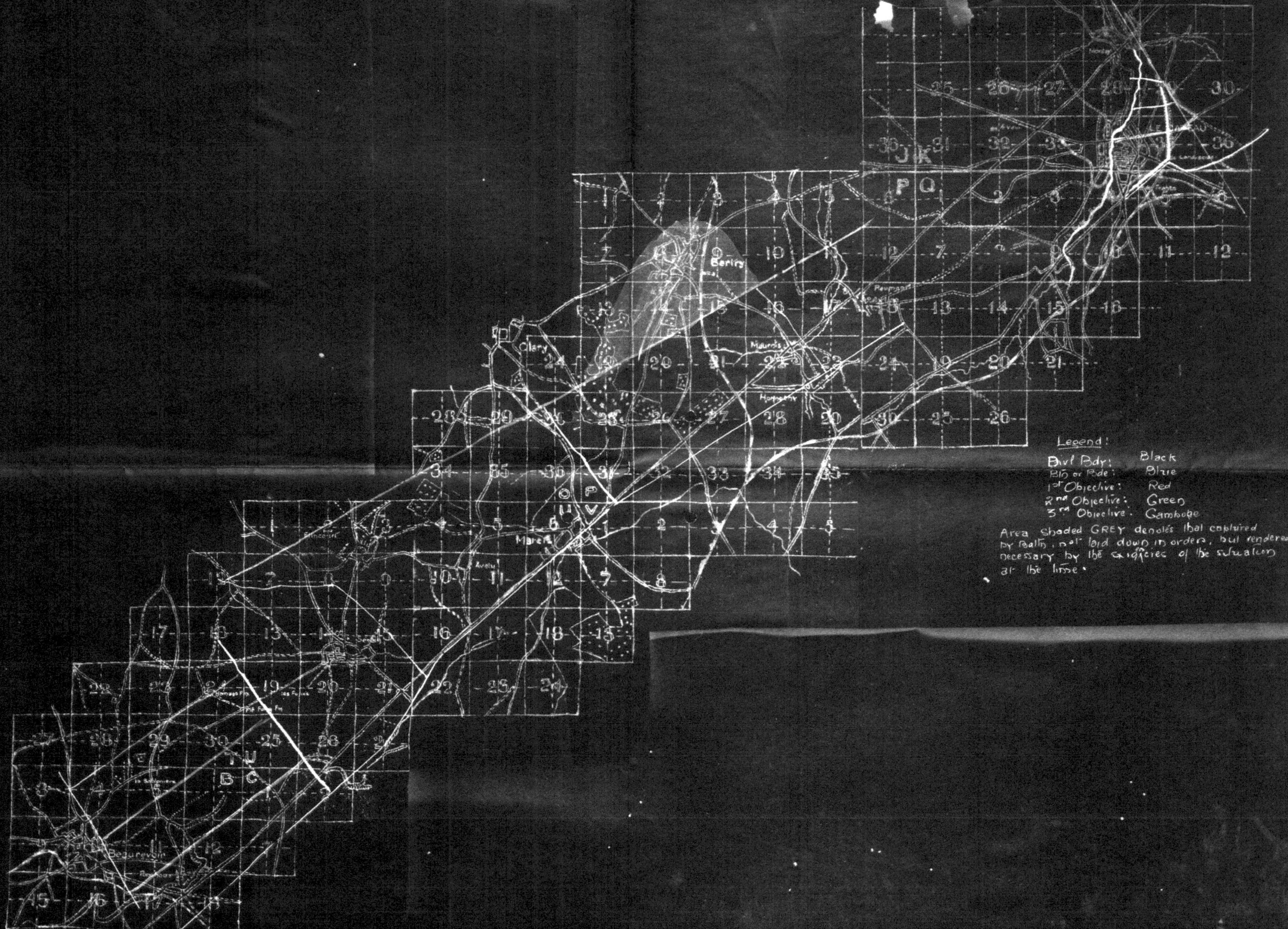
Legend:
Divl Bdy: Black
Bn or Bde: Blue
1st Objective: Red
2nd Objective: Green
3rd Objective: Gamboge
Area shaded GREY denotes that captured by Batt., not laid down in orders, but rendered necessary by the exigencies of the situation at the time.
Bertry
Clary
Maurois
Honnechy
Maretz
Beaurevoir
Reumont

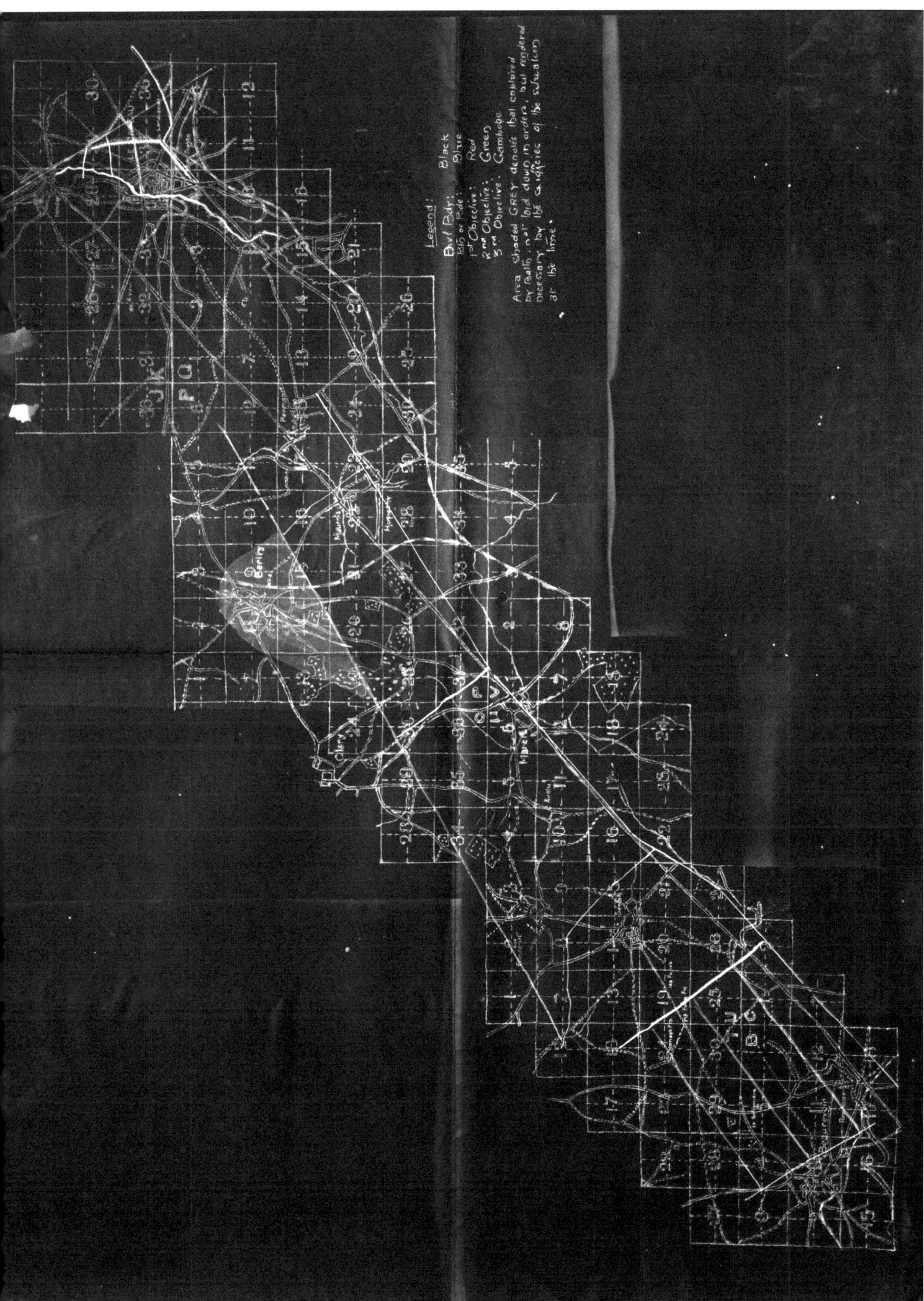

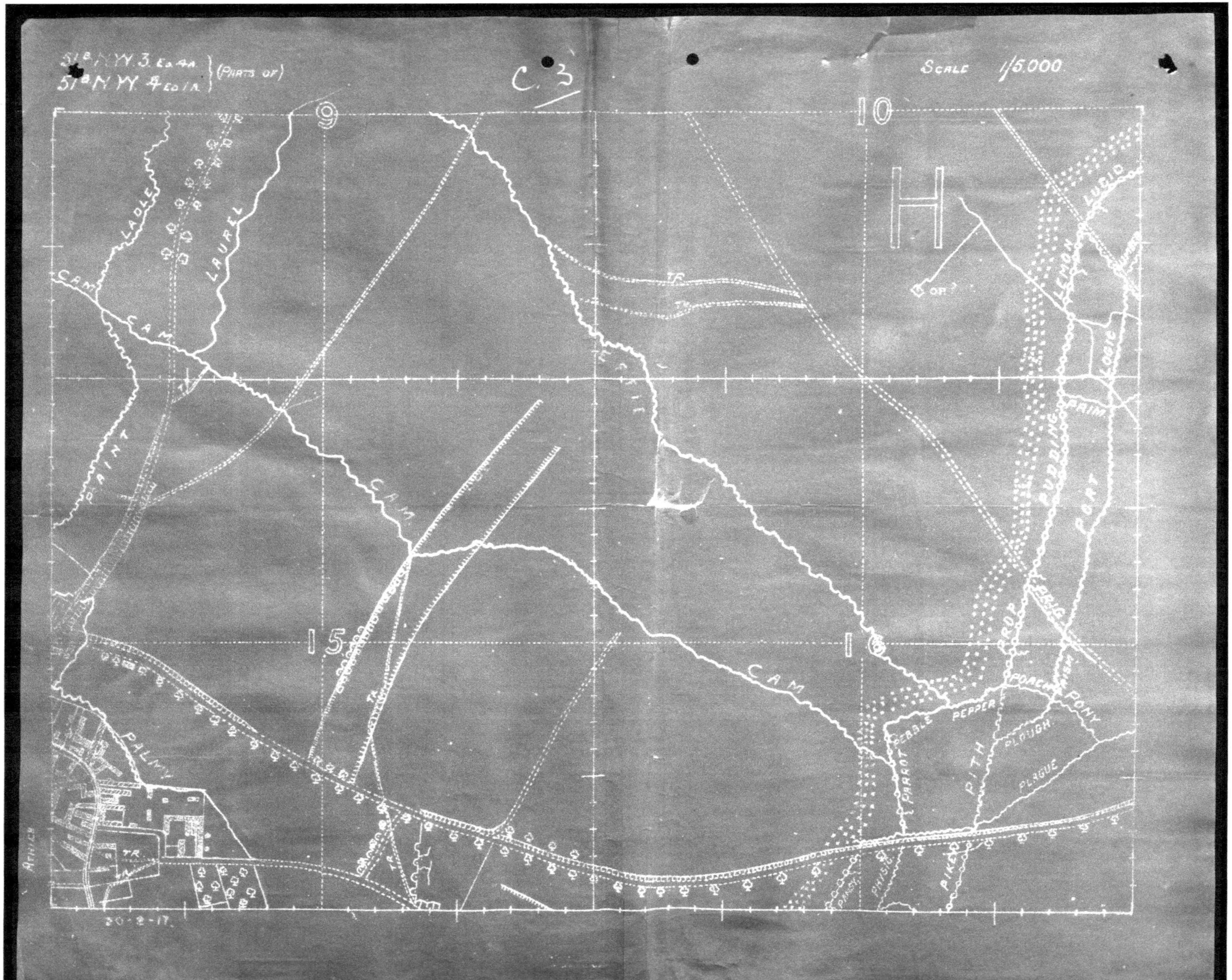
51B N.W. 3 Ed 4A
51B N.W. 4 Ed 1A
(Parts of)
C.3
Scale 1/5.000
9
10
15
16
H
CAM
LADLE
LAUREL
PAINT
CAM
CAM
LUCID
LEMON
LOGIC
PRIM
PUDDING
PORT
PROP
BRIG
PORCH
PONY
PEPPER
PEBBLE
PARROT
PITH
PLOUGH
PLAGUE
PIKE
PHYSIC
PALMY
TR.
20-2-17.

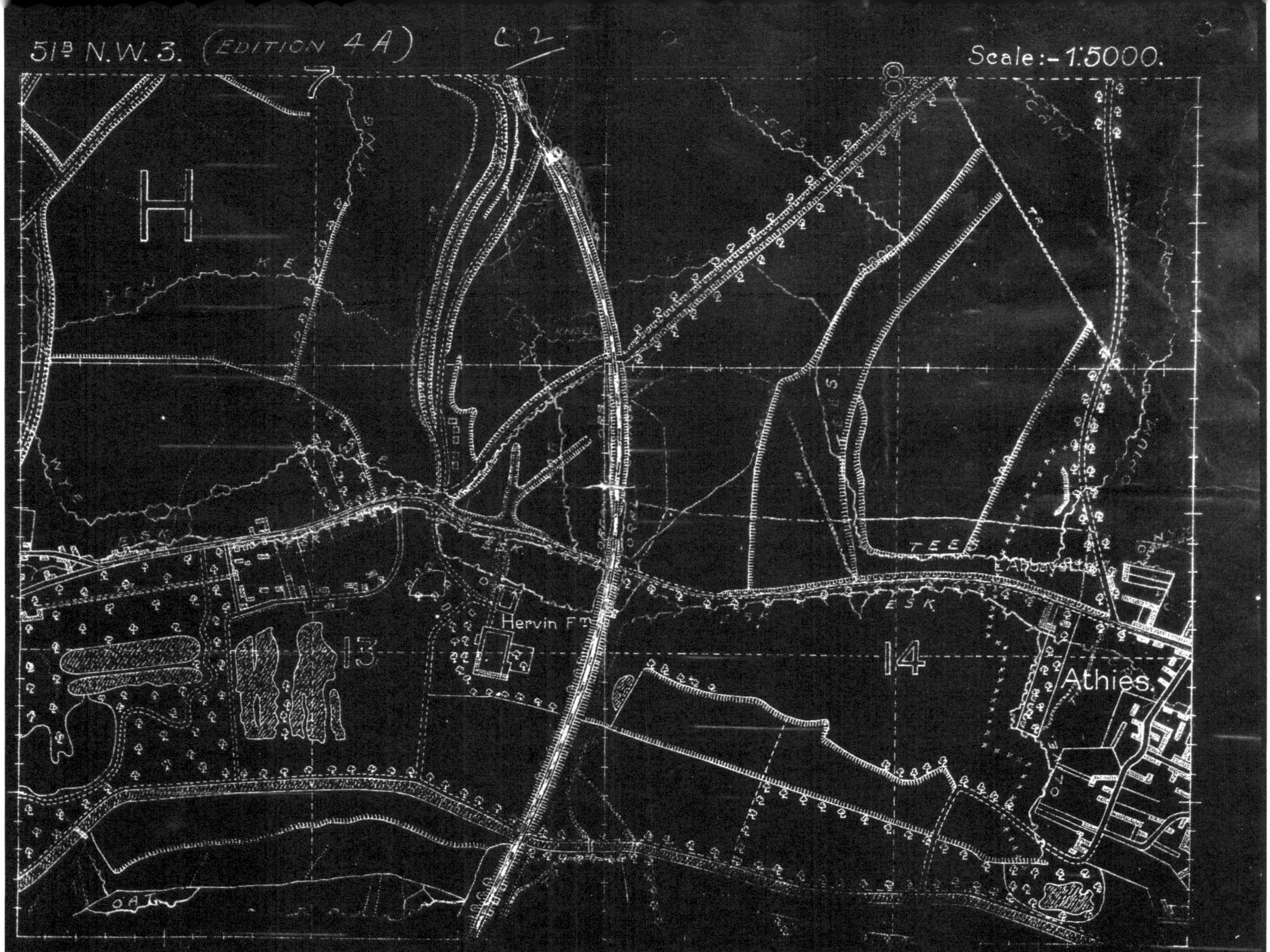

51B N.W. 3. (EDITION 4 A)
C.2
Scale:- 1:5000.
7
8
H
13
14
Hervin Fm.
Athies.
ESK
TEE
TEES
KEN
WYE
OAT
CAM
Abbeville

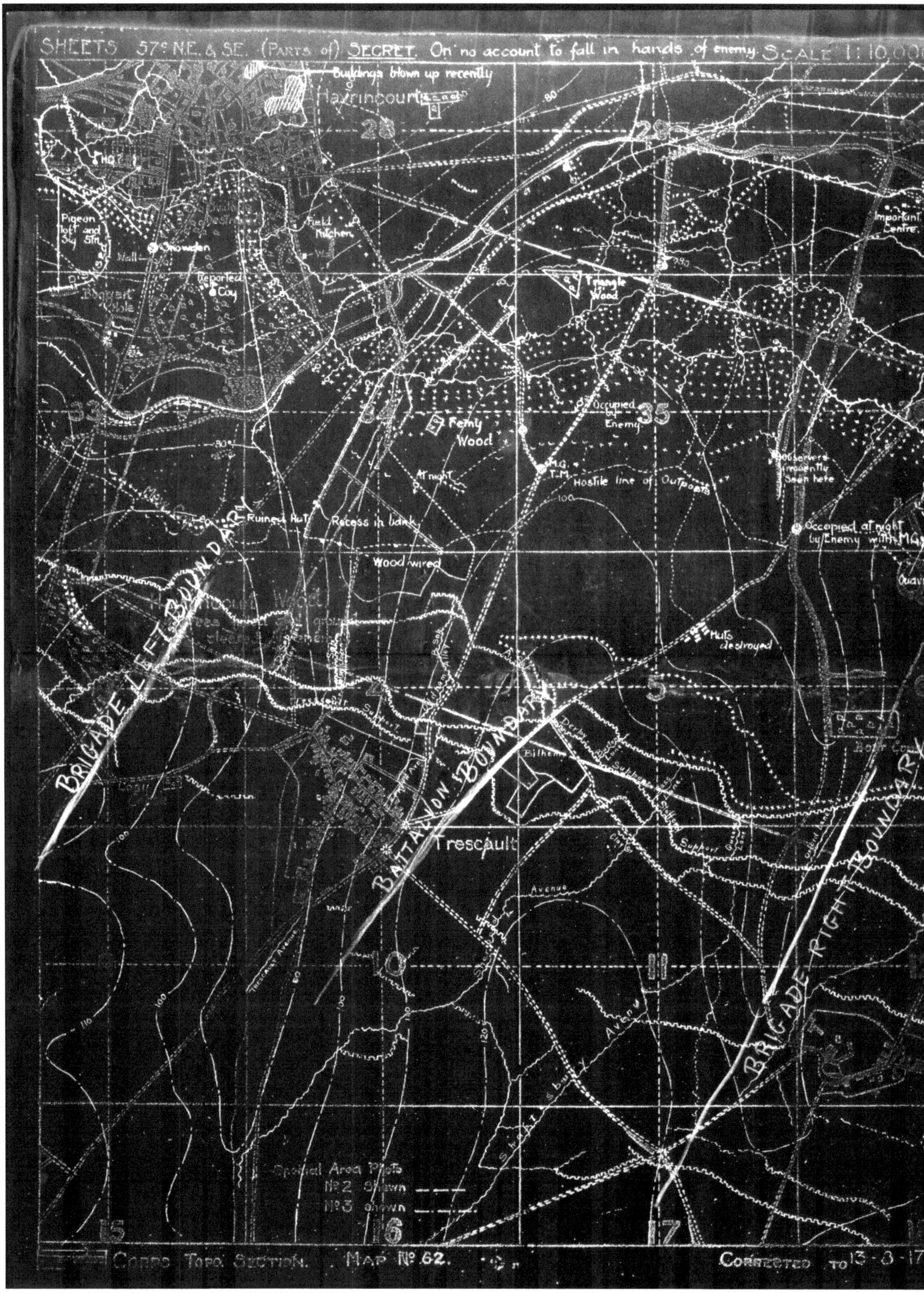
SHEETS 57c N.E. & S.E. (PARTS of) SECRET. On no account to fall in hands of enemy SCALE 1:10,000
Buildings blown up recently
Havrincourt
Pigeon loft and Sig Stn
Snowden
Field Kitchen
Reported Coy
Triangle Wood
Important Centre
Occupied by Enemy
Femy Wood
At night
M.G. T.M.
Hostile line of Outposts
Observers frequently seen here
Ruined Hut
Recess in bank
Occupied at night by Enemy with M.G.
Wood wired
Huts destroyed
BRIGADE LEFT BOUNDARY
BATTALION BOUNDARY
BRIGADE RIGHT BOUNDARY
Bilhem
Trescault
Trescault Avenue
Avenue
Special Area Photo
No 2 Shewn
No 3 Shewn
CORPS TOPO. SECTION. MAP No 62.
CORRECTED TO 13-3-17

1:10 000
R. 4.
EDITION I.
Scale 1:10,000.
18·9·17.
T.S. Nº 552.
APPROX. BRITISH FRONT LINE, 21ST AUG. 1917
APPROXIMATE FORMING UP LINE
LANGEMARCK
BOUNDARY
Zonnebeke
S' Gravenstafel
Winnipeg
Windmill Cabt
Station
Alma
Gallipoli
Toronto
Fokker Fm
Keir Fm
Somme
Nile
Boetleer
Aviatik
Dear Ho
Dump Ho
Wimbledon
Van Meulen
Otto Fm
Delva Fm
Van Isackere Fm
Beck House
Potsdam
Muhle
Albatross Fm
Hindu Cott
Schuler Fm
Clifton
Wurst Fm
Olive Ho
Springfield
Bremen Redoubt

9

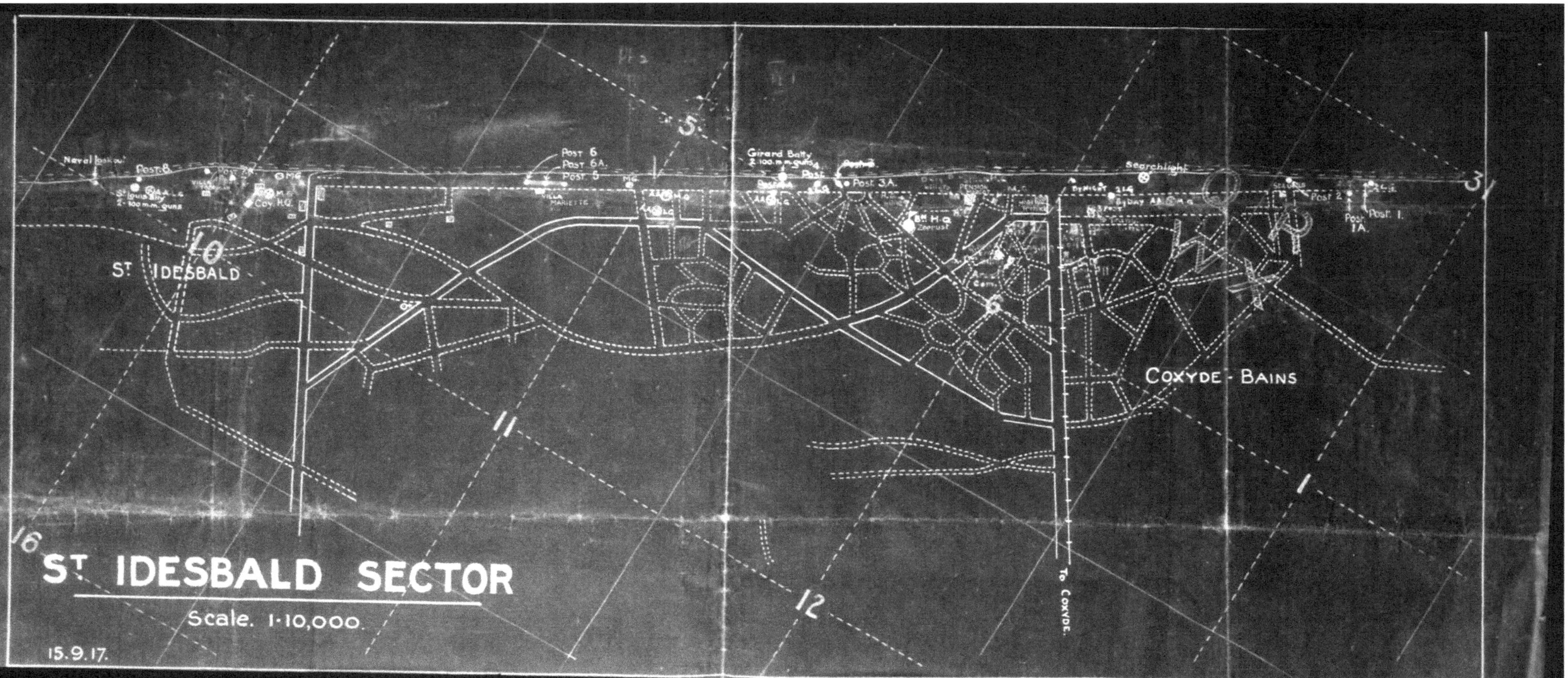
ST IDESBALD SECTOR
Scale. 1·10,000.
15.9.17.
ST IDESBALD
COXYDE - BAINS
To COXYDE.
Naval lookout
Post 8.
Post 6
Post 6A.
Post 5
Girard Batty
2.100 m.m. guns
Post 3A.
Searchlight
Post 2
Post 1.
Post 1A.
Coy. H.Q.
Bn. H.Q.
Villa Mariette
5
6
10
11
12
16
31
1

www.ingramcontent.com/pod-product-compliance
Lightning Source LLC
Chambersburg PA
CBHW060838010526
44108CB00047B/2836
9781474507776